Zafer Fehmi Yörük

Identity Crisis in Turkey

A Genealogical Inquiry into the Exclusion of the "Others"

LAP LAMBERT Academic Publishing

Zafer Fehmi Yörük

Identity Crisis in Turkey

Impressum/Imprint (nur für Deutschland/ only for Germany)
Bibliografische Information der Deutschen Nationalbibliothek: Die Deutsche Nationalbibliothek
verzeichnet diese Publikation in der Deutschen Nationalbibliografie; detaillierte bibliografische
Daten sind im Internet über http://dnb.d-nb.de abrufbar.
Alle in diesem Buch genannten Marken und Produktnamen unterliegen warenzeichen-, marken-
oder patentrechtlichem Schutz bzw. sind Warenzeichen oder eingetragene Warenzeichen der
jeweiligen Inhaber. Die Wiedergabe von Marken, Produktnamen, Gebrauchsnamen,
Handelsnamen, Warenbezeichnungen u.s.w. in diesem Werk berechtigt auch ohne besondere
Kennzeichnung nicht zu der Annahme, dass solche Namen im Sinne der Warenzeichen- und
Markenschutzgesetzgebung als frei zu betrachten wären und daher von jedermann benutzt
werden dürften.

Coverbild: www.ingimage.com

Verlag: LAP LAMBERT Academic Publishing AG & Co. KG
Dudweiler Landstr. 99, 66123 Saarbrücken, Deutschland
Telefon +49 681 3720-310, Telefax +49 681 3720-3109
Email: info@lap-publishing.com

Herstellung in Deutschland:
Schaltungsdienst Lange o.H.G., Berlin
Books on Demand GmbH, Norderstedt
Reha GmbH, Saarbrücken
Amazon Distribution GmbH, Leipzig
ISBN: 978-3-8383-4833-9

Imprint (only for USA, GB)
Bibliographic information published by the Deutsche Nationalbibliothek: The Deutsche
Nationalbibliothek lists this publication in the Deutsche Nationalbibliografie; detailed
bibliographic data are available in the Internet at http://dnb.d-nb.de.
Any brand names and product names mentioned in this book are subject to trademark, brand
or patent protection and are trademarks or registered trademarks of their respective holders.
The use of brand names, product names, common names, trade names, product descriptions
etc. even without a particular marking in this works is in no way to be construed to mean that
such names may be regarded as unrestricted in respect of trademark and brand protection
legislation and could thus be used by anyone.

Cover image: www.ingimage.com

Publisher: LAP LAMBERT Academic Publishing AG & Co. KG
Dudweiler Landstr. 99, 66123 Saarbrücken, Germany
Phone +49 681 3720-310, Fax +49 681 3720-3109
Email: info@lap-publishing.com

Printed in the U.S.A.
Printed in the U.K. by (see last page)
ISBN: 978-3-8383-4833-9

CONTENTS

1

2

ACKNOWLEDGEMENTS

I am grateful to Professor Ernesto Laclau, Dr Aletta Norval, Dr Jason Glynos, Dr Kathryn Dean, Saniye Aldemir, Osman Akinhay, Halil Ertugrul and Hanifi Araz for their invaluable contributions to this work.

Special thanks to Hüseyin Özdemir for the cover picture and Paul Cathal for proofreading.

INTRODUCTION

I. The Turk's broken finger and the Aims of Research

The Iranian director Abbas Kiarostami's award winning film, *A Taste of Cherry*, is about a man in a mid-life crisis, who is determined to commit suicide but is in desperate need of a helping hand because of the peculiar way that he chooses to do it. After a long search around the suburbs of Tehran, which results in being refused by two candidates – a soldier from Kurdistan and an Islamic cleric from Afghanistan – the suicidal character finally finds the man he has been looking for. This collaborator turns out to be a wise man with a repertoire of stories around the theme of death instinct, one of which is about a Turk:

'A Turk goes to see a doctor. He tells him: "when I touch my finger to my body, my body hurts. When I touch my head, it hurts; my legs, they hurt; my belly and my hand, they both hurt." The doctor examines him and then tells him: "Your body is fine but your finger is broken!"

And inherent in 'the moral' of this story is a rather harsh verdict on the Turks:

'My dear man, your mind is ill. But there is nothing wrong with you. Change your outlook!'

Although this statement is more revealing of the Turkish image in Persian identity than being an appropriate description of Turkishness, the story itself can be useful as a metaphor of what this research is about: Firstly 'the Turk', who enters this text as the main object of analysis in the form of Turkish political identity. Secondly, the 'broken finger', that is, an essential problem or a set of primordial problems which have been circled around and around by this subject, but is still lacking appropriate signification, for with this very broken finger, the Turk is unable to 'hit the real'.[1]

In order to explicate the meaning of this statement, and the aims of this research, I will quote below a recent affair, 'The Minority Report Affair', as a symptomatic exhibit of what is meant by a prohibited primordial problem.

I.1. The Minority Report Affair: Turkish Identity in Crisis

On 1 November 2004, a report on the 'minority rights in Turkey', authered by the Minority Rights and Cultural Rights Committee of Human Rights Advisory Group of the Prime Minister, was presented to the press. The report analysed the Lousanne Treaty and the points of failure in its implementation regarding minority rights, including in particular the linguistic obstruction of the use of Kurdish. The report also proposed using the phrase 'of Turkey' rather than 'Turkish' in the definition of national identity, as a gesture of respect to the country's ethnic heterogeneity. During the presentation of the report by the Committee

---

[1] This is Bruce Fink's description of the state of the (neurotic) analysand, where the analyst's pointing to the analysand where s/he has 'hit the real' could open up a path for the analysand's further interpretation.

6

Chairman, Professor Ibrahim Kaboglu, the leader of an ultra nationalist trades union confederation, Fahrettin Yokus, grabbed the papers from the professor's hand and tore them down. A few days after this event the deputy Chief of Staff, General Basbug, declared that the 'Turkish Armed Forces cannot tolerate a debate on the unitary state structure of Turkey'. Prime Minister Recep Tayyip Erdogan failed to defend the authors by claiming that he never authorised the Committee for such a report. Professor Kabaoglu said: 'With this affair, there remains neither opinion nor its freedom'.[2] On 10th November, during the commemoration of Ataturk's death, President Ahmet Necdet Sezer sealed the matter by denouncing the report as 'an interpretation which does not match the facts'. He said, 'the pronunciation of matters that had been resolved by the Lousanne Treaty as if they were problems is a hopeless attempt' and concluded with a threat: 'our history is full of examples of the failure of those attempts on our unity and indivisible integrity.'[3]

This affair and the discourses that have since developed around it represent a typical symptom of the Turkish identity crisis, when read against the background of the major political developments of the last two decades, including the following: Firstly, although the Prime Minister denies it, the Minority Report is part of Turkey's compliance program with the European Union criteria. Secondly, the emergence of minority rights as an issue in Turkish politics - and the denial of it - is closely related to the emergence of the Kurdish liberation movement that has challenged the republican order since the mid-1980s. Thirdly - and this is not immediately recognisable – the secularist bloc has interpreted the report as the manifesto of an anti-Kemalist bloc consisting of foreign forces, 'separatists' and the Islamists, by

---

[2] *Nokta* 8 November 2004.
[3] *Cumhuriyet*, 11 November 2004.

emphasising the fact that the Report has been produced by a government commission.[4] The Minority Report Affair thus represents a symptomatic recognition of three major challenges against the republican social order that have become tangible in the last two decades: integration with the European Union which requires structural reforms, especially regarding political democratisation and the improvement of human rights in compliance with the Copenhagen criteria; the rise of political Islam with the prospect of the political system's relaxation at the expense of official secularism; and the politico-military activities of the Kurdish movement with a 'minimum program' of recognition as a separate identity dressed with cultural rights and political representation.[5] The invigoration of the Turkish 'establishment's defence mechanisms in the form of angry condemnations can mean that the Minority Report did 'hit the real' by emphasising the necessity of a redefinition of the identity of the Turkish political subject and Turkish polity.

I.2. Research Question

The Minority Report was suppressed and an opportunity to discuss its contents was thus wasted. Instead of this, the media, politicians right, centre and left, and the military vocally denounced it. What can be discussed in these circumstances is this suppression, that is, the Affair rather than the Report itself. In other words, although the Report is an attempt to 'hit the real', its reception assumed the form of a series of symptomatic detours around this real,

---

[4] 'The spokesmen of the Nakshibbendi-Suleymanci coalition are marching in tune with the EU fairy-tale, in breach of the nation-state's sovereignty that was established by Ataturk.' (Hikmet Cetinkaya, *Cumhuriyet*, 11 November 2004.) Cetinkaya treats the Report in this article as the manifesto of the Islamists' aim to replace the society based on the Kemalist nation-state with a society of *umma*.

[5] I derive this 'minimum program' from a recent text (9 December 2004) 'What do the Kurds Want in Turkey' produced by the Kurdish Institute and signed by the prominent Kurdish figures from Turkey, including Leyla Zana, the former MP, which was published by *International Herald Tribune* and *Le Monde*.

8

that not only fail to touch the primordial problems that constitute the real of Turkish identity, but also aim to prohibit their enunciation. In fact, this affair is one of many symptomatic phenomena around the same problems that have recurred time and again during recent decades, the most traumatic of them being the anti-Islamist military coup of 28 February 1997 and the suppression of the Kurdish rebellion.

Here it is necessary to note that to assume these symptomatic phenomena as exclusively confined to the space of an 'official ideology', or 'state discourse' or government policies, will flow considering the popular participation in the various prohibitions and acts of suppression. The state-civil society (or centre-periphery) distinction, if the 'state' is assumed as an elite centre 'imposing' its will on the 'periphery', is not stable, at least in the Turkish experience and it is dissolvable around the term 'identity'. In classical terms, identity is the space in which the 'official', 'dominant' and 'popular' ideologies congregate and disperse to form the popular perceptions of self and the other and to provide popular discourses with a shared grammar. In Gramscian terms, the suppression of the Kurdish rebellion and of the Islamist revival and the politico-linguistic prohibitions that accompany these practices were various expressions of the 'national-popular will'.[6]

The Minority Report Affair can also be read as a demonstration of this combined dispersal and congregation. The Report was commissioned to civilian academics (civil society) by the government (State). It was torn down by the leader of a 'civil society' organisation and this attack was backed by the main-stream media, another civil society institution, and the

---

[6] Practices motivated by a hegemonic articulation of ideology and common sense and performed collectively by the state and civil society.

9

military and the President, that is, the State. The Minority Report Affair is therefore a spectacular demonstration, performed by various components of modern Turkish identity, with the 'active consent' of the audience, of the built-in psychic defence mechanisms of Turkishness, which paradoxically reveal the malfunctioning of the Turkish subject and the symbolic order.

What is therefore meant by the analysis of the Affair itself is to pose the following as one of the leading research questions: 'what kind of identity perceptions - of the self and the other - accompany these symptomatic responses to the Kurdish and Islamic demands of recognition?' Pursuing this question requires an analysis of the contemporary symptoms, which, in their very attempt at exclusion and obliteration, repeatedly gesture to a shared location of 'the outside' and 'the past'. Consequently, what is required in the analysis of what is present 'here and now' is above all an inquiry into this simultaneously present and absent space of the excluded. The traces to be followed begin with what returns to the discourse as metaphorical hints or 'slips of tongue': the 'outside' and the 'past' of the speaking subject.[7] This approach, which I shall call a symptomal reading of the present crisis requires the inclusion of an attempt to write a 'history of the present'.[8] I shall not claim to have written in this text a history of the 'others' of Turkish identity, but I will do my best to focus on the discourses about the other, and to collect and register all the available data produced by these others. This method is based on an understanding of the primal principle of the Foucauldian methods of archaeology and genealogy: understanding any identity is only possible through

---

[7] For instance, 'going back', 'Arab' (Chapter 3) and 'Armenian' (Chapter 2).
[8] With the above comments, I have already identified two main methodological premises – psychoanalysis and genealogy – of this research. I will explicate the meaning and the application of these methods further in this chapter.

an understanding of the outside of that identity, mainly through the discourses of the identity about its others. To put it another way, the outside and the past of Turkish identity present 'the royal road' to the untouchable real, for it is precisely around this impossible kernel – of what is lacking and what is excluded – that all of these symptomatic phenomena operate. In other words, given the Lacanian definition of the real[9], the real of the Turkish identity does not exist, it is impossible, but it produces a number of traumatic effects, including the prohibition to speak of it.[10] Hitting the real thus consists of 'preserving the traces of all historical traumas, dreams and catastrophes which the ruling ideology ... would prefer to obliterate'.[11] Grounding itself in this programmatic statement, the overall aim of this research can be described as providing the appropriate tools for the enunciation of the sediments of the repressed, disavowed and foreclosed traumas that are constitutive of modern Turkishness, and paradoxically the re-staging – or the fear of re-staging – of which is the main cause of the contemporary crisis.

This research will be premised upon a recognition of contemporary dislocations of Turkish social order as signifying a political identity crisis, and aim to make this crisis intelligible through political analysis.[12] The argument will therefore advance at three levels, which correspond to three primary aims of this research. First, an inquiry into the modern perceptions of Turkish identity; second, an inquiry into the mechanisms, nature and the spaces of exclusion that have been crucial in the demarcation of the borders of Turkish identity; and third, the analysis of the traces of constitutive traumas, dreams and catastrophes,

---

[9] The real is the impossible, because it is impossible to imagine, impossible to integrate into symbolic register and impossible to attain in any way (Evans 1996: 160).
[10] See Zizek 1989: 164.
[11] Zizek 1991: 273.

which have repeatedly tried to be 'forgotten', prohibited, excluded or obliterated through the functioning of various defence mechanisms that constitute the Turkish political psyche.[13]

Summing up the above introduction, the main research question that this study has been organised around is as follows: What are the mechanisms that prevent the accommodation by the Turkish polity of contemporary political and discursive challenges and the identity claims enveloped in these challenges? An adequate response to this question immediately necessitates a query around the following questions:

- How can the constitutive features of Turkish political identity be defined?
  - What are the main axes around which the modern perceptions of identity emerged in Turkey?
  - What is the nature of the discursive practices that contributed to these perceptions to lead to the emergence of the Turkish identity?
  - What role did exclusion play in this constitution, and which mechanisms of exclusion did accompany the construction of modern Turkish identity?
- To what degree and in what forms have these features been challenged in the history of modern Turkey, prior to the emergence of the symptoms of contemporary crisis?
- What are the distinguishing features of the contemporary crisis; or to put it differently, to what extent can the current crisis of the Turkish political order be defined as a crisis of Turkish political identity?

---

[12] See the summary of thesis argument in Section V below.
[13] I will clarify in section III of this chapter what is meant by the notion of 'political psyche'.

12

- How can the current challenges be situated around the main constitutive axes of Turkish political identity?

- In what respects do the contemporary discourses of opposition challenge the constitutive discourses?

- To what extent and at which nodal points do the contemporary challenges destabilise or demonstrate the potential to destabilise the modern perceptions of identity in Turkey?

- What is the relationship between the contemporary challenges and the discourses, mechanisms and practices of exclusion through which the modern Turkish identity was defined?

In what follows in this introductory chapter, I will firstly review the available literature on the questions of Turkish political identity and the current crisis; I will then move on to explicate respectively theoretical resources and evidentiary sources of this research; and conclude by presenting a summary of thesis argument and chapter breakdown.

II. Literature Review

Although the phenomenon of identity has become a paradigm of social and political research in recent decades, there exists very limited literature consisting of scholarly works on Turkish identity. Most of these works of anthropology or social anthropology are grounded in a notion of identity as an exclusively cultural phenomenon. The very limited literature on political identity, on the other hand, has significant limitations regarding the definition of political identity and its links with the contemporary crisis. In this section, I will review and criticise both the anthropologic and political literature on Turkish identity

II.1. Social Anthropology Studies

Bozkurt Guvenc's *Turkish Identity* (1993) attempts to give a comprehensive account of history and present of the 'Turks' from their origins in Central Asia to the Seljuks, Ottomans and the modern republic. Guvenc proposes a synthesis that would bring together all the historical elements of Turkish history and the Anatolian civilisations. There is however very limited discussion regarding the quest for identity and the ongoing identity crisis. Instead, Guvenc seems to be primarily concerned with presenting a neo-Kemalist cultural alternative to the 'Turk-Islam Synthesis'[14]. One of the problems involved in this proposal is the 'agent' that would implement Guvenc's synthesis, that is, the Turkish State.[15] Guvenc's alternative 'synthesis' inevitably produces a new grand-narrative of Turkish history, which implicitly claims that Turkishness of the present is the result of a series of multi-lateral historical influences.[16] This may be true, but it is also true that the constitutive discourses of Turkish identity do not begin with the Turks' 'prehistory'. In the light of the body of scholarly research on national identity by Anderson (1991), Hobsbawm (1990) and Balibar and Wallerstein (1994), any discourse sustaining the conventional perception of nation as an essential entity that travel through history to arrive at its teleological end (nation-state) needs to be treated as a nationalist grandnarrative.

---

[14] See Chapter 6.
[15] Given that this massive volume is among the Ministry of Culture publications, I derive that Guvenc's not so much 'secret' agent is the Turkish State.

14

Sharing this critical position, Suavi Aydin's, *The Problem of Identity, Nationhood and 'Turkish Identity'* (1998) argues against the Turkish nationalist historiography by demonstrating that 'the use of the denomination "Turk" as the ethnogenesis of the Ottomans and the Turkish-speaking inhabitants of Anatolia and Thrace dates to the second half of the 19th Century'. Aydin views the problem of Turkish identity as a consequence of the weakness of the Turkish ethnic identity, which was discursively constructed and imposed by the 'republican nomenclature' on the people.

A third study in the field of social-anthropology is *Cultural Identity Crisis in Turkey* (1992) by Cengiz Gulec. This work presents a comprehensive analysis of the discourses of Turkish identity with scholarly insight, with a main hypothesis that the views expressed within this discussion consist of expressions of a double search: first, a search for identity in republican Turkey; and second, a search for a solution to the cultural identity crisis. It is striking that despite abundant reference to the 'past', the discussion analysed by Gulec has no mention of the 'outside', that is, although the republican repression of Islamic-Ottoman past is seen as a primary problem, Gulec fails to mention the ethnic exclusion, or foreclosure of 'the Kurd' that accompanied this repression, as a source of identity and its crisis.

Guvenc's advisory position to the Turkish State rules out any possibility of an analysis of the constitutive features of the modern Turkish State, that is, the 'republican governmentality',[17]

---

[16] Guvenc's work can be interpreted as an attempt towards 'Turk-Islam-Anatolia-West Synthesis', but it is difficult to work out how and what quantity of each of these elements are to be brought together in Guvenc's recipe to reach a well-cooked perception of Turkishness of the present.
[17] See Chapter 5.

15

among the essential components of the problem of Turkish identity. The 'myth of origins', the Turkish historiography, within which Guveno's approach is situated, has been powerfully criticised by Aydin. Aydin's study, on the other hand, does not demonstrate any concern with the processes of exclusion that the construction of Turkish identity necessitated. Gulec's work seems to be partially oriented on this concern in its perception of the cultural identity crisis as a consequence of the excluded past, while failing to problematise the ethnic exclusion in the construction of Turkish identity. These inconsistencies and shortcomings are mostly due to the nature of the anthropologic approach, which, beyond an analytic concern, aims to sustain an artificial separation between the cultural and political domains.

II.2. Studies of Political Identity

Taner Akcam's *Turkish National Identity and the Armenian Question* (1992) differs from the above studies in its perception of identity as a political phenomenon. Moreover, this pioneering work relates the construction of Turkish national identity to the violent exclusion of the Armenian existence in Anatolia. Akcam's references to psychoanalysis in understanding this link are also inspiring, the premises of which are however limited to an application of Norbert Elias' holocaust analysis and German identity to the Turkish experience.[18]

Another work that promises to deal with the problem of Turkish political identity is Feroz Ahmad's *Turkey: The Quest for Identity* (2003). Instead, this book provides nothing more

---

[18] Akcam 2004.

16

than an extensive chronology of events of the 20th Century Turkish political history, hence updating the author's 1977 study on Turkish politics.

Hugh Poulton's *Top Hat, Grey Wolf and Crescent* (1997) also gives the first impression of an analysis of nationalism as the hegemonic political identity of Turkey, in its multi-split form – split between modernism, nationalism and Islam. However, although it presents a panorama of modern Turkish history, the thesis stated in the introduction, that the emergence of Turkish nationalism necessitated a transition from the 'imagined community' of Islam to that of nation, has not been pursued to illuminate the problems of contemporary Turkish politics. This is due to Poulton's failure to engage with the empirical data that he presents to identify the changes in the imagination of the community for the diverse discourses of nationalism. The title of the conclusion of the book ('Nationalist Schizophrenia') is an example of its inconsistency, since the chapter fails to explain the relationship between national identity and a psychoanalytic category like schizophrenia. Poulton's empirical-descriptive method thus instead of developing an appropriate analysis, ends up, like Ahmad, with providing a chronological archive to be analysed.

The motive behind the above studies on political identity has probably been the contemporary crisis of Turkish politics and identity, yet none of them demonstrate any clear concern with this crisis. This is precisely the point where Fikret Baskaya's *Bankruptcy of Paradigm* (1990) is distinguished. Baskaya argues in this work that the bankrupt paradigm is the republican/Kemalist ideology. Moreover, Baskaya demonstrates how this bankruptcy is related to the impossibility of sustaining the exclusion of the Kurdish identity. Baskaya,

17

however, does not extend his analysis to the crisis of Turkish political identity for two reasons. Firstly, as an economist, his main concern is to identify the obstacles to Turkey's development; and secondly, Baskaya describes the ideological formation of modern Turkey in terms of the 'artificial' imposition of an 'official ideology' over people. The current crisis is therefore isolated to the space of an official ideology, and not a 'national-popular' crisis as such.

Contrary to Baskaya's description, the identity and discourse oriented approach of this research will demonstrate that the whole field of Turkish politics has become the site of an identity crisis[19], a crisis of Turkish identity. Moreover, this crisis will be related to the ethnic exclusion that Akcam's work traces back to the construction of Turkish identity. In the next section, I will introduce the theoretical resources to be consulted, which will clarify the novelty of this study: this research will be a first attempt of its kind that will undertake an analysis of modern Turkish history in terms of identity politics.

The above works, which constitute the rather limited literature on Turkish identity, will be engaged further in greater detail in appropriate parts of the thesis. There is, on the other hand, an extensive body of literature concerning the particular issues to be dealt with in each chapter. This literature will be considered in greater length throughout this study, by being questioned and criticised wherever appropriate.

---

[19] 'A split of self-images, a loss of centrality, a sense of dispersion and confusion, and a fear of dissolution" is the description of this term by Erik Erikson (1959: 122-3).

III. Theoretical Resources

The primary theoretical stance of this research is premised upon the interpretation of political process in terms of interactive relations between various identities, that is, identity politics. The contemporary preoccupation of political science with identity politics and along with it the questions of recognition, multiculturalism, gender, ethnicity, religion, etc. seems to be echoing Erikson's assertion that 'identity is as strategic in our time as the study of sexuality was in Freud's time.' An identity-oriented approach to politics requires above all a Hegelian insight to view politics as a battle for recognition, driven by a desire for recognition by the other, through which political identities emerge and develop.[20] William Connolly's contribution through his work (1991) on Identity/Difference to this Hegelian insight consists in the introduction of a discourse analytic dimension.

III.1. Identity, Hegemony and Genealogy

Along with these theoretical contributions to the analysis of political identities, what has been recognised globally in recent decades in addition to the centrality of identity to political process is twofold: firstly, the social and political character of every identity; and secondly, the impossibility of attainment of closed, self-contained and absolute identities.[21] As Laclau (1994: 3) argues, the realisation of an originary and insurmountable lack of identity is what produces the desire for identification, leading to a political practice that plays a crucial role in structuring the field of politics. The field of politics is structured through the intersection of

---

[20] See Hegel (1977), Kojeve (1969), Taylor (1989 and 1992) and Butler (1987).
[21] Stavrakakis 2000.

19

the desire of identification with the ideological 'interpellation'[22] of individuals to certain subject positions. The precise link between the ideology's call and the individual's desire for identification is hegemony, which operates above all to achieve a 'naturalised' closure or 'suture' of the subject to the ideology. If identity is what is ultimately impossible, the logic of hegemony is what furnishes the grounds of its imagination as a possibility.

There are two further implications of this theoretical stance: First, if hegemony is the name of that political operation which brings ideologies down to earth, to the 'common sense' level, to achieve identification, then 'identity', or national identity to be precise, is what destabilises the State-civil society and centre-periphery dualities.[23] Similarly, the classical distinctions between 'official', 'dominant' and 'popular' ideologies are dissolved within the body of national identity as a discursive construct that emerge from the congregation at certain nodal points of various discourses to disperse through the social and form a collective 'national-popular' grammar.[24] Second, the hegemonic construction of identity does not merely consist in maintaining identification with the Other; it necessitates at the same time demarcation, that is, constitution of the boundaries that differentiate a social identity from the others.[25] Social

---

[22] Althusser 1977.

[23] It is more legitimate to state that these dualities are also relational, each requiring the existence of the other; they coexist not as an unproblematic and unified totality but to form the body of national identity as a simultaneous process of regulation and dispersion (See Laclau and Mouffe 1985). Consequently, the contemporary crisis is not confined to the site of the official ideology of a nomenclature as such but the whole discursive field of politics, including official, dominant and popular components, has become the site of an identity crisis. C.f. Navaro-Yashin's (2002) argument on Foucauldian and Lacanian premises that the distinction between state and 'civil society' is unstable and is dissolvable around the term 'public' through a deconstructive intervention.

[24] Gramsci's notion of 'active consent' as the precondition of the achievement of hegemonic power or 'integral state', in which ideology disperses through 'common sense' to provide the grammar of 'national-popular will', can therefore be rephrased in terms of 'national identity' (See Gramsci 1971).

[25] This process of simultaneous introjection and projection can also be observed in the Lacanian understanding of the object of psychoanalysis, which is neither the individual nor the 'man' but 'what he is lacking' (Stavrakakis 1998: 36). These assertions are further linked to the comments above on lacking identity and the consequent desire of identification. If the language of psychoanalysis is persistently dragging us time and again

20

identities exist within a 'logic of difference' and their totality as a social order – or 'system' – can only be defined in terms of difference from the 'other', with reference to a 'constitutive outside'.[26] There is therefore always a 'real' space beyond identity, consisting of what has been necessarily externalised and excluded, that is, the outside of identity.[27]

The above theoretical resources will serve as the analytic tools of understanding the constitutive features of modern Turkish identity, by providing an explanation of the hegemonic operation of modernist nationalism to achieve both identification and demarcation/externalisation. The investigation of the modern perceptions of Turkish identity as formed by hegemonic processes of articulation and dispersion will be supported by an

---

towards a (lacking) field of 'lack', of the absence of identity and subject, then the subject is left with the 'mirror of the other' as the sole medium to imagine himself to be existing as a presence. In fact, the mirror occupies the centre of the stage in the constitution of identity on what Lacan calls the 'imaginary' register. The imaginary is the realm of the illusions of identity, sameness, similarity on the one hand and autonomy and wholeness on the other. While the formers are affirmative of the lack and alienation involved even in this process of illusion, the latters produce the effects of coherence, stability and omnipotence. It is this split that is immediately translated into aggressive tension by the infant: 'the imaginary is clearly the prime source of aggressivity in human affairs' (Stavrakakis 1998: 18). This split nature of imaginary register could only be repaired through the simultaneous functioning of linguistic representation, that is, the symbolic order.

[26] This means that the outside fulfils two crucial and contradictory roles at the same time. On the one hand, it is antagonistic, it 'blocks' the full constitution of the objectivity to which it is opposed, and on the other, given that this objectivity is merely relational and would not be what it is outside the relationship with the force opposing it, the outside is also the condition of its existence (Laclau 1990: 17).

[27] Here, I refer to the Lacanian notion of reality, which does not consist only of imaginary and symbolic registers, but includes the functioning of what is excluded from these registers dominated by the symbolic order, that is, the real. The real is what resists symbolisation and escapes the language after symbolisation as a surplus and as such, it represents the limits and the failure of symbolisation. The structures of psychosis and perversion affirm on the other hand that the real is also the location of what has been excluded, exclusion taking in these cases the form of foreclosure and disavowal, by the ego. Like repression, foreclosure and disavowal are linked to traumatic perceptions and developed by the ego as defence mechanisms aiming to erase the traces of their memory (Laplanche and Pontalis 2004). These forms of defence however lead to malfunctioning of the subject and the symbolic order. Foreclosure blocks the formation of symbolic register, since what is foreclosed is precisely what constitutes the symbolic order, that is, the name-of-the-father; while in disavowal, the simultaneous denial and acceptance of what is disavowed radically split the subject (Ich-Schpaldung). The real is the impossible, because it is impossible to imagine, impossible to integrate into symbolic register and impossible to attain in any way (Evans 1996: 160). It is this impossibility which lends the real its essentially traumatic character. Hallucination and delusion, characteristics of the triggered psychosis, appear as the witness of the existence of this parallel-traumatic universe to human reality. What is observed in such cases is the return from without of what has been abolished internally (Freud quoted by Evans 1996: 66), or the reappearance in the order of the real of whatever has been refused in the symbolic order. The order of the real is in a sense

inquiry into the mechanisms, nature and the spaces of exclusion that have been crucial in the demarcation of the borders of Turkish Identity. Consequently, Foucault's genealogical stance of writing 'a history of the present' constitutes the overall structure of this research. The genealogies of modernisation, secularisation and nationalisation, which will be designed around the present concern with the identity crisis, will attempt to provide adequate answers to the question of how these issues became problematic and how their particular form can be dissolved and transfigured.[28] These histories of the present will inevitably include histories of exclusion and the excluded, that is to say that this genealogical inquiry into Turkish identity is only possible through making the outside of Turkishness intelligible, mainly through the analysis of the discourses of identity about its others. In Foucauldian words, writing a history of the present necessitates above all writing the histories of the others. Consequently, this research will focus in consecutive chapters on the moments and the techniques of exclusion; the precise 'things' that have been excluded and the specific forms of exclusion associated with certain psychic structures as the constitutive elements of modern Turkish identity.

Moreover, difference, like identity, is not absolute and guaranteed in any way: it can only be discursively constructed, due mostly to the fact that the other always already exists within identity.[29] In this case, the discursive separation of the self from the other implies a split in the self, which necessitates the operation of psychic defence mechanisms of repression, denial and foreclosure. Following the observation of this 'family resemblance' between the practices of exclusion inherent in the process of identification and the psychic defence

---

crucial for the identity of the symbolic order and human reality, for it is the real that marks the absolute limits of symbolisation. The real, in this sense, is the 'constitutive outside' of symbolic reality.
[28] Foucault 1991: 30-1.

mechanisms, it becomes necessary to clarify my theoretical stance regarding the question of the relevance of psychoanalytic concepts for political analysis, which I will elaborate on before concluding this theoretical introduction.

III.2. The Psychic Dimension of Identity Politics: Torn Country/Split Identity

The reader would have noticed by now the operation of psychoanalytic categories – including symptom, the centrality of 'lack' in the production of 'desire' and the Lacanian concept of human reality as an articulated totality of the three registers of the symbolic, the imaginary and the real – in the above introduction of the main methodological premises. The use of these categories requires justification through a clear demonstration of the relevance for the field of political science of an analytic method developed mainly for clinical practice. Much of this justification has been elaborated in detail by Stavrakakis (1998), where a special emphasis has been placed on the dangers of 'psychologism' and consequently on the boundaries that aim to limit the political scientist's interest in Lacanian psychoanalytic theory to deriving certain concepts that can be useful in approaching and accounting for our socio-political reality and for 'the political *tout court*'.[30] While this theoretical stance is fully agreed and adopted in this research, the concept of 'political psyche' and the psychoanalytic reading of the sociological model based on 'centre-periphery' distinction, which together constitute the main tenets of accounting for both the construction and crisis of Turkish socio-political field and along with it the modern Turkish identity, require particular elaboration, which will be attempted in the paragraphs below.

---

[29] The foreclosure of the Kurd or the Armenian refers to the ethnic ambiguity of Turkishness; the repression of the Islamic/Ottoman 'past' refers to the Oriental dimension of modern Turkish identity.

'Men make their own history', this was the essential motto of the Enlightenment in its bid against the conventional teleology of the Judeo-Christian metanarrative. Since the hegemonic emergence of this profane perception, questions around the human subject have dominated philosophical inquiry in various fields of 'human sciences', including ethics, law, politics, economics and sociology. The immediate solution of the 'moderns' consisted of the 'reoccupation'[31] of the void left from divinity by 'reason' and 'rationality'. Human subjectivity was thus imagined as possessing a built-in rationality. The precondition of maintaining this perception however was to generalise the categories of the mad and the criminal in order to account for the irrational or unreasonable behaviour as mental and behavioural deviations eligible for 'correction' and 'punishment' through various therapeutic and disciplinary interventions. However, the scandalous secret of modernity, which Michel Foucault has elaborately surfaced, is that these 'rational' and 'reasonable' practices also involve extensively irrational, unreasonable, mad and criminal aspects.[32] Foucault's discovery, which necessitates a serious rethinking of the notions of modernity, power and legitimacy, would have been impossible without the groundbreaking contributions by psychoanalysis to the interpretation of human behaviour. To put simply, for the purposes of my theoretical argument, Freudian psychoanalysis informs every field of scientific research by demonstrating that each statement or enunciation and therefore each discourse accommodates an unconscious dimension in addition to the conscious/rational 'meaning'. When illuminated by the light of psychoanalysis, scientific research in the socio-political

---

[30] Stavrakakis 1998: 8.
[31] See Blumenberg (1987).

24

field can no longer be conducted with the conventional approaches centred around a perception of human subjectivity in terms of 'thinking cogito', preoccupied with the problems of consciousness. One way out of the conventional inconsistency is to introduce the psychic dimension of socio-political reality, which will be both complementary and deconstructive[33] for the concept of 'society'[34] imagined by the modern scholarship as a closed system consisting of an aggregate of rational/conscious subjects.[35] The term political psyche is also grounded upon these premises not as an 'essence' as such but to affirm that each political identity, which is constituted at the nodal points where a variety of discursive practices congregate (identification), inevitably accommodates an unconscious dimension, as much as its rational/conscious content.[36]

The concept of political identity can therefore be reintroduced as the site of the articulation of political subjectivity with political psyche through which a number of imagined dualities, including primarily the subject/psyche duality, can be destabilised and deconstructed. This psychoanalytic stance opens the way for understanding the reciprocity between the contemporary identity crisis in Turkey and the symptomatic triggering of defence mechanisms. The Turkish identity crisis could therefore become intelligible through an investigation of the traces of constitutive traumas, dreams and catastrophes, which have

---

[32] Daily press reports rather than an intensive study of Foucault's *Madness and Civilisation* and *Discipline and Punish* are sufficient to see the mad and criminal practices involved in the American-British occupation of Iraq, the manifest aim of which was a 'reasonable' overthrow of a 'mad and criminal dictator'.

[33] Here, I rely on the definition of 'supplement' by Jacques Derrida (1981).

[34] C.f. Laclau 1990a.

[35] including also those who are waiting to gain consciousness through 'progress'.

[36] It is important to note here that as the name of the psychic dimension of human subjectivity, 'psyche' is not exclusively located in the unconscious or in the Id as opposed to consciousness or the location of the ego and superego, but cuts across these levels and is partially accommodated by each of them (see, Leledakis 1995).

25

repeatedly tried to be 'forgotten', prohibited, excluded or obliterated through the functioning of various defence mechanisms that constitute Turkish political psyche.

So far, I have presented the term identity as a category that overrides – and deconstructs – a series of conventionally assumed distinctions. This perception however does not claim that these distinctions and dualities are groundless, and although political identities aim to quilt over them, given the objective, as much as the imaginary and analytic, validity of these distinctions, the nature of any identity is inevitably that it is split.[37] The coordinates of this split in the Turkish subject can only be derived from the dislocated objectivity, for it is the desire to construct the social objectivity as a fullness that produces the political subject in the first place. A description of the dislocated structure of modern Turkey has been attempted by Samuel Huntington in his presentation of Turkey as the prototype of a 'torn country' – torn in the middle of what he calls 'the clash of civilisations':

> The late twentieth century leaders of Turkey have followed in the Ataturk tradition and defined Turkey as a modern, secular, Western nation state. They allied Turkey with the West in NATO and in the Gulf War; they applied for membership in the European Community. At the same time, however, elements in Turkish society have supported an Islamic revival and have argued that Turkey is basically a Middle Eastern Muslim society. In addition, while Turkey has defined Turkey as a Western society, the elite of the West refuses to accept Turkey as such.[38]

---

[37] The split can be observed between the analytic domains of cultural and political; in identification and its primordial impossibility, in the split between the self and the other and that between social and the individual, subjectivity and psyche, and conscious and unconscious. Identity can be claimed to be 'neither/nor' of any of these dualities but in its practical incarnation as political subject it is inevitably split between the choices of 'either/or'.
[38] Huntington 1993.

26

Although this 'geopolitical' description fails to demonstrate any awareness of a further major conflict that 'tears apart' contemporary Turkish society, that is, the Kurdish rebellion, the term 'torn country' is more promising than the author's intentions, and is open to the following interpretation: Turkey is a torn country because – or therefore – Turkish identity is a torn or split identity. Among the vast literature on modern Turkish history, the approach which comes closest to account for the split nature of that objectivity called Turkish society is the 'centre-periphery' model introduced by Serif Mardin (1975). Unlike the modernisation school which rests upon a forecast of ultimate superseding of the modernity/tradition dualism through economic and political development, Mardin interprets Turkey's modern history in terms of ongoing tensions and interactive relations between centre (modernity) and periphery (tradition), which does not necessarily lead to an *aufhebung* as such. This research incorporates to a large extent this revisionist Weberian stance, but only with a significant psychoanalytic twist, which takes the process of repression in the constitution (or affirmation) of the 'periphery', and its radical otherness to the 'centre', into account. The dual nature of the social gained a split character with the transition to modernity, for this duality was achieved (or an already existing duality renewed) through the mobilisation and the subsequent repression of the periphery.[39] The suppression of the mobilised periphery requires an interpretation in psychoanalytic terms as 'repression', because the modernist elite, in moulding the model of modernisation in their personality, had to externalise primarily the traditional components of their own selves through a process of repression. The

---

[39] The mobilisation of the Muslim periphery reached its peak during the National Struggle of 1919-1922 and was followed by its physical and discursive repression (see Chapter 1). The subsequent mobilisation and repression is arguably a universal model of transition to modern polity since the French revolution, for what happened in France between 1789 and 1871 was the popular mobilisation of a variety of disadvantaged groups against monarchy and 'ancient regime' by the bourgeois leadership followed by their repression (see Guerin 1946 and Marx and Engels 'The Address to the Central Committee of the Communist Leage').

model that they presented has to a large extent been an appeal to the 'nation' for the repetition of this neurosis, that is, this act of repression committed by the 'leaders', as the precondition of becoming a 'modern nation'. In other words, most of what has been achieved in the name of modernisation in Turkey is the dispersal of the 'repressed tradition' through the periphery's 'common sense'. The process that we have been witnessing since the mid-1980s consists primarily of the traumatic results of the unleashed energies driven by the revival of repressed identities and traditions, under the conditions of a new global orientation characterised by a nearly fatal erosion of the modern grandnarratives of progress and modernisation. The symptomatic nature of this 'setting free' becomes intelligible when understood in terms of that neurotic mechanism of 'return of the repressed', in which the repressed unconscious of the modernised identity has been returning, and taking the immediate form of a conflict between secularism and Islamism. What is proposed here is an amendment of the centre-periphery topology of the social of Turkey – in favour of a topology shaped in terms of consciousness and unconscious based on an affirmation of the radical otherness of the unconscious of the split social as bearing the potential of leading to traumatic dislocations of the social reality, analogous to the psychoanalytic process of 'return of the repressed'.

While it is relevant to note here that with this 'psychic dimension of the social', the term 'political psyche' also gains its analytic value,[40] it is still necessary to stress that rather than

---

[40] The inadequacy of the agent-structure or society-subject model with its preoccupation with the problems of consciousness requires an enrichment with the dimension of 'psychic structure' and 'political psyche' with an emphasis on the unconscious processes that operate beneath the immediately visible 'social structure' or 'symbolic order'.

proposing a psychoanalytic model of politics as such, what I propose is merely adding a psychoanalytic dimension to an existing model.[41]

If discourse analysis can be defined along with Zizek (1989: 125) as 'symptomal reading' then discourse analysis is the exact name of the methodological model presented in this section, consisting of the articulation of three major resources (discourse theory, psychoanalysis and genealogy), since what will be attempted by this research is a 'symptomal reading' of the contemporary identity crisis to reveal the sediments of condensed and displaced (or 'forgotten' through the mechanisms of repression, denial and foreclosure) traumas beneath (or historically behind or 'outside') the symptomatic and metaphoric expressions of the dislocated social by the traumatised political subject.

One of the immediate benefits of this symptomal reading that this research demonstrates is the analysis in Chapter 2 of the association of the signifiers 'Armenian' and the 'Kurd' in the contemporary discourses of Turkish politics as an unconscious reference to the originary

---

[41] A comprehensive psychoanalytic model of political interpretation can legitimately be developed, with no more than the usual problems involved in any model of political/social interpretation. There are at least two usual problems of any such theoretical modelling. Firstly, like the rest of the models, it will fail to be exhaustive and inevitably leave out certain dimensions of the social and political reality. Secondly, it will be an understanding of the reality through a metaphor, the metaphor in this case resting upon the trilogy of the id/ego/superego or the consciousness/unconscious dualism. So, if we take Sigmund Freud's programmatic statement literally, 'we can deal with peoples as we do with an individual neurotic' ("The Truth of Religion' in Freud 1939: 128), we can legitimately end up by introducing another metaphorical model of the social, the metaphor being a psychiatric patient suffering from neurosis. This would be a legitimate model knowing that all models represent the understanding of social reality through various metaphors, which ultimately fail to correspond fully to the reality. The psychiatric patient metaphor would not be less appropriate than the metaphor of a construction site (base and superstructure) or building/builder duality (structure/agency) or the Enlightenment model of human body (body politique a la Rousseau or Leviathan a la Hobbes or the 'Physiocrats'), etc., in understanding the social. The problem is not so much falling into the trap of 'psychoanalytic reductionism' but the fact that all the metaphors under the sun for the 'reduction' of the social have already been exhausted. This footnote can be read as an attempt to pursue what is involved in Stavrakakis' programmatic conclusion on the same issue: 'The important question is not "reduction or no-reduction" but "what kind of reduction?" In order to create a distance from crude reduction, it is necessary to operate within the field of reduction; it is necessary to *reduce reduction* to its own *impossibility*'. (Stavrakakis 1999: 142.)

act of physical elimination of the non-Muslim elements of Anatolia accompanied by a psychic obliteration of the trauma of the Empire's catastrophic collapse, I argue that 'Armenian' was the signifier of this foreclosed originary trauma and the Kurdish resistence against assimilation by the modern Turkish identity in the formative years of the republic served to trigger the pathologies specific to the mechanism of foreclosure thus making it possible for the 'Kurd' to replace the 'Armenian' as the signifier ejected from the unconscious of the Turkish political subject. In Chapter 2, Chapter 6 and Conclusion, I demonstrate on these grounds that this metonymic association of the signifiers 'Kurd' and 'Armenian' in the political discourses of modern Turkish identity explains the necessarily violent nature of any encounter between the Turkish national identity and the Kurdish identity claims through the republican history, given the pathologies appropriate to a constitutive feature of the modern Turkish identity, that is, the mechanism of foreclosure.[42]

Upon the above theoretical-methodological premises the main hypothesis of this study is as follows: 'The resistance to the accommodation of contemporary political and discursive practices of opposition and the denial of the identity claims enveloped in these practices are the constitutive characters of Turkish political identity.' Consequently, the contemporary conjuncture in which the excluded discourses and practices have powerfully challenged the structural conventions of Turkish political order is distinguished with its character of being an identity crisis. It is an organic crisis[43], that is, an epistemic, or 'paradigmatic'[44], crisis of legitimacy, hegemony and above all a crisis of Turkish political identity. This study will

---

[42] See Chapter 2.
[43] As opposed to a cyclical notion of crisis, which recurs due to the inherent contradictions of national and international character of capitalist economy (See Gramsci 1971: 210-8 and Norval 1996: 116-7).
[44] See Baskaya

30

pursue this overall hypothesis by testing the following sub-hypotheses against evidentiary data:

a) The contemporary crisis is revealing of dislocations of Turkish political order around the main axes of the modern identity perceptions, including the issues of modernisation, nationalisation and secularisation.

b) The constitutive discourses of Turkish identity, nationalism, westernism and secularism have been tangibly challenged since the emergence of the contemporary crisis.

c) The current discursive challenges radically destabilise the existing conventions of identity and difference, which have gathered a diversity of political discourses under the modern Turkish polity and sutured a variety of subject positions to a shared perception of Turkish identity.

d) The power and the specific character of the contemporary crisis arise from the fact that it advances through the emergence of certain discursive practices that are closely related to those identity perceptions, which have been the subject of discourses, mechanisms and practices of exclusion in the definition of modern Turkish identity. Because of this, the contemporary crisis could be defined as the symptomatic consequence of the return of the 'others' of modern Turkish identity.

IV. Evidentiary Sources

The methodology of this research will consequently include an extensive study of the formation and the dynamics of destabilisation of modern Turkish identity. The time-scope of the evidentiary material to be analysed expands over a century. Consequently, the selection

31

and the organisation of the material of analysis, which I will list below, has been an important part of this study.

A number of scholarly works on late Ottoman and republican history[45], and scholarly reflections on the rise of Islamism[46] and Kurdish identity[47] have constituted the background reading for the preparation of this project. The archival research that has been conducted includes daily monitoring of Turkey's mainstream and peripheral (Islamist) and 'subversive' (Kurdish) media, including newspapers and TV channels from 1985 to the present[48]. A collection of the reports on Turkey in the English language media[49] constitutes another important group of evidentiary sources. A number of books by various journalists provide extensive information on the rise of Islamism[50] and the challenge of Kurdish political identity[51] to be analysed in this research.

---

[45] Including Caglar Keyder (1987), Sungur Savran (1992), Bernard Lewis (1968) and Serif Mardin (1975 and 1991a) and Sina Aksin (1997 – 5 volumes).
[46] Haldun Gulalp (2002 and 2003), Nilufer Gole (1996), Jenny White (2002) and Elizabeth Ozdalga (1998).
[47] Kemal Kirisci and Gareth Winrow (1997), Henry J. Barkey and Graham Fuller (1998), Baskin Oran (2000 and 2002).
[48] Islamist newspapers include *Zaman, Vakit* (formerly *Akit*), *Milli Gazete* and *Yeni Safak;* Islamist journals *Soz, Imza, Mektup, Son Karar* are the main sources that have been monitored; Kurdish daily *Ozgur Gundem* (published in various names, including *Gundem, Yeni Gundem* and *Demokrasi,* after being banned by Turkish courts, and under the name *Ozgur Politika* in Europe), the Kurdish TV channel *Med TV* (operates currently under the name *Medya TV* after being banned in Europe upon Turkish government's request), the weekly *Ozgur Ulke* and the PKK's journals *Serxwebun* and *Berxwedan* are the Kurdish sources.
[49] Including in particular *Le Monde Diplomatique, The Guardian International, BBC World Service, Financial Times, Independent, The Economist* and *International Herald Tribune.*
[50] Rusen Cakir's books on political Islam (1991) and Welfare Party (1995) and the *New York Times* correspondent Stephan Kinzer's *Crescent and Star* (2001) are three significant references of this research.
[51] Left-Kemalist journalist Ugur Mumcu's unfinished project (Mumcu 1992 and 1995 - disturbed by the author's assassination in an 'unresolved murder') on Kurdish rebellions in republican history, former Turkey correspondent of *The Guardian* Jonathan Rugman's *Ataturk's Children* (1996 - co-authored by photojournalist Roger Hutchings), Nadire Mater's *Memedin Kitabi* (1999), Hasan Cemal's *Kurtler* (2003) and Rafet Balli's *Kurt Dosyasi* (1991) will be referred to in the context of Kurdish question.

Since the excluded identities are given special emphasis as a method of understanding Turkish identity, periodicals and other publications by the pro-Kurdish and Islamist political groups, parties and writers have also been monitored. In addition to reflecting on the writings of the vanguards of the Islamist movement in republican history, including Necip Fazil Kisakurek and Said-i Nursi, contemporary Islamist writer Abdurrahman Dilipak's works on modern Turkish history will receive special attention. Regarding the pro-Kurdish literature, Ismail Besikci's scholarly works require particular attention since these works pioneered the Turkish academy's recent interest in the Kurdish question. Although they are marked by the theoretical limitations of the era, they still initiate an opening towards a concern with identity and ideology in an environment predominantly obsessed by 'economic base', modernisation and Kemalist developmentalism or alternatively (the lack of) liberalism. Following on Besikci's concerns, Yegen (1999) provides an Althuserian analysis, informed by Foucault's 'structuralist' assertions, of the Turkish state discourse and discursive practices of the Kemalist period on the Kurdish question. Kurdish academic Hamit Bozarslan's articles (2000 & 2002) problematise two main issues involved in the Kurdish revival: firstly, the ambiguity of boundaries between Kemalism and Kurdish nationalist discourse, and secondly, the dominance of violence as the sole language of the Turkish encounter with Kurdish identity. All the above literature on the periphery of Turkish identity will be engaged when appropriate throughout this research.

While the genealogical emphasis of this research will be on these discourses of the excluded, the discourses of the 'centre', including discourses of exclusion and the recent decades' symptomatic expressions of the Turkish identity in turmoil[52], will be analysed in their relation to the discourses of the excluded 'periphery'.

Before concluding this list of evidentiary sources, it is necessary to state three different sources, which support various tenets of this study. Firstly, Serif Mardin's sociological interest in the religious periphery in his studies on republican history[53] provided the conduct of this research with extensive insight. Secondly, Etienne Copeaux's analysis of history curricula in republican Turkey[54] with its emphasis on the discourses of exclusion in different schools of Turkish historiography contributed greatly to this research's analytic exaction of the absolute boundaries that separate Turkish identity from its others. Finally, Ahmet Yildiz's (2000) powerful analysis of the link between the Kurdish exclusion and the emergence of an ethnic oriented nationalist discourse in the formative years of the Turkish republic has been incorporated to constitute the background to the main arguments of this research.

V. Summary of Thesis Argument and Chapter Breakdown

Given its central research problem, this thesis will be structured as a study of the resistance of the Turkish body politic to the accommodation of contemporary political and discursive practices of opposition and the denial of identity claims enveloped in these practices. Consequently, the analysis of the distinguishing features of the contemporary conjuncture in which the excluded discourses and practices have powerfully challenged the structural

---

[52] These will include statements by the prominent figures of the Turkish State and official texts, such as the constitution, laws and regulations, along with the commentary by the prominent figures of the mainstream press and media.
[53] See Mardin 1969, 1981, 1991 and 1992.

34

conventions of Turkish political order will lead to a main argument that the contemporary crisis is an organic crisis, that is, an epistemic crisis of legitimacy, hegemony and above all a crisis of Turkish political identity. To support this argument, evidence will be produced to argue that the three coordinates – modernisation, secularisation and nationalisation – at the conjuncture of which modern Turkish identity emerged in the transition from the 19th Century to the 20th have become problematic once again in the transition to a new century. These issues have become problematic as a consequence of a tangible revival in the last two decades of those identities, which had been excluded from modern Turkishness in the constitution of the latter. The formation of the mechanisms of exclusion as the built-in components of modern Turkish identity was necessitated by the traumatic experience of the gradual but catastrophic disintegration of the Ottoman Empire through the 19th Century. It is this tight fit through traumatic perceptions between the construction of Turkishness as a modern and secular national identity and the exclusion of those 'unfit' elements which has been responsible for the current identity crisis, since through this crisis it has become impossible to sustain the denial of ethnic heterogeneity and the repression of the religious affiliations of Turkish society.

The psychoanalytic method, consisting mainly of establishing the origin of the trauma that lies at the roots of a present symptom, the ego's erasing of the memory of this traumatic experience through repression, denial or foreclosure, and the inevitability of the return of this excluded element to trigger off pathologies appropriate to these defense mechanisms, is incorporated in the structure of this theoretical research. The initial chapters that follow consider the dynamics of exclusion embedded in the processes of secularisation (Chapter 1)

eaux 1998.

35

and nationalisation (Chapter 2), to be followed by two chapters that focus on the institutionalisation of the appropriate defense mechanisms that led to the consolidation of these exclusionary practices in the republican discursive formation. The first four chapters of this thesis therefore focus on the analysis of 'repression', to be followed by three chapters which consider the various manifestations of the inevitable process of 'the return of the repressed'. Consequently, while Chapter 5 documents the manifestations of the inconsistencies of the republican identity design in the politico-philosophical discussion on the quest for identity through the republican history, Chapter 6 concentrates on the genealogies of the excluded identities and the consequences of their irruption onto the republican discursive surface. In the Conclusion, consequences of the contemporary experiences of 'the return of the repressed' are considered to lead to an argument for a redesign of the politico-discursive order of republican Turkey. I shall explicate furher this overall structure through a detailed presentation of the chapter by chapter development of the thesis' argument in the paragraphs below.

Given the constitutive and destructive roles of exclusion and its impossibility, a genealogical inquiry in the moments of exclusion of the recently 'returning' identities must be holding the key to an understanding of the contemporary crisis. Consequently, I will develop my argument through the genealogies of secularisation and nationalisation in the two subsequent chapters to follow. These chapters will be primarily devoted to finding adequate answers to the questions of what precisely has been excluded and what forms and mechanisms were involved in the moments of their exclusion. Additionally, the argument in these chapters will identify the conditions in which the operation of exclusionary mechanisms became necessary for the construction of the specific design of modern Turkish identity. The building of this specific form of modern identity corresponded to the constitution of the republican power, which I will consider in terms of the three constitutive axes of modern national identity in chapters 3 and 4. In chapter 3, the argument will elaborate mainly on the meaning of the sustained status of the myth of Ataturk for modern Turkishness. I will argue that this exceptional place mainly consists in the function of this myth as much being a positive cult of identification as being the signifier of demarcation of the boundaries that separate the 'modern Turk' from his others. In Chapter 4, I will conduct an inquiry into the construction of the republican regime, which involved a hardening and deepening of the exclusionary processes through 'republican discursive practices' of specifically designed 'republican institutions'. The analysis to be conducted in this chapter along with that of Chapter 3 will present the reader a description of 'republican governmentality', as a constant process of articulation, which, while producing and reproducing the centre-periphery duality has also welded together the opposing sides of this dual totality within a broad concept of Turkish identity. The next chapter (Chapter 5) will advance this argument by demonstrating that the politico-philosophical discussion on the quest for identity under the discursive horizon of nationalism and Kemalism, while emphasising this duality of the split social, has failed to problematise the nationalist boundaries of Turkishness and included in their discourse the symptoms related to the problems originating from the processes of externalisation in the constitution of these absolute boundaries. The aim of the course of argument in chapter 6 is threefold: Firstly, the genealogies of the excluded identities through which metaphorical criticisms of the deficiencies of Turkish social order were accumulated in those spaces beneath and outside the symbolic order, as the prelude to their return. Secondly, establishing

37

the peculiarities of the contemporary crisis in its difference from the previous crises that have been observed in republican history, which will enable its description as an identity crisis accompanying the organic crisis of republican governmentality. It is within the context of such a crisis that the traumatic experience of the return of the repressed and foreclosed identities will be situated. And thirdly, a return of focus on the returning identities in order to explicate the form in which they have been returning and the traumatic impact of the revival of their challenge on the Turkish symbolic order and identity. Finally, in the Conclusion, I will argue that the contemporary suppression of the returning identities has necessitated the processes of a second nationalisation and a second secularisation of the socio-political field of republican Turkey. I will demonstrate that these processes have been driven by fear of a re-staging of the traumatic experience of the catastrophic collapse of the Ottoman Empire and consequently aimed to restore the built-in defence mechanisms of Turkish identity, hence reinforcing the 'fortresses and trenches' of republican governmentality. I will then inquire into the consequences of this double suppression by identifying the political frontiers redrawn in this process and the present conditions of the re-suppressed identities. The evaluation of the present situation will lead to an argument in conclusion that the radically dislocated symbolic order of republican Turkey necessitates a redesign of the politico-discursive order, based on a radical rethinking of the political subjectivity and political identity.

38

CHAPTER 1

DE-ISLAMISATION: A GENEALOGY OF THE 'REPRESSED'

Introduction: Madness and Secularisation

On 10 November 1994, during the Ataturk commemoration ceremony in Anitkabir, Ankara, a man suddenly appeared among the press photographers and TV crews and shouted: 'These stones cannot bring you salvation. I invite you to Koran. Worship God not the idols.' He continued this 'assault' by chanting in Arabic, 'There is only one God; God is great' until being carried away from the scene by four security guards.[55] The religious man, Mahmut Kacar, was charged with 'Defamation of Ataturk' requiring one to three year imprisonment.[56] President Suleyman Demirel, who was at the head of the ceremony referred Kacar as *meczup* (insane), a term which was immediately taken up and popularised by the media and medical authorities:

'Psychiatrists: 'Either a militant or insane'

Psychiatrists analysing the Anıtkabir aggressor's behaviour, declare that he is either a fundamentalist militant or mentally ill. Dr Arif Verimli, Assistant Professor of Psychiatry and the governor of Bakırköy Hospital for Mental, Psychological and Neurological Disorders, states that Kaçar's psychiatric examination is necessary. (...)

'By insinuating that he had been assigned to this duty by God, he demonstrates the portrait of a mentally ill person', (...) states Dr Verimli and adds: 'As a person who lives with Atatürk and who understands Him, I am very upset about what happened'.[57]

---

[55] *Milliyet*, Friday, 11 November 1994, European edition.
[56] *Milliyet*, Saturday, 12 November 1994, European edition.
[57] *Milliyet*, Saturday, 12 November 1994, European edition..

Demirel's term, 'insane', to label any such protest involving Islamic tones soon gained popularity. In 1999, following another identical 'assault' during 10 November ceremony by Salih Kaya, Demirel refused to comment for the media on the incident stating, 'what can I tell you about an insane man?'[58]

The importance of the Anitkabir incidents of 'return of the insane' of the mid 1990s lies in that they were staged against the background of an ongoing political battle between the secularists and Islamists. More importantly, a discourse analytic approach to these incidents would reveal the split character of contemporary Turkey, since if we do not feel obliged to accept the President's assertion that the Anitkabir protestors were insane and therefore there is nothing to analyse in their discourse, then the analysis of this affair would require two separate analyses of two incommensurable discourses: the discourse of the President, the psychiatrist and the media on the one side, and the discourse of the 'insane', on the other.

I shall begin with the 'insane militants' discourse. They protest Ataturk's commemoration ceremony at the site of Ataturk's mausoleum. They protest worshipping 'stones and idols', and as an alternative they present the Holy Book, the Koran. Their reference is therefore Islam, and if this is the discursive horizon under which they imagine themselves, a short look at the relationship between Islam and monuments is necessary.

In Muslim art, apart from rare use in miniatures, the human figure was prohibited. The roots of this hostility lie in the fact that Prophet Muhammad began his movement by destroying the idols located in the Caabe. Islam is an originally anti-fetishist movement, in which any form of representation of human figures is an offence to God, for the obvious reason that creating the human figure had to be the exceptional right of the Creator and not His creatures.[59] Unlike Christianity, therefore, there was no tradition in Islam of the public display of the representation of the sacred bodies of kings and saints in the form of statues and

---

[58] Foreign Ministry, Information Bureau 1999.

40

monuments.[60] Monumental buildings had been built in the name of Sultans and other important figures but they categorically excluded representations of body or face.

The first radical assault to this Islamic convention was carried out by Mustafa Kemal in 1926, when he ordered his statue to be erected in Sarayburnu, Istanbul.[61] Within a matter of a few years, dozens of Ataturk monuments rose around the country mainly in the major city squares. The statues would then disseminate to the smaller city centres and town squares, eventually becoming the measurement of the touch of the state in a location, including villages. There were some vandalising attacks by Muslim activists particularly in provincial towns and in the early 1950s a special 'Protection of Ataturk's Personality' law introduced heavy penalties in order to prevent further attacks.[62] The maintenance and wellbeing of the Ataturk statues and busts have been the major concerns of annual Gogolian inspections to provincial towns by state officials. The size of the statue is usually appropriate to the size of the town that hosts it but is also a matter of inter-town competition, since in addition to the present size of the town, the size of the Ataturk statue is also an expression of the prospects and ambitions of the townspeople in question.[63]

---

[59] Islam's stance against artistic representations of human form is comparable to the contemporary conservative-Christian stance against cloning.

[60] The exceptions to this rule in the history of the Muslim art were the drawings and paintings known as gravures and miniatures, popular forms of particularly Persian and Ottoman artistic expression, where two-dimensional human representations were allowed. On the other hand, three-dimensional representations, as in sculpture, were never attempted until the 19th century.

[61] Before Ataturk, the reformist Sultan Abdülaziz influenced by the sculptures he had seen in Vienna, ordered C. F. Fuller to make a statue of himself. This sculpture, representing Abdulaziz mounted was completed in 1871 but could never be erected, and was kept in a remote corner of the Palace under severe criticism from the public expressed through the religious scholars.

[62] See Appendix 1.

[63] I have reached this speculative conclusion after inquiring about a giant Ataturk statue in Dalyan, a small tourist resort at a remote corner of the Aegean coast. Local people, including the boat captains who take the tourists to the beach through the canal and the owner of the largest café in the town square told me that they all contributed to the building of this monument, because they demanded the official administrative status of a 'district', which would mean more government investment and more jobs for the local people.

This certainly was not the original idea Ataturk often referred to his monuments as the initiation of a fine art movement. Behind this rhetoric, however, a careful engineering of a personality cult was evident. Ataturk was one of the few republican leaders since Napoleon to commission the erection of his own statues during his lifetime.[64] Atatürk died on 10 November 1938 and his body, after being (unsuccessfully) mummied, was provisionally put in a mausoleum in the Ethnography Museum in Ankara. A monumental mausoleum was built at another location in Ankara (Anitkabir) in the mean time, which was completed in 1953 and Atatürk's body was transferred there. Following a decade of interval between 1950 and 1960, the proliferation of the bodies of Ataturk gained a new impetus and Ataturk statue, losing most of its hostile connotation of infidels' icon, became part of folk culture.[65]

The main purpose of this background information is to argue that the insane militants' protests are not incomprehensible within the logic of Islam. It is perfectly logical that for any good Muslim who follows the orders of the Koran and Muhammad's practices, Kemalist fetishism as represented by Ataturk iconography is unacceptable. Much of the question mark in the Anitkabir affair therefore needs to be placed on the other side's discourse. Why does an act of religious protest have to be excluded from the logic of political terminology of power and opposition and placed discursively outside of any logic by being called 'insane'?

---

[64] Stalin, for example, built his empire arguably with Lenin's statues after the latter's death. In fact, a similar charge can be claimed for Ataturk's inheritor Inonu, given that there were more busts and statues of Ataturk erected under his reign between 1939 and 1950 compared to the number of those erected during Ataturk's time.
[65] Humour has been a productive resource for the provincial population of coping with the crusade of icons: Ataturk statues' popular name is 'Stone Mustafa'. It is important to note however that for people the icon and the man are two different things. They would talk about Gazi Pasha or Mustafa Kemal Pasha with great respect referring to the personality of Ataturk, unlike his concrete representations.

42

Part of the answers to this question can be found in the meaning of Ataturk's body and his memorial personality in particular and the national monuments in general for the President, the mainstream media, and the psychiatrists and alike.[66] Lerner (1991) argues that the aim of the modern nationalist monument is to unite a heroic past with a national present in a secular frame. Heroes of the past must continue to live in an afterlife that belongs to the nation. The space, geography, the country of the nation becomes a text on which a heroic national tradition is inscribed through the representation/exhibition of the heroes' bodies.[67] This national afterlife is the only territory on which yesterday's heroes can meet the people of today. Since the living members of the nation cannot enter this afterlife, the task of statue-mania is to recycle the heroes of the past, who exist in the national afterlife through the streets and among the living. In the streets, the citizen continually confronts the ancestors

---

[66] The explanation of this discourse could begin with the psychiatrist's declaration that he does not only understand Ataturk but he manifestly believes that he does live with him; a statement which necessitates clinical intervention, considering that Atatürk had passed away decades before this delusion!

[67] This nationalist space also includes the invaded territory. Lerner demonstrates that for Napoleon building victory monuments was synonymous with baptising the occupied cities. In this context, the return of the offending Ataturk iconography in early 1980s in the Kurdish towns and provincial centres becomes comprehensible. The junta of the 1980 coup felt the urge to procreate more bodies of Ataturk in order to secure that the Kurds had no way out of the Turkish state's rule. In this renewed campaign of statue-mania, aesthetic problems inevitably emerged. Licensed sculptures and the Fine Arts Academy had difficulty in coping with the pressures of high demand and consequently, unlicensed businessmen who provide the same body without delay and with cut prices began to win most of the provincial contracts. The monstrous result of the further vulgarisation of the already vulgar Ataturk business is the 'ugly giant' overlooking the E5 Motorway at the eastern approach to Istanbul. The location is an atelier producing mainly for province by offering discounts. The owner of the business describes the 'giant' Ataturk as his father's masterpiece:

> He made the largest one-man statue of not only Turkey but the whole world, which means that in a sense he ressuttitated Ataturk. (...) This statue, made of cement and covered over with bronze, is 8.5 metres tall and it weighs 45 tons (Balcioglu 1991: 374).

Imagine the scene of an archaeological excavation a few thousand years ahead, in that portion of the world which is currently Turkey: the future's archaeologists face the clumsy copies of the same man arising from under the earth. Only from within such a fantasy can the Turkish psyche be intelligible, which is born with Ataturk, live with Ataturk, die in a hospital ward under the wall on which an Ataturk portrait is attached knowing that his sons will arrange his funeral in the funeral directorate's office under the image of Ataturk. The image and the body inevitably produce peculiar desires. Many middle aged, enlightened and married Turkish women tend to have an Ataturk portrait at home; and the men's obsession with the Ataturk objects is even greater. Hence the rather lengthy reflections in this introduction.

who make him know what he is - a participant in the victory parade through time of the nation.[68]

The Anitkabir Affair is therefore a confrontation over the meaning of the national monument: is it a government service that maintains the unity and historical integrity of the people of Turkey or an offence on the Islamic conventions, the 'real grounds' that bring the same people together? This contest, although explains the political/ideological conflict involved in the Anitkabir affair, does not account for the dominant portrayal of this incident in terms of reason and insanity, which categorically refuses the possibility of a political interpretation, and offers instead a psychiatric one. Consequently, the dominant discourse requires further analysis as an exclusionary practice, which has to identify primarily the designed form and the space reserved for the excluded identity. The key to making the 'return of the insane' intelligible therefore lies in the problematisation of the term 'insanity', that is, a genealogical inquiry into the emergence and development of the conditions in which it has become possible for the secularist subject to perceive and describe political behaviour driven by religious identity as insanity. The secularist subject (the President, the psychiatrist and the media) speaks from within a secular discursive environment, which not only legitimises and naturalises the confinement of religious-political behaviour and identity to the degraded side of a reason/insanity dichotomy, but constructs the secularist subject and provides her with the tools of enunciation of this dichotomy.

The analysis in this chapter will therefore consist of an inquiry into this dichotomy, with its conditions of emergence and development, and of the site to which the 'insane' is discursively confined. I will argue that this discursive dualism, which splits reason and insanity, also separates secularism from Islam, republican Turkey from her Ottoman past, the West from the East, modernity from tradition, centre from periphery and so on; and that it corresponds to Turkey's socio-political reality; in fact it is constitutive of this reality as a split objectivity. The nature of this separation, the fact that it refers to a mental division, will also lead this chapter's argument for the relevance of the psychoanalytic categories of

---

[68] Lerner 1991.

44

repression and return of the repressed in the analysis of the exclusion of Islamic identity and its recent revival. The argument is therefore as follows: The Return of the Insane is one of many symptomatic appearances of a process of The Return of the Repressed.

The above analytic stance is also expected to be revealing of the reasons, in addition to the conditions, for the exclusion, instead of recognition as a form of expression of Islamic political subjectivity, of religious protest from the logic of the symbolic order to be placed outside of any logic through psychiatric labelling. In order to make the conditions of this exclusion intelligible, I will outline in the first section the main features of the general setting, which preceded the repression of the Islamic identity, to argue that the Ottoman encounter with the West particularly in the 19th Century created the circumstances of an identity crisis. The analysis in the second section will situate the gradual erosion of the status of Islam in the development of Ottoman identity crisis. I will argue that Islam's erosion intensified within the context of a hegemony struggle between the pro-westernisation reformists and Islamists or two confronting 'epistemes' each claiming to be the true grounds for the assertion of those rules by which true and false can be decided upon.[69] The scenery of the Turkish transition from one Regime of Truth premised mainly upon a religious episteme to another premised upon secular reason will become clearer with the inquiry in the third section into the constitution of Kemalist secularism through the exclusion of Islamic discourse. Under the rules of Kemalist discourse, the emphasis on 'civilisation', science and reason went hand in hand with a growing association of religion with irrationality, 'mindlessness', immaturity and 'superstition', in addition to the connotations derived from the Enlightenment's standard secular logic, including 'tradition', 'darkness', 'backwardness', 'regression', etc. From this inquiry into the Kemalist techniques of exclusion of religious identity, an argument will develop to make the case for understanding the process of exclusion in terms of the psychic mechanism of repression.

I. The Challenge of the West: Modernisation and Ottoman Identity Crisis

---

[69] Foucault 1980: 130.

In this section, I will outline the trajectory of the Ottoman decline and the subsequent collapse, with particular reference to the changing meaning of the encounter with the West. I will present a theoretical model of organic/identity crisis, according to which I will comment on the late Ottoman social transitions in terms of an identity crisis in the following subsection.

I.1. The Meaning of the West

In the 'classical age' of the medieval Empire of the Ottomans, definition of the West did not constitute a problem for neither the 'state class' nor the subjects of the Ottoman Sultan. Ottomans looked down on the West. Ottoman Sultans, until Abdulaziz in 19th Century, never visited any foreign country, apart from the purposes of conquest; they never accepted any gifts from any foreign sovereign and; until the 18th Century the Empire did not have diplomatic missions abroad. In the Imperial eyes of the Ottomans, Christian Kingdoms and Empires had no legitimacy and the Christian countries of Europe were referred to as *darulharb*, that is, lands subject to *jihad*,or lands to be conquered in due course.

This conventional nature of the Ottoman encounter with the West began to change with the defeat of the Ottoman army at the outskirts of besieged Vienna in 1683. Ottomans came to realise that their strength was not absolute any more; the Ottoman military might was relativised through the scientific advances that the European states were engaged in and that they had to measure their strength against that of the Christian world before continuing to challenge the West.

The pragmatic elites of the Empire decided to opt for a long and painful process of modernisation, which they hoped would bring back the military and administrative strength of the Empire and secure the Ottomans a place among the emerging Great Powers, that is, being recognised by the West as one of them. 'If we do not imitate Europe at once, no option but returning to Asia will be left', the Navy Commander Halil Pasha reported to the Sultan on his return from Russia in 1830.[70] This is only one sample of dozens of 'risale's, that is reports to Sultan, by Ottoman foreign envoys on the theme of the reasons of European superiority and how to catch up with it.

Both modernisation – or 'imitation' as boldly phrased above - and seeking recognition in the relationship with the west had dangerous repercussions for two primary reasons.

Firstly, Ottoman reforms commenced with a perception of the West as a source of identification as opposed to the conventional meaning of it as a source of hostile differentiation. This change of perception implied a redefinition of the West, including the position of the Ottoman social order *vis-à-vis* the West, fundamentally different from that of the conventional Ottoman discourse. This radical change of mentality was not possible within the particular logic of the available system of meanings. Consequently, the westernising reforms led to an antagonistic split initially of the administrative structure to spread gradually through the social field.

---

[70] Güvenç 1993: 203.

47

Secondly, and symmetrically, the modern discourse of the 'great powers' was built on the assumption of an ontological difference of the Orient from the west, which the modern west had largely inherited from the Christian perception of the world. The Orient, which conventionally meant a threat to Christianity, became, in the modern discourse, the subject of conquest, that is an object to colonise, 'rationalise' and 'civilise', while maintaining its ontological status as a source of threat to 'reason' and 'civilisation'. For six centuries, the Ottoman Empire had represented the oriental challenge to the west, and its decline was naturally viewed as a golden opportunity for the elimination of any future possibility of the re-emergence of this threat, while putting this chaotic entity, which was now called 'the sick man of Europe' under the domination of 'reason' and 'civilisation'.[71]

The reformist/conservative split accompanied by the failure of recognition by the West led the late Ottoman social order to acquire the features of a dislocated structure in a state of organic crisis accompanied by an identity crisis. To explain this point further, I shall firstly introduce below the notion of organic crisis.

I.2. Ideology-Common Sense and Organic/Identity Crisis

---

[71] For Michel Foucault, the hegemony of medical discourse in the nineteenth century accompanied a conception of society as a body that needed to be protected against "illnesses" in a quasi-medical sense. This is how, according to Foucault, the methods of asepsis-criminology, eugenics and the quarantining of the "degenerates" were born, leading to the employment of "remedies and therapeutic devices (…) such as the segregation of the sick, the monitoring of the contagious and the exclusion of delinquents" (Foucault 1980: 55). The term, "The Sick Man of Europe", similarly implies the need both to be segregated and to be cured, that is, to be kept away from Europe, whilst being subjected to therapy and correction from this entity. This is arguably also the contemporary European attitude towards Turkey, "of Europe" but "sick". In the Ottoman case, though, the European "cure" consisted merely of postponing the inevitable death of the "Sick Man", within a 'Great Game' of the shifting balances of power among the "Great Powers": a politico-military game, a.k.a. the 'Eastern Question', of gradually ripping the Empire into pieces.

48

Antonio Gramsci asserts that ideologies,

> have a validity which is 'psychological'; they 'organise' human masses, and create
> the terrain on which men move, acquire consciousness of their position, struggle,
> etc.[72]

From this definition, one can move further, as Althusser does, to assert that the main function of ideology is 'interpellation', that is, the act of identification, which transforms the individuals into subjects.[73] Leaving aside the linguistic and psychoanalytic background of this assertion, it is possible to define ideology as something which provides one with identity through a 'natural' process, in which this identity is produced and reproduced in the mundane reality of everyday life. Naturalisation is achieved if an ideology has successfully dispersed through the social body and penetrated the languages of what Gramsci calls 'common sense'.

Laclau and Mouffe's description of the social as a discursive system of differences, in which hegemonic ideological intervention plays a primary role in fixing the meaning of each element of the signifying chain as a social identity at certain nodal points, has been developed on these Gramscian premises. The social is structured as an aggregate of networks of identity/difference through a naturalised dispersal of the hegemonic discourses at the level of 'common sense'. Within a clearly defined discursive territory, social identities have a relational character; they can be defined only in their difference from one another. This territory of social identities is not merely an aggregate of different egos, but of different subject positions. Identity formation is therefore primarily the 'identification' of individuals with certain subject positions, furnished by the system. Laclau and Mouffe further argue that the social as a closed system can only be defined with reference to its outside, that is, to its

---

[72] Gramsci 1970: 177.
[73] Althusser 1977.

49

difference from other systems. The act of hegemonic closure thus sets the boundaries of the territory of social identities as opposed to its 'constitutive outside' In other words, society can exist only as partially constituted and partially threatened, or as an 'imagined totality' as long as this imaginary can be renewed through constant ideological operations that 'quilt' the structural destabilisation accompanied by dislocations. To rephrase the Gramscian model of organic crisis as an identity crisis by employing the above analytic assertions, the following can be stated: An organic/identity crisis refers to a double crisis: firstly, a crisis within a given discursive territory, where the dislocated structure can no longer be quilted by the available system of meanings; and secondly, a crisis emerging from the impossibility of the definition of the boundaries of this territory due to the ambiguity of its 'outside'.

The end result of this double crisis is usually a growing ambiguity of the subject positions leading to further tangible functional defects and disturbances in the existing networks of identity/difference. At these moments of crisis, the necessity of the rearticulation of the signifying chain of differences opens up a space of 'metaphors', where surplus meanings, which cannot be expressed within the existing symbolic order, are condensed. In this 'mythical space', various critiques of the existing order are condensed, displaced and overdetermined, as in the Freudian notion of dreamwork, leading to the production of alternative systems of meaning. These alternative systems, which Laclau calls 'social imaginaries', attempt to rearticulate a system of meanings to present the totality of the existing order as a negativity.[74] The dislocated structure thus evolves into a territory of social antagonisms, which opens the way for a social transition.

The transition from Ottoman Empire to republican Turkey, which I shall consider below, demonstrates the features of such an identity crisis and soco-political transformation.

I.3. The Ottoman Identity Crisis

The contextual dimension of the Ottoman identity crisis, the crisis of the system's identity, consisted of the impossibility of the definition of the boundaries of the Ottoman discursive territory due to the ambiguity of its 'outside' as a consequence of the changing perception of the West. This contextual crisis deepened further with the destabilisation of subject positions, which led to the emergence of new antagonisms within this ambiguous territory.

According to the early reformist discourse, the Empire could remain intact and its economic integration with Europe would bring about benefits as well as long term prosperity. This, however, would prove not be the case; the westernising reforms further contributed to the Ottoman decline, which soon turned into disintegration and near collapse.

The Ottoman Empire became officially European with the signing of Paris Treaty on 30 March 1856, and was admitted in the European Concert. This was a result of the Empire's alliance in the Crimean War with Britain and France and the declaration of a reform package on 18 February 1856, which promised further improvement of Christian minority rights. However, this admission only meant a provisional halt in the trend of territory loss. As the Ottoman state tried to hold on, far beyond their political and military strength, to their far-flung, polyglot Empire, the European powers continued to move from all sides: Austria to Bosnia (1878), Russia to Kars (1878), Britain to Cyprus (1878) and Egypt (1882), France to Tunisia (1881), and Italy to Libya and the Dodecanese (1912). The Empire was

---

[74] Laclau 1990: 64.

systematically losing land to the West, a process leading towards the materialisation of a catastrophic scenario of a total 'Christian invasion of the Muslim Ottoman soil'.

The European influence on the Balkan nationalities also hastened the Ottoman decline. Initially, in the late 18th Century, the French brought about their ideas of liberty and nationalism to the non-Muslim communities of particularly the European portion of imperial land. Russia was quick to counter this with propaganda of pan-Slavism, which primarily targeted the Serbs. In the early 19th Century, Serbs in the Balkans, Wahhabis in the Arab Peninsula and Governor Muhammad Ali in Egypt were all in rebellion against Empire. In 1821, the Greek War of Independence broke out to conclude with the founding of an independent Greece in 1830. This would be followed by Bulgarian independence and a consequent exodus of Muslim minorities from Balkans to Anatolia. The 1877 Ottoman-Russian war brought about the loss of more lands and another exodus, this time from the Caucuses.

Moreover, the Empire's opening up to the West for modernisation, and her integration with the international networks of trade through the 18th and 19th Centuries resulted in the 'peripheralisation of the Empire's economy'.[75] The 1838 trade convention with Britain, which was followed by treaties with other European states with similar provision within a few years, turned the Empire into a free trade zone. 'By mid-century the trade pattern had attained a composition reflecting the core-periphery division of labour underlying the free trade doctrine: imports consisted in large part of manufactured consumer goods, while various foodstuffs and raw materials -none of overwhelming importance - were exported'.[76] The result was the collapse of conventional local industries, particularly urban manufacturing. Traditional economic order was thus sacrificed by bureaucratic reformism.

Capitalist integration produced further indigenous effects by destabilising subject positions. The reform movement aimed, along with the modernisation of the Ottoman administration through better communication and transport, to secure commercial and industrial activities

---

[75] See, Keyder 1987.

52

throughout the Empire, which would lay down the necessary conditions for the integration of the Ottoman economy into European capitalist networks. Given that for various cultural-historical reasons, the commercial classes that had emerged to link the Empire to the West were predominantly non-Muslims, composed of Greeks, Armenians, Levantines and Jews, economic reform consisted primarily in new legislation to restructure the conventional terms of the relationship between the Ottoman State and its non-Muslim subjects. The 19th Century reforms brought about by the *Tanzimat* (1839) and *Islahat* (1856) decrees aimed at ending the disadvantaged position of these *millets* vis-à-vis the Muslims. Their immediate consequence however was the economic subordination of the politically dominant Muslim Turkish elements to the non-Muslim *millets*.

It did not take long for this dislocated political economy to lead to a conflict between local producers, craftsmen, peasants and Muslim traders on the one side and on the other, the agents of international capital, that is, the emerging non-Muslim Ottoman bourgeoisie. In these circumstances, ethnic/religious antagonisms rapidly developed throughout the multinational empire, which made it impossible to maintain the social order within the context of the conventional *millet* system.

According to Erikson, an identity crisis consists of 'a split of self-images, a loss of centrality, a sense of dispersion and confusion, and a fear of dissolution'.[77] This is precisely the description of the state of the Ottoman social order from the beginning of the 19th Century onwards, in parallel to the recognition of the superiority of the West and increasing Western influence through bureaucratic reform. The crisis deepened following the 1873 downturn of the world economy, a disastrous famine in Anatolia in 1874 and the subsequent bankruptcy of the State Treasury in 1875, and was increasingly perceived as an identity crisis, particularly by the Muslim Turkish subjects and sectors of the Ottoman élite.

Within the dislocated Ottoman order, the conventional networks of identity/difference had been irreparably shattered, and the hegemony of the Ottoman elite along with the status of

---

[76] Keyder 1987: 31.
[77] Erikson 1980: 122-3.

the 'dominant nation' was at stake in addition to the sustained threat from the 'Great Powers'. The damaged structure, and the impossibility of quilting it, necessitated a redefinition of the whole system and its 'other', which was impossible within the existing symbolic order. Consequently, a mythical space opened up to lead to the production of new social imaginaries, consisting primarily of the discourses of 'salvation of the sublime state'.[78]

I.4. The Problem of the West

The consequences of the destabilisation of the meaning of the West was therefore such that the problem of the West entered in the late Ottoman discursive field as a faultline that shook and split this field. The failed recognition and the emerging Ottoman organic crisis gave birth to discourses of salvation by bringing forth the necessity to redesign the politico-discursive order for the 20th Century, including the definition of the political subject, nation and political identity. Until the emergence of modern Turkey out of these attempts to redesign the politico-discursive field, which took its final form in Kemalist nationalism, Islam maintained its exceptional status as the ultimate ground of all political discourse and the sole source of legitimacy. There was, however, an accompanying movement of secularisation through the 19th Century that gradually eroded this exceptional status. In the next section, I will consider the trajectory of this erosion, as accompanying the dissolution of the Ottoman regime of truth.

II. The dissolution of the Ottoman 'Regime of Truth'

In this section, I will outline the moments of erosion of Islam's status as the 'episteme' of the Ottoman 'Regime of Truth', which corresponded to the descent in the status of the *Ulema*, in parallel to Ottoman modernisation. I will firstly clarify what I mean by Islam's status and the Ottoman 'Regime of Truth' by presenting a portrait of the Ottoman regime at the outset of

---

[78] In 1904, the Turkist ideologue, Yusuf Akcura, analysed these discourses - Ottomanism, Islamism and Turkism - under the title of 'Three Modes of Politics' (See, Yoruk 1996 and 1997.)

modernisation and then demonstrate the locations of the blows that this regime suffered in its modernisation attempt. In the second subsection below, I will present the New Ottomans' discourse, which not only initiated the introduction of Enlightenment notions to the Ottoman mentalities, intelligentsia and public alike, but also developed a criticism of the reform movement from a restorationist stance. The ambivalent New Ottoman discourse was largely adopted by the 'Absolutist' restoration of Sultan Abdulhamid II, to be materialised in an attempt to mould an Islamic nation that would be enlightened and modern at the same time, out of the Muslim elements of the Empire. The secularisation of the Empire's administration was almost complete when the Young Turk revolution of 1908 opened the Second Constitutional era. Although on the surface, Islam maintained its status as the episteme of the Imperial regime, the erosion of this status was evident in the emergence of Ottomanism and nationalism with claims of furnishing the grounds of all political discourse and the promise of 'salvation'. The discursive contest that commenced in these circumstances necessitated the emergence of Islamism as a modern discourse to defend Islam's privileged status and to re-present the religious episteme as a discourse of salvation. The argument of this section will be that despite these moments of erosion, Islam's discursive location for the competing discourses was far away from the republican exclusion of it as a reactionary and irrational obstacle to Turkish Enlightenment.

II.1. The Islamic Episteme

The place of Islam in the conventional Ottoman social and political structures was no doubt significant although not enough to declare the Ottoman State a typical theocratic monarchy.

The Ottoman elite was organised as a Sunni Muslim state over a multi-religious society, and affiliated to the *Hanefi* sub-sect of the Sunni faith as the essential ideological framework of the state's official administration.[79] This discursive structure required and allowed the existence of an extensive and strong class of Islamic scholars *(Ilmiye)* within the state class *(askeriye)*. *Ulema* (men of *ilmiye)* consisted of *Medrese* graduates, the equivalent of universities of modern times, and manned primarily the ranks of the judicial organisation of the Empire. Scholars, teachers, physicians, religious staff, mathematicians, philosophers, astronomy scientists and astrologists, musicologists, librarians and some of the administrative staff were also *ilmiye* members in the conventional Ottoman order.[80] The *ilmiye* was strong and extensive but subordinate at the same time, due to the Hanefi faith's sublimation of the state. While Ottoman Sultans had to obtain the approval of *Sheyhülislam,* the head *ilmiye,* for all their decrees and administrative decisions, Ottoman State philosophy defined *Sheyhülislam* as a civil servant acting to assist the *Caliph[81]*, that is, the Ottoman Sultan.[82] When the Ottomans faced the challenge of Europe from the late 17th Century onwards, the changing terms of encounter with the West led the Islamic thinkers around the world towards a reform in Islam.[83] When the leading Muslim reformer Jamal al-Din al-Afghani arrived in Istanbul in 1869 to attend the Sultan's Court, considerable steps towards reforming the State

---

[79] Hanefi judicial tradition had two immediate advantages: firstly, it provided a relatively liberal interpretation of Sunni *Sharia*, suitable for ruling a multi-faith society, and secondly, it was based on the primacy of the State over the orthodoxy of the faith. Political authority was over and above everything and the State was the sublime authority, the affairs of which could not be debated or criticised (Akyol: 1999, 204). Despite these reservations, it certainly is still correct to assert that Islam was the Ottoman order's discursive universe of legitimation.
[80] Mardin 1992: 169-70.
[81] Ottoman sultans had gained the title of *Caliph* in the 16th Century following the conquest of Egypt but this title had never been emphasised until late 19th Century; and when it was emphasised this looked more like political manoeuvring than a sincerely pious recollection.
[82] Elmalili Hamdi Efendi quoted in Akyol 1999: 203. Akyol argues on this premises that the Ottoman *ilmiye,* unlike the Iranian *Mullahs,* could not become an independent force comparable to the power of the Church and clerical classes of Medieval Europe. See also Inalcik 1973: 94.
[83] See Appendix 2.

had already been taken in line with al-Afghani's motto, 'Islamic states had to strengthen their statehood with science and technology in response to the West's challenge.' In this modernist Islamic outlook, Ottoman *ulema* failed to perceive the underlying secular logic of administrative modernisation as an immediate threat and sided with the westernising reforms of the 19th Century.

The engine of the reforms was the third section of the *askeriye*, namely *kalemiye*, the Palace bureaucracy. *Kalemiye* had their own secular training at *Enderun* School, which consisted mainly of apprenticeship to a civil servant. Ottoman civil servants' *raison d'état* required pragmatism and differed in that sense from the *ulema's* Islamic idealism. The secularist program of reforming the military, administrative and economic spheres of the Ottoman social order resulted in the exclusion of the *ulema* by mid 19th Century from the central decision making process, while maintaining a marginal role in the judicial structure and education system.[84] The secularisation of the political and public spheres and mentalities, which was given a manifest start by the *Tanzimat* Decree of 1839 have been gradually expanding through the Imperial spheres by the inevitable consequence of pushing the cadres and mentalities of Islam out of these spheres. And as the spheres of law, science and academy were moving away from religion, *ulema*, as the traditional intelligentsia were losing their status. Paradoxically, these developments largely took place with the *ulema's* consent: they were convinced of the necessity of secular modernisation for the Ottoman State, their

---

[84] As Mardin (1991: 45) outlines, the first blow came in 1826, when the administration of the religious charity trusts were taken from the *ulema* to go under the control of a new ministry controlled by the Palace bureaucracy. A vital source of income for the *ulema* had thus been cut off. Reformists then introduced secular courts to operate on the side of the traditional *Sher'i* courts. In order to train personnel for the secular institutions of the *Tanzimat* regime, a secular education reform began in 1846 with the formation of the Ministry of Education. The spheres of legal, scientific and academic affairs were gradually moving away from religion and along with this development, the traditional intellectuals of the Ottoman Empire were withering away.

condition of existence, to reclaim its might against the 'modern crusade', while such modernisation paradoxically necessitated the end of their 'natural' status

II.2. Ottoman Enlightenment: The New Ottomans and 'Pan-Islamism'

It would therefore be a simplified definition to present the 'longest century of the Empire'[85] as the field of a *Kulturkamph* between the modernist secular bureaucracy and new intelligentsia on the one side, and the traditional *ulema* on the other.[86] Moreover, the strongest criticism of 'atheist *Tanzimat* Pashas' and their 'Christianisation' reforms was raised not by the *ulema* but came from among the newly emerging secular intelligentsia, namely the New Ottomans.[87] This group of intellectuals, most of whom were chosen by the Ottoman elite to be educated in western norms to become the first generation of *Tanzimat* intellectuals, developed a three-fold *Tanzimat* criticism. Firstly, *Tanzimat* reforms were implemented from above through authoritarian methods; they had to be improved to include the principles of liberty and people's sovereignty.[88] Secondly, reformism had to aim to bridge the gap between the people and the elite, and avoid breaching popular conventions. The New Ottomans observed the opposite in the Tanzimat elite's blind admiration and clumsy

---

[85] Ortaylı 1995.
[86] Mardin 1992: 184.
[87] The prominent figures of this generation, Sinasi, Namik Kemal and Ziya Pasha, emerged either from the secular civil servant training of the *Enderun* School, or the Ottoman Translation Bureau and all had spent some time in Europe as outcasts. They were influenced by Victor Hugo's romanticism and maintained contact with prominent literary figures like Lamartine. They derived from revolutionary France progressive secularist views but they were also concerned with the widening gap between the pro-western elite and the people. Consequently, as much as introducing the republican notion of liberty into the reform movement, the New Ottomans were also concerned with a definition of the people of the Empire and desired to forge a nexus with them. They launched the first periodical publications in the Empire's history, by which they criticised the Tanzimat Pashas' dictatorial regime and proposed for the first time the formation of constitutional monarchy as a remedy.
[88] See Aksin 1987, Berkes 1964 and Mardin 1983.

imitation of the Western forms. Thirdly, Islam had to be restored as a social bond among the Empire's Muslim population and a pan-Islamist perspective had to be adopted.[89] Pan-Islamism (*Ittihad-ı Islam*) was essentially perceived as a remedy for the Empire's disintegration, through the constitution of an Ottoman identity grounded upon a discourse of religious proto-nationalism, in the similar fashion with pan-Germanism and more with Pan-Slavism.[90]

II.3. Restoration: From 'Islam' to 'Islamism'

Most of the New Ottoman proposals regarding restoration through pan-Islamism were put in practice by the last of the absolutist monarchs, Sultan Abdulhamid II; after the elimination of the New Ottoman officers and intellectuals who dethroned Sultan Abdulaziz to declare Abdulhamid II as the first Sultan of their Constitutional Monarchy.[91] In this subsection, I will evaluate Abdulhamid's policies, which articulated elements of Islamism, modernism and nationalism in an attempt at absolutist consolidation.

Pan-Islamism and Islamisation

---

[89] Despite this emphasis on religion, the New Ottomans' views cannot be defined as a defence of the *ancien régime*. They were modernists in the sense that they were more influenced by the secular views on religion as a social bond of a modern society than the conventional view of Islam as the sole source of legitimation of the state.

[90] Turköne 1991: 227-8, 183.

[91] The New Ottoman palace coup brought about the Constitution of 1876 and, after some confusion, Abdülhamid II to the throne. In 1877, the Ottoman Constitutional Monarchy declared war to the Russians to swiftly lose most of her eastern European portions of land. The Russian War and the subsequent Berlin Treaty

Abdülhamid's Islamist policies, consisting of focusing on the restoration of the ties with the Muslim population and the consequent populist appeal to the Muslim population's conservative reaction against the *Tanzimat* reforms, achieved the consolidation of the State's power.[92] Islamism mainly implied a domestic policy based on an Islamic identity, which would provide a nexus for various ethnic groups, such as Arabs, Turks, the Kurds and Circassians, grounded upon notions of religious patriotism and loyalty to the Caliph, while connecting countries far from the Empire's Capital, such as Tunisia, Egypt and Yemen, firmly to the central government.[93] This discourse was backed by an economic program that aimed to repair the economic damage inflicted on the Muslim groups by *Tanzimat* modernisation. Consequently, domestic politico-financial attention turned towards Anatolia and the Arabic provinces to shift the resources to these Muslim populated regions through public investment (irrigation, transport, draining the marshes, etc.),[94] and new trade privileges for Muslim petty-producers to counter the *de facto* privileges of non-Muslim merchants.[95] In addition to the material infrastructural investment, symbolic investment constituted an important part of the Hamidian policies.[96]

---

provided Abdülhamid an excuse to topple the leader of the coup, Midhad Pasha, and to suspend the Constitution, while preparing the material grounds for Pan-Islamist policies.

[92] Keyder 1987: 52-3.

[93] The demographic transformation through the loss of land, which decreased the proportion of non-Muslims to 20%, provided suitable conditions for this policy shift. Besides, the lands that had been lost systematically since the 18th Century were predominantly Christian and over two million Muslims had been displaced and migrated from Crimea, Caucasus, Balkans and other former periphery to the Ottoman hinterland, Anatolia, between 1850s and early 20th Century (Keyder 1987: 80).

[94] This turn was hoped to compensate within a few decades for the lost sources of income from the Balkans (Cevdet Pasha in Cetinsaya 2001: 271).

[95] Keyder 1987: 52.

[96] Abdülhamid's novelty lied, according to Mardin, in his deep understanding of the symbolic mechanisms, and particularly of the symbolic effects of architecture (Mardin 1991: 93). He commissioned the construction of a railway linking Damascus with Mecca, projected in 1903 and completed in 1908 with German assistance. More than its economic value, this project probably had extensive symbolic value with its emphasis on the 'Chaliph' as protector of the Pilgrimage (Hourani 1970: 196). Abdulhamid also initiated a construction campaign throughout the Empire of public buildings of a peculiar architectural style, including schools, barracks, weapon factories, train stations, etc. The Arabic element of the Ottoman population was also glorified in the Hamidian discourse particularly in the distribution of Imperial Honours to contain Arabic secessionism led by the Wahabi

Along with the underlying political modernisation and recentralisation, the Hamidian Islamisation led in practice to the formation of the first modern Islamic state in history.[97] The new alliance between the Muslim subjects and the Ottoman bureaucracy, grounded upon an Islamic identity, would largely be maintained under the CUP rule, with the exclusion of the Arabs and Albanians, leading to the formation of an 'historic bloc' to fight the 'National Struggle' in the next century. The foundations of the future republican Turkey's nation were in fact laid down by the pan-Islamist discourse.

Islamisation via Volk Islam

The primary problem that was involved in this project of building a Muslim nation out of the *unsur-u asli*[98] was that Anatolia and the Arabic provinces contained a divergently multi-faith population. This material had to be moulded around a common identity of Islam, in fact, the Sunni-Hanefi version of it.[99] Abdülhamid II viewed various Islamic faiths other than the Sunni as deviations from the truth of Islam, a consequence of the people's ignorance, and initiated a policy of Sunnification particularly in Anatolia.

Sunnification was not to be carried out merely from above but involved a peculiar mass mobilisation technique through the promotion of Volk Islam. In addition to the prominent

---

movement. Abdülhamid's policies towards the Kurds were also significant: He sided with the Kurdish tribal chiefs in the conflict against Christians in Kurdish provinces, and legalised Kurdish banditry by forming *Hamidiye* Regiments.

[97] The degree of governmentality that Abdülhamid managed to achieve in a disintegrating Empire through the development of technologies of political mobilisation and control led many generations of Islamist and conservative political thinkers' admiration of Abdulhamid's model.

[98] 'The main element', meaning the Muslim population.

Islamic reformers, including one of the founders of modern political Islam, Jamal al-Din al-Afghani[100], provincial *ulema* and the leaders of Sufi orders began to frequent the Palace. One of the most influential and most conservative of these orders was the *Nakshibendi*, which had been expanding particularly through the Kurdish population of the Empire since the 17th Century.[101] The Sultan promoted the opening of *Nakshibendi* lodges in Istanbul and *Nakshibendi* 'missionaries' would accompany Sunni religious officials around the imperial lands in the Hamidian attempt to inculcate the 'ignorant' Muslim population.[102] Abdulhamid's promotion of *Nakshibendism*, was also linked to his pan-Islamist perspective, given that *Nakshibendi* was the most popular sufi order among the Indian Muslims, which had become a symbol of tradition's resistance against the effects of modernisation imposed by the British colonialism. This practice of the 'centralisation of the periphery' or the 'peripherialisation of the centre', although served well for the immediate task of consolidation, was also radically

---

[99] Çetinsaya 2001: 271.

[100] Hourani 1970: 111-2.

[101] See Deringil 1998. Nakshibendism was brought in the Ottoman lands in early 19th Century by Mevlana Khalid, who arrived from India to Kurdistan in 1811. In a very short time, Nakshibendism became the most popular Sufi sect particularly among the Sunni Kurds, who were predominantly Shafi, the most conservative sect of the Sunni faith. Nakshibendism had developed among the Indian Muslims as a doctrine of traditional resistance against the effects of modernisation imposed by the British colonialism. Its rapid popularity among the Kurds in the age of Ottoman modernisation, was followed by its expansion through other Muslim groups of the Empire. Abdulhamid II brought this *tarikat* to the centre of the Empire as part of his Panislamist policies by inviting *Nakshibendi* sheikhs to his palace in Istanbul as consultants in imperial decisions. Sultan also promoted the opening of *Nakshibendi* lodges in Istanbul. This was in effect a practice of the 'centralisation of the periphery' or the 'peripherialisation of the centre' (See also Appendix 4).

[102] Colonisation through religious conversion was not a novel tactic for the Ottomans. Bektashi dervishes, for example, were given the title of *Gazi* and land was allocated to them for the formation of their lodges in the occupied lands (Barkan 1942 and Melikoff 1999). Abdulhamid's move was however differed in two ways from this early colonisation tactics. Firstly, the early colonisation was inclined towards Bektashism, a liberal Shiite faith, probably to ease the conversation process, while the dynasty was officially Sunni. In contrast, Abdulhamid was attempting a religious standardisation around Sunni faith and he deployed one of the most conservative orders for this purpose: the *Nakshibendi*. Secondly, the target of this new conversation was not the Christian subjects or newly occupied lands; the urge for re-colonisation of the Empire's remaining soil was rather ironic. A way of understanding this is to claim that Abdulhamid was trying to counter the Christian missionary action within the Empire (see Acikel 2000) but a better explanation would be understanding this as an attempt of reconstitution of a lost hegemony (Deringil 1998) by deploying methods derived both from the inherited Imperial experience and the experience of Christian missionary activities.

modifying the conventional balances between the Ottoman elite and the popular level[103] by unleashing the energies of the 'alienated periphery',[104] thus opening the way for conservative resistance against any further secular modernisation. This destabilised equilibrium explains to a large extent the reasons of the 1920s' Kemalist/Islamist confrontation, which led to the repression of the periphery accompanied by a violent crackdown of particularly the *Nakshibendi* order.

Secularisation under Islamisation

While implementing the policy of Islamisation, Abdulhamid had no objections to the technological and administrative modernisation, and furthered this process as a requirement of centralisation.[105] However, an irreversible consequence of modernisation of the governmental sphere, particularly the advance of secular education, was the spread of secular

---

[103]This balance is referred to as the 'alienation of the order' (Kucukomer 1994) the trajectory of which can be described as follows: There are several indicators to assert that the Ottoman dynasty was originally an Alevi-Bektashi family like almost all the other Turkoman clans of the time (13th Century). Bektashi dervishes played the role of the spiritual leaders and advisors to early Ottoman chiefs from Osman to Mehmet II. They were also given the title of *Gazi* and land was allocated to them for the formation of their lodges in the occupied lands (Barkan 1942 and Melikoff 1999). Roughly from Mehmet II's reign (1452?-14??) onwards, Sunnification of the State gained momentum leading to the alienation of the state from the Turkoman clans of Anatolia. This situation turned into a conflict in the 16th Century when the Safavid Persian Shah called the Anatolian Alevis under his authority. The Alevi massacre by Selim II, which followed this politicisation of the Alevi population, is still alive in the collective memory of Turkey's Alevis. After the massacre, Bektashi dervishes continued to operate particularly in the Balkans and a gradual separation between Bektashi order and the Alevi masses of Kurdish and Turkoman origin of east and central Anatolia took place (Melikof 1999). (Kunt 1988: 106, Akyol 1999: 34 and Melikoff 1994: 31) The Janissaries, on the other hand, survived as an exclusively Bektasi force within the state, until the abolition of Janissary system by Sultan Mahmut II in 1826. Ottoman sultans and the *askeriye* maintained their links with the Mevlevi faith after the Alevi massacre, but by then the Mevlevi lodge had already been popularly criticised as an elitist sect (Güner 1991: 247-250). The conventional balance therefore implied that the Ottoman elite including the ruling dynasty and the *ulema* differentiated themselves from the folk-Islam practices with a claim of representing the true Islam.

[104] This practice of the 'centralisation of the periphery' or the 'peripherialisation of the centre' was arguably repeated by Ozal more than a century after Abdulhamid II and followed by Erbakan in a rather stark style by an invitation of *tarikat* sheikhs to a Ramadan dinner at prime ministerial residence, which would provoke a Kemalist coup in 1997 (see Conclusion). Both Ozal and Erbakan belonged to the Nakshibendi order, which explains the influence of this order in Turkey.

[105] Abdulhamid's motto was 'a mosque and a school in every village'.

mentalities. In fact, Sultan's deployment of Islamist discourse reveals a silent recognition that Islam was no longer the 'natural' *epistémè* of the imperial horizon. The transformation of the Muslim subjects into a 'Muslim nation' was more a modern project looking towards the future and modelling itself after the practices of modern nationalism than the resuscitation of the past. In this project Islamism was progressively deployed as a modern discourse of identity building. The absolute status of Islam might not be regained but Islamism could contest with other modern discourses to win the upper hand over a modernising society. After Abdülhamid, Islamism increasingly gained the features of a modern political discourse, which paradoxically required the recognition of Islam's eroded status.[106] Being so, *Islam* transformed itself into *Islamism* from its conventional divine status to be articulated in modern politics.

Therefore, the Islamist Sultan's policies were paradoxically generating the ideological gravediggers of the episteme of Islam in three ways. Firstly, the administrative modernisation increasingly produced and popularised secular mentalities. Secondly, Islamism increasingly became a profane modern discourse. And thirdly, the project of monarchic consolidation took more after the modern nationalist experiences than the pre-reform Ottoman order. The logic of nationalism inevitably included a separatist attack on the religious episteme by urging the dissolution of larger religious entities into smaller, linguistically or ethnically imagined or invented units. Abdulhamid's Islamism thus paradoxically served to erode further the Islamic

---

[106] Turköne's research (1994: 19) vindicates this point, where he states that Islamism functioned under Abdülhamid as a source of legitimation after passing through a silent *de facto* secularisation - secularisation in the sense that reshaping Islam as a profane political discourse, as God's word coming down to earth in the conditions of modernity so as to be used as a source of legitimation and mobilisation.

64

episteme and reinforced the grounds for the secular and nationalist discourses to confront the logic of Islam

.

Abdulhamid was not merely creating his ideological gravediggers but the modernisation of transport and telecommunications also increased the speed of dissemination of dissident libertarian ideas.[107] A constitutional movement led by Young Turks in exile with an anti-absolutist discourse, which preached *hürriyet* (liberty) against *istibdat* (oppression), in which elements of the rivals of Islamism, that is, Ottomanism and Turkism, were articulated, was forging its hegemony among the intelligentsia, including the Islamist sectors of it.[108]

II.4. Modern Islamism

The rehabilitation of Islam, which began under Abdülhamid II after decades of indifference by the *Tanzimat* reformers, continued in the Second Constitutional era both in the policies of the CUP[109] led governments and in the powerful scholarly argumens of the Islamists. Islam prevailed as the main source of legitimacy in the lively political atmosphere of Istanbul, where political ideas of westernism, nationalism, liberalism and socialism supported by philosophical currents of positivism, rationalism, materialism, idealism, along with Islamism,

---

[107] An ironic example of unintended consequences of Abdülhamid II's authoritarian strategies of control and censorship is Mehmed Talat Pasha, who struggled in the CUP ranks against Abdülhamid II. Talat Pasha made his career in the Sultan's new communications apparatus as the General Director of Telegram Administration and played a crucial role in the post-Hamidian governments. The more centralised and the more authoritarian the system, the more the opposition used the advantages of the centralised system (Açıkel 2000). By modernising the educational, administrative and military system, Abdülhamid was literally producing his 'grave diggers'.

[108] At the turn of the century, sermons against the 'Islamist' Sultan's absolutism, on the grounds of the principle of consultation in Islam (mesveret), could be heard in Istanbul's mosques on any Friday lunchtime.

[109] Committee of Union and Progress (*Ittihad ve Terakki Cemiyeti*): the political organisation of the Young Turks.

were in daily engagement in the politico-philosophical debate through various journals.
Young Turks had published Journals abroad titled *Içtihad* and *Sura-yı Ümmet* (Council of the
umma)[110], through which they argued that Islam was an expression of both the constitution
and liberty. Both westernism and Turkism of this period had to employ an Islamic grammar
in their arguments.[111]

Islamism emerged as a political and intellectual movement at the turn of the century from a
critique of the consequences of *Tanzimat* era and westernisation. The ranks of the Islamist
movement consisted not exclusively of the *ulema* but mostly of the members of new
intelligentsia, including the graduates of the *Tanzimat* schools. The politicisation of Islam in
the form of an Islamist current was also necessitated by the challenge of the discourses of
westernisation, Ottomanism and Turkism against the Muslim 'common sense' and the
'episteme' of Islam of the Ottoman order. In this environment, Islam had to reclaim its
exceptional status in society through political debate, like any modern political discourse.

The debate among discourses of salvation during the Constitutional era was largely
determined by the critique of *Tanzimat* reformism within the context of modernisation, the
differentiation of the Islamist discourse between reformist and conservative wings, and the
ascent of the logic of nationalism as the only feasible project of salvation. In turn, this debate,
which I will consider under the three topics below, largely determined the fate of Islam.

The Problem of Westernisation: Technique vs. Imitation

---

[110] *Ümmet* included all the followers of Prophet Muhammad, the larger community of Muslims of the world.
[111] Tunaya, 67-69 & 73-75.

The problem of overcoming the humiliated 'national' pride[112] divided the Islamist discourse between reformism and conservatism, but more significantly it led to a discussion over the meaning of 'civilisation' and 'technique'.

The westernist journal *Ictihad* introduced a distinction between technical and 'real' civilisations, and admitted that the West was superior in technical civilisation. In terms of real civilisation, however, the West could not compete with Islam. Technical civilisation could be transferred and lent by one country to another, real civilisation could not. Ottomans should therefore try to borrow and transfer whatever they could from the West in terms of technical knowledge, but when it came to questions of cultural values, norms, customs and beliefs, they should keep to their own Islamic heritage. The solution to the problems facing the Ottomans lay in being able to keep the concepts of technical and real civilisation apart, something that, according to westernist Celal Nuri, the Tanzimat reformers had failed to do.[113]

This differentiation was denounced by the editor of *Ictihad*, Dr. Abdullah Cevdet, as a hopeless attempt. Cevdet argued that 'If you speak of civilisation, there is just one, and that is in the west. One is either in it or out of it; there is no way in between.' Therefore, the European civilisation had to be imported 'with both its roses and its thorns'.[114] Abdullah Cevdet's proposal, however, did not perceive Islam as an obstacle to 'civilisation'; instead he proposed a reform of Islam:

---

[112] The infamous symptom of a century of humiliation in the encounter with the West is Bihruz Bey, the anti-hero of one of the renowned post-*Tanzimat* novels: *Araba Sevdasi* by Recaizade Ekrem. Bihruz Bey is not alienated from his roots; he is, at the outset, totally ignorant about his roots as a result of his inadequacies (the lyrics that he cites to seduce a blond are from a poem admiring a brunette). Bihruz Bey tries to quilt over his lack of roots by imitating the Western customs; but the drama that he attempts to stage ends up as nothing better than a farce. Bihruz's sole achievement is to move away from conventional mores and customs, which he calls 'Barbarian'. However, there is no goal that this distancing leads him to; the place where Bihruz reaches is not the West but a void. Bihruz represents the post-*Tanzimat* reflection by the late Ottoman salvation discourses on the early reform movement. The masochistic *Tanzimat* Pashas granted the West, the traditional other of the Ottomans, the status of a sadistic Big Other, whose excessive desires could never be satisfied. Salvation discourses of Turkism, Islamism and Ottomanism aggreed on the perception of Bihruz Bey as the scapegoat of failed westernisation representing the inevitable outcome of the *Tanzimat* elite's blind admiration towards Christianity and the West.
[113] See Özdalga 1998: 10.
[114] Abdullah Cevdet's statement of 1913 is quoted in Lewis 1968: 236.

I have seen after long experiences that if the light came from the Christian world, the Muslim soul would shut all their doors to it. Because of this, we assume the duty of injecting a new flow of blood in the Muslim veins. We need to search for the progressive institutions within the institutions of Islam and these institutions are already present within Islam in abundance.[115]

Reformist and Conservative Islamism

We can identify two wings of the Islamist discourse from the outset, although both expressed similar positions on certain issues, and neither side represented a monolithic unity on every issue. The reformist wing, organised around the journals *Sirat-ı Müstakim* and later *Sebilü'r Resad*, essentially followed the tracks of the Islamic reformers Al Afghani and Muhammad Abduh. Reformist Islamists consisted of the new intelligentsia (graduates of *Tanzimat* schools) and some members of the *ilmiye*. They supported the parliamentary system set up by the constitution claiming that it coincided with the original message of *mesveret* (consultation) in Islam. Most of them emphasised the necessity of reopening the 'gate of *Içtihad*'[116] in order for Islam to embrace the modern developments. Their main criticism was the 'imitationist' policies of the pro-western reformers, particularly the *Tanzimat* bureaucracy, who they believed, had brought about destruction to Ottoman society as a result of their blind appreciation of the West. Their views were blended with Al-Afghani's and

---

[115] *Içtihad* 1905, cited by Mardin 1983: 171.
[116] Içtihad means interpretation based on individual study and connotes one of the authoritative sources of God's will. Based on the Koran, the Sunna (lessons to be learned from the life practices of the Prophet), the other accepted forms of interpretation were reasoning by analogy (kiyas) and consensus of the 'doctors of law' (icma). The gate of Içtihad had been closed down in late 10th Century and since then Islamic thinkers with a more philosophical bent had called for a reopening of this gate in order for Islam to prevail in changing conditions. (Özdalga 1998: 6)

Abdülhamid's stand of taking the science and technology of the west under the horizon of the Islamic culture. They supported the structural reforms in the *Medrese* system, arguing that these 'divine' institutions had been degenerated and fell behind the time.[117]

The conservative Islamists shared many of the Islamic reformists' views on the criticism of *Tanzimat*'s 'imitation'. They however strongly opposed the opening up the path for *Içtihad* arguing that what was needed was the reestablishment of strict control over the Muslims' compliance with the Islamic rules, since the main reason for the decline was moving away from the orders of the Koran and *Sharia*. The conservative wing included the 'fundamentalist' Sufi dervishes, provincial *ulema* and a group of Islamic scholars from the traditional *ulema*.[118] These were precisely the groups of people dominated by the Volk Islam mentalities that had been brought together by Sultan Abdülhamid II. Traditional Islamists published a newspaper, *Volkan*, and formed an association, *Ittihad-ı Islam*, both of which would be indicted of being behind the 31 March Affair, which I shall consider further below.

Umma vs Nation

Islamists powerfully challenged the Turkist current with charges of 'racial discrimination'. Babanzade Ahmed Naim in *Sebilürresad* and Süleyman Nazif in *Içtihad* confronted the Turkists, with principles of Islam. Ahmed Naim stated that nationalism and Turkism were against the *Sharia* because Islam prohibited the 'ethnic cause'. Islamist reformer and poet

---

[117] Tunaya 2003: 49-81.
[118] Including, for example, the future Sheikh-ul Islam Musa Kazim

Mehmed Akif (Ersoy) addressed the congregations at Beyazıt Mosque in Istanbul with anti-nationalist speeches:

'Community of Muslims; you are not Arabs, or Turks, or Albanians, or Kurds, or Laz, or Circassians! You are affiliated to only one nation, which is the grand nation of Islam. Without leaving Islam, you cannot pursue the ethnic cause. One cannot remain a Muslim and be in the pursuit of an ethnic cause'.[119]

Turkist writer Agaoglu Ahmed fought back by claiming that Islam did not prohibit 'nation' but 'tribalism'. According to Agaoglu, the initial aim of Prophet Muhammad was also to create a community of Islam based on nationality through the unification of the Arab nation. Agaoglu argued that contrary to Islamists' claims, serving a nation in Mohammed's practice meant serving Islam. The journal of the Turkists of the constitutional period was *Türk Yurdu*, but in order to appeal to the pious public, the Turkists also published *Islam Mecmuası* (Islam Magazine) which declared that it was 'working for the Muslims' interests' and aimed 'a life with religion and a religion with life'. In this magazine, Islamic solutions were sought for contemporary problems, while the possibilities of a peculiarly Turkish Islam were contemplated. When the Turkist magazine of *Islam Mecmuası* is researched, the boundaries separating Islamism and Turkism become very ambiguous.[120] A synthesis of the two currents, which Tunaya names 'Islamist Turkism', also emerged through this discussion. Said Halim Pasha, a reformist Islamist, argued that since the time was 'the age of nations', it was

---

[119] Akif in Tunaya 2003: 71. Akif was deeply concerned with the loss of Empire's lands in the Balkans, but he was particularly upset about the Albanian declaration of independence in 1911. Ottomans never imagined Muslim Albanians as the 'other', and Akif an ethnic Albanian by birth, saw the Albanian separation as a traumatic result of a senseless epidemic, that is, nationalism:

Your nationality is Islam … what is ethnicity!
You should have embraced your nation and stood by it
What is Albania? Is it mentioned in the *Sharia*?
It is blasphemy and nothing else to put forward your ethnicity. (Ünlü & Özcan 1987: 77.)

[120] Akgün and Çalış 2002: 592-3.

impossible to unite Muslims as one nation. Instead, a long-term strategy of forming a federation of the 'Islamic Family' leading to the unity of Muslim nations was necessary.[121] Said Halim Pasha derived this conclusion from his criticism in *Buhranlarimiz* ('Our Crises') of the *Tanzimat* reformism:

In order to ascend as a nation, we were obliged to derive from western civilisation. (...) This led to that false contemplation that 'for salvation, we are bound to imitate the western nations'. (...) [We need to] derive from the term 'Turk', a social and political entity as strong as the connotation of the terms French, English and German.[122]

The motto of Turkish nationalism would also bare Islamic affiliations. In Ziya Gokalp's *Türklesmek, Islamlasmak, Muasırlasmak*, the three notions were presented as complimentary to each other. Islamisation was part of the project of civilisation and nationalisation. Here, Gökalp's notion of Islamisation presented a synthesis between Al Afghani's Islamic Puritanism and the New Ottomans' defence of the sphere of religion as the primary cement of modern society.

The Islamists' fight against the principle of 'nation' was a hegemony struggle to maintain Islam as 'Islam', as a regime of truth, against the threat of its relativisation as one of many modern and particular political discourses of the time. This debate over the acceptance or refusal of the term 'nation' would be lost with the growing popularity through time of 'nation' and 'nationalism', which accompanied the rapid nationalisation of the late-Ottoman discursive territory[123] as a necessity for salvation under the conditions of modernity, only to open up a new linguistic struggle over the definition of its content, 'nation of Islam' or the

---

[121] Tunaya 2002: 73.
[122] Said Halim Pasha in Alkan 2002: 462-4).
[123] See Chapter 3.

71

'dominant nation' vs. 'the Turk' or 'civilised nation'. This second battle was fought between Islam and Kemalism, which will be considered in the next section.

II.5. The Turning Point: 31 March Affair[124]

The discursive construction of Islam by the secular discourses of salvation as a negativity became possible after the suppression of the 31 March rebellion. The 31 March (13 April 1909) Affair that broke out as a military mutiny in Istanbul built itself on a number of discontents,[125] and was participated in by the elements of conservative Islamism, including a number of Sufi sheikhs and a fraction of the *ulema*, including some *Medrese* teachers and students. The mutineers marched to the Parliament, killed two deputies and a naval officer and 'liberated' Istanbul from the CUP power for 10 days. The mutiny was then quelled by the troops loyal to CUP, Sultan Abdulhamid II was dethroned and the CUP's control over the Ottoman State was tightened, which would lead to a one party dictatorship. Eight mutineers were executed after the suppression of the revolt, including the leading figure of the conservative Islamists and the editor of *Volkan* newspaper Dervish Vahdeti.[126] The conservative Islamist *Ittihadı Islam* Party and the liberal *Ahrar* Party[127] were outlawed.

---

[124] See also Appendix 3.

[125] The immediate reason was the growing conflict within the ranks of the Ottoman army between officers without military college training, whose careers were threatened by the government and the graduates of military colleges who manned the ranks of the CUP. The CUP led government also decided to end the Medrese students' exemption from military service and the leading CUP members such as Ahmed Riza gave anti-ulema speeches at the Parliament. On 6/7 April 1909, an opposition journalist, Hasan Fehmi, whose newspaper *Serbesti* had published the claims of a financial scandal involving the CUP, was murdered as he was crossing Galata Bridge on the Golden Horn in Istanbul. The assassin escaped, which raised a vocal suspicion that he must have been linked with the CUP. Hasan Fehmi's funeral turned into a large-scale anti-government demonstration.

[126] Aksin 1972.

[127] *Ahrar* Party's leader Prince Sabahaddin, formerly the leader of the liberal wing of the CUP, was briefly detained after the suppression of the revolt, but released without charges. The CUP leadership interpreted the revolt both a Hamidian plot and Prince Sabahaddin's bid for power. With the closure of the *Ahrar* Party, the consequences of the revolt served to the CUP's aim of suppressing the liberals.

31 March Affair had important consequences for the Islamist discourse. Firstly, the reformist and conservative wings experienced a radical split. Reformist Islamism distanced itself from the rebels by denouncing the revolt as reactionary mob action.[128] A declaration condemning the revolt by the "Cemiyet-i Ilmiyye-i Islamiye" (Islamic Scholars Association) was published by the Islamist journal *Sirat-ı Müstakim*. These Islamist reflections on the 31 March Affair could not however prevent discursive associations of all forms of Islamism and the reactionary revolt. After 31 March, the modernist-reformist discourses of salvation moved further away from Islam and the Islamist discourse. The image of a 'reactionary threat', ready to smash the gains of modernisation, and its association with religion in the form of Islamic fanaticism were leading to the mental registration of the Affair in terms of revolution/counter-revolution, progress/reaction, fanaticism/reason, Islam/modernism, etc. dichotomies. It was through this differentiation that the modern secular identity could completely free itself from Islam to construct itself through a de-Islamised discourse: 31 March Affair thus served as the constitutive trauma of a specific modern secular identity.[129]

II.6. Conclusions

In this section, I have outlined the process of the Islam's loss of its status as the absolute referential universe, that is the episteme of 'a regime of truth', to become a modern political discourse engaging in a contest with others for hegemony. Pan-Islamism and the accompanying notion of *umma*, the Hamidian Islamic state model, understanding

---

[128] One of their leading figures Mehmed Akif defined the Affair as 'a tragic incident, which is religious on surface but political and reactionary in reality'.

modernisation in terms of the adoption of the technique and not the culture of the West, and the responses to the increasing nationalisation of the ideological universe and with it the growing popularity of the term 'nation' for the redesign of late-Ottoman society, are the main themes that emerged through this process to determine the future struggle between Islamists and secularists. Political developments, particularly the 31 March Affair, also furnished the grounds of this confrontation by making it possible for the secular discourses of salvation to move out of the discursive horizon of Islam.

III. The Kemalist Watershed

Kemalism radically turned the tables with a comprehensive attempt to end the dual character of the symbolic order, through a confrontation with all expressions of Islam as a political identity. The Kemalist discourse and the republican symbolic order were shaped through this confrontation, the moments of which I will consider in this section. I will firstly demonstrate how the Kemalist repression was preceded by a mobilisation of the periphery in the national struggle. I will then consider the problem of the perception of the nation as the main issue that differentiated the Kemalist core from the Islamic periphery, over which a struggle for hegemony was fought between Kemalism and Islamism. This struggle was concluded by the repression of the Islamic identity in two subsequent steps, including the liquidation of the *ulema* and the criminalisation of Volk Islam practices, which I will consider in subsections III.3 and III.4. In the fifth subsection, I will consider the secular reforms, which went beyond

---

[129] Ataturk, in his biographical references, always claimed that he led the "operation army" to Istanbul to quell the 31 March revolt, which is not true. His claim to this particular incident is interesting when it is read as the

the fields of education and state affairs in general to overcome the dual structure of the social in toto at the expense of the Islamic conventions and on behalf of secular identity. I will argue that the Kemalist association of modernisation and secularism with 'civilisation' and 'reason', and the discursive construction of Islam as their opposite, constitute the origins of the contemporary associations by secularist discourse of Islamist political action with insanity. The argument in conclusion will imply that the Kemalist suppression of Islamic identity and the secularisation of the republican socio-political field through the repression of Islamic identity, while achieved the abolition of Islam in the symbolic order, led to the constitution of modern Turkey as a split structure, split between a conscious Kemalist core and an unconscious periphery. I will argue further that this split structure determined the split nature of republican Turkish identity: modern Turkishness was constituted as a split identity through the repression of the Islamic/Oriental components of Turkishness.

III.1. The Mobilisation of the 'periphery'

'National struggle' was fought by a coalition between the Muslim notables of Anatolia and the military-intellectual patriots of mostly CUP origin[130] General Mustafa Kemal, a junior figure in the CUP but a 'popular hero' since the 1915 defence of Gallipoli, sparked the movement and took the upper hand in the coalition as the Turkish forces under his command stopped the Greek army in central Anatolia. This success was grounded upon an abundant deployment of Islamic symbols to mobilise the Muslim masses.[131] The Kemalist hegemony

---

constituve trauma of the modern-secular psyche.

[130] See Appendix 3.

[131] For example, Mustafa Kemal countered the *fatwa* of the Istanbul authorities, which denounced national struggle with one by the mufti of Ankara, baptising the national struggle a Holy War. In a proclamation on 16

was built over the national struggle on the basis of a number of promises: 1- the salvation of Sultan/Caliph, 'who was held captive by the foreign occupiers in Istanbul', 2- the liberation of the 'motherland', the geographical borders of which were drawn by the 'National Pact' as adopted in the last session of the Ottoman Parliament. 3- the reinstitution of the Muslims as the 'dominant nation' within these borders.

The Islamic character of the national movement is particularly evident in the fact that the first National Assembly consisted exclusively of the Muslim deputies, unlike the Ottoman Parliaments which reflected the multicultural character of the Empire. The declaration dated 21 April 1920 calling the Grand National Assembly to meet, authored by General Mustafa Kemal, emphasised the aim to take advantage of the holy Friday, that prior to the opening all the deputies would pray at Hacı Bayram Mosque, 'to be enlightened with the divine glory of the Koran'. 'After the prayers', the declaration read, 'the deputies will carry in procession the hair from the beard of the Prophet and the sacred banner of Mohammed to the parliament building.' 'Before entering the building', declaration continued, 'prayers will be performed and sheep will be sacrificed while Koran and *Hadis* will be recited aloud. There will be prayers for the salvation, prosperity and independence of our Caliph and Sultan, our religion and state, our land and nation'.[132] Such manifest use of religion for political ends would be declared by Mustafa Kemal in February 1925 as a crime to be treated as treason.[133]

March 1920, Kemal said, 'God's help and protection are with us in the sacred struggle which we have entered upon our fatherland and salvation' (Toprak 1981: 63). The Ankara Government declared numerous times their loyalty to the Sultan/Caliph and urged the people of Anatolia not to be deceived by the negative propaganda by the Istanbul government and the occupying powers.
[132] 'In our history, no parliamentary opening ceremony had such fanatically conservative religious character. Were those extraordinary outbursts after the announcement of *fatwas* thought to be an insurance against the rebellions that broke out here and there? Whatever the reason may be, separating belief and conservatism from the opening day of the parliament would be a more sober decision. Neither choosing a Friday nor so much hubbub was necessary. A good prayer would make a better impression. Since such dose of conservatism was

The Kemalist mobilisation of periphery through an Islamic discourse resulted in the domination of the first National Assembly by conservative Volk Islam figures. The prominent figures of the Islamist intelligentsia also participated enthusiastically in the National Struggle. Leading Islamist Mehmed Akif wrote the lyrics of the 'Anthem of Salvation' which was adopted as the national anthem by unanimous resolution of the Grand National Assembly on 1 March 1921. Islamists joined the Grand National Assembly as deputies and performed sermons in the mosques around Anatolia calling Muslims to rally behind the nationalist movement. *Sebilurresad* transferred its headquarters from Istanbul to Ankara to participate in the mobilisation of periphery.

III.2. Defining Nation

The Islamist intellectuals' participation in the national struggle did not mean total surrender to Kemalist nationalism. They fought a linguistic battle through the national struggle against Kemalism on the fixing of the floating signifier 'millet' (nation) with a content. When the national struggle was fought 'millet' was used equivocally to signify both *Anasır-ı Islam* (Islamic elements) and the Turks as one of these elements. The main rhetoric was built over the fact that the former dominant nation (*millet-i hakime*) of the Empire had been turned into an oppressed nation (*mazlum millet*) by the foreign powers, and was under the threat of becoming subordinate to the non-Muslim elements.

---

not sustainable for the leadership, its counter-reaction could be more dangerous. The National Assembly opens with a very religious, in fact a very dervish-style, ceremony.' Edirne Deputy Kazim Karabekir (Karabekir 1988: 627.)
[133] Koçak 1995: 100.

Nevertheless, the Islamists' active participation in the Anatolian movement was a step back from the uncompromising stance of the constitutional era Islamism (see above), signalling the 'nationalisation of Islam'. An indication of this linguistic surrender was Mehmed Akif's Anthem of Salvation, in which he used the term 'millet' four times and 'irk' (race) twice: that 'nation which worship God' (millet = Muslims); and the 'heroic race' (irk = Turks). The right to salvation, that Akif proposes in this anthem, is not of the Turks (irk) but of the Muslims (millet). In fact, three famous lines of the anthem, where Akif speaks to the Crescent, suggest that the crescent was upset with this 'heroic race', probably due to the downturn in the Ottoman military stand against the Christian West. Akif degraded Turkism and what is contemporarily called nationalism as a 'racial cause' or an 'ethnic cause', and when he talked about millet, he firmly meant 'the nation of Islam'. However, although he continued to refer to Turkishness as 'irk' (race) in the anthem, a differentiation is observable from the anti-nationalist preacher of the Beyazit Mosque[134] to the poet who glorifies a 'heroic race'.

Akif obviously had to realise by 1920 the victory of the principle of nation, which he continued to view as ethnicity or race, over the principle of religion and consequently viewed the involvement in the 'national struggle' of one particular race of the greater Muslim nation as necessary, given that this was a struggle against the Christian existence in Anatolia. Christian existence in Anatolia was certainly the driving force for the Muslim participation in the national struggle. Another religious figure, Said-i Kurdi (a.k.a Said-i Nursi and Bediüzzaman) preached to the Kurdish people to side with the Kemalists in the name of Islam.

The equivocal use of nation, and the struggle between the Islamists and Kemalists to fix it with their particular content, continued throughout the national struggle. When the national struggle was fought, 'millet' was used ambiguously to signify both *Anasır-ı Islam* (Islamic elements) and the Turks as one of these elements. The main rhetoric was built on the fact that former dominant nation (*millet-i hakime*) of the Empire had turned into an oppressed nation (*mazlum millet*) as a result of the intervention of the foreign powers, and was exposed to the threat of becoming subordinate to the non-Muslim elements. Mustafa Kemal employed an equivocal discourse benefiting from the term's built in ambivalence, when using keywords like *millet* (nation), *milletdas* (fellow national), *dindas* (religious brother), *irade-i milliye* (national will) and *hakimiyet-i milliye* (national sovereignty).[135] He underlined in numerous occasions the religious grounds of nation and emphasised his respect for ethnic heterogeneity, particularly in the opening speech of the third term of the Assembly. Kemal also used the terms Turkey and Turk almost synonymously, insinuating that they signified other Muslim elements, too.[136] The boundaries that separated *millet* from its outside were agreed upon to be religion by all the elements of the 'historic bloc'. This delimitation for the code 'millet' was deployed in the mass population transfers with Greece in accordance with the Lausanne Treaty, in which religion, rather than ethnicity or language, was the criterion for differentiating populations.[137]

---

[134] See Section II above.
[135] Yıldız 2001: 129.
[136] Yıldız 2001: 129.
[137] The lively discussion on the content of the terms 'nation', Anatolia, Turk and Turkey in various sessions of the Assembly are referred to in Yıldız 2001: 130-1.

III.3. The Liquidation of the *Ulema*

The Kemalist leadership consisting mainly of members of the military bureaucratic elite managed to maintain its hegemony in the National Assembly during the three year long military conflict with the occupying Greek forces and the Istanbul sponsored rebels. However, the historic bloc of mobilised periphery and the military elite split immediately after the conclusion of the military conflict in September 1922. Islamist deputies in the Assembly had long sensed Kemal's aspirations to replace the Sultanate and Caliphate with his personal dictatorship and viewed the Ankara government's decision of 1 November 1922 to abolish the Sultanate as the first step in Kemal's project. The political frontiers were being reshaped in parallel to the growing antagonism between the Kemalist and Islamist components of the nationalist 'historic bloc'.[138] Mustafa Kemal and his supporters had observed the potential political ability of the Islamists in mobilising people, through both the Islamic establishment led by *ulema* and folk Islam represented by the Sufi orders. With the

---

[138] The ongoing cracks in the historic bloc revealing its fragility suddenly surfaced in the parliament immediately after the definite military success. The Ankara government declared on 1 November 1922 the abolition of the Sultanate and sent the Sultan to exile, while the Sultan's cousin, was elected as the Caliph. On 21 November the Turkish peace conference opened in Lausanne, which was suspended in a deadlock on 4 February 1923. Between this date and 1 April, the Grand National Assembly fiercely debated two issues: 1- the imminent concessions to be given from the 'national pact', particularly the government's willingness to give up Mosul and 2- the motion for the abolition of the Caliphate. On the first point Mustafa Kemal made the following U-turn:

> The national pact has never drawn borders as this line or that line. What draw those borders are the nation's interests and the sublime assembly's decisions. (Demirbas1995: 66)

Hüseyin Avni, a leader of the 'Second Group' responded to these comments:

> Pasha, sit at the head of your army. You have no other duty. I recognise this duty as sacred as you do. If you wish I would come and serve as your disciple. Whatever it may cost, perform your duty as the Head Commander: raise our flag in our borders and point your bayonet to the English throat (Demirbas 1995: 67).

Another leader of the pro-Islamist 'Second Group' was Ali Sükrü, who addressed the Assembly with powerful pro-Caliphate speeches. On 6 March 1923, Mustafa Kemal accused Ali Sükrü of harming the national interest. On 26 March Ali Sükrü disappeared and on 29 March his body was found in a shallow grave not far from Mustafa Kemal's villa on Çankaya hill (Mango 1999: 381). Kemal's bodyguard Lame Osman would take the blame and was executed.

dissolution on 1 April 1923 of the Grand National Assembly, Kemalist leadership abolished the most important means of expression of this crack within the historic bloc.

The new parliament, consisting of deputies selected personally by Mustafa Kemal,[139] approved the Lausanne Treaty, declared Turkey a republic on 29 October 1923 and abolished the Caliphate on 3 March 1924. The unity of education law that passed the same day effectively ended religious education.[140] Another motion passed the same day abolished the office of *Seyhülislam*. On 8 April, religious courts were abolished. The *ulema* were thus made completely redundant within a matter of months.

III.4. Repressing the Periphery: Kurdish Rebellion as Religious Reaction

The *ulema's* liquidation was however the lesser part of the difficult task of repression of the mobilised periphery. The Kemalist crackdown had to target the Volk Islam in order to clear the way for the secular reforms. The attack on popular religion commenced as part of the counter-insurgency measures in the wake of the 1925 Kurdish rebellion. In preparation, Kemal persistently labelled the Kurdish rebellion a reactionary religious affair rather than a

---

[139] Mango 1999: 385.

[140] With the introduction of Unity of Education Law in 1924, religious education was taken under the state's control. The Administration of Religious Affairs (Diyanet Isleri Baskanligi) was also founded as part of the same reform. Religious personnel were reorganised under this administration as civil servants. In order to train new religious personnel, imam-hatip schools were opened in Istanbul and twenty-eight other provincial centres. A new Faculty of Theology was also set up at the Darülfunun in 1924. However, this line of schooling lacked popular participation. By 1926, twenty imam-hatip schools were remaining and in 1932, the number of these schools dropped to two, one in Istanbul and one in Konya. The number of students in these schools was also reduced from 2,258 in 1924 to ten by 1932. In 1933, Faculty of Theology was closed down and turned into an Institute for Islamic Research. After the third congress of the RPP in 1931, where the principle of secularism was included in the party programme, the government declared that religion only concerned the individual conscience. Religious education was the responsibility of the family, not the state. As a result, religion was abolished from primary and secondary school curricula in 1935 (Jaschke 1972: 74-83).

national uprising. The Sheikh Said rebellion thus resulted in the repression of the periphery to accompany the foreclosure of the Kurdish identity.[141]

Mustafa Kemal made a public statement on 7 March and attributed the rebellion to criminals who tried to hide their intentions under the mask of religion, and who had relied on activities all over the country aimed at weakening the authority of the state.[142] Opening the new session of the assembly in November 1925, he described the rebellion as the work of 'reactionary tendencies and preparations'. In the closing passage of his six-day speech (1927) he spoke of the rebellion as an uprising of ignorance, fanaticism and general hostility towards the republican administration and the 'modern movement' and accused the opposition Progressive Republican Party of becoming a source of hope for reactionaries.

It is true that Sheikh Said was a senior *Nakshibendi* figure, who declared himself *Emirülmücahidin* (Commander of Warriors of the Faith) and made it known that his aim was to restore the *Sharia*, violated by a 'godless government'. But he and the rebellious Kurdish leaders had sought a separate dispensation for their people, as admitted by the Prime Minister and the Independence Court's sentence.[143] Mustafa Kemal, on the other hand, glorified the suppression of the Kurdish rebellion not as a counter-insurgency operation but as 'a war of ideas': 'For the first time in Turkish history, our soldiers went to war for their ideals, for a noble cause'.[144] Kemal's choice was therefore to declare an ideological war against 'reaction'.

---

[141] See Chapter 2.
[142] Mango 1999: 423-5. In fact, Mustafa Kemal had ceased to refer to the Kurds by name in his public speeches since the proclamation of the republic.
[143] During the discussion at the Assembly on 25 February, Prime Minister Fethi (Okyar) acknowledged that in this case the political purpose was Kurdish separatism. Ismet (Inönü), who replaced Fethi, after the latter resigned over the counter-insurgency methods stating, 'I will not dip my hands in blood by choosing unnecessary violence', viewed the matter initially as a confrontation between an inferior and a superior ethnicity. 'We must turkify the inhabitants of our country at any price', uttered Ismet, 'and we will annihilate those who oppose the Turks or 'le turquisme'' (Simsir 1991: 58).
[144] Cited in Tunaya: 614.

His description of the problem of ethnic heterogeneity is important in the association of Islam with reaction:

There are citizens and members of our nation inside the political and social entity of contemporary Turkish nation, to whom the propaganda of the ideas of being Kurdish, Cyrcassian and even Laz are attempted. But these misnomers, which were the products of the past ages of tyranny, failed to have any influence - apart from suffering - on any members of the nation except for a few brainless reactionaries used by the enemy. Because, the people of these communities like Turkish society in general share the same common past, history, morals and law.[145]

The discursive association of religion with rebellion served an additional end, as important as the denial of Kurdish identity: the association of Islam with 'backwardness', 'reactionary fanaticism', 'counter-revolution' and 'irrationality' as opposed to 'civilisation', 'progress', 'revolution' and 'Reason'. Islam was no longer an alternative 'regime of truth', since Reason had replaced religion as the global principle of modernity. Nor was it any longer a social bond that tied the society together, since in the age of nationalism, religion was replaced with nation. Religion was a matter of individual conscience and had no communal functions. Calls for a return to *Sharia* or Caliphate by 'a few brainless reactionaries' could therefore achieve nothing but 'suffering'.

III.5. Secular Reforms and the Kemalist 'Regime of Truth'

The Kemalist regime thus insisted that the Sheikh Said rebellion of 1925 was a counterrevolutionary attempt mobilised by religious propaganda. The Maintenance of Order Law and the Independence Tribunals would be used against both the leaders of the rebellion and any potential Islamic opposition. In the wake of the Sheikh Said rebellion a new bill was passed in the Grand National Assembly on 25 February 1925, as an addendum to the 'Law of Treason' stating that the use of religion for political ends was a crime to be treated as treason[146] and Mustafa Kemal proposed to his Assembly to pass a 'hat law', which banned other headgear including fez. A law to dissolve Sufi orders and close down Dervish lodges and shrines accompanied the hat law.

Sweeping secularist reforms continued at full speed after the suppression of local resistances to 'hat revolution', through Independence Tribunals' sentences. A further consequence of the suppression of the Sheikh Said rebellion was the liquidation of the political opposition with the closure of the Progressive Republican Party and the trial of its leading members at Independence Tribunals, which concluded with a number of death sentences. A monolithic one-party dictatorship under the personal command of Mustafa Kemal was established. The agent of change, the RPP led by Mustafa Kemal, seemed to have been set completely free to reshape society in its own image.

Kemalist secularism is officially defined as the separation of the state's pursuits from the sphere of religion. It is however evident from Mustafa Kemal's statements that secularism meant more than this in practice. Firstly, such a separation could not be put in practice without breaking down the cultural and moral influence of religion over social life.[147] Secondly, in the Kemalist discursive practices, the pursuits of the state lacked the clear boundaries that separate 'political society' from the sphere of 'civil pursuits'. Kemalism wanted to build a *civilised* society', which was not necessarily imagined as a *civil* society'. Consequently, given the popularity of religion, an autonomous civil sphere could only exist as a threat to the Kemalist will to civilisation. The 1929 Great Depression served further the expansion of these state pursuits by leading to the construction of a public sector economy through a state-led industrialisation campaign on the grounds of the newly adopted principle of étatism. With this over-inflated state at hand, the conquest of all remnants of civil

---

[145] Inan 1969: 23.
[146] Koçak 1995: 100.
[147] Parla 1991: 150.

84

society[148], and their transformation through 'civilisation' and etatisation, became a feasible Kemalist project. The term 'civilisation' was deployed as synonymous with secularisation, that is, the breaking down of traditional communities and conservative mentalities (conservatism and ignorance - *taassub ve cehil)[149]* through education, which would above all transform the modern Turkish subjects' sense of belonging from both the immediate conservative community and the imagined community of Islam to the Turkish nation and the civilised West. This nation of modern subjects would then march into civilisation under the tutelage of the Kemalist State armed with the grand narratives of national development, progress and modernisation.

III.6. Repression and Unconscious

It is important to specify the spatial location of religion in this discursive constitution of republican Turkey and modern nationalist subject. Let us first turn to the Islamist discourse's description of this location:

> The Ottoman cultural heritage that had been thrown in the rubbish bin of the republic
>
> could make itself felt only as a diminishing deep current confined to (...) the old
>
> wooden houses, (...) certain cafés and second hand book collector shops'.[150]

Islam, which once 'hovered over and above society' as the sole source of politics, morals, aesthetics and even sciences, was pushed down to the depths of the social, both spiritually

---

[148] The economic activity had already been destroyed by the liquidation of Christian minorities. A national economy project was implemented by the CUP government aiming to replace the emptied positions of Christian subjects in the economic networks with Muslim ones. This project was disturbed with the outbreak of World War I. The decisions of Izmir Economic Congress (1923) indicated a continuation with the national economy project, which could not be pursued due mainly to the lack of resources. Kemalists did not really inherit a civil society from the Empire but only the remnants of it, in the form of urban and rural pious, conservative communities. The 1929 great depression served largely in the shaping of a peculiar Kemalist project, which resembled both the Soviet experience on the one hand and European fascism and national socialism on the other. I shall consider the development of the Kemalist project in detail in the next chapter.
[149] See Atatürk 1962: 890.

What is observed from the above outline of the trajectory of the Kemalist repression of Islamic identity is that in the Kemalist republican discourse, it became possible to associate Islam, which had been the irrefutable referential source of any truth for the Ottoman State and society for six centuries, with a mental deficiency, that is, insanity. In the constitution of the republican discursive horizon around a strong will to 'civilise', Islamic identity was carefully situated in a space of exclusion to constitute the dark, superstitious, insane and primitive side of a 'radiant', 'rational' and 'civilised' republican identity; if so, the Islamic identity constitutes the unconscious of the republican identity. It therefore becomes possible to assert that the discursive dualism, which splits reason and insanity, and which corresponds in the secularist discourse to the dualism that separates secularism from Islam, or the secular core from the religious periphery, is open to a reading in terms of a psychic dualism which separates the conscious from unconscious.

IV. Conclusions

This chapter consists of a problematisation, through a genealogy of the exclusion of the Islamic discourse in the construction of modern Turkish identity, of the contemporary secular discourse, which manifestly situates religious protest outside the symbolic order. I have argued that this exclusion was preceded by the organic crisis of the Ottoman order, which in turn was a result of the changing terms of encounter with the West and the accompanying change in the perceptions of the West. I have then considered the moments of the gradual erosion of the status of Islam as the ultimate ground of all political discourse and the sole source of legitimacy – as the episteme of the Ottoman regime of truth – and the consequent emergence of Islamism as a modern political discourse. I have however argued that despite these moments of erosion, Islam's discursive location for the competing discourses of salvation of the Empire was far from the republican exclusion of it as a reactionary and irrational obstacle to Turkish Enlightenment. I have, on the other hand, demonstrated that political developments, including the Hamidian mobilisation of Volk Islam and the 31 March Affair, laid down the grounds of a movement towards such an exclusion.

Nevertheless, the comprehensive exclusion of Islam was a consequence of the Kemalist attempt at overcoming the dual character of the social on behalf of the secular identity. The constitution of Islam as the opposite of reason, among a number of attributes, was part of the Kemalist techniques of exclusion. From the inquiry into the Kemalist techniques of exclusion of religious identity, an argument has developed to make the case for understanding the process of exclusion in terms of the psychic mechanism of repression. This implies that the Kemalist exclusion of Islamic identity and the secularisation of the republican socio-political field, while achieved the abolition of Islam in the symbolic order, led to the constitution of modern Turkey as a split structure, split between a conscious Kemalist core and an unconscious periphery. Kemalism thus built itself on the deepening of the faultline that entered the Turkish socio-political field through pro-West reformist discourses. As I have argued, this split structure determined the split nature of republican Turkish identity: modern Turkishness was constituted as a split identity through the repression of the Islamic/Oriental components of Turkishness.

The moment the term Turkish identity is pronounced one is therefore referring to a split, and as such to at least two identities. The conscious core, or the Kemalist/republican centre[154], generates a reality where the task of 'civilisation' and the cult of Ataturk constitute a regime of truth corresponding to the republican symbolic order. The unconscious consists on the other hand of the 'popular religion' or common sense' nationalism of Muslim Anatolia, where the sediments of the repressed, including non-western elements, the Ottoman past and Islamic identity, remain to flow as 'a deep current'. Kemalism, although excludes Islamic identity, does not deny it; instead it situates the Islamic identity within the perspective of modernisation, as something to be superseded through modernisation. The 'deep current' would continue to flow as the repressed dimension of the Kemalist psyche, as the

---

[154] Mardin 1975.

unconscious component of modern Turkish identity: the inescapable sediments of the *ancien regime*. Therefore, the two levels, the conscious core and the unconscious periphery, although radically different from each other, do coexist as the complementary elements of the same national identity.

CHAPTER 2

FIN-DE-SIECLE NATIONALISATION OF THE TURKISH DISCURSIVE TERRITORY

Introducing the Symptom: June 1999, Isle of Imrali

Terrorist organisation's ringleader is being tried...

Mudanya Governor provides lunch and dinner for the martyrs' families. Governor states that the Mudanya residents opened their houses for the accommodation of 50 martyr families since the beginning of the Ocalan trial on 29 May.[155]

In the courtroom, the families of the killed soldiers shouted at Ocalan and his lawyers: "**Armenian** seed Vampire Apo".[156]

Lawyer of Prosecution Fuat Turgut referring to his 'sources', said that he had information confirming that Ocalan's father was an **Armenian** and demanded the court to ask the defendant whether or not his father was Armenian.

Martyr relative Ilhami Cicek: "The name of the defendant *who is non-Turkish and non-Muslim should be changed to his real name.*"[157]

---

[155] Anatolian News Agency, 2 June 1999.
[156] Hurriyet, 5 June 1999.
[157] Anatolian News Agency, 2 June 1999.

The Ocalan trial was the peak-point of a series of hysterical anti-Kurdish symptoms of the 1990s Turkey acted out at football matches, soldier farewell ceremonies, martyr funerals and any nationalist gathering of an official or unofficial character. This hysteria was certainly one of the inevitable consequences of the 15 year long undeclared war in north Kurdistan, which haunted the popular masses in spite of the official attempts to present the event in terms of 'state security' as opposed to 'national war'.[158]

An analysis of the above symptom in terms of a cause and effect model would certainly be accurate.[159] It is, above all, a symptomatic articulation of the Turkish response to a major challenge of the 1980s and 1990s against the republican social order - the politico-military activities of the Kurdish movement with a 'minimum program' of recognition as a separate identity dressed with cultural rights and political representation. However, within the limits of this line of analysis, an accurate explanation of the specific form of the Turkish response remains unaccounted for. The form of Turkish encounter with the Kurdish identity leads to the following question: 'Why, instead of the recognition of Kurdish identity and accommodation of Kurdish demands through the democratisation of the political order, the claims and demands to this effect since mid-1980s had to be countered by such violence costing the lives of over 30,000 people, mostly Kurdish civilians, systematic human rights violations and the displacement of over a million Kurdish inhabitants?' In the search for an answer to this

---

[158] See, Laciner 1999. The escalating war has also seen rise in the racist attacks on the Kurds, particularly in the West of Turkey. In late 1992, two Kurdish youths were rescued from a lynch mob in Alanya and there were attacks on Kurdish property. In Igdir, there were anti-Kurdish riots after HEP gained a seat on the municipal council in Novemer 1992. On 13 July 1993, an anti-Kurdish riot broke out in Ezine, Canakkale. In April 1998, ultra-nationalist mob attacked the corpses of the PKK guerrillas in Antalya, protesting their burial in 'Turkish soil'. The corpses were excavated from the graveyards by the local council to be reburied in an unknown location.

question, I will ground my argument upon the thesis that the metaphorical references to 'the Armenian' in the traumatised Turkish subject's discourse mentioned above is the key to the understanding of this violent intolerance. A rephrasing of the above question will therefore help to emphasise the specific concern of this chapter: 'what are the mechanisms that lead to the national-popular discourse's association of Ocalan with the Armenian?' This question can be answered by writing a 'history of the present' through a joint problematisation of two attempts of 'separatism' and their suppression in modern Turkish history: the Armenian question and the Kurdish question.

The argument in this chapter will be based upon an understanding of the nationalist ideology in psychoanalytic terms. It is therefore necessary to assert at the outset that the psychic defence mechanism of foreclosure and its consequences, which will be extensively discussed in this chapter, need to be seen as a universal feature of any national identity, or, that nationalism is structured like psychosis. Nations are produced primarily in the imaginary register as coherent and autonomous entities[160] to be crystallised through the operation of nationalist discourses, which interpellate a certain group of people to identification with a national identity. As Ernest Renan (1990) put it in the 19th Century, the process of nationalisation has to include a process of forgetting, which can be read as repression. Similarly, Tom Nairn (1977: 359) associated nationalism with neurosis, since it is the discourse of uneven development perceived traumatically as a pathologic failure. In psychoanalytic theory, neurosis is the outcome of repression and therefore Nairn's assertion

---

[159] Studies on the Kurdish conflict are firmly based, without exception, on an outline of a history of this conflict in terms of a chain of causalities (See Olson, Bruinessen, Berkey and Fuller, Kirisci, Poulton).
[160] Anderson 1991.

is complementary to Renan's argument. Another aspect of nationalism, that is, the constant reference to the outside of the nation (other nations) in persistently antagonistic terms blended mostly with anxiety and paranoia, which is crucial for the structuration of the national territory as an autonomous entity, has managed to escape psychoanalytic theorisation of nationalism. This aspect can be understood in terms of the ultimately inevitable failure of identification,[161] and the consequent aggressive tension.[162] The realisation of an originary and insurmountable lack of identity not only produces the desire of identification, and the structuration of the field of politics but also leads to a desire to master over the ultimate failure in the encounter with the limits of symbolisation. The desire to master this excessive element, which bars 'reality' within certain boundaries, in turn leads to the production of fantasy.[163] The fantasy of the nationalist discourse is unexceptionally related to the 'other nations', the extremes of the phantasmatic scenario being to master these others or the fear of falling under the others' domination. This constantly referred to phantasmatic outside can be read as the order of the real, the location primarily of the identities necessarily excluded from the constitution of the 'national reality'. The suppression of the ethnic/linguistic/religious heterogeneity in the constitution of any nation[164] necessarily includes the operation of the psychic mechanism of foreclosure and the nationalist fantasy is its metaphorical expression. Given the nature of foreclosure, that the excluded element is not

---

[161] Laclau 1994: 3 and Stavrakakis 2000.

[162] The same is arguably the nature of any 'social imaginary'. If, given its psyhoanalytic nature, the imaginary register is the realm of the illusions of identity, sameness, similarity on the one hand and autonomy and wholeness on the other. While the formers are affirmative of the lack and alienation involved even in this process of illusion, the latters produce the effects of coherence, stability and omnipotence. It is this split that is immediately translated into aggressive tension by the infant: 'the imaginary is clearly the prime source of aggressivity in human affairs' (Stavrakakis 1998: 18).

[163] Stavrakakis 2000a: 101.

[164] Gellner (1983: 48) points out violence, exclusion and assimilation as the built-in features of any nationalism; similarly Nairn (1977: 105) argues that nationality constitutes the basis of both 'national liberation' and 'narrow nationalism', both the principle of self-determination and fascism.

merely the theme of fantasy but exists in the order of the real, 'living through' the nationalist fantasy sooner or later, or the return of the foreclosed from the order of the real, is inevitable. This is but the description of the moment of entry into psychosis with the onset of hallucinations and delusions. Nationalism is therefore structured like psychosis since the imagination of nations necessitates the construction of 'other nations', as the obverse of the 'nation' in antagonistic terms, or, as 'Hallucinated Communities'.

This chapter will continue the analysis of Turkish identity crisis by reflecting on the moments of exclusion imminent in the nationalisation of the Ottoman discursive horizon. I will demonstrate that these moments of exclusion and the specific forms of enunciation of this experience have been constitutive of the Turkish political identity. On these grounds, the formation of Turkish political identity will be considered in terms of the development of an 'historic bloc' that formed the social base, or the 'economic-corporate' content, of the myth of 'nation' and the nationalist social imaginary, accompanying a protracted process of the discursive externalisation of the signifier 'Armenian', in parallel to the physical liquidation of the non-Muslim elements. In the first section, I will analyse this process and specify the characteristics of the emergent Turkish identity in the eve of the formation of republican Turkey. Republican Turkey was formed through a Kemalist *coupure epistemologique* initiating a split between the secular/modernist ruling ideology on the one side and the popular 'nation of Islam' on the other, as considered in Chapter 1. The national character of the additional split between the Kurdish identity and the republican perception of Turkishness was denied and, instead of being accounted for as what it was, pronounced by the republican discourse in terms of the primal split between religious and secularist identities. In the second section, I will consider this denial in terms of foreclosure of the fears peculiar to the military/bureaucratic elite consisting of a condensed scenario of disintegration of the 'nation' through 'reactionary' religious agitation, which demarcates the boundaries of a specifically republican Turkish psyche. I will then consider in the third section the functioning of associations of 'the Kurd' with 'the Armenian' to argue that this metonymy has a psychological value and provides a nexus between the republican core and the popular level to furnish a national-popular territory. The overall argument of this chapter is that these primary moments of externalisation are in effect moments of the traumatic encounter of Turkish political psyche with the real, accompanied by 'real' human tragedy of extensive dimension, that is, the massacre of over a million inhabitants of Anatolia.

I. Milletisation through de-Christianisation

'Killing Twice'

January 27, Auschwitz's Liberation Day, was declared in 2001 to be Britain's first Holocaust Day. The genocides in Bosnia, Cambodia and Rwanda were remembered along with the Jewish holocaust, while the Armenians were entirely excluded from the ceremony. However, after intense pressure, the British government had to make a concession: a few Armenians were invited to the event and mention would be made to the hundreds of thousands of deaths in 1915. As expected, this rather limited recognition of the Armenian suffering provoked immediate anger from the Turkish authorities and public.[165]

---

[165] A Turkish paper published an exceptionally overt threat to 'kill twice': "Let it be clear to world public opinion: in the past we punished all the infamous half-castes who, not content with profiting from our lands, attacked our

By the end of the year 2000, the Armenian genocide has been acknowledged by the European Parliament, along with France, Sweden, the Vatican and Italy. Of the major powers, only the US, Canada and Britain still hold back. Formerly, the Turkish government threatened to deny the US use of its air bases if the President agreed formally to accept the massacres as genocide.

In 1990, Turkish Ambassador to US, Nuzhet Kandemir claimed the Armenian deaths were 'a result of a tragic civil war initiated by Armenian nationalists'. In order to maintain this 'thesis' globally, a war of position at the academic level has also been fought by students, academics and diplomats alike.[166] 'Many of the Turkish efforts', comments Akcam (2001), 'aimed to obscure the facts, rather than dispute a false charge.'

Thomas Bürgenthal, an Auschwitz survivor, lawyer and member of the UN Human Right Committee, says: "I don't know why the Turks can't admit it, express sorrow and go on. That's the worst. You do all these things to the victim and then you say it never happened. That is killing them twice'.[167]

---

possessions, the lives and honour of the Turks. We know that our forefathers were right and, if there were such threats again today, we would not hesitate to do what was necessary" (*Akit*, 12 February 2001).

[166] Julia Pascal (2001) reports that Turkey had offered funding for academic programmes in the universities such as Princeton and Georgetown. In 1998, UCLA's history department voted to reject a $1m offer to endow a programme in Turkish and Ottoman studies because it was conditional on their denying the Armenian genocide. In August 2000, Turkey tried to suppress a Microsoft online encyclopaedia entry. The Chronicle of Higher Education reports that the Turkish government threatened Microsoft with serious reprisals unless all mention of the Armenian genocide was removed. Professor Colin Tatz, director for the Centre for Comparative Genocide at Macquaire University, Sydney, Australia, claims that Turkey has used 'a mix of academic sophistication and diplomatic thuggery ... to put both memory and history into reverse gear'.

[167] Pascal 2001.

Julia Pascal's answer to this question is that the stakes involved in the persistent Turkish denial of genocide consist mainly of economic interests: the consequences of an acknowledgement of the Armenian genocide may legitimate land claims and legalise reparations.

Pascal is wrong. The size of government resources invested so far in the suppression of the Armenian issue is a proof that there is not a necessarily rational link between political behaviour and economic interest. In fact, a further passage from Pascal's article makes it very difficult to sustain an economic interest argument: 'Turkish-born Armenian author, Agop Hacikyan was called up in 1955 to military service in Izmir. As a soldier in uniform, he remembers stopping to go to the public toilet. Looking down, he saw that the urinal had been constructed from Armenian gravestones. Forty years after the mass murders, Turks were happily making people urinate on Armenian graves'.[168] With an economic interest paradigm, building toilets from Armenian gravestones, converting churches into manufactures and cowsheds around the country and a variety of similar practices aiming mainly to destroy and degrade the traces of non-Muslim presence in Turkey, will be difficult to explain. Besides, these are not official but popular practices being traditionalised by ordinary Muslim Turks' 'common sense'.[169]

The persistent denial of the Armenian massacre and the ever-present popular resentment towards the 'Armenian' signify much higher stakes than Pascal imagines. The Turkish fear consists in the fact that deconstruction of the Armenian taboo is likely to reveal that Turkish

---

[168] Pascal 2001.

98

identity, rather than heroism and self-sacrifice, as has been authored and tutored to so many republican generations, is grounded upon ethnic cleansing supported by cold-blooded demographic engineering.[170] Denial, far beyond economic concerns, is necessary for the reproduction of Turkish reality; overt avowal, on the other hand, is likely to lead to the unravelling of the 'Borromean Knot', which holds this reality together. I will therefore argue in this section that the psychic function of the Armenian massacre, and the taboo of the Armenian attached to it – as observed in the simultaneous denial of the Armenian massacre and the degradation of the Armenian people – signifies a traumatic faultline, which is simultaneously constitutive and destabilising for the Turkish identity.

If the Armenian taboo is constitutive, then exploring the meaning of the signifier 'Armenian' for Turkish identity – which requires above all an inquiry into the elimination of the Armenian people at the turn of the century – may be holding the key to an analytic comprehension of this identity as a combination of the political psyche and political subjectivity. The use of this key involves the revisiting of the moments of constitution of Turkishness and its encounter with the Armenian identity, which I will present in the subsections below as interactive events of history.

I will firstly situate the process of dissolution of the imperial symbolic order through the operation of the floating signifier *millet* within the context of Ottoman identity crisis outlined in chapter 1. I will then identify the three segments of Muslim-Turkish community, who were

---

[169] These popular practices occasionally outraged even the top figures of the ruling elite. See, for instance, Kemal's chronic F. R. Atay's comments in September 1922 (Atay 1980: 325).
[170] Akcam argues that the heroes of 'National Struggle' are in fact 'thieves and murderers', or 'genocide and robbery convicts' (Akcam 2001).

increasingly driven towards each other by a shared 'victim psychology'. In the next subsection, I will analyse the movements of these segments as leading to the formation of an 'historic bloc' around a 'myth' of salvation, which initiated the elaboration of a nationalist 'social imaginary'. The analysis will focus on the consequences of this movement in the design of Turkish national identity, including in particular the processes of externalisation involved in this movement and the accompanying mechanisms of exclusion that emerged as the integral components of this identity. In the final subsection below, I will outline the main features of Turkish identity prior to Kemalist secularisation in the wake of the conclusion of 'national struggle'. I will argue that these features are constitutive of Turkish political psyche, or a crude greater identity perception which unite the conscious (secularist) core (or the modern centre) and the repressed unconscious (Islamic) periphery, which the republican order has avoided to symbolise. I will then conclude this section with a discussion on Pascal's remarks above on the degradation of the non-Muslim 'memory traces'. I will present an argument in conclusion that the popular anti-Armenian rituals have a value, which is psychological and are therefore historically necessary for the reproduction of the Turkish identity. This necessity stems from the specific features of Turkish identity, the definition of which has had to rely heavily on an outside, that is to say that the possibility of Turkishness is largely dependent upon the discursive representations of what had been excluded from the absolute psychic boundaries of Turkishness.

I.1. From Dominant Nation to Oppressed Nation

Scholars, who have researched the 'peculiarity of the East', have developed the notions of 'Oriental Despotism' (Hegel, Montesquieu, Wittfogel), 'Asiatic Mode of Production' (Marx), 'Tributary Mode of Production' (Samir Amin), etc., to define the non-western societies of the Medieval Age.[171] All these definitions share an emphasis on the importance of tax collection in the socio-economic structure of these societies. The Ottoman Empire was no exception: any socio-economic history of the Empire is bound to be written, above all, as a history of crises and reformation of successive regimes of taxation. The late 16th Century witnessed such a crisis and a consequent transition from taxes in kind to taxes in cash. Another development, resulting from a number of indigenous and exogenous factors, the ascending role of the *ulema* along with the ascendance of the *Sheria* to replace the Sultan's Law as the primary judicial point of reference, also commenced around this time.

Historians agree in marking these simultaneous developments as the beginning of the end of the classical age of the Empire, leading to a transition from the classical division of society between the state class (*askeriye*) and the people (*reaya*), to a division between religious communities (*millets*). The new tax regime viewed the Ottoman population as an aggregate of communities rather than individuals. The obligations were now placed onto not individuals but to units such as villages, communities, guilds and cities as a whole through which taxes were collected. The growing primacy of the *Sheria* in the legal system in the expense of the Sultan's Law, on the other hand, led the non-Muslim subjects consult increasingly their religious leaders for disputes among themselves, rather than the *Khadis*, the Ottoman judges. Following the transfer to the religious communities of power and responsibility of the conduct of their own legal and educational matters, the central

---

Turner 1978.

administration acknowledged in the 18th Century the *millet* system, a system based on religious communities *(millets)*. The transition to *millet* system was a novelty in the sense that for a non-Muslim his *millet* rather than the Ottoman administration became the most important social-political organisation.[172] For the non-Muslim population of the Empire, *millet* would gradually become the name for the main source of their communal identification, in social, cultural and, later, political senses.[173]

Moreover, *millet* system laid the grounds for the 19th Century Ottoman identity crisis[174] with the proliferation of nationalisms. A term, *millet,* which had been originally introduced to signify religious communities' liability to the State, would become a floating signifier through time to mark initially the autonomy of these communities *vis-à-vis* the State, and evolve gradually to mean 'nation' in Turkish in the heyday of nationalism.[175]

The Ottoman ruling class, the conventional *millet-i hakime* (dominant nation) and the Muslim migrants from the outlying imperial lands in the Balkans and those fleeing the Russification policies to seek refuge in the Empire all experienced this process of the Empire's disintegration through *milletisation* as a common trauma.[176] This shared traumatic perception brought together these three groups of 'victims' in an 'historic bloc' to form the

---

[172] Kunt 1997: 67-8.
[173] "Milla" is an Arabic word, meaning "a word" in its origin, and therefore a human community who accepts a certain word or a book of revelations. "Milla" is the synonym of "logos" in Greek. In Qoran and in its later usage, it signifies a more definite community than "umma". It is used both to signify Muslim community and non-Muslims, religious communities and the secessionist groups in the Muslim world. In the Ottoman Empire, the word "millet" is used to signify religious communities. The essential difference between 'millets' is thought to be religious differences rather than ethnic ones. For instance, the largest non-muslim millet, "Rum", consisted of Serbians, Bulgarians, Albanians, Arabs and Greeks who were members of Greek Orthodox Church Community. Similarly the Muslim millet consisted of Turks, Albanians, Kurds and Arabs. (Lewis 1968: 62.)
[174] See Chapter 1.
[175] For the dissolution of the *millet* system alongside the traditional class positions, see Karpat 1973.
[176] See Appendix 4.

102

nucleus of the Turkish nation. In the next subsection, I will consider the stages of formation and development of this 'historic bloc', each of which was closely related to the externalisation of the elements that resisted articulation by the proto-nationalist myth of the 'Empire's salvation'.

I.2. The emergence of the Nation as an 'Historic Bloc'

The identity of Turkishness was born as the identity of an 'historic bloc', which emerged and developed through a war against the ethnic and religious plurality of Anatolia. The history of transition from Empire to republic was, in effect, the polarisation of the late Ottoman discursive horizon in the Schimittian sense, that is, a redefinition of the political scenery in terms of an antagonistic division between friends and foes.[177]

1. The Hamidian Grounds

The first stage was Abdulhamid II's absolutist reign between 1876 and 1908, during which the Sultan's 'moral and cultural leadership' accompanied by a discourse of Pan-Islamism was restored over an alliance between the ruling elite and the Muslim elements at the 'economic-corporate' level. Sultan promoted the economic wellbeing of the displaced craftsmen, Muslim merchants, landowners and notables against the non-Muslim subjects of the Empire.[178]

---

[177] See, Mouffe 1993: 50
[178] See Chapter 1 for a detailed account of Abdulhamid II's policies.

The defeat in the 1877-78 Russian War and the terms of the Berlin Accord imposed in its aftermath served to strengthen the solidarity between the official and popular levels around an anti-non-Muslim sentiment. The emerging conflict was partly due to the dispute on land claims accompanying the settlement of the Muslim migrants in Anatolia, the unpronounced 'last shelter' of the Empire, next to the traditionally non-Muslim habitat particularly in the East Anatolia. The tensions of the settlement of Muslim Cyrcassians, who had emigrated en masse since the Crimean War on the Armenian land, gained momentum with the Kurds' participation in the conflict on the anti-Armenian side in the wake of the Russian War.[179] The status of the Armenians, who traditionally occupied high positions in the Palace bureaucracy, and were called *millet-i sadıka* ('the loyal nation') because of their loyalty to the Empire's interests, was in decline, pushing the Armenian *millet* further under the influence of nationalist currents, triggering off further the Turkish-Muslim hostility. The conflict began to gain the character of a civil war in parallel to the popularisation of the Hamidian discourse of salvation consisting of a call for identification with an entity premised primarily upon the otherness of the non-Muslim subjects, who were increasingly associating their demands for equal rights with centrifugal aspirations.

2. The Ottomanist Interval

---

[179] In the wake of the defeat against Russia, Abdulhamid legalised Kurdish banditry by the formation of *Hamidiye* regiments, with the excuse of the need for the protection of the Muslim population from the Armenians. Then in 1894, he ordered a counter-insurgency operation on Sassun mountains against the Armenian *Hunchak* party agitators in which *Hamidiye* regiments were deployed alongside Ottoman troops, and which resulted in the destruction and forcible evacuation of many Armenian villages. Finally, in 1895 and 1896, in Istanbul and in the Armenian provinces, Muslim population, whose fanaticism was generated for the occasion, was incited to kill and pillage Armenians. Chailand and Ternon estimate the number of the Armenian victims of these events as three hundred thousand. (Chailand & Ternon 1983: 28.)

The Young Turk program was grounded extensively on the principle *of Ittihad-i Anasir*, the unity of the Ottoman subjects, under an Ottoman identity imagined through equal rights for all subjects. Appealing to the democrats of Europe, they articulated the demands of equality and liberty of the Christian millets alienated under the Hamidian policies in an anti-absolutist discourse supporting a myth of Ottomanism, which promised equality and federation among various ethnic and religious groups of the realm.[180]

Consequently, the Young Turk revolution of 1908 brought in a spirit of Ottoman fraternity[181] as reflected on the composition of the first parliament: of 288 deputies that convened in Istanbul there were 147 Turks, 60 Arabs, 27 Albanians, 26 Greeks, 14 Armenians, 10 Slavs and 4 Jews. There were, however, certain limits to this fraternity: the 'historic bloc' consisting of Muslim-Turkish population of the imperial land, the migrated Muslim population from the outlying Ottoman lands and Turkic-Muslim peoples seeking refuge in Anatolia from Russification policies, under the 'moral and intellectual leadership' of the ruling bureaucracy, began to formulate its particular stance defining in effect the boundaries of CUP's liberté. Huseyin Cahit (Yalcin) issued in the pro-CUP newspaper *Tanin* as early as 1908 a warning to the minorities against a parliamentary composition, which would threaten

---

[180] The Armenian *Dashnak* Party participated in the Young Turk congresses abroad and *Ittihad ve Terakki* published declarations denouncing Abdulhamid regime for oppressing its Armenian subjects in 1894 and 1896. Similarly, the uprising of Crete islanders was hailed in the *Ittihad ve Terakki* publication *Mesveret* as a 'cause of rights and justice'. Pro-Islamist writer-journalist Abdurrahman Dilipak mentions these practices of Young Turks to insinuate treason (Dilipak1991: 36-9), affirming the contemporary Islamist discourse's reinforced loyalty to the late Ottoman 'historic bloc'.

[181] An explosion of joy ... erupted in Constantinople and in the big cities of the Empire. For several days, processions of demonstrators brandishing placards in various languages flowed through the streets. The *mullah* embraced the Armenian priest and all races mixed together. Turks, Armenians, Greeks and Jews celebrated the coming of a new age in which all would live together peacefully on Ottoman soil (Chaliand & Ternon 1983: 30).

the Turkish-Muslim colour of the government.[182] The myth of 'imperial salvation', which had served as a surface of inscription for a variety of discourses, including pan-Turkism, pan-Islamism and Ottomanism, that brought together an 'historic bloc', was increasingly being overdetermined by a specific content, Turkism, as the manifest form of the late Ottoman 'social imaginary'.

This evolution led to a rigorous criticism of other contents of the dream of salvation, particularly Ottomanism.[183] This criticism in turn led to the emergence of a religio-linguistic definition of the 'Turk' based on a 'nationalist common sense':
While the Turkish peasant grasped very well the boundaries of nationality with the expression 'whose language goes along with my language and whose religion goes along with my religion', intellectual misters gave importance neither to language nor to religion.[184]
The religio-linguistic boundaries of the nation were further narrowed through an elaborate addition of the Arabic-Muslim elements to the list of the excluded along with Christian subjects.[185] The Turkist criticism of the Ottomanist and pan-Islamist articulations was allowing Turkishness to be presented as a separate entity, resisting as much to identification with the extensive Muslim community (umma) as to unity with non-Islamic identity.

3. The Turkist power and Turkification

---

[182] 'The Turks are the conquerors of this country, with great heroism and self-sacrifice. (...) Whatever may be said, millet-i hakime of the country is the Turks and will remain to be the Turks' (quoted in Yildiz, 2001: 312).
[183] 'After the declaration of the Constitution, I had exchanged ideas with most of our notables. Their ideas were more or less focusing all on the following conclusion: "Ottomanism is a collective nationality, which means neither Turkism nor merely being Muslim. Every individual living under the government of the Ottoman State belongs to the Ottoman nationality!" However, this idea was in fact a crude dream born in the brains moulded by anti-nationalist Tanzimat education. (...) While the Turkish peasant grasped very well the boundaries of nationality with the expression 'whose language goes along with my language and whose religion goes along with my religion...", intellectual misters gave importance neither to language nor to religion (Seyfettin [1912] 1988: 9-10).
[184] Seyfettin [1912] 1988: 10.
[185] The leading Turkist intellectual, Yusuf Akcura stated thus: 'What kind of a common denominator can a Christian Serb farmer in Kosovo share with a nomadic Muslim Arab at the Nejd desert?' (Georgeon 1986: 131-2.)

Turkism, which emerged originally as a discourse of the oppressed among the Muslims in Russia in the specific form of Pan-Turkism, went through a transformation to be utilised in the pragmatic debates among the Ottoman intellectuals around the question of reinstalling the Sublime State's authority over its subjects.[186]

The Ottoman defeat in 1912 against the Balkan alliance consisting of the armies of Greece, Bulgaria, Montenegro and Serbia, all former Ottoman *millets*, was the tragic turning point,[187] leading the Young Turk discourse and policies to shift from Ottomanism to Turkism.[188] The CUP of the Young Turk movement, which seized the State and formed a one party dictatorship out of the ideals of liberté, egalité, fraternité of 1908 revolution, realised by this defeat that the problem they were facing was part of a global question of nationalisation.[189]

---

[186] Suleyman Seyfi Ogun draws a distinction between these two vicissitudes of Turkism and identifies a State (Staatgeist) and Civil Society (Volkgeist), or Cultural and Political nationalisms distinction in this original differentiation, which leads him in conclusion to declare that Kemalism was anything but nationalist. (Ogun 1997: 216-28.) Such a distinction can only be sustained by ignoring the ambiguous character of the late Ottoman discursive horizon, and the consequential processes of condensation and displacement between these discourses. First of all, Ogun's perception of *millet-i hakime* discourse based on Sunni Turkish dominance being an exclusively a state oriented discourse flaws in the light of the historical experience of popular possession of this mentality by the Muslim masses of the Empire. What is witnessed in a reading of this history is also an ambiguity between the levels which Ogun so carefully differentiates, that is, the domains of the state/civil society, political/cultural, and also the discourses that are supposed to be corresponding to these differences, e.g. dominant nation's nationalism/oppressed nation's nationalism. In fact, Yusuf Akcura, who Ogun presents as the champion of the *volkgeist* nationalism, wrote one of the most *staatgeist* natured texts of Turkish nationalism ('Three Modes of Politics'). In this 1904 essay, Akcura defends Turkism against Islamism and Ottomanism almost exclusively in terms of its practicality and utility for the State. Secondly, the ambiguity around the meanings were so extensive that not only the variations of the same discourse but discourses defined as serving completely different projects of emancipation were often intertwined. *Ittihad ve Terakki*'s discourse, for instance, can be both identified as Pan-Turkist or Pan-Islamist or none. Similarly, at the level of the 'oppressed nation', separate meanings that were articulated within these two distinct discourses were already subject to disarticulations and rearticulations at the popular level of 'common sense', as in the case of Russian Muslims. When the term 'myth' as a surface of inscription for a variety of metaphorical discourses of emancipation trying to hegemonise the mythical space and with it the emerging 'historic bloc' is introduced, an appropriate description of the scene of late Ottoman discursive horizon can be obtained.
[187] Ottomans' traumatic-perception of the event was starkly enunciated by Mehmed Akif, the future poet of the National anthem, and I quote his 'poetic' description of Balkan Question below for his sentiments sum up the collective mentality of both the 'dominant' and 'oppressed' wings of the 'nation':
Karadagh bandit, Serbian donkey, Bulgarian snake,
Then the Greek dog, surrounded the country,
Shattered our entire army,
Grabbed our land and expelled us (Ersoy 1987: 77).
[188] The association of the state élite with Turkism had already taken place with the entry into the 20th Century. In fact, Arabic, Armenian and Greek sources usually trace the beginning of the Turkist period of the Ottoman state to 1908 revolution, whereas the Ottomanist policies were not officially left aside until 1912.

In fact, by 1913, Armenian and Greek demands had also moved far beyond seeking their rights as equal subjects according to the international treaties, towards claims of independence. When Turkism was declared as the official ideology by the CUP, the Ottomanisation project had long been shelved by all walks of Ottoman society and replaced by centrifugal nationalisms.[190] Under these conditions, the situation was increasingly interpreted in terms of 'uneven development', considering the Turks as the disadvantaged latecomers, who had no sympathisers and no 'protectors' in the pursuit of their goals. Anatolia had thus become the field of antagonisms with the Christian population defining themselves in their opposition to the Turkish-Muslim rule and relying primarily on hopes of exogenous protection and intervention, while the Turks had to rely solely on their own 'nationalisation' and more importantly their state apparatus of force and violence.[191]

In 1913, a secret CUP communiqué declared the exhaustion of their attempts of coexistence with other nationalities under the banner of Ottomanism and announced the adoption of a project of reconstruction of the Ottoman State on the basis of *unsur-u asli* ('the essential element'), a term signifying Muslim Turks.[192] This turn accompanied the escalation of the Turkist thinker Ziya Gokalp to the top of the CUP as the ideological leader. Gokalp had

---

[189] In the title of *Müdafaa-i Milliye Cemiyeti*, an association founded during the Balkan wars, the term *milli* was used for the first time to mean 'national' (Yildiz 2001: 74).
[190] [After reading the Armenian publications of the beginning of the Century, demanding independence, his father talks to the author Suleyman Nazif]:
"... I did not know that the dimensions of the Armenian problem were so threatening. I thought this problem was limited to reform and justice demands. I now see that these demands had come from a deeper source. This cannot be prevented and will lead to a disaster for the Armenians. (Suleyman Nazif, 'The Armenian Country', reprinted in Bayar 1967: 1671-6.)
[191] 'The main item of the secret meetings' agenda at the Ministry of War was the liquidation of the non-Turkish elements amassed at strategic locations and were loyal to negative outside influences. (...) These meetings continued through May, June and August 1914'. (Extract from Esref Kuscubasi's Memoirs, in Bayar 1967: 1573.) Kuscubasi was the founder and the head of *Ittihad ve Terakki*'s secret service, *Teskilat-i Mahsusa* ('Special Organisation') and in these meetings, attended exclusively by *Ittihad* leadership and the chiefs of *Mahsusa*, military, administrative and political measures were worked out for this liquidation plan. While the military measures consisted of direct intervention for forcible deportation, political and economic measures aimed primarily to mobilise Turkish Muslim public to reclaim their dominance as the 'essential element' in Anatolia through participation in the liquidation of the other elements (See Akcam 1991 & 2004).
[192] In this nationalist turn, the recent forcible deportation of over 400,000 Muslims from the Balkans played an important role. *Ittihad ve Terakki* leaders, in a sense, decided to retaliate for this exodus from the non-Muslims with the same methods that had been used by former Ottoman subjects of non-Muslim origin in the Balkans (See, Toynbee 1970: 138).

108

persistently argued that the policy of Ottomanisation was in reality a policy of Turkification in disguise and should be replaced with a policy of manifest Turkism.[193]

A grand project of Turkification of Anatolia commenced with an aim to break down both the economic strength and political orientations of primarily the Greeks and Armenians, which constituted a considerable portion of population,[194] since such an existence was viewed as the greatest threat to the integrity of Anatolia, the 'last shelter' of the Ottoman 'essential element'. The initial step was a concerted attack in 1914 in the eve of the World War I on Greek presence in Trace and West Anatolia. *Teskilat-i Mahsusa*, the CUP's secret service, initiated undercover operations to 'thin out the Greek population' through forcible deportation and massacre.[195] The properties and businesses of the deportees would be taken over by Turkish-Muslim elements under the supervision of Celal Bayar, then a leading figure of the *Mahsusa*, assigned to the post of general secretary of Izmir governor during this operation.[196] The head of *Mahsusa*, Esref Kuscubasi, glorifies in his memoirs this operation as 'the conquest of *gavur* Izmir by 'serious, determined ... and pure-clean patriots.'[197]

These 'serious, determined, pure and clean patriots' of *Teskilati Mahsusa* then staged the second leg of the project, that is, the liquidation of the Armenians.[198] Their agents prepared the scene for the deportation through massacres in Armenian villages and by mobilising the Muslim population of East Anatolia to terrorise the Armenian population. The CUP decree for the Armenian deportation was implemented throughout Anatolia between May and August 1915. The destination of this journey had been declared to be the concentration

---

[193] Duru 1949: 61-2.

[194] 40% in the eve of the First World War, according to Church registries – Yildiz 2001: 112

[195] Akcam has documented all the available evidence regarding the Greek liquidation to conclude that the number of the displaced added up to 1,150,000, in addition to around 500,000 massacred by the Turkish mobs sponsored by the CUP government (Akcam 2004: 145-9).

[196] See, Akçam 1992: 150-3 and Bayar 1967: 1568-1582. One of the boldest manifestations of the link between the late-Ottoman ethnic cleansing and republican Turkey is the fact that one of the major actors of the former, Celal Bayar (*Teskilati Mahsusa* code name 'Galip Hodja') became the third President of Republic of Turkey in 1950. Akcam (1992, 2001 and 2004) extends this list of linkage to tens of top republican bureaucrats.

[197] Kuscubasi in Bayar 1967: 1577 &1581.

[198] The technicalities involved in the definition of genocide is beyond this research's concerns. My concern is limited to demonstrate a shared 'state tradition' and 'popular mentality', which had to play a major role in the formation and reproduction of a specific Turkish political psyche to accompany a specific Turkish political subjectivity. What is significant about the Armenian liquidation, along with the immense humane loss, is the

camps in Aleppo, but fewer than 100,000 survived the exodus; the rest, 'at least 600,000', according to the *Encyclopaedia Britannica*, were either massacred by the guards or organised looters or died during the journey.

4. Historic Bloc's final victory: 'National Struggle'

The finalisation of the 'purification' of Anatolia would be delayed until September 1922, when the invading Greek army was conclusively defeated by the national forces led by Mustafa Kemal and forced to withdraw from Anatolia. With the army, hundreds of thousands of Greek civilians had to flee their homeland, the Aegean region. Turkification was concluded by the agreement with Greece after the war, on the exchange of population by which the remnants of Greek Orthodox population were deported in exchange of Muslim immigrants from Balkans.[199] The 'final solution' was thus achieved and the Anatolian population was homogenised with the reduction of the non-Muslim elements to negligibility.

In this process of 'purification' of Anatolia, Muslim population played an active role, with both sentimental – taking the revenge of a hundred years of humiliation – and economic instincts – taking over the property and businesses, or pillaging non-Muslim property. The fear of being deprived of the land and property extracted from the non-Muslim minorities after their liquidation on the side of the Muslim population,[200] and the fear of persecution by the Allies for charges of genocide on the side of the *Teskilat-i Mahsusa* figures, played a constitutive role in the renewal of the 'historic bloc' uniting the former reformist bureaucracy

---

very disavowal of the event, its absence, for instance, from the official history teaching in Turkey, and the persistent avoidance and repression of the pronunciation of it.

[199] 'It is a queer coincidence', comments Celal Bayar, the former head of the *Mahsusa* operation in Izmir, 'that the completion of this 'deportation' attempt and movement in the future according to the Lausanne Treaty, would fall onto my shoulders in the capacity of the 'Minister of Population Exchange, Settlement and Construction'.' (Bayar 1967: 1569.) It was not solely Bayar of the ethnic purification project to become an active participant and leading figure in the 'National Struggle': This movement led by General Mustafa Kemal was to a large extent a continuation of the purification project regarding its organising cadres, participating elements, aims and sentiments. Akçam documents this continuity in his pioneering 1992 work (see Akçam 1992 and Akcam 2004). Prior to Akcam, Zürcher demonstrated the extensive role of the *Ittihad ve Terakki* and *Teskilat-ı Mahsusa* cadres in the formation of the 'National Movement' in Anatolia. (see Zürcher, 1984.)

[200] In addition to manifest statements by the public to this effect, the fact that the nuclei of the 'national struggle', Defence of Rights Associations, first emerged in the regions where the Armenian and Greek liquidation had occurred is evidence to the popular fears, hence the meaning of the 'rights' to be 'defended' (See Baskaya 1991).

and the Muslim Anatolian notables under the Kemalist leadership to conduct the National Struggle.[201]

Consequently, the primary aim of the 'national struggle' was to put a decisive end to the existence of Christian minorities in this newly declared homeland. This aim is evident in the programs of the local organisations that preceded Mustafa Kemal's passage to Anatolia; the resolutions of Erzurum (23 July 1919) and Sivas Congresses[202] (4 September 1919), held by the delegates of these local organisations; and the fact that the elections to the first assembly in Ankara excluded the Christians.[203] Measures passed by the Istanbul government on 8 January 1920 for the restitution of Armenian possessions were cancelled on 14 September 1922 in the National Assembly.[204] The best articulation of the aims of the 'national struggle' is probably Mustafa Kemal's address to Clicia farmers in 1923 in the wake of the victory:

> Armenians have no place in this noble country. Your country is yours, it belong to Turks. This country was the Turks' land in history and therefore it is Turkish and it will remain Turkish to the eternity. (…) This fertile land is purely Turks' country.[205]

I.3. Results of Nationalisation: Turkish Political Psyche and Popular Foreclosure

Centuries long history of Ottoman Empire, after dissolving in parallel to the evolution of the term *millet,* ended with the formation of the Turkish Republic out of its ashes. The painful organic crisis of the Empire, that traumatic experience of catastrophic collapse, also furnished for the Turkish Muslim elements and the ruling elite the grounds for composing a nation through the articulation of a new Turkish identity. This groundwork involved a

---

[201] Akcam (1992 & 2004) documents in detail the link between the genocide charges and convictions and participation in the 'national struggle' for the CUP cadres.

[202] The decision of defence taken in the Erzurum Congress was thought exclusively against the formation of Armenian and Greek entities and the movements of the Allies were viewed in this context. Erzurum Congress carefully avoided to give the impression of a hostile position against the occupying Allies (Selek 1963: 383). Sivas Congress resolution no 2 states that the aim of the Anatolia and Rumelia Defence of Rights Association was to prevent activities which aimed the formation of Greek and Armenian entities in Ottoman lands.

[203] The first assembly, which met on 23 April 1920, unlike the ethnic plurality of the late Ottoman parliaments, consisted exclusively of Muslim deputies.

[204] Akcam 2001.

[205] Atatürk 1989: 130. In the Clicia (Adana) region, the surviving Armenians returned with the occupation forces to take back what belonged to them. So the notables fell in with the national liberation movement, and

popular civil war with active government participation leading to the de-Christianisation of Anatolia, after its 'baptising' as 'Anadolu', the 'last shelter' of the Empire's Muslim subjects.

The above conclusions have been derived through an alternative periodisation of modern Turkish history and consequently inherent in this section is a three-fold historiography argument. Firstly, the assertion that modern Turkey emerged through a 'national struggle' is accepted under the title of 'nationalisation', but the origins and development of this struggle have been traced to the 1878 Berlin Accord, much earlier than the official version's[206] date of 1919. Secondly, the focus of attention has been shifted from the official version's obsession with the international relations and the State's affairs[207] towards an interest in the domestic affairs and societal transformations. Even with the official emphases above, there is not much reason to fail to account for the manifest fin-de-siécle desire to de-Christianise Anatolia, which was generated by permanent international conflict and the constant contraction of the Ottoman land and led to a popular and semi-official civil war. Thirdly, the official version emphasises the fact that the history of the Ottoman decline involved a series of failed defensive battles until the 'national struggle's success in defending Anatolia against the 'imperialist powers'. The same period of history, however, involves a successful offensive war systematically fought by a 'nation of Islam' and the Ottoman State against the non-Muslim inhabitants of Anatolia. It is through this protracted ethno-religious offence, which began with the Ottoman State's 1894 Sassun operation and the subsequent Armenian pogroms of 1895-6 in Istanbul and Eastern Anatolia, continued with the 1914 liquidation of the Greek population in the Aegean and the Thrace, reached to its peak with the Armenian 'exodus' of 1915 and concluded with the 1922 population exchange with Greece, that Anatolia was baptised 'Anadolu'.

---

even organised it in some places. Some of them were close to Mustafa Kemal himself: for example Lame Osman who later became commander of his personal guard (Akcam 2001).

[206] By 'official version' I do not only refer to the directly official sources of historiography but to a much wider dispersed field of history scholarship, which produce, reproduce and disseminate this official version to be deployed in the discourses of power and opposition alike. Among the vast literature to this effect, Bernard Lewis (1968) and Stanford J. Shaw and Ezel Kural Shaw (1977) are the standard international texts on Turkey.

[207] The fear from politics is arguably responsible for this obsession, given that the political science departments of state universities still operate under the name 'international relations' or 'administrative sciences', avoiding the name 'politics'.

This historiography argument is accompanied by a psychoanalytic argument that through the protracted 'national struggle' Turkish identity emerged with certain built-in psychic mechanisms, to shape the psychic dimension of the popular Turkish identity, that is, the Turkish political psyche. This structure consisted of a condensed and displaced articulation of the traumatic perceptions of the three components of the historic bloc of the experience of the Empire's collapse, which I will outline below.

The Ottoman elite's perception of Ottoman collapse – including centuries long defeat and contraction, accompanied by indigestion of transition from a mighty Empire straddling three continents to a nation-state squeezed and split between two continents – entered in the Turkish identity formation as a generalisation of the elite's fears – including fears of annihilation – in terms of a geopolitical paranoia. Sediments of the traumatic experience of the catastrophic collapse of the Ottoman Empire, the constitutive trauma of Turkish identity, are visible in the ongoing expressions of the 'Sèvres Syndrome'.[208] The foundational myth of Turkish political identity contained a deep security concern vindicated by a certainty of being encircled by internal and external foes, permanently engaged in a 'master plan' to block Turkey's development and prosperity.[209] This nationalist perception has served to legitimise the brutal crackdown of any dissident movement in modern history, including in particular the late 1960s and 1970s socialist movement and the Kurdish movement of the last two decades.

---

[208] After the conclusion of the World War I, a delegation of the Ottoman Sultan signed the treaty of Sèvres in August 1920. This treaty provided for a partition of the Ottoman Empire leaving only parts of Anatolia with Istanbul as capital for the Turks. At the same time Turkey's republican forces were fighting against Greek occupation forces which landed in May 1919 in Izmir with the consent of the Allies. After almost ten years of constant warfare, Turkey was about to disappear from the political map due to territorial claims of Russia, Britain, France, Italy, Greece and Armenia. This situation is what is referred to as the Sèvres Syndrome (See Oran 2000).

[209] Among the vast literature of official paranoia from textbooks to government policy programs, the most striking is probably the following recollection of Murat Belge (1992) from a speech given to the political detainees by a colonel in 1971: 'In the north, our traditional archenemy 'communist' Russia; in the west their poker and our old enemy Bulgaria; next to them our worst enemy Greece; in the south two anti-Turkish Arab countries, Iraq and Syria'. Then it was the east's turn. The Shah was in power and there were no problems between Turkey and Iran. Our borders had remained the same since 1639. The colonel said, 'I never liked these Farsis'. There had to be a way of being surrounded by the enemies.

The period of nationalisation was similarly experienced as a trauma by the Muslim population of the outlying imperial lands in the Balkans and the Russian Muslims suffering from the Tsarist policies of Russification, who migrated to Anatolia in their millions.[210] The desire to repress the traumatic memory of humiliation and suffering, led to sublimation in terms of discourses of salvation (pan-Turkism and pan-Islamism) while the same desire was increasingly manifested through a compensatory discourse of revenge to be materialised in the de-Christianisation of Anatolia. While discourses of sublimation have been maintained in modern identity as elements of Turkish political subjectivity, the desires of compensation and revenge entered in the structure of modern identity as the formative features of the Turkish political psyche.

The trauma of the Empire's Turkish Muslim subjects, on the other hand, consisted of their economic subordination in the 19th Century to the emergent non-Muslim commercial bourgeoisie. This 'injustice' generated a common mentality grounded upon the desire of reinstitution of the Muslim majority as both economic and political 'dominant nation' of Turkey. '[T]he lords and masters of this country are the Turks. Those who are not of pure Turkish stock have only one right in the Turkish land, it is the right to be servants and slaves' (Mahmut Esat Bozkurt 1930: 3). Resentment of those other than Turks was the inevitable consequence of the dominant nation's desire.

Turkish political psyche, which had been shaped through centuries long humiliation of the Ottoman pride, was therefore composed of a paranoid mentality that would dominate the interpretation of both domestic and international politics and a desire of revenge and compensation from the resented others of the identity. This composition was the condensed and displaced manifestation of a latent primal desire to maintain collective amnesia, that is, to erase the traces of an undesirable recent past including the dissolution of the Empire and the fear of annihilation. The collective desire of forgetting, which was materialised in the specific form of 'ejection' of the memory traces of a traumatic collective experience[211], is discernible in terms of the psychic defence mechanism of foreclosure.

---

[210] Caglar Keyder (1987: 80) estimates this figure to be around two million.
[211] Which differs from 'burrying in the unconscious', that is, repression (see Evans 1996: 65).

114

In strictly clinical terms, the foreclosed signifier needs to be the signifier of father and this foreclosure is responsible for psychosis, which manifestly places certain boundaries to the applicability of the psychoanalytic category of foreclosure to political analysis. A detour of Lacan's journey to the theorisation of foreclosure would however be revealing of further possibilities of the use of the term.[212] Besides, if as Lacan said, 'it is not what the name of the father is that counts than what it does',[213] which is to bind together the three orders of the real, the symbolic and the imaginary, then the function of the excluded other can be considered in these terms. In fact, Slovoj Zizek points out a late-Lacanian possibility of political theorisation grounded upon foreclosure,[214] emphasising the function of the excluded other:

> [I]n the last years of his teaching, Lacan gave universal function to this function of foreclosure: there is a certain foreclosure proper to the order of signifier as such; whenever we have a symbolic structure it is structured around a certain void, it implies the foreclosure of a key signifier.[215]

---

[212] Returning to Freud's analysis of the Wolf Man, what is revealed there is that the analysand 'rejected castration' (Grigg 1998: 52). Lacan's comment on this case in his 1954 seminar reads, 'it is castration that is foreclosed.' Later, in the Seminar Book III (1955-6) Lacan shifts his focus on the foreclosure of the Name-of-the-Father, concluding that the foreclosure of castration is secondary to this original foreclosure (Grigg 1998: 53-4).

[213] It is not impossible to link the Turkish foreclosure of the signifiers 'Armenian' and 'Kurd' to the foreclosure of the Father. Anatolia is named as the 'Motherland', which opens up the Turkish nation-building to a reading of a struggle by the 'latecomers' on the ownership of this 'mother' against its original owners, or the 'real fathers', including the other religions and the other ethnicities. Such an attempt of psychoanalytic reading would however force the analogy too far, since what we speak of here is not individual psyche but the psychic dimension of a specific discourse, a specific utterance of the paranoidic structure of a form of subjectivity or identity, all of which are linked to the notion of collectivity as much as individuality. It is because of these absolute limitations of psychoanalytic analogy that I choose not to incorporate in this research the recent attempts to explain the Turkish mentalities towards the Kurds in terms of 'social hysteria' (see Akcam 2004). A term like social or collective hysteria represents an attempt beyond analogy to a 'psychoanalytic closure', which includes a desire to 'glue' political analysis with psychoanalysis, the social with the individual, in an inconsistent way. A second reason for not finding these attempts valuable is that the mechanism of hysteria, as a form of neurosis, which has to consist of the repression of a representation (Freud) or a signifier (Lacan), falls short to account for the abolition of the ethno-religious heterogeneity of Anatolia in the Turkish symbolic order. Besides the violent collusion of the 'Turkish reality' with the Kurd's or the Armenian's return from the 'outer shadows', that is, the real, cannot be understood in terms of hysteria.

[214] Zizek's example is Lacan's understanding of woman as a symptom, that is, as the real, of man: 'Woman does not exist, her signifier is originally foreclosed, and that is why she returns as a symptom of man' (Zizek 1989: 73)

[215] Zizek 1989: 72-3.

The excluded other, a key signifier, which is at the same time a traumatic point that resists symbolisation[216] and necessitates foreclosure, can be perceived as that constitutive void.

Foreclosure, a defence mechanism specific to the psychotic structure, involves the radical rejection of a particular element from the symbolic order. In Freud's words, 'the ego rejects the incompatible idea with its affect and behaves as if the idea had never occurred to the ego at all'.[217] Lacan points out the location of this rejected idea (signifier) as the Real. The physical expulsion of the Christian existence from the 'motherland' and from the 'national reality' symbolised for the Turkish political psyche the purge of the incompatible memory traces of a period of trauma. Through the operation of this defence mechanism, a peculiar type of behaviour in political, cultural, scientific, social and popular life, or a peculiar 'reality', emerged by the name of Turkish identity to behave as if the ethno-religious plurality of Anatolia had never been the case. The Turkish foreclosure has not merely served to purge a period of trauma from the redesigned national identity; it has also operated to obliterate any traces of its memory; any initiative that could impinge on this organised amnesia has been systematically stifled.

The specific object, the signifier, of this act of foreclosure, the metaphor of the nation's scarred memory of its birth trauma, is 'the Armenian'. For 29 Muslim ethnicities of Anatolia, of which the victorious historic bloc was composed, most of whom not native Turkish speakers, the term *millet* did not signify much beyond an entity understood in terms of a religious identity.[218] In these circumstances, the discursive marker of early nationalism, or the cement of the new national identity, was religion, and the nodal point that brought together the vicissitudes of nationalist imaginary was non-Muslim menace, along with the

---

[216] Stavrakakis 1999: 65.
[217] Laplanche and Pontalis 2004: 166.
[218] The over-quoted dialogue between a veteran officer and a peasant during the National struggle in Yakup Kadri Karaosmanoglu's *Yaban* (The Alien) is revealing in this context and deserves yet another citing:
We know sir, you are one of them, but...
Who are 'them'?
You know, Kemal Pasha's lot...
How can one be a Turk and not on the side of Kemal Pasha?
But sir, we are not Turkish.
So, what are you?
We are Muslims, thanks to God, the Almighty... The ones you mention live over there in Haymana.
(Karaosmanoglu 1960: 131.)

consequent 'historical necessity' of the liquidation of non-Muslim population of Anatolia, as the constitutive event of national identity. The discursive externalisation of 'the Armenian' was constitutive above all of the boundaries separating the 'nation' from the 'enemy'. Through the foreclosure of the collective trauma, the excluded Armenian has therefore fulfilled a constitutive function as the 'real' of Turkish identity. The foreclosed fear of annihilation symbolised by 'the Armenian' is the precise void, the 'impossible kernel' around which the modern Turkish identity was structured. 'The Armenian', and related to it, the paranoid perceptions of 'non-Muslim menace', 'foreign conspiracy', 'external and internal enemies', etc., all placing an exceptional emphasis on the 'ejected real', have operated as the crucial building-brick of the emerging Turkish national identity.

The sustained hatred, signifying a disturbance with psychic dimensions that determines the Turkish perceptions of 'the Armenian', is partly a result of the ambiguity of objectivity, that is, the difficulty involved from the outset in specifying an entity to be called Turkish. 'The Armenian', or the 'real' of the Turk, operates as Turkish identity's 'constitutive outside' to be constantly overemphasised as a defence mechanism against the problems associated with the primordial lack of an 'inside' as such.

A further lack revealed through the mention of 'the Armenian' is the possession of the 'motherland'. A significant proportion of the historical inhabitants of the newly declared 'motherland' of the Turkish-Muslim nation had been various non-Muslim ethnicities, including, among others, Greeks and the Armenians. Deserving the motherland necessitated a life and death struggle to neutralise the claims of these 'pretenders' to the same land. The Anatolian cultural heritage, beginning with the traces of the recent Christian existence, the traumatic mirror of the historical otherness of this 'mother' to the Muslim Turks, has consequently been a primary casualty. The urinal of an Izmir toilet made of Armenian gravestones is but only one of many tragic examples of this cultural destruction.

Therefore, the externalisation of 'the Armenian' played a constitutive role in the politico-discursive articulation of the 'nation' by signifying through its absence what the nation is not. The popular anti-Armenian practices and the sustained hatred have a value, which is

117

psychological, and are therefore historically necessary for the reproduction of the Turkish identity. This necessity stems from the specific features of Turkish identity, the definition of which has had to rely heavily on an outside, on what had been excluded from the absolute psychic boundaries of Turkishness. Turkish identity has only been possible through the non-Muslim menace to the 'motherland', that is, the possibility of a re-staging of the nation's constitutive trauma to materialise the fear of losing the nation's 'last shelter'.

The above psychoanalytic argument can therefore lead to a modification – and correction – of Pascal's economistic response to the question of 'why should a nation be killed twice?' For Turkish political psyche, to symbolically reproduce through degrading rituals and practices the historical event of violent liquidation of the Armenian existence in Anatolia, and the simultaneous denial of the historical factuality of the event, are crucial necessities. It is through these practices and persistent denial that the Turkish 'reality' has been reproduced. To put it bluntly, the 'nation' does not exist and the hallucinated 'Armenian' is its symptom.

II. The Other Within: Moments of Foreclosure

Republican Turkey was formed through a Kemalist *coupure epistemologique* initiating a split between the secular/modernist ruling ideology on the one side and the popular 'nation of Islam' on the other, as considered in Chapter 1. An additional, unpronounced experience of violent split between the Kurdish identity and the republican perception of Turkishness operated at the background of this rupture. The moments of the Kurdish resistance to Kemalist power went hand in hand with moments of suppression and exclusion accompanied by an increasingly deliberate failure of any reference to the Kurdishness of the suppressed and excluded. In this section, I will consider this experience and its denial in terms of foreclosure consisting of the expulsion from the republican symbolic order of the signifier Kurd. This 'ejection' foreclosed the fears peculiar to the military/bureaucratic elite, consisting of a condensed scenario of disintegration of the 'nation' through 'reactionary' religious agitation. With this foreclosure, a second battle commenced for the secularisation and the Turkification of the Anatolian 'nation of Islam' leading to the demarcation of the psychic boundaries of a specifically republican Turkish identity.

118

The primary problem that the republican order had to face from the outset was the multi-ethnic character of the 'nation of Islam', that is, the Anatolian population in the wake of the externalisation of the non-Muslim *millets*. A tendency, which threatened the unity of the 'dominant nation' or the 'nation of Islam' of the collapsing Empire was in fact present before the republic. The first shock was experienced with Albania's declaration of independence from the Ottoman Empire in 1911. Ottomans never imagined Muslim Albanians as another nation and viewed the Albanian separation as a traumatic result of a senseless epidemic, that is, nationalism.[219] The 'plague', which had expanded towards the Muslim *millets* of the Empire after the non-Muslim ones, continued with the 'Arab betrayal', that is, the Wahhabi uprising against the Ottoman government during the World War I. The 'last shelter', Anatolia, although imagined in the nationalist discourse as the 'motherland' of a harmonious nation, was in reality demonstrated, even after the purge en-masse of Christian elements, a colourful ethnic diversity, consisting of the Kurds, Laz, Cyracassians, Safardic Jews and various migrant ethnicities such as Pomaks, Tartars, Gypsies and Muslim Bosnians, all had their own mother-tongues other than Turkish. In this fragile environment for nationalism, the early resistance of the Kurds to assimilation as Turks at the moment of the constitution of the symbolic order was perceived by the nationalist leadership as a traumatic re-staging of the late-Ottoman trauma. The Kurdish resistance presented a threat to the sensitive equilibrium among 29 Muslim ethnicities with a sudden domino effect, which would leave virtually nothing to ground the new national identity on. In the sub-sections below, the cycle of resistance and repression in the formative years of the republic will be analysed as leading to the republican nationalist declaration of foreclosure. I will firstly consider the Kurdish participation in the 'national struggle' and move on to demonstrate that a Kurdish resistance also emerged in parallel to the formation of a Kemalist central authority with increasing emphasis on Turkish nationalism. I will then analyse the suppression of this resistance and its long-term consequences in terms of foreclosure.

---

[219] The Islamist poet Akif's following lines are telling of this frustration:
'What is Albania? Is it mentioned in the *Sharia*?
It is blasphemy and nothing else to put forward your ethnicity.'
(Ünlü & Özcan 1987: 77.)

II.1. The Kurds and the 'National Struggle'

The Kurds were conventionally part of the Muslim *millet* and they chose to participate in the 'nation of Islam' during the nationalisation of the late Ottoman discursive horizon. Led by tribal lords and religious Sheiks and provoked by the Ottoman administration, army or agents, the Kurds played an active role from the outset in de-Armenisation of Kurdistan.[220] The primary motive of the Kurdish mobilisation was to prevent the possibility of the establishment of a Greater Armenia, which included Kurdistan.[221] The first attempt to found a state with the name Kurdistan in 1880 was also motivated by the Armenian conflict. The chief aim of this Kurdish rebellion led by Sheikh Ubeydullah was to resist the implication of 1878 Berlin Accord, which according to Ubeydullah implicated an Armenian state and the British protection for the Christian Kurds.[222] Ubeydullah's Kurdistan was suppressed, but the Ottoman State's sponsoring of anti-Armenian preaching and activities continued.

Following the defeat of the Ottoman Empire in the First World War, and the subsequent Mudros Armistice, Kurdish sheikhs and aghas, who had confiscated immense wealth from the liquidated Armenians, including land and property,[223] became deeply concerned with the prospect of what had remained from the Armenian population backed by the Allies reclaiming their land and property.[224] Besides, an Armenian state was already in the process of formation at the eastern borders between Russia and Ottoman lands. Kurdistan's feudal aghas, who had participated in the Armenian massacre, were the first to ally with Mustafa Kemal's movement. Kemalists, too, were anxious to secure the Kurdish support, since the

---

[220] In Palu, Urfa, Erzurum, Arapkir, Maras, Sivas and Diyarbekir, Kurdish masses, along with Hamidiye regiments and Ottoman forces, were actively involved in decades of killing, looting, plunder and vandalism (Ahmad 1994: 152-3). One line of Turkish "defence" for the Armenian massacre is blaming the event on the Kurds. Sultan Abdulhamid and later the nationalist authorities of republican administration have uttered several times that what happened in the East was some kind of civil war between the Kurds and Armenians. It is important to note that the argument to be pursued here has nothing to with this line of jenoside "justification". Kurdish mobilisation against the Armenians was only one leg of a multidimensional event. The most important of these dimensions is the Ottoman governments' active involvement and provocation from the outset to the bitter end. For a detailed study on the limits of Kurdish involvement in the de-Armenisation of the east, see Ahmad 1994: 145-184.

[221] 'It is heartbreaking to see the land of Jazira and Botan, I mean the fatherland of the Kurds, being turned into a home for Armenians', uttered Kurdish poet Hajj Kader Y Koy around this time (in Ahmad 1994: 159).

[222] 'Armenians will establish an independent state in Van and the Nasturians will declare themselves British subjects.' The Sheikh added: 'I shall not tolerate such a thing even if it requires arming the women'.

[223] Kutlay 1996: 265-6.

first battle to be fought by the national forces was against the Armenian army in the east, until the signing of Gümrü Treaty on 2 December 1920. Mustafa Kemal, conscious of the Kurdish sensitivity on the Armenian issue, decided to launch his national movement in Kurdistan. The first Article of the Amasya Declaration of the National Movement (1919) stated clearly that 'national and social rights of the Kurds will be recognised'.[225] In his personal letters to the Kurdish notables in the organising months of the National Struggle, Kemal emphasised the Armenian menace and the importance of the unity of the 'Muslim Ottoman nation'.[226] There was considerable Kurdish representation in Sivas Congress and the Grand National Assembly in Ankara. In one of his first addresses to the newly gathered assembly, Kemal argued that the assembly was not composed of the representatives of Turks, Kurds, Circassians and the Laz, but rather the representatives of a strongly unified Islamic community.[227] As a consequence of this 'spirit of Islamic fraternity', majority of the Kurdish tribes remained loyal to the 'National Movement', and Kurdish troops participated in a number of battles fought by the National Forces.

Kurdish intelligentsia of Istanbul watched these developments cautiously. They had opposed the Kurdish participation in the Armenian massacres and warned the Kurds in their publications against collaboration with official policies of genocide.[228] In the years following the Ottoman defeat in the First World War *Kurdistan Teali Cemiyeti* (a.k.a. "Kurdistan Club") was founded as a platform of Kurdish intelligentsia. This organisation built relations with the Armenian organisations and intervened in the discussion on Allied plans of the partitioning of the Ottoman lands with projects of an independent and unified Kurdistan. One of the leading figures of the Club, Sherif Pasha, participated in Paris Conference and Sèvres Treaty as the Kurdish delegate. However, the Club's pro-Armenian stance only served the Kurdish intellectuals' further alienation from the Muslim population of Kurdistan. Kurdish

---

[224] Kutlay 1996: 292.
[225] Baskaya 1991: 63.
[226] See Baskaya (1991: 63) and Kutlay (1996: 142). Akcam (1992: 158) concludes that, 'the Kurdish-Turkish unity became possible thanks to the common fear of Armenians.
[227] Barkey & Fuller, 1998: 9.
[228] Ahmad 1994: 171.

notables lobbied Europe through telegrams protesting Sherif Pasha's participation in the negotiations of Paris Conference and Sèvres Treaty as the Kurdish delegate.[229]

There were, however, attempts to connect Istanbul with Kurdistan. A Kurdish Club was founded in Diyarbakir in 1919, prior to Kemal's arrival in region, with aims similar to the Istanbul Club. Initially, most of the Diyarbakir dwellers[230] affiliated to the Club. In a similar development, in 1920, village headmen of Mus, Bitlis and Bingol regions collected petitions for 'Kurdish national democratic rights' to be presented to the Paris Conference.[231] Kemal was cautious from the outset towards the Diyarbakir Club and orchestrated a campaign against its leading members claiming that they were in close collaboration with Captain Noel, a British agent assigned to Kurdistan, against the National Movement. In 1921, the Kurdish Club was shut down by the Kemalist administration without any resistance.[232] Instead of defending the Club, Diyarbakir notables seemed to have been won over by the Kemalist project.[233]

The natural and cultural differences between the modern Kurdish intelligentsia of Istanbul and the masses of Kurdistan finally degenerated into a cleavage between the supporters of the Sèvres Treaty, on the one side, and its pro-Kemalist opponents on the other. Sèvres Treaty promised autonomy to Kurdistan 'with a view to full independence' along with an independent Armenia, while the Kemalist national movement stood against this treaty for the formation of an independent Turkey which would include Kurdistan. Kurdish notables,

---

[229] Said-i Kurdi's letter to Sherif Pasha during Paris Conference sums up the sentiments dominated Kurdistan notables' psychology:
    The Kurds, who had lived as self-sacrificing and courageous supporters of Islam for four and a half centuries ... cannot act in breach of their religion by signing peace treaties with our historical and vital enemy in the expense of the Muslim community. (Göldas, 1991: 33.)
This 'historical and vital enemy' is certainly Armenians. The Istanbul based Kurdish intelligentsia seemed hopelessly alienated from the people of Kurdistan led by tribal lords and religious leaders, on the issue of the future of Kurdistan.
[230] Pirinccizades were the only tribe that did not affiliate to the club. Kutlay (1997) claims that this was due to their involvement in the Armenian massacre.
[231] Mumcu 1992: 57.
[232] Baskaya 1991: 63.
[233] 'Ekrem Cemil Pasha, who had come to Diyarbekir from Istanbul for the Club's activities, could not even walk safely on the street. He faced difficulty in visiting and staying in the neighbouring towns. The Diyarbekir of two years ago had gone and was replaced with a different, hostile Diyarbekir' (Kutlay 1996: 144). Ekrem Cemil was later handed over to Ankara authorities by a tribal leader and faced trial at the Independence Court (Göktas 1991: 33).

anxious not to lose their gains from de-Armenision of Ottoman *vatan* took the latter position while *Teali* politicians emphasised from the outset the Kemalist-nationalist threat to Kurdish identity, warning these notables against 'falling into Mustafa Kemal's trap' (Cemil Pasha 1992: 36.)

II.2. The Kurdish Resistance

The Muslim Kurdish masses rallied behind the Kemalist leadership and participated in the 'national struggle'. There was however a rarely mentioned exception, further to the *Teali* intelligentsia: the Alevi-Kurdish clan Kocgiri, who rose against the Kemalist authority in 1921 during the 'national struggle'. The Kocgiri rebellion[234] was a relatively small scale one, with limited participation of the West Dersim region's Alevi Kurds, and quelled swiftly by the Kemalist government, with tragic humanitarian consequences.[235] This early resistance to Kemalist centralisation also surfaced the Sunni/Alevi cleavage within the Kurdish identity: although the West Dersim declaration[236] was nationalist and not religious by any criteria, Sunni Kurds remained indifferent to its appeal. This division between Alevi and Sunni Kurds would prevail as one of the determinants of the Kurdish political identity in Turkey.

Kocgiri rebellion was a warning shot for the Kurds to question the Kemalist leadership's intentions regarding the status of Kurdistan. 'The Law on the Autonomy of Kurdistan' of 10 February 1922, which passed in the Grand National Assembly, against fierce opposition from the Kurdish deputies,[237] was a consequence of this awakening and the consequent pressure from the Kurdish deputies.[238]

---

[234] See Appendix 5.

[235] Out of the 135 villages that homed the Koçgiri clan, 132 villages were torched to the ground; thousands of civilians were killed. Laz militias led by infamous butcher of Armenians, Lame Osman, were deployed along with the national army commanded by notorious Nurettin Pasha. The anti-Alevi and anti-Kurdish sentiments of the Sunni Laz people were appealed by the Kemalist administration to promote a genocide-like massacre of the Alevi Kurds of Kocgiri and Dersim. Survivors were deported to central Anatolia, particularly to the Sariz district of Kayseri.

[236] See See Appendix 4.

[237] The reason for this opposition was the weak and cosmetic character of autonomy proposed by the motion. (See Olson 1989: 70)

[238] The autonomy law however was never implemented. In fact, the fact that such a law had ever passed in the parliament has been officially denied to date; destroyed minutes of the parliamentary session of 10 February 1922 (a lack) being the sole proof of such a law (Kutlay 1997: 158).

The Sheikh Said Rebellion

If Koçgiri rebellion represented a test of strength between a tribal group and the central authority, then Sheikh Said rebellion of 1925 was almost an all out battle between the Turkish government and the Kurds of Turkey. Although some crucial tribal participation failed to take place due to the Alevi/Sunni divisions, it succeeded, to a large extent, in bringing together all three elements of Kurdish identity, that is, the Sheikhs/tribal leaders, military units and Istanbul based intelligentsia.[239] The former Kurdish deputies of the Ankara parliament, who had been alienated from the parliament by Mustafa Kemal's 'election coup' in April 1923[240] and Kurdish officers of the Tribal Regiments of the 7th Army, who had been re-recruited to the republican armed forces, both participated in the formation of the *Azadi* in Erzurum in 1922 along with *Teali* intelligentsia and local religious leaders, including Sheikh Said himself. All three sectors of Kurdish nationalism thus gathered under the roof of *Azadi* in a bid to resist the Kemalist breach of Kurdish expectations.

However, when they eventually united, it was, in a nutshell, too late: the opportunities of the power vacuum brought about by the conditions of the post-World War collapse of the Empire had already been wasted by the Kurds, and the episode of National Struggle was concluded by the formation of a strong central authority armed with a Turkist discourse as well as weapons made in the Soviet Union, to complete the Turkification of Anatolia. "We must turkify the inhabitants of our country at any price", uttered Ismet Inönü in the wake of the suppression of the rebellion, "and we will annihilate those who oppose the Turks or 'le turquisme'".[241]

---

[239] See Appendix 6.
[240] With this coup, Kemal began to determine the entire list of parliamentary candidates prior to the elections. In the 1923 'elections', he got rid of the parliamentary opposition to the abolition of Caliphate and Sultanate, and decreased the Kurdish parliamentary representation almost to nil: only a negligible minority of the appointed deputies for Kurdish constituencies were of Kurdish origin.(see Frey, 1965: 184-192.)
[241] Simsir 1991: 58.

124

Of the three sectors of Kurdish identity, the sheikhs' leadership signified the intertwined character of religion and nationalism in Kurdish discourse,[242] which led to the emergence of an ongoing debate on whether the Sheikh Said rebellion was a nationalist movement or a religious one. The official Turkish discourse denied the movement's Kurdish character and classified it as a reactionary movement sponsored by the Great Powers,[243] while the regime's Independence Tribunal found the rebels guilty of 'acting with the motivation of founding an independent Kurdistan'.[244]

The counter insurgency operation against the Sheikh Said rebellion was more costly in human and financial terms than the National Struggle.[245] The rebellious leaders were captured and hanged[246] and severe reprisals were taken in those districts that had participated in the uprising. Martin Van Bruinessen quotes Kurdish sources stating that military operations resulted in the pillaging of more than two hundred villages, the destruction of over eight thousand houses, and fifteen thousand deaths.[247] Its consequences for the Kurds were catastrophic, almost amounting to 'annihilation' through physical elimination of the entire Kurdish leadership and the destruction of all sources of Kurdish identity.

'With the suppression of the Sheikh Said rebellion, the Republic and the Kemalist approach hoped to bury the Kurdish question', said Abdullah Ocalan in a 1991 interview.[248] This attempt was carried out on all fronts: military suppression of successive rebellions until 1938;

---

[242] Islam, and particularly the orthodox Shafi sect of its Sunni interpretation, has been an effective component of Kurdish identity. This character explains not only how the aim of protecting Caliphate could bring together the westernised *Teali* intellectuals with religious sheikhs, but also one of the essential divisions of identity within the Kurdish population, that between Alevis and Shafis, and the consequent silence towards the suppression of the Kocgiri rebellion.

[243] The title of late journalist Ugur Mumcu's investigative book on this rebellion is enough to guess its contents: "The Kurdish Islamic Rebellion". (Mumcu 1992.)

[244] There is one point missing in this debate: while the Turkish side emphasises the religious character of the Kurdish movement in order to label it 'reactionary', no one seems to have thought on the *Kurdish character of the Islamic movement* in Turkey (see Appendix 7), which also explains the Kemalists' primary appeal to the Kurdish identity in the mobilisation of the 'national struggle'.

[245] Tunçay 1981: 136.

[246] 47 executions were carried out on 29 June 1925 in addition to 6 executions on 27 May 1925.

[247] Bruinessen 1994: 149. David McDowall's findings regarding the number of deaths are between 40,000 to 250,000. These differences and the ambiguity in the number of losses are essentially due to the lack of any statistics, given that the first republican census was carried out in 1927, and the destablised Kurdish provinces of the time did not trust the authorities for a number of reasons to register their births and deaths (see, McDowell 1992: 37).

[248] Balli 1991: 217.

official decrees to reduce Kurdishness to the degree of 'nonentity', and on the political-cultural front, a policy of assimilation closely associated with the republican Turkish historiography and literature, based on painstaking elaborations to 'prove' the Turkish origins of Anatolian people.[249]

II.3. The Republican Foreclosure

The Kemalist technique of exclusion of the Kurdish identity, which Ocalan refers to as 'burial' and the Kurds call the 'policy of denial', is a sophisticated one and requires lengthy analysis, since it is through this analysis that the contemporary official and popular practices and mentalities regarding the Kurdish question can become intelligible.

As demonstrated above, the Kemalist movement began with the mobilisation of the Kurds in the East Anatolia. The multi-ethnic composition of Turkey was not seen as an obstacle against the realisation of the national project, based on a perception of 'nation of Islam'. In addition to Mustafa Kemal's speeches of the time emphasising 'the brotherhood of the Turks and the Kurds',[250] in the minutes of the assembly sessions, the terms Kurds and Kurdistan are frequently observed, and important programatic documents of national struggle included promises of Kurdish self-determination[251] and a law on the autonomy of Kurdistan also passed the assembly on 10 February 1922. During the peace negotiations in Lausanne, the Turkish delegation led by Ismet insisted that the Ankara government represented the Kurds as much as the Turks and therefore minority rights for the Kurds should not have been an issue.[252]

---

[249] I will consider the Turkish History Thesis and Sun Language Theory in Chapter 4.
[250] Yegen 1999: 114-5.
[251] Kutlay 1991: 138.
[252] Yegen 1999: 117. In his six day speech (1927), Mustafa Kemal referred to the absence of the Kurdish issue in Lausanne treaty as an achievement of the nationalist government: '*In Lousanne:* certainly not allowed to be mentioned' (Ataturk 1980: 50).

126

The Kemalist recognition of the Kurds remarkably shifted towards denial from 1923 onwards, when Kemal began to avoid the words Kurds or Kurdistan. Article 88 of the 1924 Constitution ruled for the first time that 'everyone in Turkey be called a Turk, regarding citizenship status, and regardless of religion and race'.[253]

The first manifesto of the Kemalist *coupure epistemologique* is Kemal's declaration on 7 March 1925 attributing the Sheikh Said rebellion, instead of the manifest Kurdish aspirations of separation from the newly formed republic, to criminals who tried to hide their intentions under the mask of religion, and who had relied on activities all over the country aimed at weakening the authority of the state.[254] The elaborate wording of this statement indicted the pro-*Sharia* resistance along with the opposition Progressive Republican Party for the rebellion but there was not a single reference to the Kurdish character of the event. In the opening speech of the new session of the assembly in November 1925, Kemal clarified his description of the rebellion as the result of 'reactionary tendencies and preparations'. A wave of secularisation, beginning with the 'hat law' commenced after this speech. In the closing passage of his six-day speech Kemal spoke of the rebellion as an uprising of ignorance, fanaticism and general hostility towards the republican administration and the 'modern movement' and accused the outlawed opposition Progressive Republican Party of becoming a source of hope for reactionaries. He therefore initiated what the Kurds called later the policy of denial (of the existence of a separate Kurdish people). The ministry of education would follow Kemal's linguistic silence with a decree in December 1926 to prohibit the use of ethnic names such as Kurd, Laz or Circassian, as they harmed Turkish unity.[255]

The Kemalist rupture thus consisted of a deliberate silence regarding the signifier 'Kurd', accompanied by attempts of metonymy favouring the repressed Islam and the 'ancient regime' as substitutes to the signifier Kurd. Moreover, this 'symbolic' refusal to assimilate

---

[253] Kili and Gozubuyuk, 1985.
[254] Mango 1999: 423-5. This speech was given in the aftermath of the parliamentary approval of a draconian 'Maintenance of Order Law', according to which not only the Kurdish leadership was eliminated but also the Progressive Republican Party was dissolved on 3 June 1925.
[255] Mango 1999: 428.

the signifier Kurd was an asymmetric reflection of the 'real' Kurdish resistance against assimilation to the Turkish identity. Exploring the nature of this 'real' can lead to grasp the nature of the Kemalist foreclosure.

In the previous section, I have argued that 'the Armenian' is the foreclosed real of the Muslim/Turkish identity. Chronologically, the emergence of this real preceded the symbolic constitution of the Turkish nation, and this temporality is one of the rationales behind the argument of 'the Armenian' being constitutive of Turkish identity.[256] The Armenian is therefore the 'primitive' or 'pre-symbolic' real, the inassimilable fear of castration (Ottoman dismemberment) that could never be absorbed by the symbolic,[257] and consequently the epicentre of all the symbolic constructions related to the Turkish identity.

The republican real, on the other hand, in which the Kemalist symbolisation of 'national reality' was to introduce a cut,[258] consisted of a multi-ethnic 'nation of Islam'. We have seen in the previous chapter that the Kemalist *coupure epistemologique* repressed and buried in the unconscious the religious character of this 'real nation'. Its multi-ethnic character, however, necessitated for the republican nationalist project yet another foreclosure :

> There are citizens and members of our nation inside the political and social entity of contemporary Turkish nation, to whom the propaganda of the ideas of being Kurdish, Cyrcassian and even Laz are attempted. But these misnomers, which were the products of the past ages of tyranny, failed to have any influence - apart from suffering - on any members of the nation except for a few brainless reactionaries used by the enemy. Because, the people of these communities like Turkish society in general share the same common past, history, morals and law.[259]

The ethnic heterogeneity of the 'real nation' therefore belonged to a negativised past ('ages of tyranny') while a positivised 'common past and history' invented[260] along with the

---

[256] This dimension of temporality can best be observed in the popular and official attempts of justification of the Armenian genocide ('we did it but they had done it first' – Akcam 2004: 236).
[257] Here, I borrow from Fink (1995) the chronological scheme of the 'two reals', consisting of a pre-symbolic r1 a post-symbolisation r2.
[258] Evans 1996: 159.
[259] Ataturk in Inan 1969: 23.
[260] This invention included the 'Turkish History Thesis', which I will consider in the consecutive chapters to follow.

128

'common morals and law' as the nexuses of popular identification with the 'contemporary Turkish nation'. It is precisely at this moment of the Kemalist call for a collective and selective amnesia that 'the Kurd' appeared to resist symbolisation. The Kemalist silence regarding the name of the Kurd thus corresponds to the real, that crude surplus, which is tangibly present after symbolisation. The Kurd qua Kurd could not be assimilated to the 'harmonised' chain of signification of Turkish reality; it could only be the theme of traumatic perception of the republican nationalist psyche.

Although foreclosure is a psychic defence mechanism of the threatened ego, it simultaneously leads to a major psychic malfunction, psychosis, by leaving a hole in the symbolic order, which can never be filled. What this primordial hole affirms is the ever presence of the incompatible idea that had been purged from the symbolic register, in the order of the real. Sooner or later, when the foreclosed element reappears in the real, the subject is unable to assimilate it.[261] This is the case with the signifier Kurd, which has been the subject of exhaustive attempts of failed assimilation by the republican subject in terms of 'religious reaction', 'foreign provocation', 'tribal resistance to modernisation', 'regional underdevelopment', 'smuggling' and 'banditry'.[262] This list can be enriched by a number of terms such as 'national security', 'a handful of terrorists' or 'south-east question', common denominator of all being a persistent and failed desire to metonymy, to produce a substitute for the Kurd or Kurdistan with signifiers available under the republican discursive horizon. Besides, all these 'names of the Kurd' have been associated with persistent state violence, including the overt legalisation of murder[263], various forms of firmly documented atrocities and human rights violations,[264] comparable to entry into psychosis with the onset of hallucinations and delusions. The triggering function of the Kurd stems from a situation where the reappearance of the Kurd could only occur as an appearance from outside the

---

[261] Evans 1996: 65.

[262] Yegen 1999.

[263] Special Law No. 1850 of 1930 reads: 'Murders and other actions committed individually or collectively between 20 June 1930 and 10 December 1930 by the representatives of the state or the province, by the military or civil authorities, by the local guards and militiamen, or by any civilian having helped the above or acted on their behalf, during the pursuit and extermination of the revolts which broke out in Ercis, Zilan, Agri and the surrounding areas, including Pulumur and Erzincan province and the area of the First Inspectorate, will not be considered as crimes' (Kendal 1980: 65).

[264] Early surveys include the foreign envoys' communiqués, which have been replaced since the late 1980s, by comprehensive regular reports of national and international human rights organisations.

symbolic order. And this 'collusion with the inassimilable signifier'[265], the encounter with the shadow of the 'real horrific Kurdistan'[266], dislocates the social objectivity.[267]

The above argument implies that the 'republican Turkish nation' does not exist and the hallucinated 'Kurd' is its symptom, which explains the necessity of the foreclosure of the Kurd for the republican identity. However, as I have argued in the previous chapter, the Turkish identity was born as a split identity between a Kemalist conscious core and a repressed periphery, and the republican design of Turkish identity was fairly alien to the repressed national-popular level particularly at the moment of the Kurdish exclusion. Kurdish resistance to Kemalist assimilation was raised not from the outside but inside of this 'nation of Islam'. The question therefore arises as follows: If the Kurd is the foreclosed obverse of the firm texture of the Kemalist/republican nation, then what does it mean for the peripheralised national-popular identity that had constituted itself through the exclusion of the Christian existence in the 'motherland'? In the next section, I will search for an appropriate answer to this question in an attempt to demonstrate that the official representations of the phantom of the Kurd have successfully built a psychic bond between the two levels.

III. The Kurd as the Armenian

This chapter's reflection on the Armenian and the Kurdish exclusions as the moments of formation of Turkish political identity has so far introduced an analysis of this process in terms of two subsequent foreclosures (f1 and f2). This analysis has based itself upon Fink's temporal scheme of the 'two reals', consisting of a pre-symbolic real (r1) and a post-symbolisation real (r2) (Fink 1995). I then placed in this scheme, the two stages of the emergence of Turkish identity, firstly the emergence of an Ottoman nation of Islam (f1) from a multi-faith society (r1) and secondly the emergence of a republican Turkish nation (f2)

---

[265] Evans 1996: 65.
[266] This was one of the very rare pronunciations of the 'real' nightmare scenario from the top of the Kemalist elite: constitution of a 'real horrific Kurdistan' was pointed out as the main danger by the Prime Minister Ismet Inonu in his 1935 East report (cited by Mumcu 1995: 118).
[267] Stavrakakis 1999: 130.

from a multi-ethnic nation of Islam (r2).[268] Stavrakakis (1999: 47-9) emphasises the pedagogic value of Fink's scheme as an approach which is legitimate and fruitful, arguing however that it risks to substitute retrospectively the pre-symbolic r1, 'a terrain which cannot be approached adequately any more', with the post-symbolic consequences of the failure of symbolisation, that is, the encounter with r2 and the subsequent emergence of fantasy and illusion.[269] If this analysis is to base on the Lacanian definition of the real as the terrain of the impossible, 'because it is impossible to imagine, impossible to integrate into symbolic register and impossible to attain in any way',[270] then Stavrakakis' criticism of chronological classification of the real has to be taken into account.

Returning to Turkish 'reality', the question to determine the theoretical and analytic tasks at this stage therefore emerges as follows: how can a foreclosure-based perception of republican history other than a chronological chain of consecutive foreclosures be elaborated?

III.1. Kurdish Resistance: Limits of Republican Assimilation

In response to the above question, an analytic distinction between the predominantly Muslim identity of the repressed 'periphery' (i1) and the republican Turkish identity of the 'centre' (i2) as constituted by two distinct foreclosures (respectively f1 and f2) can be introduced. This model firmly describes the two identities with their absolute psychic boundaries, but assumes a clear-cut duality to prevail through republican history. This, in fact, has not been the case: the two levels have been in constant interaction through time.[271] Consequently, the i1 and i2 have constantly influenced, 'contaminated' and modified each other and demonstrated the ability of operating as a unified political subjectivity around the issues of

---

[268] This scheme can be enriched by an emphasis on the relationship between the desire or joussaince and foreclosure to introduce d1, j1, d2 and j2 to the analysis.

[269] Stavrakakis argues that this retrospective claim of 'a description of what the pre-symbolic real really is' contradicts with the Lacanian definition of the real (Stavrakakis 1999: 49).

[270] Evans 1996: 160.

[271] The emergence of hybrid political projects such as the 'conservative liberalism' of DP, AP and AKP, 'populist ultra-nationalism' of MHP and 'moderate/tolerant secularism' of the DSP, with the common aim to mediate between the republican project of creating a civilised nation in its own Kemalist image and the Islamist project of re-seizing the State, is one example. Another example is the changing nature of history textbooks through decades, where Kemalism was gradually and elaborately synthesised with a Turk-Islam synthesis discourse (See Copeaux 1998: 194-197).

'national security'. What is required therefore is an analytic model that accounts for the fluidity of the notions of core (consciousness) and periphery (unconscious) and the consequent instability of the boundaries separating the i1 and i2.

This analytic model requires a perception of Turkish political identity (I) as an amalgam of the two levels,[272] constituted by the foreclosure of the trauma of the catastrophic collapse through the exclusion of the Christian identity. 'The Armenian' survives this analysis as the condensed metaphor and the taboo of the inassimilable fear of castration (Ottoman dismemberment) that could never be absorbed by the symbolic on the one hand, and, on the other, operates as the post-symbolic phantasmatic mirror, that is, the Turkish hypothesis of the 'primitive' or 'pre-symbolic' real, the epicentre of all the symbolic constructions related to the Turkish identity. Therefore the violent suppression of the Kurdish resistance to assimilation and the accompanying foreclosure of the signifier Kurd are suitable for a reading as the Kemalist symptoms of the return of the incompatible idea from the order of the real. In this case, the Kemalist collusion with the Kurd becomes comparable to triggered psychosis, rather than the emergence of the psychotic structure. Since the Turkish foreclosure, that is, the untouchable event of the exclusion of the Christian existence, the fear of the recurrence of the primal trauma in the form of Kurdish identity (perceived as the exorcised phantom or the spectral resuscitation of 'the Armenian') has served to maintain the integrity of Turkish political psyche.

The Kemalist techniques of exclusion of the Kurdish identity do not consist merely of a 'symbolic' refusal to assimilate the signifier Kurd and the 'real' violence against the Kurdish identity. An important task of the republican 'passive revolution' that the Kemalists conducted to hegemonise their periphery has been the dissemination of their perception of the 'Kurdish threat' throughout the 'common sense' level, with an aim in effect to popularise a Kemalist 'hallucination'. The Kemalist 'passive revolution' emphasised the considerable tension that was involved in the encounter between the popular 'nation' and Kurdish identity politics, due to the fact that a dimension of Kurdish politics has been open to the centrifugal

---

[272] With this model, the description of Identity as a simultaneously unifying and deconstructive element, which operates to dissolve the imagined 'absolute' status of dichotomies of state/civil society, centre/periphery and Kemalist-secularism/Islam, also gains some substance (see Introduction).

tendencies including claims to separation and independence, and each enunciation of this dimension has had the potential to evoke the foreclosed memories of the nation's constitutive trauma. Consequently, each appearance of the Kurd qua Kurd in the outer shadows of 'the real horrific Kurdistan'[273], that is, the real, could have triggered off Turkish paranoia time and again. In short, the national-popular perception of the Kurdish resistance was suitable for an association of 'the Kurd' with 'the Armenian'. Attempts to secure this association have served to build a psychic bond between the core and the repressed periphery through recourse to 'the Armenian' in the official representations of the phantom of the Kurd.

An early case of this psychic association of 'the Kurd' with 'the Armenian' was the 1937-1938 Dersim operation.[274] In the subsection below, I will consider the representations of the Dersim Kurds in the Kemalist press, State officials' discourse and the field commanders' orders as the manifestations of this association as a peculiar Kemalist technique of mobilisation/manipulation of the repressed periphery for the task of Kurdish exclusion.

III.2. Turkish Political Psyche at Work: Dersim Operation

Dersim operation was the result of the nine 'East Reports' authored between 1926 and 1936 by important members of the republican elite to be submitted to the republican authorities, and the special law for Dersim region, Tunceli Law, which passed the Parliament on 25 December 1935. The law changed the name of this mountainous Eastern region from Dersim to Tunceli[275] and put the province under the administration of a military governor with extraordinary powers. The aim of these state efforts was to end the de facto autonomy of this portion of Anatolia and integrate it into the 'motherland'. Its population, the Alevi Kurds, would be Turkified through methods of demographic engineering.[276] The operation began in March 1937 and continued until November 1938, with the massacre of more than 10,000

---

[273] This was one of the very rare pronunciations of the 'real' nightmare scenario from the top of the Kemalist elite: constitution of a 'real horrific Kurdistan' was pointed out as the main danger by the Prime Minister Ismet Inonu in his 1935 East report (cited by Mumcu 1995: 118).

[274] This ability to function in unity has also been affirmed in the popular anti-communist movement, 'the Cyprus cause', Maras massacre of 1978 and during the Kurdish conflict and the trial of the Kurdish leader Abdullah Ocalan in 1999.

[275] Literally the 'Land of Bronze' referring to an invented myth that Turks lived in the region in the Bronze Age.

[276] For an elaboration on the methods of integration through demographic engineering see Chapter 4.

Alevi Kurds.[277] Villages were systematically destroyed and tens of thousands of people were deported to various regions of Anatolia according to the Resettlement Law of 1934.

The peculiarity of the Dersim operation is that it went far beyond the State practices of quelling a revolt and witnessed to an unprecedentedly excessive use of violence. According to Martin van Bruinessen, what happened in Dersim is ethnocide which manifestly aimed 'the destruction of Kurdish ethnic identity'.[278] Mobilisation of the conscripts for such excessive violence, including the sadistic massacre of entire families could not have been possible merely through military coercion of orders or the declaration of 'a war of ideals for a noble cause'.[279] Nor would the economic argument, the fact that soldiers were allowed to sack the Alevi corpses,[280] be a sufficient explanation of such mobilisation. Taking into account the psychic dimension of the incentives, on the other hand, may provide an explanation, for which the peculiarities of Dersim region have to be outlined first.

People of Dersim are not orthodox Muslims. They belong to the Alevi faith, in fact an original version of it. In the 16th Century a gradual divorce between the Bektashi order and the Anatolian Alevis of Kurdish and Turkmen alike began,[281] and the conditions of Dersim which was almost literally closed to outside world due to environmental conditions allowed an original religious development. Dersim's Alevism can be legitimately called a version of Gregorian Christianity, due to Armenian influence and blood lineage,[282] expressed in Shiite Islam's grammar. The inhabitants of this agnostic island surrounded by pious Muslim tribes of both Kurdish and Turkish descent developed a consequent sense of identity. Although they are popularly called Kurdish, they prefer to call themselves Alevi referring to their religion instead of ethnicity, or Dımıli or Zaza after the language they speak, or Dersimi (of Dersim).

---

[277] Kurdish sources speak of tens of thousands including women, children and the elderly. We probably will never learn the full dimensions of atrocities of the 'civilisation' of Dersim.
[278] Bruinessen 1994.
[279] Mustafa Kemal glorified the counter-insurgency operation against the 1925 Sheikh Said rebellion with these words (cited in Tunaya 2003: 149).
[280] On most of these corpses they found jewellery and most returned home better off. See, Kalman 1995: 393.
[281] Melikof 1999.
[282] See, Bruinessen (1994), Kalman (1995): 32-4.

The State discourse during the Dersim operation have frequent references to these peculiarities, some of which, including the discourses of the field officer, the governor, the press and the highest regional authority, will be considered below.

"The officer ordered: do not leave any of these Alevis alive. (...) It was important in those days to kill Alevis, because this opened the path to Heaven,"[283] states A. Demirtas, who performed active duty as a private in the Dersim operation. This refers to the centuries old motto of Muslim fanaticism that 'in God's eyes, killing one Kizilbas[284] is a better deed than performing Hadj (pilgrimage to Kaaba in Mecca) five times'. The Dersim massacre was therefore made possible by the State's gesture towards the other of the other, to the field of common sense fantasies. For a taste of the images appearing on the screen of anti-Alevi fantasy, I shall quote passages from a text dated 1931 written by the governor of Erzincan, on the customs of Dersim Kurds:

> Every year, following the 20th of January, they perform certain rituals; they gather in a house leaving unmarried boys and girls aside. They call this 'cem'. (...) Persons, who are not of the Alevi faith cannot be present in these gatherings. If there is a Turkish guest in the village during the period of the rituals, they will do their best not to reveal their secret to him; for instance, two or three persons among them

---

[283] Witness Account of a soldier (A. Demirtas of Kars, published in Kalman 1995: 393). I try my best to refrain from quoting any episode of the genocidal orgy described in this interview and other witness accounts quoted in the above work and elsewhere.

[284] The term Kizilbas, was first became known as the name of the Turkoman tribal troops devoted to the fifteenth century Iranian Safavi religious leader, Shaikh Haidar Ibn Junaid. The Safavis rose in the Ardebil region on the south-western shores of the Caspian, before seizing control of the Persian empire. The Kizilbash tribes formed the crack troops in contest with the Ottomans for control of Anatolia in the late fifteenth and early sixteenth century. The struggle for Anatolia between Ottoman and Persian empires took on a strongly religious hue, between Sunni and Shi'i Islam. Although the Ottoman Sunnis triumphed, a large number of pastoralist tribes in central and eastern Anatolia remained adherents of 'Kizilbash' beliefs, cut off from Shi'i Persia. Originally the Kizilbas, tribes seem to have been Turkoman rather than Kurdish. It is unclear whether Kurdish tribes embraced this form of Islam from neighbouring Turkoman tribes or whether Turkoman tribes acquired Kurdish cultural characteristics. The probable truth is that both factors came into play, particularly with political marriages between the progeny of neighbouring tribal chiefs. Be all that as it may, clearly the Bektasis and Kizilbas, (Alevi Kurds) have a common origin in the ferment of Muslim and other religious ideas current in eastern Iran in the early middle ages. With repeated disorders in eastern Anatolia, frequently inspired by dissident religious movements, there remained a strong feeling that those tribespeople who adhered to Kizilbash beliefs were not 'proper' Ottomans. This feeling increased dramatically in the second half of the nineteenth century when the Ottoman sultans deliberately fostered Sunni Islam as a bulwark against foreign influence. The main regional focus for this Islamic revival was central and eastern Anatolia. The Kizilbas,, finding themselves openly reviled and their name increasingly used as a term of abuse, quietly dropped their historic name in favour of the more anodyne term: Alevi.

accompany the guest until he goes to sleep. When he is asleep they go back and join the ritual (Kemali 1992: 153-7).

Cem ritual of Alevis, in which men and women participated as equals, unlike the orthodox Muslim prayers, has been a rich source for the production of incestuous group sex fantasies referred to as *mumsöndü alemi* (candle-out party), popularly believed among the Sunnis.

Ali Kemali's opinion on the Alevi religious leaders is as follows:

Seyits and Dedes are intelligent but ignorant and confusing. Their hair and beard are mixed together and almost all of them are covered with dirt. Because they never wash and clean their body due to their belief, they emit such a nasty smell that to be near them is a torture (Kemali 1992: 153).

It is needless to contend that the above observation is itself a description of the governor's fantasy or a deliberate lie, a conscious attempt of externalisation. The other of the other, that is, the Alevi of the Kurds, was therefore constructed with the help of fantasy, ready to lead to the revival of 'common sense' hostility. The 'enemy', the Kurdish bandit, was not merely returning from the non-symbolised outside of the republican subject, that is the foreclosed real of the republican discourse, but from the real of the 'nation of Islam', that is, from outside the absolute psychic boundaries of the Turkish identity. This discourse on the real, 'the real horrific Kurdistan', was further associated with that signifier of the metaphoric taboo of Turkish silence on the expulsion of the non-Muslim identities from the entire territory of Turkish political psyche – 'the Armenian' towards which the Turk felt compelled to act in such a way that it never existed at all:

'Armenian books found in Seyit Riza's tent'

In Seyit Riza's tent, numerous books in Armenian were found. Most of them are religious books. (...)

There is ample evidence that these books have been held in hand and read. Some pages are marked. Some notes were taken at the margins.[285]

This article is from the government's newspaper *Ulus* published in the wake of the capture of Seyit Riza, the spiritual leader of the Dersim tribes.[286] The best example of the official

---

[285] *Ulus*, 7 October 1937.
[286] I shall recall here that the military operations in Dersim did not end but escalated after the capture of Seyit Riza, mainly with the aim of 'correcting' the civilians, and lasted another year.

136

association of Dersim with the Armenians is the statements in the eve of the Dersim operation of General Abdullah Alpdogan, the regional commander, governor and inspector general at one and the same time:

Some of them use the Armenian names for the villages and neighbourhoods that they live in. (...) They are Turks, but they are not even aware of their own history. [They have been deceived by the Americans] who tore them away from the Turkish society claiming that the Kurdish and Kizilbas blood is Armenian blood, and thus including them in the Armenian nation. (...) The Kurdish community of Tunceli was made Armenian.

I had commanded a regiment of the army which had suppressed the Koçgiri rebellion [1921]. We had seen crosses hanging on the necks of children in the Koçgiri villages. (...)

The plotting of the outsiders continue: Muses is a French agent and an Armenian of Tunceli origin. (...) He carries out propaganda to form a separate state in Tunceli. (...) He wants a gun to be fired against the State and a revolt start.[287]

This speech given by a top member of the state apparatus is a full scale gesture towards the real, the constitutive trauma of the Turkish identity, a gesture towards the denied memoirs of that prolonged agony, the catastrophic collapse of the Ottoman Empire, including the paranoid experience of the threat of 'Great Powers'. More significantly, it is a gesture towards the Armenian and with it an invitation to a schizoid recollection that Anatolia is neither 'Ana' nor 'dolu'. It is the moment when the foreclosed Armenian, the inassimilable signifier, reappears in the real; it is therefore the moment of entry into psychosis. Even if the people of Dersim did not 'fire a gun on the State', something had already been triggered somewhere deep under.

The excessive massacre of the Kurds in Dersim, beyond being a symptom of the republican will to territorial integrity and national homogeneity, is therefore revealing of the psychic function of the return of the Armenian from the order of the real to appear as the phantom of the Kurd. This linkage provided a nexus that united the republican core and the repressed periphery to mobilise for national-popular tasks. It is precisely this totality of the conscious-

---

[287] Alpdogan's speech on December 1936 quoted in Mumcu 1995: 156-7

rational centre and the repressed periphery on the one hand, and of the political psyche and political subjectivity on the other that is referred to as Turkish political identity in this research.

III.3. The 'Imrali Symptom' revisited

The popular exclusion of the Kurds has therefore become possible by the coding the Kurds with the signifier 'Armenian'. The Kurdish national movement of the 1980s and 1990s was similarly linked in the popular psyche to 'the Armenian', as the 'ontological enemy', 'the subcontractor of that "master-plan" of the disintegration of Turkey'.[288] Seeing 'the Armenian' in the person of Abdullah Ocalan, the captured leader of the Kurdish rebellion, is therefore intelligible as a traumatic perception of what is appearing in the order of the real.

This real refers to the constitutive trauma of Turkish identity and the accompanying fear of total disintegration, which was partially overcome by the conclusion of the 'national struggle' by being ejected from the symbolic universe of the new identity. The Kurdish revolt of 1925, which appeared at the outset of the formation of modern republic to mark the limitations of the republican symbolisation and manifest a primordial lack of identification with the 'nation', served above all to evoke this constitutive fear. As a result, the signifier Kurd was overtly ejected from the symbolic universe with the personal intervention of Mustafa Kemal, the father-Turk. From 1925 onwards, the Kurds along with the land of the Kurds, Kurdistan, have disappeared from Turkey's symbolic order, while the foreclosed 'real Kurd' did continue to exist outside this universe. When the recent Kurdish revolt made the denied 'real Kurd' visible once again through the corner of the Turk's eye, something analogous to the onset of hallucinations and delusions took place. With the delusional return of the inassimilable signifier Kurd from the order of the real, the accumulated traumas that structure Turkish political psyche have been revived and triggered leading to the escalation of state violence against the Kurds and to the popular hysterical symptoms to accompany this episode of violence.

---

[288] Bora 2002: 918.

The above analysis of the necessarily violent nature of the Turkish encounter with the Kurdish identity further enables us to provide a three-fold explanation for the association of Ocalan with the Armenian in the national-popular discourse. Firstly, Ocalan has to be 'Armenian' because of the Kemalist linguistic prohibition of the Kurd, which, while prohibiting the Kurd, has at the same time encouraged the popular associations of the Kurd with the Armenian. Secondly, Ocalan has to be 'Armenian' because the popular religion, or 'common sense' nationalism, imagines the Turkish nation as a totality of all Muslim elements within the border of Turkish republic. The only way to violently externalise an element of the 'nation of Islam' is this association with the outside of this 'nation', that is, the Armenian. Finally, Ocalan has to be 'Armenian' because 'the Kurd', beyond its immediate denotation, is a metaphorical connotation for 'the Turk' of his constitutive/primal trauma, that is that life-and-death struggle of the Ottoman elite and the Muslim masses of the Empire against non-Muslim identity.

IV. Conclusion: Hallucinated Communities

In this chapter, I have inquired into the emergence of modern Turkish identity by considering the processes and mechanisms of exclusion. I have argued that the late Ottoman and republican nationalisation involved the constitution of the mechanism of foreclosure as a primary feature of Turkish political psyche and Turkish identity. I have demonstrated how the exclusion of non-Muslim identity was constitutive of an historic bloc organised around a religious identity to form the nucleus of Turkishness. The evolution of this proto-nation into the modern/secular Turkish identity became possible with the repression of the Islamic identity, as analysed in chapter 1. I have argued that this repression was simultaneous with the suppression of the 1925 Kurdish rebellion and was accompanied by another exclusion, that is, the foreclosure of the signifier Kurd. This foreclosure has also been constitutive in that it consisted of a call to various Muslim ethnicities to be assimilated by the designed Turkish identity. I have then argued that the Kemalist foreclosure has to be considered as a paranoidic symptom of the reappearance of the foreclosed constitutive trauma in the order of the real. This line of analysis takes into account the interaction between the analytic categories of core and periphery, which is particularly evident in the national-popular association of the Kurdish question with the Armenian foreclosure, as demonstrated in the above analyses of the Dersim operation and the recent symptomatic expressions of anti-Ocalan hysteria. The overall argument of this chapter is that the moments of exclusion are in effect the moments of the traumatic encounter of Turkish political psyche with the real leading to a 'real' human tragedy of extensive dimension, that is, the massacre of over a million inhabitants of Anatolia. Furthermore, the maintenance of Turkish identity through republican history required the maintenance of the built-in psychic defence mechanisms and a readiness to re-stage this human tragedy whenever the Turkish identity felt that its integrity is under threat. In response to the question on the specifically violent nature of encounter with the Kurdish identity, it is therefore legitimate to assert that Turkish identity is structured like psychosis and the Kurd is its 'hallucinated community'.

CHAPTER 3: KEMALISM AND MODERN TURKISH IDENTITY

Kemalism is one of the fields on which a vast literature of political and historical discussion is available. A model of modernisation from above, a successful case of secularisation of a Muslim society, a bureaucratic-corporatist societal model and a republican monarchy, are a few but many descriptions of Kemalism. There is also a strong claim by the left-liberal scholars that Kemalism is a linear continuation of the late-Ottoman institutions and the accompanying modalities of power, which has been strongly opposed by scholars who emphasise the republican rupture as a revolution from above. In this chapter, I will treat Kemalism as a discursive practice, which would fit in any and all of these descriptions. The most striking feature of Kemalism, which many accounts tend to overlook, is probably its peculiarly Turkish character:[289] Kemalism is the only original Turkish contribution to the modern social science literature, and a keyword to which the terms Turkey and Turkish are closely related.[290] The tight fit between Turkishness and Kemalism is grounded upon a mutual relationship: Kemalism made Turkey as much as it is 'made in Turkey'.

This mutual relationship is due to the fact that Kemalism emerged from the late-Ottoman process of modernisation, secularisation and nationalisation as a discourse that promised to materialise these 'national' tasks under the conditions of the post-World War I Turkey, which primarily required political institutionalisation and the constitution of modern, secular and national political subjectivity. I have argued in the preceding chapters that this constitution necessitated certain practices of exclusion, which I have analysed in terms of the psychoanalytic notions of repression (modernisation/secularisation) and foreclosure (nationalisation). The making of modern political subjectivity necessitated exclusion, which required in turn the incorporation of these psychic defence mechanisms. Kemalism, therefore, consisted primarily of an appeal for identification with these defence mechanisms along with a modern, secular and national modality with both conscious and unconscious dimensions.

---

[289] I have noticed during my two decades of stay in Britain that any average British citizen knows Ataturk, doner kebab and, since the mid-1990s, the football team 'Galatasaray' about Turkey.
[290] Reincarnation of an originally Kemalist model can be observed in the experiences of Ba'thism, Nasserism and even Peronism with their variations.

In this chapter I will inquire into the success of this appeal, which has made and sustained Kemalism as an undeniable determinant of Turkish political identity. I will argue that this hegemonic success is primarily due to the production and implementation of clear responses to the questions that the Ottoman identity crisis had put forward.

As the most pressing of these questions, I will proceed by considering the dichotomy of nation and its outside. Firstly, I will comment on the emergence of the Kemalist discourse by situating the Kemalist subject's desire to nationalise as emerged from the lack in the Other, that is the lacking Turkish nation as an objective entity. The role of the myth of Ataturk in the making of this lacking entity will be considered in two subsections. Firstly, I will argue that the myth of salvation and the accompanying vacancy of 'national hero' preceded the emergence of a nationalist social imaginary and that the first rigorous response that Kemalism produced through the intervention of 'national hero' was on the question of the ambiguous object of 'salvation'. I will develop this argument by following the trajectory of the inflation of Kemal's personality cult to escalate to the position of an 'empty signifier' representing a 'lack', a lacking universality, that is, the nation to be 'liberated'. Secondly, I will specify the nature of the Kemalist intervention into the question of 'Quest-ce qu'une nation?' as demarcation. Kemalism provided a clear definition of the boundaries of the republican discursive territory[291] to be drawn according to a dichotomy of nation, present and future on the one side and 'outside' and the past on the other. Understanding what is Kemalist in Turkish political identity therefore necessitates an analysis to expose these boundaries within which this identity has attempted to fit.

In the second section, I will consider the problem of modernisation and its Kemalist solution. I will recall the dislocatory effects of the necessity and the ideal of westernisation (civilisation) for the Ottoman order, and consider the Kemalist response as a synthesis of intertwined drives of modernisation and nationalisation. In the first subsection, the results of early westernisation and its nationalist criticism will be considered. Kemalism will then be presented as a second westernisation attempt, which took into account both the early failure

---

[291] The discursive definition corresponded to the definition of physical boundaries of the national territory.

142

and its nationalist criticism. I will argue that Kemalism's primarily demarcating function for Turkish identity is observable in the construction of the boundaries between a negativised past on the one side and the present and future of the 'nation', on the other.

In the third section, I will analyse Kemalism as a nodal point that binds together a vast diversity of discursive elements, moments and networks, including statements, signifiers, meanings, perceptions of identity/difference and subject positions, under its discursive horizon, that is, the republican symbolic order. I will begin with analysing the Kemalist attempts to reoccupy the divine space left out from the exclusion of the Islamic discourse from the republican universe, in which Kemalism tends to turn into its opposite, that is, a religious discourse. I will argue that it is within this divine space that the Republican Regime of Truth with its Kemalist episteme replaced the Ottoman Regime of Truth with its Islamic episteme. I will then inquire into the nature of Kemal's intervention as the 'Father-Turk' in the process of formation of the republican discursive universe. I will argue that the significance of Kemal's name is analogous to the paternal function in the child's introduction into the symbolic order. The importance of this intervention, which constituted and hegemonised the modern Turkish discursive universe, and with it the modern Turkish subject, also lies in the endurance of this paternal-pedagogical vision to determine the logic of state-society relations of republican Turkey. I will then consider the problems of identity that Kemalism produced or reproduced while trying to develop adequate responses to the Ottoman identity crisis. These problems, in addition to the reproduction of the divine space, consist of the overemphasised patriarchal function in the constitution and maintenance of modern Turkish identity, leading to the maintenance of state/society division inherited from Ottoman society, and the constant reproduction of Turkish neurosis, due to the impossibility of bridging the cleavage between the modern and traditional identities.

In conclusion, I will argue that one of the primary errors of studies on modern Turkish politics is to underestimate the hegemonic power of Kemalism as the discursive horizon of republican Turkey, as the nodal point that has tied together a republican Turkish reality and as a discourse that has functioned in terms of 'identification in the last instance' for Turkish political subjectivity. This power of Kemalism stems, in Gramscian terms,[292] from the fact that as an ideology, Kemalism has a validity which is 'psychological'; it 'organises' the Turkish subjectivity, and create the terrain on which the Turkish subject moves, acquires consciousness of their position, struggles, etc.. In Foucauldian terms, as a modality of modern power, Kemalism, is capable not solely of 'exclusion, blockage and repression', but also of 'producing effects at the level of desire'.[293] In psychoanalytic terms, the overemphasised paternal function of Kemalism opens up the possibility of an analysis of the making of Turkish political subjectivity in terms of entry to the symbolic order. The making of the Turkish subject always consists of prohibitions because Kemalism overwrites itself on a larger field of identity, by performing a cut on the imaginary identification with a 'nation of Islam'; the Kemalist identification therefore includes a primal loss of a sense of imaginary wholeness. However. Kemalist symbolic order, the field of law and order constituted by the name-of-Ataturk, is also productive, because, like any symbolic order it provides the object-world with meanings and turns the ego into a subject, who is able to perceive and produce meanings.

I. Nationalisation via Kemalisation

In this section, I will account on the emergence of the Kemalist discourse by situating the Kemalist subject's desire to nationalise as emerged from the lack in the Other, that is the lacking Turkish nation as an objective entity. Understanding what is Kemalist in Turkish political identity therefore necessitates an analysis to expose these boundaries within which this identity has attempted to fit. The role of the myth of Ataturk in the making of this objectivity will be considered in two subsections. Firstly, I will follow the trajectory of Kemal's inflated personality cult to the position of an 'empty signifier' representing a 'lack', a lacking universality, that is, the nation to be 'liberated'. Secondly, I will specify the nature of the Kemalist intervention into the question of 'Quest-ce qu'une nation?' as demarcation. Kemalism provided a clear definition of the boundaries of the republican discursive territory to be drawn according to a dichotomy of nation, present and future on the one side and

---

[292] Gramsci 1970: 177.
[293] Foucault, 1980: 59.

144

'outside' and the past on the other. I will argue in conclusion that the peculiarity of Kemal's intervention consists firstly in providing the myth of salvation with a content ('nation') to be liberated, following his escalation to the status of an empty signifier through filling in the vacancy of 'national hero'; and secondly, in his mapping out the physical and discursive boundaries of this nation as opposed to its outside.

I.1. Kemal as an 'empty signifier'

Kemalism as a specific political discourse did not exist before the formation of Kemalist hegemony. The Kemalist overdetermination of the post-Ottoman mythical space occurred during the 'national struggle' as the affirmation of the modernist military bureaucracy's hegemony over that 'historic bloc' which carried out this struggle. Kemalism, however, was not born in a void; it contained many elements of the late-Ottoman mythical space, which consisted of various discourses of 'salvation'.[294]

The 'desire of salvation', which had emerged against the background of traumatic disintegration was materialised through a prolonged 'national struggle' by an 'historic bloc' consisting of the modernist military-bureaucratic elite and the Turkish-Muslim masses. I have demonstrated in Chapter 2 how this struggle led to a situation by which 'Anatolia was made a pure Muslim/Turkish land'.[295] In other words, the mythical space of 'salvation', which served as a surface of inscription of various contents, was overdetermined by one of these contents to be transformed into a social imaginary of nationalism.[296] The Kemalist leadership emerged, when the military-bureaucratic hegemony over Muslim-Turkish subjects was at stake following the conclusion of their last bid to halt the collapse of the Empire by embarking on the World War I with the Allied invasion of all the remnants of the Ottoman

---

[294] I have considered the emergence and evolution of this mythical space in the previous chapters relating the late-Ottoman 'dreams of salvation' to the Ottoman identity crisis. In Chapter 1, I have considered the battle between the secularist and Islamist discourses in the 'longest century of the Empire', which continued in the formative years of the republic. And in Chapter 2, I have narrated the ruling bureaucracy's disposal of the Ottomanist discourse in favour of an amalgam of Turkism and Islamism. Through these developments, the literal content of the late Ottoman dreams of salvation, that is, 'the salvation of the sublime state', was gradually transformed and overdetermined by the manifest desire of formation of a modern nation-state.
[295] Atay 1980: 450.
[296] For the dissolution of myths and the emergence of social imaginaries see, Laclau 1990: 61; and Howarth, et. al. (eds.) 2000: 14-6.

soil.[297] This was arguably the catastrophic moment when the obverse of the late-Ottoman dreams of salvation had come true with the logical conclusion of the process of disintegration in the total dismemberment of the Ottoman land and 'nation'.[298]

In these circumstances, Kemalism presented itself not as the particular discourse of the remnants of Ottoman military bureaucracy to maintain their power in modern conditions, but as the only feasible manifestation of the 'national-popular' desire of salvation in the post-World War I conditions. Kemal's escalation to the status of a 'national hero' became possible after emptying out this military bureaucratic content, which made possible the hegemonic presentation of a particular will as the 'general will' of the national-popular camp. This implies that the emergence of Kemal as the 'national hero' was the emergence of an empty signifier which incarnated the lacking security, coherence and integrity of *vatan* (homeland) and *millet* (nation).

The trajectory of Mustafa Kemal's escalation to the position of a 'national hero' as the leader of the nationalist bloc can be observed in the memoirs of Yakup Kadri Karaosmanoglu, in an essay titled *Atatürk:* 'We opened our eyes to the world in an atmosphere of catastrophe and collapse. Our early youth passed with longing for a national hero.' This longing for a hero grew even further with the hopes that the CUP awoke but failed to keep up with: 'As we were in our twenties, we no longer believed in anyone or anything.' The years Karaosmanoglu refers to are the years of the second constitutional era (1908-1918). Despite these disappointments, Karaosmanoglu and his generation found a hearth and a holy man to seek refuge: 'in fact, we found a temple to seek refuge under its roof: the Turkish Hearth. A strange man in this building looking like a Buddha statue kept on forecasting the arrival of a saviour and a day of salvation.' This Buddha that sat in the Turkish Hearth building was Ziya Gokalp, who had considerable intellectual influence on Karaosmanoglu's generation. 'However, this poet assigned the title of national hero to Enver Pasha right in the wake of the

---

[297] Although the CUP was behind the organisation of the local committees of the Anatolia and Rumelia Defence of Rights Association (see Zurcher 1984), its leading members were either on the run or in exile, being held responsible for the Armenian massacre by the British led tribunals in Istanbul. Furthermore, the CUP cadres, which governed the country during the disastrous defeats between 1908 and 1918, considerably lost their credibility in the eyes of the other components of the historic bloc.

Sarikamis disaster.[299] Who knows, he might have got tired of waiting... But we suffered from another disappointment with this move by the CUP's ideologue and lost half of our belief in his intellectual sincerity.' It is obvious that although this generation found some peace in the wording of Gokalp, what they needed was no longer a man of letters but a man of action. Finally, Karaosmanoglu found what he had waited for in Mustafa Kemal's passage to Anatolia and the declaration of the determination of Ankara government to implement the 'national pact'[300]: 'Like a sailor reciting his last prayers in a sinking boat, I am constantly reciting his name by myself: Mustafa Kemal, Mustafa Kemal. And my heart found a deep feeling of security and peace.'[301]

What we observe in Karaosmanoglu's account is the process of emergence of the intertwined signifiers 'salvation' and 'national hero' to represent the absence of security, coherence and integrity of the late Ottoman social objectivity. The CUP discourse raised popular expectations to inflate the connotations of these empty signifiers further. However, the CUP's bid in entering the War on the Germans' side proved to be a mistake with disastrous consequences. The inflated hopes were shattered further by the signing of Mudros Armistice, Sévres Treaty, the occupation of Istanbul by the Entente forces and the landing of the Greek forces in western Anatolia. In these conditions, Mustafa Kemal, a junior figure of the CUP[302] and a successful commander of the battle of Gallipoli, emerged as the 'national hero', who was able to promise and deliver the long expected 'salvation':

> History has proved incontrovertibly that success in great enterprises requires the presence of a leader of unshakeable capacity and power (...) There is no claim that the person that was required by the situation at hand (...) had to be myself. However, one among the sons of this land had to come to the fore.[303]

---

[298] For the Muslim-Turkish subjects of the Empire this was the moment of total disorder, analogous to the Argentine of the 1960s. (See Laclau 1996: 55 & 42-3.)

[299] In Sarikamis, in the eastern border of contemporary Turkey, the Ottoman army suffered a disastrous defeat against the Russian forces as the opening battle of the World War I.

[300] The 'National Pact' was adopted by the Ottoman Parliament in Istanbul on 17 February 1920, which declared 'Turkey' as the homeland of the nation to be liberated.

[301] Karaosmanoglu 1983: 36.

[302] Similarly, Peron was not involved in the process of disintegration in the 1960s. Laclau argues that this absence furnished ideal conditions for Peron to become an 'empty signifier' (Laclau 1996: 54-5).

[303] Atatürk 1960: 44-5, 47.

Kemal thus became the 'empty signifier' incarnating the moment of universality of 'salvation' that unified the Turkish/Muslim popular camp.[304] The dissociation of Kemal's name from the CUP leadership, turned into an advantage in the eyes of both the Muslim-Turkish masses and the Entente powers in the post-World War I conditions: he was neither responsible for the defeat, nor had he been involved in the Armenian genocide.[305] Kemal's escalation to the status of the expected 'national hero', however, cannot solely be explained by suitable consequences. Mustafa Kemal's 'unshakeable capacity and power' was also a result of his indisputable military talent and admirable political manoeuvring. An example of this talent and manoeuvring was the propaganda war around the Inonu 'victories'.[306] On 1 April, Ismet sent a telegram to Mustafa Kemal announcing: 'The enemy has abandoned the battlefield to our arms, leaving thousands of dead behind'. Kemal replied to Ismet by stating: 'It was not only the enemy you have defeated, but fate itself – the ill-starred fate of our nation'.[307] The reference to collective memory in this message is obvious: in Inonu, not only the Greek advance but the traumatic sequence of defeats that had led to the Ottoman collapse was halted.[308] The battles of Inonu were thus invented as the sole successful attempt of a chain of defensive battles that ended in defeat for over a century; as the first shade of hope that the national-popular dream of salvation could have come true.

---

[304] According to Andrew Mango, Kemalism was born on 24 December 1919 in the Anatolian town of Kirsehir, when Kemal addressed a group of Turkoman tribesmen by reciting a couplet from the patriotic poet Namik Kemal which reads, 'The enemy has pressed his dagger to the breast of the motherland/Will no one arise to save his mother from her black fate?'. Kemal commented on this verse by saying, 'Another Kemal has now sprung from the nation's breast', and added: 'Even if the enemy presses his dagger to the breast of the motherland/A man will be found to save the mother from her black fate'. (Mango 1999: 262.)

[305] On 24 September 1919 Kemal made the following promise to USA Radio Gazette: 'We guarantee that there will be no new terror against the Armenians' (quoted in Simsir 1973: 171).

[306] Kemalist historiography claims that in January and March 1921, Greek forces suffered defeats and were stopped by the nationalist forces led by Ismet in Inonu, central Anatolia. However, Greek advance into Anatolia continued after these imaginary victories. The Times reported on 7 February 1921: 'Kemal produced a propaganda war out of a situation, which is not a victory by any criteria' (Cited by Dilipak 1991: 87).

[307] This well-propagated correspondence between Ismet and Kemal is quoted in Nutuk (Ataturk 1980: 386-7).

[308] This correspondence was circulated around the country and was particularly welcomed in Istanbul. In addition to celebrations, prayers were conducted around the imperial capital for the soldiers killed in the battle and Sultan sent donations to the Red Crescent for the relief of victims. What is significant here is the coded references to the sequence of defeats, which was halted for the first time.See Kutlay (quote Kutlay) See Mango 1999: 312-5. Sultan's grandson, Prince Omer Faruk, who entered Anatolia and tried to be listed for the nationalist forces in the wake of Inonu Battle, was politely refused and sent back to Istanbul by Mustafa Kemal. Kemalist historiography narrates the 'national struggle' as an anti-imperialist and anti-monarchist war in which Sultan and the Istanbul government presented as persistently plotting against the Kemalists. This narration,

Kemal's linguistic conduct of the term nation was also another success story. In addition to his equivocal deployment of the term,[309] Kemal began to develop a discourse in which *millet* gradually gained an additional content, signifying Mustafa Kemal himself, in his statements: a development difficult to notice but significant.[310] Kemal frequently pronounces his will as the nation's 'general will' and occasionally goes so far as to command the nation to do certain things.[311] This feature of Kemal's discourse, beyond obvious self-confidence involving a degree of narcissism and megalomania, was an affirmation that his personality and later the representations of his body, in the form of monumental symbols, emerged as the signifier of the 'nation', and as such, Mustafa Kemal was an empty signifier since he represented a 'lack', a lacking universality, that is, the nation to be built. The birth of modern Turkish identity was thus closely tied to the cult of Mustafa Kemal, that is, the imaginary closure and fullness of the Turkish nation. Consequently, Kemal's intervention into the problem of the 'lacking nation' deserves further consideration, which I shall undertake below.

I.2. The Kemalist Demarcation: Nation Besieged

Turkish nationalism – as in all nationalisms - preceded the (re)birth of the Turkish 'nation'. Both the 'nation' and its geographical location were ambiguous in the late Ottoman discursive territory. These two lacks in the objectivity were consequences of the fact that modern Turkish identity emerged through a transition to a nation state from a multiethnic Empire, accompanied by a constant contraction of the geographical space and demographic movements and transitions. Given the ambiguity of *vatan* and *millet*, Mustafa Kemal's personal intervention in these questions of 'objectivity', consisting of the 'nation' and its geographical territory, was crucial. The Kemalist intervention consisted primarily of an

---

which still constitutes the backbone of Turkish history textbooks, is based on Kemal's six days speech (1927) where he literally re-wrote the history of the 'national struggle' to legitimise his personal dictatorship.
[309] See, Chapter 2.
[310] The only research, which provides this insight, is Taha Parla's five-volume analysis of Kemalist discourse. See particularly Parla 1991, 1991a and 1991b. (See Parla 1991: 167 & 171-2.)
[311] "The superfluous expressions which were incompatible with the modern character of the new Turkish State and our republican order, contained in the articles 2 and 26 of the Constitution, constitute compromises to which the revolution and Republic ought to have agreed so as to satisfy the exigencies of the time. When the first favourable opportunity arises *the nation must eliminate* these superfluities from our Constitution" (Atatürk 1980: 328). So did the *nation*, that is Mustafa Kemal's handpicked parliament, two years after this 'command', after waiting for the 'first favourable opportunity', and removed the articles 2 (The religion of the Republic is Islam) and 26 (it is essential to apply the *Sheria* rules). (Also see, Parla 1991: 110 & 167.)

149

attempt to end the ambiguity of the boundaries of the national territory, including the physical borders of the 'motherland' and the discursive outside of the nation.

The geographical location of the 'nation' was a primary problem of the Turkist discourse, which had emerged outside the Ottoman lands from the Turkic communities' conflict with the pan-Slavist Russification policies.[312] Ziya Gokalp, the undisputed ideological guru of Turkish nationalism wrote as late as 1911: 'The country of the Turks is neither Turkey nor Turkestan / Their country is a great and eternal land –Turan'.[313] Even when it became a ruling discourse of the Empire under the CUP, Turkism was closely linked with a project of emancipation of the 'Turks under the Russian yoke'. A late attempt of this manifest desire was Enver's Sarikamis operation of 1914 with a pan-Turkist hope of liberating Caucuses and Central Asia[314] only to end in a great disaster. The association of Turkism and the nation's 'last shelter', Anatolia, was a relatively late event.[315] The nationalist movement led by Kemal named itself as the 'Union for the Defence of Rights of Anatolia and Rumelia' in Sivas Congress of September 1919. The name 'Turkey' was pronounced for the first time to name the territory of the 'National Pact' to be adopted by the Ottoman Parliament in Istanbul on 17 February 1920. Anatolia and an undetermined portion of the Balkans (Rumelia) were thus

---

[312] Landau 1981.

[313] Gokalp 1987: 186.

[314] Mango 1999: 141.

[315] The declaration of Anatolia as the Turk's homeland, however, was building on a historically developed sense of Anatolian patriotism. When the nomadic Turkish clans fought their way into Anatolia for the first time in the 11th Century, this patriotic sentiment was already there, as the difference of Byzantium from the Latin Christian world, regarding religion (Orthodox Christian), language, culture, government, etc. Turkish clans had been superficially converted to Islam, while preserving their Central Asian polytheist traditions. As they advanced in Anatolia, they began to adapt to a series of non-muslim mores and traditions of the Armenian, Kurdish and Greek inhabitants. The Turks' transition from warrior/nomadic clans to settled peasants took many centuries during which they learned settled life and agriculture from local non-muslim peoples. This process was further marked by mixed marriages and a consequent cultural, linguistic and even racial transformation. The Ottoman State, which was founded through the destruction of the Byzantium, paradoxically inherited the Byzantian institutions, particularly the land regime based on an exceptional relationship with free peasantry (Keyder 1989: 15). The Ottoman Anatolia could therefore be described as a post-Byzantian Turko-Hellenistic unity, located at the cultural and spatial margins separating East from the West, Islam and Othodox Christianity from Catholic Christianity, which was, as a result 'contaminated' by each. Ottoman Turks, although considered themselves as part of the larger Islamic community, always preserved their Anatolian based cultural difference from the rest of the Muslim world. At the turn of the century, Anatolian patriotism gained a specifically Islamic/Turkish connotation through the conflict with non-muslim communities. In addition to the massacres and expulsion of the Armenian/Greek ethnicities from Anatolia, the 1915 battle of Gallipoli, during which Turkish/Muslim youths were killed in their thousands for the defense of the 'homeland', strengthened this Turkish/Muslim sentiment of Anatolian patriotism. It was against this background that Anatolia, renamed 'Anadolu', was declared the Turks' homeland by the nationalist leadership.

150

baptised as 'Turkey'.[316] On 4 January 1921, Mustafa Kemal declared for the first time to *Daily Express* that 'Turkey is the land of the Turks',[317] and on 21 January 1921, the new Constitution referred to the Ankara parliament as the 'Grand National Assembly of Turkey'. This was the first official use of the term 'Turkey'. On the definition of this homeland, 'Turkey', Kemal persistently deployed a realistic discourse of 'militarily defensible homeland',[318] which he discursively defended against the 'unrealistic' late-Ottoman dreams of salvation, including Ottomanism, pan-Turkism and pan-Islamism:

> I am neither a believer in a league of all the nations of Islam, nor even in a league of the Turkish peoples. Each of us here is entitled to hold his ideals, but the government must be stable with a fixed policy, grounded on the facts and with one view and one alone – to safeguard the life and independence of the nation within its natural frontiers. Neither sentiment nor illusion must influence our policy. Away with dreams and shadows! They have cost us dear in the past.[319]

Kemal's first restriction therefore regarded physical boundaries of the homeland, which included a prohibition of the Turkist dreams of liberating *Turan,* the pan-Turkist homeland of central Asia, the dreams of reclaiming the lost Ottoman lands, and the pan-Islamist ideal of liberating and uniting the Muslims of the Middle East and Asia.

Kemalism's relationship with these 'dreams and shadows' however did not only include a straightforward rupture but continuity at the same time, which is evident in various manifestations of the Kemalist discourse signifying its religious and Turkist origins.[320] The rupture, on the other hand, consisted of the overdetermination of these desires by the goal of furnishing the republican grounds of the construction and maintenance of a modern Turkish nation, whose homeland was Anatolia. At this construction site, the second Kemalist intervention to fix the signifier nation became necessary. Kemal seems to be implying a simple argument based on his notion of militarily defensible homeland, that is, if the name of

---

[316] Foreigners had long called the Ottoman country Turkey; Turks were beginning to follow the suit, by calling Anatolia 'Turkiye'.
[317] Quoted in Dilipak 1991: 86.
[318] In 1926, Kemal commented on the Wilson's Principles: 'Poor Wilson did not understand that a frontier is not defended with bayonets, force and honour cannot be secured by any other principle' (Mango 1999: 294).
[319] Armstrong 1932: 218-9.

151

the nation's homeland was 'Turkiya', the land of the Turks, then the name of the nation was Turkish. In the 1920s, Kemal's description of 'the Turk' excluded ethnic connotations, with an emphasis on 'becoming' as opposed to 'being' Turkish.[321] Nation, argues Kemal, is 'a political and social unity consisting of citizens who are connected to each other with a shared language, culture and a common ideal.'[322] Turkishness was therefore a 'common ideal' and an overriding identity, which provided a civic (citizenship), linguistic and cultural bond to connect various ethnicities of the Muslim population, leading to political and social unity.[323]

This positive definition of nation can be viewed as a statement of *Risorgimento* nationalism. According to Andrew Vincent (1998), *Risorgimento* nationalism, the source of inspiration of Wilson's Fourteen Points, represents the liberal form of nationalism, related to the notions of national sovereignty, on the one hand, and individual liberties on the other. The key background theme was the right of self-determination by nations. The major problem with this form of nationalism, however, was that once having promulgated the idea of the self-determining nation, it was difficult to know where to halt. As President Wilson realised, how could one prevent every moderately sized community perceiving itself as a nation, and thus a state? How was one to resolve conflicts between liberal nation states and more problematically secessionist movements within liberal nation states?[324] As a manifest

---

[320] Including the population exchange, the unpronounced building blocs of the 'nation' and the religious features of the Kemalist grammar, all of which refer to the Sunni/Muslim grounds of the 'nation', on the one side, and the ethnic and utopian elements within Kemalist nationalism, which I shall refer further in this chapter.
[321] Saying is a way of becoming. Hence reads Kemal's famous motto: 'How happy he is who says I am a Turk'. What this motto excludes is an ethnic definition of Turkishness, which is evident in two ethnocentric attempts to modify it. The Turkist guru Nihal Atsiz said, 'How happy he is who is created as a Turk'. Kemalist extremist Mahmut Esat Bozkurt similarly said, 'How happy he is who is able to say I am a Turk', implying that the regime would not allow every citizen to call themselves Turkish even if they wanted to do so. (See Yildiz 2001: 212.)
[322] Afet Inan 1969: 18. This book was first published in 1930 as a textbook of secondary education. It was prepared under Ataturk's close supervision and some chapters were written by Ataturk himself. The chapter on nations and nationalism is one of these (Yildiz 2001: 221).
[323] This attempted sublimation of Turkishness was rather a difficult task. Although Turkism had become the official ideology of the ruling CUP in 1912, it was mostly the discourse of a section of the late Ottoman élite, overridden by Islamic identity at the common sense level. The peasant population of Anatolia were not willing to call themselves Turks, while at the 'high culture' level the situation was even worse. The claim that Ottomans were Turks could only be found in European, Arabic and Persian discourses, as a degrading gesture towards the 'barbarian' nature of this state and culture. Similarly, in the conventional Ottoman discourse, the term 'Turk' signified a series of negative attributes, including barbarism and inferiority.
[324] Vincent 1998: 248-9.

solution to this problem, Kemal proposed the following regarding the fate of those non-Turkish-speaking Muslim populations of the 'militarily defensible homeland':

There are citizens and members of our nation inside the political and social entity of contemporary Turkish nation, to whom the propaganda of the ideas of being Kurdish, Cyrcassian and even Laz are attempted. But these misnomers, which were the products of the past ages of tyranny, failed to have any influence - apart from suffering - on any members of the nation except for a few brainless reactionaries used by the enemy. Because, the people of these communities like Turkish society in general share the same common past, history, morals and law.[325]

This statement is a peculiar example of Kemal's discourse, which makes the crucial role of his personal intervention in the formation of the new symbolic order plausible. Firstly, he calls various Muslim ethnicities of Anatolia to identify themselves with Turkishness, on the basis of a 'common past, history, morality and law'. Secondly, any resistance to this symbolic assimilation is related to the negativised Ottoman past ('ages of tyranny'), religious discourse ('brainless reactionaries') and the outside threat ('enemy agents').

The Kemalist intervention therefore includes an overt call for a simultaneous amnesia and recollection. The negative past, the object of amnesia, consists of ethnic histories and Ottoman history, which blurs and blocks the recollection of a positive common past, upon which the present has become possible and a common future to be constructed. This simultaneous forgetting and remembering, as Ernest Renan argued more than a century ago, is a universal nationalist principle:

The essence of a nation is that all the individuals that form the nation, in addition to having many things in common, must also forget many things. All French citizens are obliged to have already forgotten the Saint-Barthelemy and the 13th Century Midi massacres. There are not even ten families in France who can prove their descent from Frank origins.[326]

---

[325] Inan 1969: 23.
[326] Renan 1990.

153

Kemalist discourse implies that there are in fact two histories that the same group of people have lived through, one is their 'proper' history and the other is an alien group's history that they, the Turks, had been forcibly dragged in. This idea of two pasts is grounded upon Ziya Gökalp's thesis that Turks have a glorified pre-Islamic past and that under Ottoman rule, Turkish identity was oppressed by a cosmopolitan elite. What was Ottoman was in fact alien to the Turks' essence. Consequently, leaving the Ottoman past becomes an act of national liberation, since it is associated with emancipation of a nation from the culture of the oppressor, 'ages of tyranny', in its search for self-identity.[327] The Gokalpian connection is observable in Kemal's assertion in his citizen education textbook that 'the Turks were a great nation before adopting Islam'[328] and in one of the main assertions of the Turkish History Thesis:

> The history of the Turkish nation, as it has up until today been known, does not consist merely of Ottoman history. Turkish history is much older and the nation which disseminated culture to all nations is the Turkish nation.[329]

The Ottoman past of the new nation should therefore not merely be excluded but also redefined as a negativity that had prevented and continued to prevent the achievement of full Turkish identity. The Other of the Turkish identity was thus constituted, which simultaneously provided the symbolic order with a closure and legitimated the official war against Islamic discourses and practices at the level of popular culture, by presenting this crucial component of common identity as a remnant of the superseded past, a 'shadow' of the Other contaminating authentic Turkishness.[330]

Kemal's discourse therefore links his prohibition of ethnic particularism in favour of nationalist universalism with a grand project of negativisation of the Ottoman past as the Other of the republican Turkey. With this linkage, repression of the ethnic heterogeneity of 'Turkiya', repression of the Islamic identity[331] and identification with the West are united under the roof of the same prohibition.

---

[327] Gökalp 1958: 32.
[328] Tezcan 1989: 18.
[329] Inan & Karal 1946: 64.
[330] For two comprehensive analyses of this negativisation, See Bora 1997: 58 and Yoruk 1998.

154

I will engage further with this constitutive act of negativisation of the Ottoman past in its relation with another major question of the late Ottoman identity crisis, that is, Westernisation. Before advancing any further, let me outline first the nature of the Kemalist intervention as analysed so far in this section.

I have pursued in this section an argument that Kemalism's hegemonic success consists of the production and implementation of rigorous responses to the questions that Ottoman identity crisis had put forward. Firstly, Kemal successfully reoccupied the position of 'national hero' left out from Enver,[332] thus responding to the pressing question of the 'agent of salvation'. Once the saviour, the subject, was thus established, the content of the myth of salvation gradually emerged. Kemal mobilised Muslim notables for a dual purpose of the salvation of the Throne and Caliphate and of the nation, which for the mobilised nation was one and the same thing. Then the emphasis gradually moved towards national sovereignty and national struggle was increasingly presented in the leaders' discourse as the realisation of the 'will of the nation', while this national will was increasingly associated with Kemal's personality. What we observe at this stage is therefore the nation as the object of salvation and Kemal's personality inflating to include the representations of both the object and subject of salvation. With the conclusion of national struggle in victory, Kemal's personality cult gained the authority to represent itself as the incarnation of the moment of salvation. At this stage, another question of Ottoman identity crisis, the definition of nation was dealt with. Kemal began with providing a realistic definition of the national territory and battled against other descriptions by appealing to the nation to exorcise these rival myths of salvation. Kemal then named the nation in terms of Turkish identity, which he evidently imagined as overriding the ethnic diversity of the 'nation of Islam'. Kemalist social imaginary thus overdetermined the mythical space of salvation, but rather than developing a concrete definition of Turkishness, Kemalism provided a discursive framework for national identity. I will argue in the concluding section of this chapter that this flexibility, which is concerned with emphasising what the nation is not rather than what it is, explains as much the obsession

---

[331] see Chapter 1.
[332] This reoccupation of personality cult is evident in Yakup Kadri's writings above. Kemal's reoccupation is also obvious in the fact that on arrival in Ankara to launch the national assembly in April 1920, he was

with the security that Kemalist Turkey inherited from the disintegration of the Empire as Kemalism's success in surviving as Turkey's discursive horizon through decades. Kemalism's responses to the questions of the Ottoman identity crisis therefore led to a clear definition of the republican territory both physical and discursive. The discursive definition consisted of nation with its present and future standing against its 'outside' and the past. Being Turkish means the exclusion of what remains outside the physical borders of Turkey. It means the exclusion of the dreams of imperial salvation along with the irredentist ideals of Turan and the salvation of Muslim nations. Being Turkish further requires the exclusion of ethnic particularism. Finally all these 'others' of identity are presented as various incarnations of the 'shadows of the ages of tyranny'. Therefore, being Turkish means above all the exclusion of the Ottoman past, that is, the metaphor by which all the excluded are articulated.

II. Nationalisation via Westernisation

The problem of modernisation, perceived as the incorporation of the 'West' and presented as 'civilisation', had been one of the faultlines around which the late Ottoman Empire had been shaken from its foundations, experienced a discursive and physical split and finally collapsed. Kemalism did not only inherit this problem but was formed around a specific form of response to the questions stemming from the problem of westernisation to be shaped around technique/culture and culture/civilisation dichotomies. I will argue that this response consisted of a tense equilibrium between the goals of westernisation and nationalisation. I will begin with recalling the dislocatory effects of the necessity and the ideal of westernisation (civilisation) for the Ottoman order, and then consider the emergence of Kemalist response from within the critiques of Ottoman westernisation. I will demonstrate how Kemalism emerged as an attempt of incorporating the discourse of 'civilisation' with nationalism, following on Ziya Gokalp's theoretical tracks, which had situated the problem of civilisation and culture within the context of universalism and particularism. I will conclude this section by arguing that Kemalism overcome the tensions between nationalism

---

welcomed by the military band playing a tune made for Enver; the verse had been modified to replace Enver Pasha to 'Kemal Pasha.'

and civilisation through a temporal exclusion. The Kemalist negativisation of the Ottoman past reconstructed the dichotomies of 'civilisation/Orient' and 'present and future/past' in terms of a 'nation/alien' dichotomy. The peculiarity of Kemalism lies in its rigorous negativisation of the Ottoman past by relating this to a nationalist grandnarrative of alienation and contamination by foreign influences of a 'national essence', which enabled it to present the Kemalist *coupure epistemologique* as an act of national emancipation.

II.1. 'Unhappy Recognition'

I have argued in chapter I that the Ottoman modernisation, which emerged as a task following the changing terms of encounter with the West, produced immediately a reformist/conservative split to be deepened by the failure of recognition by the West. This cleavage developed further through reform attempts to lead the late Ottoman social order to acquire the features of a dislocated structure in a state of organic crisis accompanied by an identity crisis. The West therefore entered in the late Ottoman discursive field as a faultline to radically shake and split, that is, to dislocate the Ottoman social order.

The infamous symptom of a century of humiliation in the encounter with the West is Bihruz Bey, the anti-hero of one of the renowned post-Tanzimat novels: *Araba Sevdasi* by Recaizade Ekrem.[333] Bihruz Bey is not alienated from his roots; he is totally ignorant about his roots from the beginning as a result of his inadequacies (the lyrics that he cites to seduce a blond are from a poem admiring a brunette). Bihruz Bey tries to quilt over his lack of roots by imitating the Western customs; but the drama that he attempts to stage ends up as nothing better than a farce. Bihruz's sole achievement is to move away from conventional mores and customs, which he calls 'Barbarian'. However, there is no goal that this distancing leads him to; the place in which Bihruz ends up is not the West but a void.

Bihruz or the bruises inflicted by Bihruz on the Ottoman pride is present in the New Ottomans', particularly Namik Kemal's, discourse as the subject of hatred, in the form of

---

[333] For a thorough analysis of the critique of the pro-western character in Tanzimat novel see Serif Mardin, 'Tanzimattan sonra asiri Batililasma', in Mardin 1991: 21-79.

'decedent Tanzimat Pashas'. The source of 'moral humiliation' and 'inferiority feeling' that Tekin Alp and Atay mention (see, below) is not the popular embarrassment from Bihruz's degrading look on people and traditions, but the popular shame and the bruises that the Bihruz symptom inflicted on the collective pride. The masochistic elites of Tanzimat granted the west, the traditional other of the Ottomans, the status of the sadistic Big Other, whose excessive desires could never be satisfied.[334] For the Islamists, Bihruz Bey was the inevitable consequence of blind admiration towards Christianity and the West, a symptom of Tanzimat's failure to distinguish between technical and cultural aspects of western civilisation.[335] The pro-Westernisation ideologue, Dr. Abdullah Cevdet, rigorously criticised the technique/culture duality: 'If you speak of civilisation, there is just one, and that is in the west. One is either in it or out of it; there is no way in between. Civilisation must be imported with both its roses and its thorns.'[336] There was, on the other hand, a third way, a different

---

[334] Nationalists of the left and right alike have evoked a similar accusation of 'masochistic surrender' against the supporters of Turkey's inclusion in the European Union. In this discourse, the EU's Copenhagen Criteria is the *jouissance* of the Other, and the members of pro-EU lobby are those masochists who surrender themselves to these perversions of the sadistic Other. An example of this line of discourse with historical analogies is an article by a contemporary newspaper columnist specialising in popular history:
I have written several times before, 'the European Union will not admit us in, this business will be deterred again, do not be carried away with pipe dreams', and I unfortunately was right. The Europeans delayed the business to 2004 in Copenhagen and advised us to continue with the reform process.
The Copenhagen Criteria, that is, those rules that Europe impose upon us in order for us to become European are based on four demands: the stabilisation of the state institutions to guarantee democracy, the achievement of the supremacy of law not only on the paper but in practice too, the prioritisation of human rights and the protection of the minorities.
    (...)
The Copenhagen criteria were in fact 1839 Istanbul criteria, that is, the criteria that we have been asked to implement for 163 years since the declaration of Tanzimat, and for some reason we have always failed, and even when we tried, we have always been told that it was not enough.
(...)
We took the first official step with the Tanzimat declaration on 3 November 1839. We implemented on paper the criteria put forward by Europe. But the response was merely the assignment of the title of "sick man" (...)
Then the Crimean war broke out. We allied ourselves with Europe against Russia and won. We were sure that we would be Europeans. The peace conference met in February 1856 in Paris. We were expecting an admission but we were asked to do more. (...)
We implemented the conditions dictated by Europe on 18 February 1856 with the declaration of a new Reform package. This package proved to be useful for a few months. We were admitted in the European Concert, the EU of the time, and became officially European on 30 March 1856. However, we were drawn in a series of wars with European countries in a short time, in which we lost both our lands and our European identity.
Another episode of anxiety of becoming European, we experienced on 23 December 1876. (...) Turkey declared itself a Constitutional Monarchy on that day when European representatives met in Istanbul with Ottoman counterparts. However, the delegates once again raised the same list of demands. (...)
The result of all these variants of our ambitions to become European was always the same: loosing territory" (Bardakci, M. *Hürriyet*, December 2003).
[335] See Chapter I.
[336] Abdullah Cevdet's statement of 1913 is quoted in Lewis 1968: 236.

158

line of criticism of Tanzimat modernisation by the nationalist thinkers, who interpreted Bihruz Bey as a symptom of westernisation without a sense of nationhood.[337] Kemalism took up both Cevdet's full-westernisation approach and the nationalist argument on board. Tanzimat failed because it was unable to impose an uncompromising westernisation program[338] and because the Tanzimat elites lacked a nationalist stance. Modern Turkish identity was consequently born at this critical juncture of civilisation/nationalisation. So, with Serif Mardin (1991: 79), 'we can claim that Bihruz Bey syndrome has totally positive aspects, too: Turkey won her national independence on the basis of it'. Mardin's assertion will become more comprehensible with an insight of nationalism as a 'derivative discourse' as formulated by Chatterjee.

II.2. Civilisation/Nationalisation

Partha Chatterjee suggests that the logic of Orientalism also applies to nationalist thought in the Third World. His study demonstrates that Third World nationalism is a 'derivative discourse' that acts upon the basis of the categories produced by Orientalism. Underlying this point is Chatterjee's following observation:

Nationalist thought, in agreeing to become 'modern', accepts the claim to universality of this 'modern framework of knowledge'. Yet it also asserts the autonomous identity of a national culture. It thus simultaneously rejects and accepts the dominance, both epistemic and moral, of an alien culture.[339]

The Turkist discourse of Ziya Gökalp (1876-1924) was situated at the edge of this simultaneous rejection and acceptance to constitute the main theoretical framework of the republican 'will to civilisation' and nationalism. In order to inoculate nationalism into the 'civilisation' project, Gökalp, an orthodox disciple of Emile Durkheim, asserted a distinction between cultural unities based on common sentiments and modern civilisation based on

---

[337] Said Halim Pasha, 'Our Crises', quoted in Alkan 2002: 462-4 (See also Chapter 1).

[338] Karaosmanoglu (1956) argues that Ataturk was distinguished from the Tanzimat elites in his uncompromising westernist 'fundamentalism'.

[339] Chatterjee 1986: 11.

reason and positive sciences.[340] The distinction between culture (*hars*) and civilisation (*mediniyyet*) corresponds to the difference between the particular and the universal. In Gökalp's image, there is a unified western civilisation that supersedes the particular autonomous spheres of national cultures of say, Englishness, Frenchness, Germanness, etc.[341] The formation of Turkish identity should therefore go hand in hand with the task to civilise, which meant the integration of Turkishness as an autonomous cultural sphere into the universal western civilisation as one of the particular components of it.

Gökalp asserts two theses in order to present westernisation as a nationalist necessity. The first thesis, that we have already seen above, is that what is Ottoman is in fact alien to the Turks' essence, and therefore leaving the Ottoman past is an act of national emancipation from the culture of the oppressor, in its search for self-identity.[342] The second thesis builds on Abdullah Cevdet's above assertion that there is in essence only one civilisation and it is what we call western civilisation. According to Gökalp's historical narrative, there has never been in history an eastern civilisation and what we call eastern civilisation is somehow a 'degenerated' form or a 'primordial' version of western civilisation:

> Mediterranean civilisation was established in Antiquity through the efforts of Egyptian, Assyrian, Phoenician, etc. people. This civilisation, after being matured in ancient Greece, passed to the Romans, who, after inoculating this civilisation to hundreds of nations, split into the two independent states of Eastern Rome and Western Rome. This political split was, in effect, the split of the Mediterranean civilisation into eastern and western civilisations. Europeans inherited and improved the Western Roman civilisation, while the Muslim Arabs adopted not only the political institutions but the whole civilisation of the Eastern Rome. Eastern Roman civilisation thus acquired the name Eastern Civilisation after being adopted by Muslims.[343]

Implicit to this argument is not only the thesis that there is only one essential civilisation but also that there is an ontological difference between the east and west, which lies in the absence or presence of an essence capable of creating civilisations - an essence which Hegel

---

[340] Gökalp 1976: 28-9.
[341] Gökalp 1958: 25.
[342] Gökalp 1958: 32.
[343] Gökalp 1958: 50-1.

called 'Spirit'. For Gökalp, as for all Orientalist thinkers from Montesquieu to Max Weber, this essential difference is evident in the absence of 'dynamism' in the east:

Eastern nations were not able to develop their civilisation any further than its level in the Medieval Ages, because, according to the law of stagnation, unless an agent comes to change it, everything remains as it is.[344]

This 'agent', which he is careful to place outside the eastern society, is for Gökalp the graduates of the new imperial schools of engineering, medicine and administration, since they received exclusively western style education. Gökalp asserts that these western institutions were the examples according to which the whole society should be institutionalised by the agents of change, while abolishing all the eastern institutions which Gökalp calls 'the ghosts of the Medieval Age'.[345]

Kemalist discourse inherited both of these theses[346] in its attempt to materialise the Gökalpian goal of creating a Turkish nation whose ideal was to 'civilise'. Consequently, an important dimension of the Kemalist reforms consisted of the struggle of recognition by the West as one of them, as European, which the Kemalists believed would require the repression of the inherent Orient of Turkishness:

We will become civilised. We will march forward. Civilisation is a fearful fire which consumes those who ignore it (...) Don't be afraid. Change is essential, so much so that, if need be, we are prepared to sacrifice lives for its sake.[347]

Westernism, or the Kemalist will to civilisation, is in a nutshell 'desiring the desire in the Other' which can be observed from Mustafa Kemal's statement on the 'hat revolution':

We considered ourselves separate from the civilised world with a different symbol on our head. We wore the hat today. Many foreigners appreciate this. (...) Women should also wear hats. There is no other way open to us. Here is an example for you (pointing a woman): With this head, a civilised woman cannot go to Europe and mix with the community there.[348]

---

[344] Gökalp 1958: 55.
[345] Gökalp 1958: 57-60.
[346] Many objection can be raised against this continuity. Yildiz 119.
[347] Mustafa Kemal's 1925 address to people of Kastamonu, in Mango 1999: 434
[348] 'A speech in Bursa Turkish Hearth', 23 January 1925, Atatürk 1989: 229.

Following the performance of Selim Sırrı (Tarcan) of an authentic folk dance, which he had modernised in western forms, Mustafa Kemal said:

> Ladies and Gentlemen: Selim Sırrı Bey when performing the 'zeybek' dance, gave it a civilised form. (…) We can now say to the Europeans: 'we, too, have a perfect dance'.[349]

The Kemalist imaginary therefore evidently accepts both epistemic and moral superiority of the European culture and proposes a Tanzimat-like imitation. The replacement of the Arabic script with Latin letters, the abolition of Caliphate and Sharia, a shift from Muslim to the Christian calendar, the adoption of Swiss and Italian codes for civil and criminal law and the legal emancipation of women can be quoted among the Kemalist 'revolutions' to the effect of westernisation perceived as 'repetition and imitation'.

However, to see the Kemalist westernisation as a linear continuation of Tanzimat westernisation is a simplification, that political Islamist discourse, for instance, very often fall into. For Tekin Alp, Atatürk 'was a sacred hero, who assumed the mission of liberating his nation and country (…) from the *moral humiliation* that they had been subjected to for centuries'.[350] Kemalist chronologist Falih Rifki Atay also pointed out the same motivation:

> Although with some compulsion, the Turks had to be liberated from the *incurable feeling of inferiority*, that is, the acceptance that they lacked a history of civilisation, and a language of science and literature. In fact, they had to replace this inferiority feeling with *a feeling of superiority* that they were one of the nations, who had served civilisation and sciences.[351]

The republican goal of 'rising to the level of contemporary civilisations' is above all a nationalist goal, a manifestation of an attempt to cope with the collective humiliation and 'feeling of inferiority' that the elites and the nation experienced through the Ottoman disintegration, as a result of the imitation of the west. It is a manifest will to supersede the nation's constitutional trauma - the moment of *Verwerfung*, that bruised the national pride during the event of birth, that is, the nation's birth trauma - by masking the lack that this trauma revealed. Consequently, the move to westernise was accompanied by a strong nationalist discourse, taking on board the nationalist criticism of Tanzimat and deriving

---

[349] 'A speech in Izmir Girls School', 13 October 1925, Atatürk 1989: 240
[350] Tekin Alp 1998: 27.
[351] Atay 1980: 468 - my italics.

162

further from Gokalp's first thesis to assert that westernisation was in fact an act of reclamation of a lost essence. The Latin alphabet was declared by Mustafa Kemal 'the Turkish letters'[352] and the adoption of the western outfit was presented as leaving a style of dressing which was 'neither national nor universal'[353]

Kemalism therefore rehabilitates the Ottoman rationale of reform, that is, to meet the European challenge with the European means, which includes the task of recognition as a European state, or in Kemal's words, securing the Turkish nation's 'rightful place' among the 'civilised nations'. Kemalisation of the social therefore consisted of an effort of nationalisation via westernisation:

> In the process of revolutions, we could, for the first time, realise our Turkishness. (…) Within the world of Western civilisation, the Turk would become Turk just as the Italian being Italian and the German being German.[354]

The Kemalist goal designed for modern Turkey was therefore to catch up with the West and assume her 'rightful place' as a modern civilised state and society. If Islam impeded this process, then Islam itself would be tamed and the role of Islam as a crucial component of Turkishness repressed. As Mardin (1981: 208-9) observes, the loss of Arab provinces in the World War I ('Arabs' betrayal') made it possible for the nationalist discourse to jettison the Turks/Arabs/Islam linkage. As Atay put it bluntly:

> Westernisation meant at the same time Turkification, through emancipation from Arabisation.[355]

The repression of the 'Orient inside' was accompanied by a discourse of *ancien regime et revolution* to be presented with a Gokalpian detour (above) as an act of emancipation and national liberation. The presentation of westernisation as the precondition of nationalisation also required the definition of the outside of this project. The definition of this outside corresponded to the disavowal of the Ottoman past and its reconstruction as 'dark ages' ('Arabisation') leading to the negativisation of the past as the Other of republican Turkish

---

[352] 'Citizens, these notes of mine have been written by real and proper Turkish words in Turkish script. The harmony and richness of our language will show itself with the new Turkish letters.' ('A Speech on the Writing Revolution', 9/10 August 1928, in Ataturk 1989: 272.)
[353] 'Can a nation be without a national outfit? (..) Our nation deserves a civilised and international style of dressing and we will adapt this.' ('A Speech in Inebolu', 29 August 1925, in Ataturk 1989: 220.)
[354] Atay 1980: 446.

identity. Ottoman and Islam were of the past while the nation and the West belonged to the present and future. Out of the desire of identification with the West, Kemalism managed to construct itself retrospectively as a revolutionary discourse through the operation of a temporal exclusion.

III. The 'Kemalist Knot': (Re)birth of a Nation

The Kemalist operation, in addition to exclusion and demarcation, included practices of articulation aiming to constitute and hold together the republican symbolic order. One of these practices consisted of the Kemalist attempts to reoccupy the divine space left out from the exclusion of the Islamic discourse from the republican universe, which I will consider in the first subsection below. This was in effect an attempt to reproduce the Ottoman regime of truth with its Islamic episteme in modern conditions as a republican regime of truth with a Kemalist episteme. I will then inquire into the nature of Kemal's intervention as the 'Father-Turk' in the process of formation of the republican discursive universe. I will argue that the significance of Kemal's name is analogous to the paternal function in the child's introduction into the symbolic order. I will then consider the problems of identity that Kemalism produced or reproduced while trying to develop adequate responses to the Ottoman identity crisis. These problems, in addition to the reproduction of the divine space through reoccupation, consist of the overemphasised patriarchal function in the constitution and maintenance of modern Turkish identity, leading to the maintenance of state/society division inherited from Ottoman society, and the constant reproduction of Turkish neurosis, due to the impossibility of bridging the cleavage between the modern and traditional identities.

III.1. Divinisation of the National Universe: Our Oath

Every child who grow up in Republic of Turkey had to recite aloud every morning for five years in primary school the following text ('Our Oath') facing a portrait of Atatürk, the Father-Turk:
> I am a Turk, I am truthful, I am hardworking, My law: to protect the younger, to respect my elderly, and to love my country and nation more than my own self. My

---

[355] Atay 1980: 446.

ideal is to ascend and progress. I devote my existence to the Turkish existence. Hey Sublime Ataturk, who provided us with our present time: I hereby swear that I will continue to walk uninterruptedly in the path you opened up, towards the ideal you formed and the aim you showed. How happy he is who says I am a Turk! This text of "morning prayers" is a direct address to the children's psyche, aiming to write a set of unconscious references over a set of unconscious values based on religion.[356]

Benedict Anderson (1991: 5) argues that the term 'nation', rather than 'liberalism' or 'fascism', has to be thought in line with 'kinship' and 'religion'. Similarly, Carlton J. Hayes asserted that nationalism was the modern expression of an essentially universal religious sentiment. Nationalism emerged in many cases as a secular religion, which secularised the divine universe while sublimating the profane national space to the status of divinity. The attempts to fill the discursive void that was left over from the expulsion of Islamic discourses from the symbolic order of modern Turkey represent a typical example, which can be made further intelligible with reference to Hans Blumenberg's concept of 'reoccupations'. Blumenberg means by this concept the process by which particular notions, associated with the advent of a new vision and new problems, have the function of replacing ancient notions that had been formed on the ground of a different set of issues. The ancient notions impose their demands on the new ones and inevitably deform them.[357] According to Blumenberg, the metanarratives of 'philosophy of history', 'progress' and emancipation' are the products of this necessary process of 'reoccupation'.[358] They rephrase the narratives of history that belonged to the Christian theology beginning with a 'primal sin' and are forecasted to end with 'salvation' in profane terms. In other words, the terms of discourse have changed but the

---

[356] Religious values have been rarely imposed in Turkish and consequently the religious references of daily life in Turkey are to a large extent incomprehensible and therefore unconscious. An ordinary child in Turkey is brought up by registering many religious phrases in Arabic from their parents, consisting of simple citations from Koran, having absolutely no idea of what they may mean in Turkish. These phrases are usually for uttering in certain situations: 'selamunaleykum' when meeting someone, 'bismillahirrahmanirrahim' when starting to do something, 'suphanallah' when facing an unexpected situation, 'estagfurullah' when misunderstood, etc. There are many longer phrases with similar function. A catalogue of Arabic verses from Koran, particularly those cited during the prayers, are also memorised, without comprehension, by the child. With these incomprehensible signifiers in a foreign language, an unconscious referential order enters into the child's symbolic universe. Kemalist-secular indoctrination, which begins at the age of 7 targets precisely this order of unconscious references in an attempt to redesign it with Kemalist mythology.

[357] Laclau 1990: 74.

[358] Blumenberg 1987.

discursive formation remained the same with its teleological grammar. Turkish transition from a semi-theological cosmopolitan society to a republican nation is an exemplary experience. The 'introduction' to *Turkey in Photographs*, published in 1936 by the state's general directory of publications outlines this theological transition:

Kemalism is the ideological religion of the Republic of Turkey. This religion's perception of the world is European, but its basis is Turkish.

Religion/Kemalism/Nationalism gained a metonymic character in the early republican discourse with Mustafa Kemal's personal encouragement. Samsun deputy Ruseni Barkur wrote a book titled *Din Yok Milliyet Var (There is no Religion but Nation)* in 1926, which was scanned by Mustafa Kemal prior to publication. 'Our holy book is (...) our nationalism', writes Barkur and concludes with a rhetorical question: 'Is there a more honourable religion than being Turkish?' Kemal's notes in the margins read 'Well done; congratulations!' Similarly, in 1937, Ordu deputy Muhittin Baha declared the RPP's six arrows 'the Holy Book of the Turks'.[359] As Gellner observes, Kemalism was an attempt to substitute religion with nationalism, which came very close to producing a secular religion:

The spirit in which Kemalism was formulated and upheld was, at any rate in the first generation, a kind of perpetuation of High Islam. The spirit was projected onto a new doctrine. The content was new but the form and spirit were not.[360]

The replacement of religion with nationalism primarily meant the replacement of religious institutions with institutions of modern education for the dissemination of rationalism and positive sciences along with nationalist ideology. In 1923, Mustafa Kemal addressed a meeting of teachers in Samsun:

For everything in the world – for civilisation, for life, for success – the truest guide *(mursid)* in the world is knowledge *(ilim)* and science. To seek a guide other than knowledge and science is headlessness, ignorance and aberration.[361]

The word for knowledge *ilim*, like *scientia* in medieval Europe is originally the signifier of theological knowledge, while the word for guide, *mursid*, connoted the sheikh of a muslim brotherhood. What was expected from the 'army of teachers' was to operate as the dervishes of the nationalist/secularist/western culture, which involved the dissemination of the

---

[359] TBMM Zabit Ceridesi, Devre V, c. 16, 1937, p. 69.
[360] Gellner 1994: 86.
[361] Mango 1999: 412.

166

'ideological religion of the republic' through a battle against the popular Islamic beliefs and institutions. In these circumstances, Kemalist nationalism replaced the Islamic dogma for Turkish intelligentsia.[362]

Kemalism tried on the one hand to secularise and nationalise the divine universe that it inherited from the Ottoman past and on the other it was faced with the necessity of divinisation of the national universe. As Kemal himself put it, the break with the old order, beliefs and symbols 'emptied the batteries of our spiritual potentials'.[363] The main theme of the divine fantasy that emerged at this juncture is the 'Divine Other' symbolised in the body, image and gaze of Atatürk. Mustafa Kemal's revolution was accompanied by a discourse of building the leader's personality cult. In the wake of the 'national struggle', he was referred popularly as *Gazi* or *Halaskar Gazi* (the Saviour Warrior). Kemal, however, wanted to build further upon these mythical grounds. With the introduction of the surnames in 1934, he chose the surname *Atatürk* (the father of the Turks) for himself. In 1926, erecting Kemal's *übermensch* size statues commenced in provincial centres around the country, beginning with three major cities, Ankara, Istanbul and Izmir. Kemal was literally building his own myth, which he hoped to 'reoccupy' the emptied out space of divinity in the national imagery.

What this divine Other, with its materialisation in an extensive production of monuments, statues, busts and portraits, attempts to reoccupy becomes clear with an arbitrary shuffle through primary school textbooks or any 'Atatürk Poems Anthology'. The divine Other is presented in children's poetry as 'the equivalent of Sublime God' or 'the God of Turkishness' (Edip Ayel). He inspires another poet to utter the line, 'You will see that Your idol is on my heart' (F. N. Çamlıbel), leading to a divine fantasy based on an alternative national cosmology: 'Leave the Kaabe to the Arab, Çankaya is enough for us' (K. Kamu).[364]

---

[362] It was against this background that Halide Edip Adivar (1963:159-161) named the republican intelligentsia *Ulema-i Rusum* (official clergy), rather than *münevver*, the usual term for the intellectual, pointing out the continuity in the pattern of orthodox loyalty to political authority and ideology.

[363] Bozdag 1974.

[364] Çankaya is where Atatürk's residence was located. For the quotes from Ayel, Çamlıbel and Kamu's poetry and for other striking products of this series of sublimations see Aslan, 1999: 59-67.

If the existence of psyche is conditional upon the subsequent acts of repression and sublimation, that is, the co-existence of taboo and totem,[365] then the repression of religious identity (*Sharia*) and the subsequent attempt to replace it with the Ataturk cult and Kemalist dogma can be understood as an attempt to design a specifically republican psyche. The primary school ritual of 'our oath' marks this psychic intersection of repression and sublimation. The Big Other attempts to erase the repressed traditional values on the surface of the new generations' unconscious by writing over them a set of secular nationalist values. And the republican generations turn their faces every morning while reciting 'Our Oath' to the Big Other, that is, Atatürk, whose desire that they are uttering with this recital; because 'the unconscious is the discourse of the Other'.

The notion of 'reoccupation' and the necessity of secularisation of the divine universe through the divinisation of the national horizon explain the function of Ataturk's personality cult in republican Turkey. I have argued in Chapter 1 that the transition from Empire to Republic consists of a transition from one regime of truth to another accompanied by a transition from the Islamic episteme to a Kemalist one. Revisiting 'Our Oath' the republican regime of truth can be identified with the following: Turkishness, hardworking, law-obeidence, patriotism, ascendance and progress. The sole reference that guarantees the truthfulness of this regime appears to be 'sublime Ataturk', with his nationalist ideals and goals. I will argue that it is within this divine space that the Republican Regime of Truth with its Kemalist episteme replaced the Ottoman Regime of Truth with its Islamic episteme.

However, pointing out reoccupation and the accompanying religious grammar is only one way of understanding the crucial place that the cult of Ataturk maintains in modern Turkish

---

[365] The effects that the Atatürk myth was expected to produce were not limited to the reoccupation of the void that emerged from the secularisation of society. Nor can the totalitarian effect of the Orwellian Big Brother who monitors everything can exhaustively explain this expected effect. In order to understand an additional effect of the representations of Atatürk, the productive role of the gap between the way I see myself and the point from which I am being observed to appear likeable to myself in the identification process needs to be taken into account. In this context, the relationship between the nation and Atatürk could be defined as a call for imaginary identification on behalf of a certain gaze in the Other. It should also be noted that the trait of identification can also be a certain failure, weakness or guilt in the other, 'so that by pointing out the failure we can unwittingly reinforce the identification' (Zizek 1989: 106). Ataturk's appeal to the new generations certainly includes a call for identification with the Kemalism's failure in peeling off the alienating shell over the Anatolian population to expose the kernel of 'national character' (see Chapter 4).

identity. As I have argued, the Ataturk cult also needs to be seen as an 'empty signifier' representing the lacking fullness of 'nation' along with the promises of salvation, security and territory of the 'nation', that is, 'the moment of universality'. I will argue below that this empty signifier was linked to a constitutive moment of modern Turkish symbolic order, through a series of literally paternal interventions, which introduced a cut in the 'republican real'.[366] This implies that the-name-of-Ataturk has been the nodal point stitching the links of a peculiar republican reality with its specific subject, that is, modern Turkish identity. In fact, 'Our Oath' is an example of the incarnation of a lacking moment of universality as represented by the 'empty signifier' Ataturk, which brings together the idealised republican values in its recital aloud by "Ataturk's children".

After thus presenting the 'Kemalist Knot', I will investigate the weakest links of this knot where modern Turkish identity tends to unfold. I will identify three such points, each of which has largely been inherited from the *ancien regime* but have also been persistently reproduced by the new regime of truth's Kemalist episteme. (1) The reproduction of the religious mind-set and grammar, which has been dealt with above. (2) The overemphasis on the pedagogical and patriarchal relationship between Ataturk and 'his' nation. (3) The authoritarian suppression of any returns of the repressed oriental/Islamic identity, which has simultaneously quilted and reproduced and even deepened cleavages between the conscious core and 'unconscious' periphery. Therefore, Kemalism has to a large extent meant the sustainable reproduction of the split nature of Turkish identity.

III.2. The-Name-of-Ataturk

The Kemalist intervention is constitutive of the modern Turkish symbolic order and is analogous to Lacan's description of 'primal repression', which constitutes all meaning through the intervention of paternal metaphor. The Name-of-the-Father contains a prohibition (of the child's imaginary symbiotic relationship with the mother – *Non du Pere*) which is simultaneously productive, since it facilitates the child's entry into the symbolic

---

[366] See Chapter 2.

order, that is, language and community (*Nom du Pere*).[367] There is a further reason that encourage this analogy, that is, the fact that in 1934, Mustafa Kemal assumed the surname Ataturk, which literally means 'the father of the Turks'. Kemal certainly insinuated with this surname his constitutive paternal function for modern Turkish identity. As Yegen (1999: 215) demonstrates, the paternal structure is also evident in the state discourse's association of the terms that belong to paternal family discourse, including 'family', 'hearth', 'house', 'room', with terms that belong to the nationalist discourse such as 'nation', 'people' and 'Turk'. The Kemalist introduction of the paternal metaphor also built itself on Gokalp's perception of Turkish nation as children to be instructed:

> The Ottoman nation took this ill literature as its model because it was an old society. The Turkish nation which emerged from the Ottoman ruins very healthily is on the other hand young, in fact at a child's age.[368]

The surname Ataturk declares the constitution by the head of the family (nation) of modern Turkey's symbolic order. The-Name-of-Ata facilitates the subject positions of modern Turkish identity in their relation to Ataturk himself. It is constitutive, productive and, at the same time, prohibitive. The-Name-of-Ata decides 'in the last instance' what can and what cannot be spoken.

The *Non du Pere*, Ataturk's prohibition, consists of firstly the denial of the 'misnomers', the signifiers of the existence of other national identities within the Turkish symbolic order; and secondly the repression of the Ottoman past and Islamic identity, to be excluded from the articulations of 'common past, history and morality'. The *Nom du Pere*, on the other hand, the 'common law' that Ataturk calls the 'nation' to identify with, that is, modern Turkish symbolic order, imagined in terms of 'civilisation', that is, modernisation and secularisation, and nationalisation. Ataturk's law provides a discursive territory grounded upon the promises of national sovereignty, citizenship, universal suffrage, women's rights, liquidation of traditional restrictions along with pre-modern forms of exploitation, etc. These positive terms, however, are subject to delay, due to outside threats; in fact, these threats, together

---

[367] Fink 1997: 81.
[368] Gokalp quoted by Kocak 2001: 378.

170

with the-Name-of-the-Father, paradoxically serves to facilitate the definition of the Turkish discursive territory within certain boundaries, outside which 'enemies' are located.

The Kemalist discourse, or the voice of Ataturk, is therefore the *point de capiton* of modern Turkish identity. Ataturk's name (and 'Ataturk's No!') is what determines the reality of modern Turkish identity, by tying specific meanings to the signifiers of Turkish symbolic order, hence creating a foundational, unshakeable meaning.[369] It is through this stitch that the modern Turkish subject assimilates the structure of language, without which everything would come undone.

The Kemalist hegemonisation of the republican discursive horizon consisted of the inflation of the cult of Ataturk as an 'empty signifier' to symbolise the lacking national objectivity and then intervene in the field of the social reality to constitute this 'national objectivity'. This intervention contained in itself a linguistic articulation that primarily defined the geographic, political, historical and ideological boundaries of this imagined objectivity, and the psychological design of a shared unconscious through a call to the 'nation' for identification with a modern/nationalist repression. The pedagogical/paternal emphasis in state/society relations have been further linked to this generalised neurosis with certain defects, where the Kemalist knot has had to struggle hard to keep uptight.

III.3. Problems of Kemalist Pedagogy

The result of the overemphasis on the paternal function in the constitution of the subject, was a kind of fetishism regarding the nation's relationship with the 'father' or the state. Gunduz Vassaf (1984: 1-5) presents this problem as follows:

> We observe that the pre-republican history was erased from collective consciousness and the republican generations were brought up like a new born child with no history. (…) A generation, which identified with the West, adopted Western models and behaviours, and derived all their self-confidence against the experience of fundamental change from Ataturk, to whom they were bonded like a father.

---

[369] Fink 1997: 93-4.

This relationship built itself on an already existing perception of state/society (askeriye/reaya) or centre/periphery division[370] and prevailed through republican history. The long-term dual nature of republican power split between a military-bureaucratic elite, 'the guardians of the republic' on the one side, and elected politicians on the other, as observed in the constitutional status of National Security Council (NSC)[371] as an 'advisory body', is arguably a consequence of this patriarchal/pedagogic structure. What is more significant is that this modality remains to be a legitimate one for the majority of the Turks.[372] Stephen Kinzer reports asking a secular man, who voted the pro-Islamist RP, what if RP attacked secular lifestyle. The man replies: 'Don't worry, if they try to do anything like that, the army will throw them out'.

> There wasn't any real risk, they believed, because the military would prevent things from going bad. (…) This is a reassuring system because it guarantees that if voters make a mistake, generals will step in and set things right. But it also encourages Turkish voters to remain permanently immature, like children.[373]

The overemphasised paternal function does not only guarantee the endurance of Kemalist fetishism but secures political immaturity of a nation, who identify itself with Kemal's gaze overseeing the country, if not as a house or barracks anymore, as a large classroom in which the whole nation is subject to permanent tutelage and correction by the republican guardians.[374]

III.4. The Split Reproduced

'We are all sons and daughters of an identity cirisis'

---

[370] Ataturk said the following against the prospects of a plebiscite: 'To hold any kind of a referendum, which would hinder our will to rise to the level of contemporary civilisation will not be only ignorance but also treason. Before teaching literacy to the 80 per cent of its people, revolutions cannot be carried out in a country by plebiscites'. (Kocaturk 1984: 76-7.)

[371] The NSC is a constitutional body composed of the President, Prime Minister, certain cabinet ministers, Chief of Staff and the commanders of the armed forces, which meets monthly to discuss internal and external security threats and takes 'advisory' domestic and foreign policy decisions which are in effect compulsory to pursue for the elected governments.

[372] A 1999 questionnaire revealed that the most trusted institution was the military.

[373] Kinzer 2001: 67.

[374] The motto of the 'citizenship week' in military service reads: 'The best citizen is the one who fulfils his duty'.

172

Tom Nairn observes that the desire of 'repetition and imitation' (of the English/British model) is bound to failure in all nationalisms as a consequence of the 'law of uneven and combined development':

> Actual repetition and imitation are scarcely ever possible, whether politically, economically, socially or technologically, because the universe is already too much altered by the first cause one is copying.[376]

In other words, as the nationalist subject begins to radically transform his social order in accordance with a model, this universal model, the Big Other itself, is already something else. This ultimate failure of identification with the Other[377] is probably responsible for Nairn's psychopathological verdict on nationalism:

> 'Nationalism' is the pathology of modern developmental history, as inescapable as 'neurosis' in the individual, with much the same essential ambiguity attaching to it, a similar built-in capacity for descent and dementia, rooted in the dilemmas of helplessness thrust upon most of the world (the equivalent of infantilism for societies) and largely incurable.[378]

Such a psychoanalytically enriched grammar can be helpful in understanding both the split nature of the nationalist subject, as a symptom of westernisation after Bihruz Bey, and of the object of nationalisation, that is the split Turkish identity.

To constitute themselves as western, the Kemalists felt it necessary to deny any traces of the Oriental dimension of Turkishness. In doing so, they placed themselves clearly 'outside' of this 'object' out of which the modern 'subjects' were to be made. They were 'outside' for they imagined themselves within the horizon of modernity, as the 'agents' whose mission was to inoculate modernity into a traditional structure as Gökalp had proposed: Kemalists were the modernisers. But since the very term 'modernisation' is situated by definition at the spatial and temporal margin separating the traditional from the modern, the East from the West,

---

[375] Tanpinar 2001: 259.
[376] Nairn 1977: 17-8.
[377] Zizek 1989: 122.
[378] Nairn 1977: 359.

Kemalists as much as belonging to the West also belonged to the Orient. Kemalism itself was ambiguous and 'undecidable', in this regard. It was an impure entity, which threatened the purity of the very symbolic order that it so eagerly desired. In other words, in the absence of the western colonisers, Kemalist elites seem to have assumed the role of self-colonisers. Kemalist westernisation resembles to Frantz Fanon's (1967) description of the colonised intelligentsia's efforts of identification with Europe's culture, and to Edward Said's (1979) profile of the 'native orientalist' who undertakes through the discourse of modernisation the duty of adjusting the Orient to the West. This, according to Said is participation of modern Orient in self-orientalisation. Similarly, Hilmi Yavuz (1998) described Turkish modernisation as 'not Westernisation but Orientalisation'. The formation of the Kemalist subject required repression: in order to mould a modern model in his personality, the Kemalist had to exclude primarily the traditional components of his own self through a process of repression. The model that the Kemalists presented has to a large extent been an appeal to the 'nation' for the repetition of this neurosis, that is, this act of repression committed by the 'leaders', as the precondition of becoming a 'modern nation'. As Meltem Ahiska argues, 'the Turkish elites were split, because they could never achieve identification with the West's gaze':

> They had to build their identity according to a projected gaze of the West and this gaze could have never been fixed: it was always open to varying interpretations. Due to this ambiguity, [the mirror of the West] has always been the source of dissatisfaction and disappointment.[379]

The social objectivity was to a large extent constructed through the projection of this insurmountable split in Kemalist self on the 'nation'. The Kemalist elite could not escape the image of their repressed Oriental self in the mirror of the 'nation', which led them to neurotically reduce this Other to the status of an object to 'force to be civilised' through a series of 'revolutions' overtly obsessed more with the nation's appearance than the legal and institutional structures. As a result, the moment of the emergence of Turkish subject contains a primal split: a split along the axis of 'the clash of civilisations', which was immediately manifested in the physical split of 'historic bloc' that had existed roughly from the beginning

---

[379] Ahiska 2005: 128.

174

of the Abdulhamid II's reign in 1876 to the declaration of the republic.[380] Instead of 'suturing', in a Gökalpian fashion, the building stones of the split Turkishness, the Kemalist subject felt compelled to deepen this East/West cleavage further with their bureaucratic Jacobinism, driven by a will to build a new national identity based primarily on a violent repression of the East. The moment of this split was also the moment of the emergence of modern Turkish identity.

From that moment onwards, republican Turkey has demonstrated the features of a 'torn country' as described by Huntington (1993). As an early articulation of Huntington's thesis, novelist Kemal Tahir argued that since the beginning of westernisation, a society with 'dual reality' has existed in Turkey.[381] Literateur Ahmed Hamdi Tanpinar (1901-1962) described the transformation that was experienced with westernisation as a problem of 'shifting between civilisations': 'The duality that was brought about by our transition from one civilisation to the other emerged initially in the social life, then split our society into two regarding mentality and finally settled inside each individual'.[382] Tanpinar thus achieves the exceptional diagnosis of the individual as split subject and concludes: 'we are all sons and daughters of a crisis of consciousness and identity'.[383]

Since repression and the return of the repressed are the same thing,[384] what we observe from the moment of Ataturk's call to repress the 'Orient inside' onwards, is a republican history experienced as a series of repressions and subsequent returns of the repressed. The local resistances to the secular 'revolution' were the initial symptoms of the 'torn country', one of the frequently quoted of them being the Menemen Affair.

Menemen affair (23 December 1930) was a small-scale disturbance in an Aegean town near Izmir involving Dervish Mehmed, a drug addict, declaring himself the messiah in the town-square. Since this proclamation occurred after the Friday prayers in front of the mosque, an audience of some hundred men gathered around the 'messiah'. A young second lieutenant,

---

[380] See Chapters 1 and 2.
[381] Yavuz 1987: 80.
[382] Tanpinar 1970: 27.
[383] Tanpinar 2001: 259.

Kubilay, commanding a platoon of soldiers, arrived at the scene to disperse the crowd. He fired a blank on Mehmet to scare him. Unharmed, the dervish declared that he was impervious to bullets, and after producing a gun he shot and killed Kubilay. He then dragged the lieutenant's body to the mosque's courtyard, decapitated him and stuck his head on a pole to the applause of his audience. Two watchmen who opened fire on the crowd were then killed by them. The audience thus turned into rioters. A little later a military division arrived at the scene, dispersed the crowd, killing Dervish Mehmet and five others.[385]

Mustafa Kemal was reportedly outraged especially by the news that the crowd applauded Mehmet when he shot the officer. He demanded that Menemen should be declared an accursed town and razed to the ground. He also said that no mercy should be shown to the inhabitants, including women.[386] According to Mango, Ismet (Inonu) convinced Mustafa Kemal to narrow the target to the Nakshibendi order. An 82 year old Nakshibendi Sheikh, Esad Erbili, was arrested with his son in Istanbul and brought to Menemen for trial. The Sheikh died in detention before his son and twenty seven others were hanged on 4 February 1931. Most of them were poor refugees from the Balkans, brought into Turkey by population exchange. Also among the hanged were the official imam of the region's military regiment and a Jewish shopkeeper named Josef.

An exaggerated version of the above incident is an unchangeable chapter of every republican history textbook, in which the Menemen incident, or 'Kubilay incident', is narrated as a reactionary uprising. In Menemen, a monument stands at the top of a hill in memory the republican martyr Kubilay. Kubilay and Menemen are such important notions of Turkish political psyche that they have been abundantly employed in the recent arguments between the Islamists and secularists.[387] The symbolic meaning of the incident makes the murder of Kubilay a significant moment in the nation's history that could be staged again if the secular

---

[384] Evans 1996: 165.
[385] For a well-documented research arguing for the possibility of the whole Affair being a conspiracy planned and organised by the government in order to outlaw the opposition Free Republican Party, see Mazici 2001.
[386] Mango 1999: 476.
[387] On the issue of the prohibition of veiling in universities, the rector of Izmir Ege University declared his determination by saying: 'If more Kubilays are required to maintain the republic, we are ready to sacrifice our lives'. The outraged Islamist media attacked to the rector and has referred to him since this statement as Mr Kubilay. (See *Vakit*)

176

nation is not in a constant state of alarm against the threat of a reactionary upheaval. Like the '31 March Affair', the discursive construction, symbolisation and the practical consequences of this incident, including the manifest fear of a re-staging of the same scenario, that is, of its return, are telling of an act of not merely suppression or quelling of a revolt, but of an act of repression, which forms and reproduces through generations the unconscious dimension of Turkish identity.

One of the possible readings of the term 'the sick man of Europe' is therefore as follows: Turkey, in order to become 'of Europe' had to go 'sick'. The sickness involved here can be read as acute neurotic disorder, that is, each time Turkey dares to look at herself in the subjective mirror of the West, she faces the reflection of her Oriental self.[388] The result is always self-destructive: armed with power to teach, correct and penalise, the modern Turk punishes his oriental half; only to mourn further for his incomplete, unfulfilled, split self; thus returned to the traumatic moment of failure in the Western mirror, turning repetitively against his oriental self to discipline and punish further, and so on, and so forth.

IV. Conclusion

Many researchers of Turkey have been astonished by the extensive deployment of the figures and symbols related to Ataturk in contemporary Turkey. Many among them attempted to explain this as an official affair of monolithic state ideology, which is only partially correct. The extensive use of Kemalist symbols in contemporary Turkey affirms that Kemalismremains to be the hegemonic current of Turkish world of political thought.[389] As Celik argues, Kemalist horizon enabled the emergence of a multitude of subject-positions to articulate themselves with the notion of secular-modern Turkishness.[390] Insel's argument (2001: 26-7) similarly implies that Kemalism has functioned as a shield for a wide variety of

---

[388] This is due to the inevitable delay in any mirror image: 'The image that is reflected on us from the eyes of the West is in fact the image that we have previously reflected on this mirror, that is, the image of our own inconsistency... Ego is bound to see in the mirror of the Ideal his desires because of his inconsistencies and his inconsistencies because of his desires' (Kocak 2001: 398).

[389] See Bora and Gultekingil 2001: 14.

[390] Celik 2000: 198 and 2001: 90.

177

political approaches due to its suitability for a diversity of interpretations. Many groups with conflicting political tendencies have employed Ataturk's sayings and principles for the legitimation of their particular causes. Everyone can find a saying, tendency or principle in Ataturk, whose pragmatism resulted in a reservoir of sayings that could fit in any particular group's interest, on the condition that his conflicting sayings are overlooked or repressed. As a result, leftwing, rightwing, religious, atheist, democratic, westernist, Turkist, globalist, Mercantalist, pro-private enterprise, state capitalist, etc. versions of Ataturkism were able to emerge through the republican history. This flexibility becomes intelligible through the argument pursued in this chapter.

Kemalist social imaginary, after emerging from the overdetermination of the mythical space of salvation, rather than developing a concrete definition of Turkishness, provided a discursive framework for national identity. The Kemalist framework emerged mostly by defining the others of Kemalist imaginary including the dreams of imperial salvation and ethnic particularism. A diversity of discourses was allowed to operate within the boundaries set by the definition of the outside of this framework, within which Kemalism also maintained a degree of flexibility as opposed to a doctrinaire solidity:

> One day he was reviewing the principles of the RPP. I said: 'Pasha, this is by all criteria a party of revolution and a revolutionary party cannot move without an ideology, a doctrine.' He smiled as if pitying my naivety and said, 'My child, then we will stuck frozen'.[391]

This memoir implies that Kemal deliberately maintained the emptiness of the discursive territory drawn by Kemalist boundaries. This flexibility, which is concerned with emphasising what the nation is not rather than what it is, explains as much the obsession with the security that Kemalist Turkey inherited from the disintegration of the Empire as the reasons of Kemalism's success in surviving as Turkey's discursive horizon through decades. Kemalism's long-term maintenance as the main determinant of the discursive horizon of Turkey and republican Turkish identity is due to its ability to reproduce itself as an empty signifier deliberately detached from any particular content.

However, there are ultimate boundaries of the language games that could emerge under the Kemalist horizon; these boundaries correspond to those drawn by Kemal himself, as the ultimate 'authority of delimitation',[392] in his responses to the questions of the Ottoman identity crisis. I have argued that these boundaries consist of those which separate the nation with its present and future from its outside and Ottoman/Oriental past. Kemalism is therefore unsuitable for the legitimation of any discourse that fails to affirm the integrity of the Turkish nation. Similarly, any discourse that firmly stands for a fundamental shift in domestic or foreign policies in breach of the goal of 'civilisation' cannot find any legitimacy in Ataturk's principles or sayings.[393]

The systematic reproduction of the cult and ideals of Ataturk through education has also served as an important nexus for the transmission of Kemalism to successive generations. The popular identification with Ataturk myth is evident in what I shall call 'volk Kemalism', as opposed to the elites' reproduction of Kemalist symbols. Volk Kemalism consists of the popularity of Kemalist images and popular references to Ataturk at the common sense level, including folksongs, myths and attributes to Ataturk. Ataturk is popularly referred to as Mustafa Kemal Pasha, Gazi Pasha (Warrior) or Halaskar Gazi (Saviour Warrior), which led Serif Mardin (1969: 70) to observe that the celebration of the gazi has become an integrated component of the Turkish Volkislam. These titles peculiarly refer to Ataturk's military personality and are associated with Yakup Kadri's above quoted expectations of a 'national hero'. The original act of national liberation is arguably the primary link between the conscious core (State, ideology) and the unconscious periphery (society, common sense) of the republican symbolic order.

---

[391] Karaosmanoglu 1983.

[392] 'Authorities of delimitation' is one of the discursive processes that Foucault proposes as the analytic categories of the construction of the object of any discourse. These authorities include professions or authorities, who name, construct, design and demarcate an object as the object of a specific discourse. (Foucault 1989: 41-2.) The object of the Kemalist discourse is Turkish identity and Kemal himself is the ultimate authority, the referential universe of those authorities who make the decisions regarding the description, construction and demarcation of this identity.

[393] This was precisely the case with the RP led coalition's fate, which triggered a second secularisation led by the military from 28 February 1997 onwards.

In the explanation of the Turkish attachment to the myth of Ataturk, the Althusserian notion of 'determination in the last instance' could be helpful. If Marxism is not simply the explanation of all with reference to economy but the limits of it is best defined by Louis Althusser as 'determination of the economy in the last instance', then the most appropriate definition of modern Turkish identity would not be a crude 'Kemalist nation' but determination of, or identification with, Kemalism 'in the last instance'.

In this chapter, I have argued through an inquiry in the emergence of Kemalism that the peculiarity of Kemalist hegemony lies in Kemal's responses to the deficit questions of the Ottoman identity crisis, regarding nationalisation, secularisation and modernisation. I have demonstrated that these Kemalist responses consisted primarily of the definition of boundaries of the nation and its outside in both physical/geographical and temporal senses. The subsequent Kemalist task was to commence the construction of republican social order around the axes of modernisation, secularisation and nationalisation which had entered the late-Ottoman discursive universe as three faultlines and led to the dissolution and collapse of the Empire. Kemal's cult, image and gaze served as the nodal point where these three axes correlated with the 'nation' to form the republican political subjectivity. I have demonstrated that this process of construction involved an extensive deployment of the paternal metaphor, evident above all in Kemal's assumption of the surname Ataturk. The overemphasised paternal function, on the other hand, guaranteed the nation's long-term political immaturity, as opposed the notions of modern citizenship, civilisation and progress, which reveals a significant built-in inconsistency of Kemalism. The Kemalist logic further deconstructs itself with the constant reproduction of the religious grammar in its attempt to reoccupy the secularised divine sphere. A third inconsistency of Kemalism has been the vicious circle of repression of the Islamic identity and the subsequent returns of the repressed, which also reveals the underlying inconsistencies that split up the nationalist perceptions of the West hence demonstrating the ultimate limits of westernisation.

Despite these inconsistencies and failures, Kemalism continues to hover over and above republican Turkey as evident in the popularity of images, quotes, monuments and abundant representations of Ataturk's body and gaze. After demonstrating the imminent

180

inconsistencies and failures of Kemalism, understanding the sustained Kemalist effect requires further elaboration. One response to this problem could be that the trait of identification can also be a certain failure, weakness or guilt in the Other, 'so that by pointing out the failure we can unwittingly reinforce the identification'.[394]

In concluding this chapter, the following analytic observations need to be listed: Kemalism as a political discourse has primarily fulfilled a demarcating function, signifying above all the boundaries of a politico-discursive framework within which modern Turkish identity could be defined. The Kemalist operation produced and has since maintained this framework by a sustained exclusion of the Islamic identity and the ethnic heterogeneity of the 'nation' through practices of repression, foreclosure and reoccupation. Kemal's equivocal use of his cult to signify virtually nothing in particular, but at the same time everything that may be attached to a perception of 'universal', demonstrates a deliberate act of production of an empty signifier.[395] What this universality corresponds to can be best described in terms of a 'regime of truth', that is, an aggregate of rules by which the ultimate decision on true and false are made, while 'true' is loaded with certain effects of power.[396] The positive goals of the Kemalist regime of truth consisting of modernisation, secularisation and nationalisation were presented in terms of a national march from under an outdated 'dark' universe of the East to the nation's 'rightful place' under the civilised and 'radiant' universe of the Western values of Reason and Progress. Kemalism therefore is primarily a discursive framework furnishing the surface of a referential universe of a politico-discursive field in which a proliferation of discursive networks of power, identity and difference has been possible. Further analytic reflection on these discursive networks and practices becomes necessary in order to map out the constitutive features of republican power and republican political identity, which I will undertake in the next chapter.

---

[394] Zizek 1989: 106.
[395] Aletta Norval's analysis of the proliferation of discourses on Apartheid enables an analysis of Kemalism as an empty signifier: 'Apartheid may have become so naturalised, what we mean by it so obvious, that it has become an empty signifier, signifying everything and yet nothing.' (Norval 1994: 120.)
[396] Foucault 1980: 130.

181

CHAPTER 4: THE CONSTITUTION OF REPUBLICAN POLITICAL IDENTITY

In the previous chapter I have presented Ataturk as an empty signifier and emphasised his function as an 'authority of delimitation'. Therefore, Kemalism is primarily a discursive framework, which lays down the surface of a referential universe of a politico-discursive field in which a proliferation of discursive networks of power, identity and difference has been possible. The main concern of this chapter is to map out the constitutive features of republican power and republican political identity, which emerged within the Kemalist framework. The achievement of this task necessitates a focus on the analysis of those discursive networks and practices, which have been constitutive of the republican order. I will argue at the outset that Republic of Turkey is to a large extent the product of one of the symptoms of the late-Ottoman modernisation, namely militarisation. This argument stems from the fact that the military has functioned in republican history as an important political actor, concerned as much with the protection of the republican ideology as of the national territory.

Consequently, I will devote the first section of this chapter to a genealogy of Turkish militarisation to argue by referring to the discourses of educational system that Turkish identity has been constructed to a large extent as a militarist identity. After establishing that institutions of military and education are the long-term apparatuses of the republican order, I will move on to demonstrate the attempts in monoparty period of mastering over the repressed periphery, which led to the emergence of discourses and apparatuses designed particularly for this purpose. The discursive framework of these apparatuses consisted of an

182

articulation of discourses of authenticism and 'national character', which included the tendencies of villagism and peasantism, along with an ethnicist shift in the nationalist discourse. As the theoretical reservoir of these discourses, the Turkish History Thesis will be given special attention. I will analyse these practices as a 'passive revolution' attempt and assess the points of its failure. In the third section, I will account for the consequences of the republican consolidation of power with the operation of above discourses of mastering over periphery coupled with ethnic nationalism for those groups, who were not considered Turkish. I will present the Dersim operation, which involved detailed planning of the relationship between population and territory, the relations of men with things, and the adjustment of these relationships according to republican goals, as a striking case of transition to modern governmentality.

I. The genesis of republican power: Modernisation via Militarisation

This section is devoted to the analysis of the 'militarisation' of the Turkish discursive horizon in parallel to Turkish modernisation. Deriving from Foucault, I will attempt an interpretation of Turkish passage to modernity as a process of colonisation of the social sphere by a certain disciplinary modality, that is, militarism. In order to make intelligible the conditions of realisation of this 'military dream of society', I will consider the trajectory of Turkish military modernisation and the emergence of a new elite consisting of military officers, bureaucrats and intellectuals with modern mentalities at a time when the Ottoman State was going through the agony of its collapse. Following an outline of the main dynamics in which the military discourses and mentalities hegemonised the social and cultural spheres, I will consider the mechanisms that have organised and reproduced these discourses and mentalities, and maintained the central role of military in Turkish politics as the 'guardians of the republic' and militarism as a remarkable constituent of modern Turkish identity.

I.1. The disciplinary model

A significant contribution by Michel Foucault to political analysis is his emphasis on an inherent dimension of modern power: the dimension of disciplinary modalities. The model of docile, efficient and productive body of the modern individual was first born in prisons from the punitive and disciplinary practices over 'the bodies of the condemned'.[397] The penetration of the disciplinary model from various 'social quarantines' to the social as a whole, led to the formation of modern societies as disciplinary societies.[398] In addition to prisons, Foucault mentions schools, hospitals and barracks as the spaces of these social quarantines. A striking parallel between Foucault's genealogical narration of the French transition to modernity and Turkish modernisation is the fact that Turkish transition to modernity was both a cause and the consequence of the modernisation of Turkish military. Moreover, the Republic of Turkey, which was founded by the military following a military conflict, was manifestly imagined as the political structure of an 'army-nation'. Since then, the military has popularly been seen as the 'backbone' of the republic and maintained a powerful role in politics. I shall attempt in this section to make the centrality of military as an institution and militarism as a political discourse in Turkish politics intelligible through a reading of Turkish transition to modernity as the colonisation of the Turkish society by the

---

[397] Foucault 1991.
[398] Foucault 1991:217-8.

military model. Most of the points of my argument on Turkish military and republican society below will pursue the applicability in Turkish politics of the following statement by Foucault (1991: 169):

> Historians of ideas usually attribute the dream of a perfect society to the philosophers and jurists of the 18th century; but there was also a *military dream of society*; its fundamental reference was not to the state of nature but to the *meticulously subordinated cogs of a machine*, not to the primal social contract but to *permanent coercions*, not to fundamental rights but to *indefinitely progressive forms of training*, not to the general will but to *automatic docility* (my italics).

Turkish 'military dream' gathered its contents and manifestations through the Ottoman modernisation, which commenced with an attempt for the modernisation of the army, in order to end the defeats suffered in the hands of the Europeans. The conventional nature of the Ottoman encounter with the West had begun to change with the defeat of the Ottoman army at the outskirts of besieged Vienna in 1683. By 1774, the Otoman military advance in Europe had been plainly reversed. Ottomans came to realise that their strength was not absolute any more; the Ottoman military might had been relativised in parallel to the scientific advances of the European states. They therefore had to measure their strength against that of the Christian world before continuing to challenge the West. Ottoman rulers responded to the new situation by a pragmatic deployment of a famous Koranic motto that encourages the faithful to fight the devil with the devil's own tricks. The first attempt of modernisation thus began with the modernisation of the military.

The year 1789, when Sultan Selim III succeeded to the throne, is a turning point in Ottoman history as in the world history. Selim was deeply influenced by the French revolution and attempted to establish a "New Order" (*Nizam-ı Cedid*), which primarily involved a military reform. The Sultan initially tried to reform the Janissaries, who after a few months of military training, gave it up claiming that "exercise is infidel's business".[399] Upon this, Selim founded a new army called *Nizam-ı Cedid* alongside the traditional Janissary hearths, which began their training under French and Swiss officers' instructions in 1794.

Ottoman soldiers had participated enthusiastically in wars of conquest. 'These wars were sources of income both for the state and the warriors. It was therefore logical that defensive wars evoked less enthusiasm, and as the wars concluded with disastrous defeats, the will to participate in them would diminish even further. There was no concept of patriotism and in fact the lands that tried to be defended were after all Christian lands.' When deprived of their major source of income, that is, conquest, Janissaries began to get involved in trade to form small businesses. Some were also involved in racketeering of the local businesses in Istanbul. And, 'when Janissaries became people with double jobs, exercise would naturally become a burden. On the other hand, as the power of firearms increased (...) so did the importance of military exercise. (...) Janissaries, who refused to be trained, usually got nervous under fire, turned back and ran away. (...) Standing under intensive fire from the enemy required a certain discipline, a type of 'robotisation', that could only be attained through exercise'.[400]

---

[399] Aksin 1997: 80.
[400] Aksin 1997: 80-1.

186

Nizam-ı Cedid was abolished and Sultan Selim III was executed by the Janissaries, but Selim's radical cousin Mahmud II, who took the upper hand in 1808 defeated the Janissary forces and abolished their order after an all out battle in Istanbul in 1826. Mahmud managed to form another new army, *Asakir-i Mansure-i Muhammediye* (The Victorious Soldiers of Muhammad), and new secular military schools under French and English instruction. During the *Tanzimat* regime under Sultan Abdulmecid, conscription to the Ottoman army was regulated with a decree in 1843, which authorised the central administration to directly control the conscription around the country. Recruitment to the army had previously been conducted by provincial governors, as a remnant of an old Turkish/Ottoman tradition. The new regulation, which ruled a five year service for every Muslim male of the Empire marked the definite moment of transition from the conventional concept of army as a professional force, supported by the provisional mobilisation with the promise of plunder during expeditions, to the concept of national service, that is, military service as an obligation of citizenship. From then on, the barracks have served as the schools of modern nation-building.

The emergence of the model of the object of new disciplinary practices, i.e. the soldier, required the presence of a second element as the agent of disciplinary power, that is, the officer. The new army and navy required new officers trained in positive sciences, foreign languages (French) and European military strategies. In 1826 a Military Medical Academy (*Tıbbiye*) was founded, and followed by the founding of a military academy (*Harbiye*) in 1834.[401] In early 1880s, a system of military boarding schools (*Askeri Rüsdiye*), which recruited students after primary education, was introduced to be followed by the introduction

---

[401] Unat 1964: 65 & Aksin 1997: 120.

of military high schools (*Askeri Idadi*). By 1898, the number of cadets in 28 *Rüsdiyes* had reached to 8000.[402] Education in *Rüsdiyes* was secularist and of a high standard.

Most significantly, this increase in the military schooling in parallel to other *Tanzimat* schools, resulted in a transformation of the conventional Ottoman elite. A new group of military elite, both extensive and powerful, was entering into the ranks of the conventional Ottoman *askeriye* (ruling classes). They usually came from humble backgrounds, from the periphery of Ottoman society, and gained their status not by natural blood ties but through education and training. Consequently, they were more linked with the lower layers of the Empire's population and had social ambitions of upward mobilisation.[403] They obtained a positivist outlook through their education and were all concerned with the 'salvation of the Empire'.[404] This mentality of leadership, along with convictions in progress and scientific positivism would largely rule the discourse and actions of the 1890s generation of the new bureaucracy and intelligentsia, but most significantly those of the military officers.

The new class of military officers was a product of the necessary 'democratisation' of the education system, by which lower and middle class youth around the country were given the

---

[402] Mardin 1991: 57.

[403] Murat Belge describes this development as a new form of 'devshirme' (conversion) system: 'There was a condition of the conversion: a person of Serbian, Croation or Greek origin was able to rise as high as to the post of Grand Vizier, but he needed to demonstrate his complete loyalty to the state throughout his service at various ranks of bureaucracy and as its precondition he had to cut off all his ties with the community that he originated from. The *devsirme* system weakened with the Ottoman decline, but its philosophy continued to reign. (...) With the beginning of the republican era, the multi-ethnic structure did not exist anymore in Turkey, in which the former *devsirme* system would be anachronistic. Instead, the social classes would replace ethnicities as the field of the application of the conversation system. Education has been the primary mechanism of upward social mobilisation in most of the republican history. (...) The criterion, however, remains the same as the Ottoman condition: persons coming from humble backgrounds were able to improve their social condition within the political and bureaucratic hierarchy of the new era - to the extent of their full loyalty to the state, which is the precondition of their existence out of nothing' (Belge 1992: 162).

[404] Mardin 1991: 58.

opportunity to join the ranks of Ottoman elite as the officers of the Ottoman army. They were modernists armed with a European outlook and yet they were not an elite in the old sense of the word, that is, an elite alienated from people. They were in constant touch with the country through young conscripts, whom they trained and educated in the barracks. In the barracks, not only a constant touch with humble origins was maintained but also the imagery of a future social order, 'a military dream of society', was taking shape. This social imagery was a hierarchical and disciplinary one, modelled on officer-soldier relationship.[405] Disciplinary practices in the barracks had an educational aim, that is, to mould an army of modern soldiers out of masses of predominantly peasant youth. The private that the officer faced with was illiterate and had neither a notion of personal initiative, nor division of labour, nor collective identity. He usually expressed a very confused notion of religious belonging.[406] The officer viewed this religious mystic confusion as a consequence of the influence of Sufi Islamic orders throughout the country.[407] Yet, this confused man was in essence pure and innocent, and was able to be turned into an industrious and learned individual, of course, through subjection to harsh disciplinary practices. Foucault observes a similar development at an earlier stage in French history:

---

[405] This, above all, was a unilateral power relationship, based on blind obedience and subordination secured by threat of punishment, which embodied extensive violence. A recent (December 2003) human rights survey revealed that 32 % of subjects had been subjected to violence by their superiors during military service. This figure needs to be doubled given that the survey carried out among both male and female subjects, while only men are eligible for military service. (Doç. Dr. Melek Göregenli, 'Siddet, kötü muamele ve iskenceye yönelik deneyimler, tutum ve değerlendirmeler', Ege Üniversitesi Psikoloji Bölümü Sosyal Psikoloji Anabilim Dalı. Quoted in Human Rights Foundation Turkey, December 2003 Report).
[406] Mardin 1991: 54-55.
[407] The officers interpreted the situation as follows: 'Fanatic mullahs had deceived the "ignorant" private with myths and fallacies, instead of a proper religious instruction and education revealing the truth of Islam and the State'. Mardin (1991: 55) quotes a young officers' memoirs on this issue: "When I asked the question 'What is our religion? The religion that we belong to?' I was expecting a response like 'thank God we are Muslims'. However, I did not receive this answer. Some said, 'we are of the religion of Imam-i Azam', others 'we are on the side of Prophet Ali'. Some could not think of an answer. Indeed some of the men said 'we are Muslims', however, when it was asked 'who is your prophet?', there was further confusion. There were names that nobody could imagine to be the name of the prophet. One said, 'our prophet is Enver Pasha'. I asked to the very small

By the late eighteenth century, the soldier has become something that can be made; out of a formless clay, an inapt body, the machine required can be constructed; posture is gradually corrected; a calculated constraint runs slowly through each part of the body, mastering it, making it pliable, ready at all times, turning silently into the automatism of habit; in short, one has 'got rid of the peasant' and given him 'the air of a soldier'.[408]

Turkish modernisation was accompanied by discourses containing a great deal of emphasis on militarisation and discipline. Conscription and the accompanying notion of national service were the essential mechanisms that have operated to disseminate the disciplinary model based on officer-soldier relationship to become a hegemonic determinant of modern Turkish identity. I shall devote more of this section to the techniques of this dissemination and the militarist discourses that dispersed along with the expansion of the military model to become an essential element of the construction of modern Turkish identity.

I.2. Officers' Will to Power

Charles Tilly (1985) demonstrates that the formation of nation states in Europe was a result of wars. Additionally, many Third World countries were also founded through independence wars. The formation of the Turkish nation state also followed decades of war. However, after the formation of the state, the weight that each nationalist discourse assigned to the army varied. In Turkey, the army was escalated to an exceptional position, not solely as the

fraction, who knew the prophet's name, 'is our prophet still alive or dead?' and the subject took a twist which was unresolvable. Some said that he was alive, others that he was dead ...'
[408] Foucault 1991: 135.

190

protector of the 'motherland' but also the essential protector of the regime.[409] Historical reasons accompanied by an increasing trend among the officers, which I shall call 'the will to power', were responsible for this peculiarity.

The transition from Empire to republic could be read as a narration of that process in which modern army officers evolved from the position of the servants of the Ottoman state to the exclusive status of 'the ruling elite' of their own state.[410] This relationship of legal possession of the state and the lack of it is partly responsible for the Kemalist negativisation of the Ottoman past, as a history in which the Turks were alienated from their own essence, under the domination of a cosmopolitan elite.[411]

The materialisation of this 'will to power' began with the suppression of a mutiny in Istanbul in 1909, an incident known as 31st March affair.[412] The most durable consequence of this affair was its contribution to the new military elite's psyche with an image of 'the reactionary' as the other. The CUP officers viewed the 31 March incident as a counter-revolutionary attempt carried out mostly by conscripts, who had been deceived by Mullahs to turn against the CUP rule. The image of 'the reactionary', who abuse innocent masses by using religion for his political ends, thus entered the officers' political psyche, as the 'other' of the moderniser's identity. 31 March Affair was therefore the moment when the construction of the self-image of modern secularist officer was finalised, with a mission to

---

[409] Parla 1991.

[410] This move is evident in the linguistic transition from the class of 'seyfiye' (military in Ottoman Turkish) to the class of askeriye (the name for the whole ruling state class in Ottoman Turkish, while in contemporary Turkish, this term exclusively means 'military' –including conscious/unconscious connotations of its original meaning, 'the ruling class').

[411] See Chapter 3.

[412] See Chapter 1.

191

lead the 'nation' to progress, which required above all the repression of the Islamic/Oriental dimension of his own self. With these features, 31ˢᵗ March Affair also served to articulate the discourses of secularism and militarism. With the realisation of the 'military dream of society' through the colonisation of the social by the military model, the militarist/secularist officers' psyche would be promoted to the status of an integral component of modern Turkish identity.

This 'colonisation' was possible over suitable historical conditions in addition to the officers' will to power. The republic inherited simultaneously a strong state tradition and a 'missing bourgeoisie',[413] that is, a destroyed civil society, from the Ottoman Empire. The state, too, was strong in tradition but its institutions had disintegrated except for the military.[414] In a sense, the reformed Ottoman State was born as a paralysed body politique. The republic took over a strong but paralysed state tradition with the exception of a single institution, the military, which proved in leading the Greek war its efficiency. The military seized the whole state apparatus as a logical consequence of this situation and tried to reactivate the state's vast institutional structure in its own image during the formative years of the republic.[415]

---

[413] Keyder 1987.

[414] Ottoman integration with European markets had rapidly turned the country into a semi-colony with effects of economic depression. Ottoman treasury was in chronic crisis throughout the 19th century with constant accumulation of foreign debt, and in 1875 the state declared financial bankruptcy. With the introduction of the Ottoman Dette Publique (*Düyunu Umumiye*) in 1881, the conduct of most of the tax collection in the Ottoman lands was transferred from the treasury to the representatives of the foreign creditors. Financial crisis hit hard the civil servants, whose salaries, the State failed to pay regularly. Moreover, this crisis was not taking place in a consolidated system but in a country where most of the state institutions had been reformed or newly introduced during the 19th century Tanzimat movement.

[415] The political economy of integration with western capitalist markets led to a conflict between the displaced local producers, craftsmen, peasants and Muslim traders on the one side, and, on the other, the agents of international capital, that is, the emerging Ottoman bourgeoisie consisting primarily of Christian subjects of the Empire and European nationals with trading privilages (Levantines). As we have seen in chapter on nationalism, the post-Tanzimat state from Abdülhamid to Young Turks sided more and more with the formers, not solely in terms of state subsidies, tax exemptions and other economic promotions and privileges but also by encouraging and initiating the physical elimination of the latter. At the turn of the republican Turkey, although Muslim merchants had taken over the Christian property and businesses, the international trade networks were no longer operative in the country as a consequence of the War, and therefore a rapid renovation of bourgeoisie and civil society did not occur. In these conditions, the new republican state was able to practice extensive power over a

192

The officers' will to power, therefore, operated over suitable conditions provided by historical developments of a destroyed civil society and a strong state tradition, of which most of the institutions, except the military, that were supposed to maintain this strong tradition had been paralysed.

I.3. Militarist Discourse: The National Macho

The following is a primary school hymn:[416]

> Boy: "Little Ayse, little Ayse tell me what you have been doing"
>
> Girl: "I am looking after my baby and cooking food for him,
>
> I am rocking his cradle and I love my baby"
>
> Girl again: "Little soldier, little soldier show me what you have been doing"
>
> Boy: "I am looking after my rifle; fitting a bayonet on it
>
> I will put my helmet on and march to my barracks"

Each Turkish child have performed such rituals at primary school, which serve to naturalise gender roles to accompany the introjection of militarism.

To begin with, Turkish patriotism is not based on the defence of a fatherland but the 'motherland'. The identification of land with women has its origins in Islam. Koran made the

social structure consisting of a 'missing bourgeoisie' and a damaged, in fact totally destroyed, civil society. Following the Young Turks' tracks in the policies of 'national economy', the military bureaucratic leaders of the new regime overtly wanted to nurse the formation of a 'republican bourgeoisie', but their primary desire was to establish as the condition of the emergence of capitalist Turkey a 'civilised society', which was not necessarily a 'civil society'.

point of resembling women to earth as something to be cultivated and seeded, to be made fertile.[417] Nationalist literature made crucial contributions to this religious identification of land and woman. The Anatolian peninsula, for instance, which the Turks declared their homeland with the national pact of 1919, was pronounced in the early republican literature, with a clever linguistic twist, as 'Anadolu'; 'Ana' meaning mother in Turkish and 'dolu' meaning full. This linguistic twist is however also revealing of the Turkish psyche, not solely for the sexual codes but because the very need for the pronunciation of fullness as such demonstrates a denied or foreclosed awareness of a primordial lack. When land and women are one and the same thing, their defence, as well as turning them into fertile beings, is naturally an exclusively masculine duty. Compulsory military service, which is declared a duty and a right at the same time for the male population, thus naturalises the bond of citizenship between the state and population. Masculinity and state are identified through 'the most sacred duty' of military service. In this imagery, women were given the complementary role of mothering male children (as in the Ayse hymn), that is, to provide the country with soldiers.

One of the constitutive myths of Turkish nationalism, that is, the Turkish nation as an army-nation, thus contains in itself a gender based exclusion, that is, the exclusion of women from the 'nation proper'. Moreover, the definition of the male Turkish nation is closely related to domination over women. A military service story published in 1933 depicts the 'sweet dream' of Hüsmen on his last day in the barracks:

---

[416] This is one of the hymns that I remember my elder sister and brother used to recite together at home, which they learnt at school.

194

After he returned to the village and married, he would teach his wife Kezban the things that he had been taught in the military service, particularly the upright position that he always stood by holding his breath. (…) His first task would be to teach Kezban the utterance of identity. When he called her name she would rush to stand in front of him like a soldier and after saluting him she would shout: 'Kezban, daughter of Ali (…) Order me sir!'[418]

Compulsory national service therefore does not only masculinise the 'nation proper' but also defines this very masculinity as domination over women. National service is the precondition of becoming a man, both in the state discourse and folk culture. The men however do not serve as commanders during the military service. On the contrary, most of the conscripts serve as privates, who had to obey and carry out the orders, stand upright and most of the time be verbally abused and beaten up. However, after the military service, every man would become the commander of his wife and his household.[419] This way, the officer-soldier relationship, the law of the barracks, would infiltrate into and colonise the cultural sphere of the whole nation to become the hegemonic mode of socialisation. This would not fit with the classical military motto that 'every Turk is born a soldier', but the state is certainly determined to turn every Turk, male or female, into a soldier, within a carefully cut discourse of hierarchy, beginning with the gender based difference and moving from there to reproduce the traditional difference between the state and public, in republican conditions. The 'vatandas' (citizen) of the Republic in this sense, becomes a linear extension of the Ottoman 'reaya' (peasant subject).

---

[417] Al-Baqara: band 223.
[418] Quoted in Altinay and Bora 2003: 145

195

'Serif (Mardin) observed to me that in the old days, every Turkish bosom contained two souls, a *macho* and a Sufi. Kemalism had done its best to destroy the Sufi: it now had to cope with the *macho* on his own'.[420] The macho in the Turkish soul, however, was not something merely to cope with, but an aspect of Turkishness that made the nationalist power possible. Nationalist power, did not cope with or repress or exclude but provided a surface of inscription on which this macho was produced, organised and reproduced as a 'ritual of truth'. In turn, the macho provided the Turkish nationalists with a dispositive for the dispersal of the militarist discourses of nationalism. 'Macho' can be perceived as a peculiar form of masculinity, which bears the connotations of aggression and violence in addition to an overemphasis on male identity:

The Turks' boat has a red tower and the soldiers in it are lion-hearted

The enemy's boat has a blue tower and the soldiers in it are very scared

This is Turkish a nursery hymn quoted by Murat Belge[421], when demonstrating how violence is rooted in Turkish social structure, from the child's relationship with parents to the citizen's relationship with the state.[422] This culture of violence, argues Belge, has been reproduced officially, particularly in education:

In education, in the textbooks of every level, violence is encouraged with such naïveté that cannot even be called 'indirect'. In all written and oral texts of the education system, the values of war and the warrior are extremely dominant; 'heroism' is the

---

[419] Altinay and Bora 2003: 145.
[420] Gellner 1999: 87.
[421] I remember singing it in primary school.
[422] Belge 1992: 152-3.

196

essential theme. To dress children in military uniforms, to make them march (in national days, etc.) like soldiers and rituals like this are complementary to education.[423] Belge also points out that a value of 'sacrificing one's self for the nation' has been intensively elaborated in the Turkish education system, leading to a clear-cut opinion of life in terms of us/them dichotomy. It is through this dichotomy that the macho of the Turkish soul is thoroughly organised to reproduce the productive nationalist subject.

I.4. Militarisation and Governmentality

The argument in this section implies that an important symptom of Turkish modernisation was militarisation of not merely the political and social structuration that accompanied modernisation but also common sensical mentalities in which the modern Turkish identity was moulded and reproduced. Militarisation, that is, the process of colonisation of the social sphere by a certain disciplinary modality, was the realisation of the 'military dream of society' through the operation of a masculinist and hierarchical discourse. This operation has maintained the legitimacy of the position of a new military-bureaucratic elite of republican Turkey and the central role of the military in Turkish politics, not merely as the defenders of national territory but virtually as 'the guardians of the republic'. More importantly, however, the hegemony of the military discourses and mentalities has served to reproduce militarism as a significant component of modern Turkish identity. It can be legitimately asserted on these grounds that the state/citizen relationship of republican Turkey is grounded largely upon the officer/soldier relationship, as the modernised version of the conventional Ottoman State/peasant subject relationship. This model is accompanied by the constant operation of

---

[423] Belge 1992: 153.

197

patriarchal militarist discourses, by which the social has been hierarchically reproduced from

gender divisions to the subjection of the 'citizen' to the State. Moreover, this military model

is based as much on consent as on force, with its ability of producing collective 'national

popular' goals. Kemalism could be depicted as the particular discourse of the remnants of

Ottoman military bureaucracy, which managed to forge their hegemony over the elements of

an 'historic bloc' in post-World War I Turkey.[424] Since then, the legitimacy of the military

model and the hegemony of Kemalist discourse have produced and reproduced each other.

I.5. Militarism and Education

The infiltration of the militarist discourse into the social sphere can be immediately observed

in another essential institution of the republic, that is, education. To begin with, the most

abundantly used titles of Mustafa Kemal have been 'Commander in Chief' and 'the Head

Teacher'. This metonymy over the 'names-of-the-Father' and others such as 'army of

teachers' and 'military service as a hearth of education' signify the fact that discursive

practices of education and military are closely linked in Turkish practice, that is, that the

military has functioned as an educational institution while education has been organised like

a military activity to function in great deal with an ideal of the dispersal of a militarist

discourse.

Military service has been the first experience for many generations of particularly rural male

population for meeting the 'high culture', including literacy and modern rules of personal

---

[424] See Appendix 4.

198

hygiene, dining, etc., in parallel to nationalist indoctrination. The barracks have also served to practically introduce the majority of the Turks, for the first time in their lives, to a considerably large portion of their 'imagined community' from around the country. More significantly, however, education is structured like the military. These two institutions were defined in the formative years of the republic as two fronts of the same battle.[425] Mustafa Kemal outlined the form of this relationship in 1923 as follows:

> The task of the second army consisting of teachers is to teach the first army, which kill and get killed, why they kill and why they get killed.[426]

References in Kemal's discourse to the teachers as the soldiers of the state's cultural front further imply that order and discipline are prioritised in the educational institutions and operations, as in the military.

A second link between the military and education is the emphasis on their exclusively national character.[427] The only two ministries in Turkey, titles of which begin with the term "national" are the ministries of Defence and Education'. The overemphasis on the national character of military is comprehensible, since without nationalist or patriotic sentiments, military defence of the land and nation would be difficult. However, neither the military's tasks in Turkey have been limited to the defence of national territory nor the overemphasis on nationalism was limited to the military institution. An analysis of various enunciations of the early republican discourse would immediately reveal that the founders of the republic perceived education primarily in terms of nationalist indoctrination:

---

[425] See, Altinay 1999.
[426] Cited by Altinay and Bora 2003: 146.
[427] For Altinay and Bora (2003: 146), the relationship between the military and educational networks is best symbolised in the compulsory subject of 'national security'. 'National Security' courses have been part of the

Education may be understood as religious, national or international education, each having their specific aims and objectives. I will decline here to dwell on the others after stressing with determination that the education to be given by the new Turkish republic to the new generation will be national education.[428]

Ataturk's prime minister, Ismet Inonu, elaborated further on this statement in 1925 to clarify what was exactly meant by national education:

There is a Turk, who gives this land its Turkish character. However, this nation does not yet demonstrate the features of a unified nation that we desire. If this generation works consciously with sincerity under the guidance of science and life by devoting all its life, then the Turkish nation can become a complete and mature Turkish nation in cultural and social regards.[429]

Education was therefore an overt act of building and dissemination of the Turkish identity. It was a specifically national – as opposed to religious and international – practice; in other words, education was the discursive practice of the dissemination of the boundaries of republican Turkishness drawn by Kemal, the ultimate 'authority of delimitation'.

The republican education system was therefore structured as the builder of Turkish identity. It has been the most important medium between the poles of the cleavage that split the social between the conscious Kemalist core and the unconscious periphery. In this model, the teachers as the republic's 'organic intellectuals' have been assigned the duty of carrying consciousness to the 'nation'. However, rather than these Leninist party terms, the Kemalist

---

secondary school curricula since 1926; its textbooks have been prepared by the Chief of General Staff and the lectures have been held by military officers in uniforms.

[428] Ataturk's 1924 Samsun speech to teachers (Ataturk 1989: 206).
[429] Yucel 1994: 25.

discourse, as we have seen above, was inclined towards a military discourse, consisting of an 'army of teachers' conducting a war against the unconscious, in order to win over the new generations to the Kemalist consciousness.[430] Militarism is therefore the discursive framework within which education was overtly situated by the Kemalist discourse.

II. A Response to the Lack of Hegemony: Ideological Condensation

Military and education have been two apparatuses to constitute the backbone of republican power, through which modern values of the nationalist State have been introduced to successive generations. The emphasis of Kemalist discourse on the 'new generation' and the subsequent investment on republican education affirm the split character of the first generation and reveal a long-term plan to overcome this split in time, through the dissemination of a militarist-disciplinary modality and modern nationalist values. However, the task of consolidation of power could not wait the bringing up of a new generation. The problem of lacking hegemony had developed to become a pressing issue by the early 1930s when Kemal observed for a second time mounting opposition in the short lived Free Republican Party experience.[431] The Kemalist attempt to reoccupy the place of Islam in popular common sense with Ataturk's personality cult, supported by nationalist monuments, could not immediately produce the expected effects. It was not enough to ask people to

---

[430] The relationship is again mutual. While the national education served primarily to spread of republican indoctrination through the social field, the cultural capital that has been offered by education has been perceived as an opportunity for upward mobilisation, particularly by the rural youth with humble backgrounds.

[431] The first parliamentary opposition, Progressive Republican Party had been dissolved in the wake of Sheikh Said rebellion and its cadres were violently eliminated in 1926. The Free Republican Party, although founded with the personal encouragement of Mustafa Kemal, had to dissolve itself on 17 November 1930 after only three and a half months of activity.

become republican and love Ataturk.[432] The ideal of republic, which fell short of popular enthusiasm and romanticism in comparison to the power of volk Islam, was failing to generate a feeling of belonging around itself. It failed to propose a 'map of behavioural guidance' for everyday life, beyond the 'cold' ceremonies performed on national days. There was a need to find a new ideal, capable of contesting and replacing the ideal of Sharia, which would serve primarily to the enlargement of the new regime's political base.

The problem of hegemony inevitably brought forward the problem of ideology, that is, the necessity of generating a discursive nexus capable of bonding popular masses with the Kemalist elite. The demarcated signifier of Turkishness had to be filled with a positive content capable of mobilising the 'national-popular' dynamics with 'active consent' and enthusiasm. An ethnic nationalist discourse was the favoured choice of this juncture.[433] Consequently, republican discursive practices began to shift towards an attempt to generate a sense of belonging around Turkish identity on the basis of an ethnic theory, which would preach that the Turks constituted a super-family with a nexus of kinship.

Ahmet Yildiz's comprehensive work[434] on Turkish nationalism in the formative years of the republic demonstrates how an ethnicity-based nationalism dominated the 1930s Turkish State discourse. Ample reference to race, etnicity, blood, etc. can be found in Mustafa Kemal's rhetoric.[435] The ethnicity issue therefore lied at the heart of the process of nation building in

---

[432] Bozkurt 1931: 1-2.
[433] C.f. Yildiz 2001: 158-64.
[434] Yildiz 2001.
[435] Kemal was more sensitive on this issue compared to other notables of the state apparatus. One of these notables, Mahmut Esat Bozkurt, the first theorist of Kemalism, said the following on the difference between proper Turks and other citizens:

Turkey: it produced demographic discourses, discourses on national character, race and blood, discourses of history, civilisation, geography, reform, and finally, security. All these discourses were closely linked to the practices carried out by the State and the newly emerged republican discursive apparatuses.

The shift in the nationalist discourse was accompanied by a number of important governmental decisions to the effect of organising the republic as a monoparty state[436] and the introduction of etatist economic policies.[437] Mustafa Kemal marked this shift with a

'Anyone other than the proper Turks should not be leading Turkish state's business. (...) We will not believe anyone except for the Turks. (...) My personal opinion is that the lords and masters of this country are the Turks. Those who are not of pure Turkish stock have only one right in the Turkish land, it is the right to be servants and slaves' (quoted in Yildiz 2001).

[436] The objective situation of monoparty regime was legalised in the 4th Conference of the RPP in which the Party Secretary Recep Peker declared that republic of Turkey was a party-state and in 1936 the RPP was fused with the state apparatus. The Minister of Interior would be the RPP Secretary General and the provincial governors and the party representatives would be the same person. In 1937, the six arrows representing the six principles of RPP were included in the Constitution as the principles of the Republic of Turkey. The Party itself gained an authoritarian character with the formulation of a Chief system, similar to the Heidegger's führerprinziple in Germany. A prominent ideologue of Kemalist nationalism, Mahmut Esat Bozkurt, commented on the chief system as follows:

A contemporary German historian states that National Socialism and Fascism are modified forms of Mustafa Kemal's regime. This is very correct. This is a correct assertion. Kemalism is an authoritarian democracy rooted in the people. Turkish nation is like a pyramid. Its base is people and the top is the head, who also comes from the people and who we call Chief. The Chief derives his authority from people and this is what democracy is (Bozkurt: 137).

Under such a peculiar notion of democracy, workers of the new republic were denied the rights to strike and to unionise. In 1936, a labour law modelled on fascist Italian legislation prohibited unionisation and declared strikes outlawed (Keyder, 1987:14), while the infamous Tatil-i Esgal Kanunu (Code for Prohibition of Strikes) of 1909 was still in effect.

[437] The background to the etatist turn was the Great Depression of 1929. The etatist political economy developed through state enterprises, state investments particularly in industry and state control of all economic activity. The concept of central planning was imported from the Soviet model and two industrial plans were prepared with the assistance of Soviet economists. The state's monopolisation of the financial markets[437] and the introduction of monopolistic state-owned economic institutions and public industrial enterprises[437] were balanced with the RPP's manifest aim of creating a national bourgeoisie. This choice had been made as early as 1923 with the manifestation in Izmir Economy Congress of their will to implement the 'National Economy' policies of the CUP. Kemalists were the heirs of the Young Turks and they most significantly inherited a 'bourgeois' mentality from them. They wanted to build a capitalist Turkey, in which private but national entrepreneurs would generate wealth. The Tesvik-i Sanayi (Promotion of Industry) Law of 1927 was another manifestation of the same policy, which guaranteed state support for national entrepreneurs. Etatism of the 1930s and the war years, on the other hand, were viewed by the bureaucracy as a necessary turn under the conditions of the Great Depression. It was also an opportunity for expanding the Kemalist power base at the economic-corporate level, and building a strong base of infrastructure for future private enterprise (See Keyder 1987: 91-115). The function of the Kemalist economic policies could become intelligible, if we consider

speech declaring his manifest will of condensation of 'ideological state apparatuses' on the subject of the closure of Turkish Hearths:

There are some periods in the history of nations when all moral and material forces must be gathered together and made to work in the same direction to reach definite goals.[438]

Turkish etatism was supported by discourses with strong emphasis on development and progress. The RPP declared in its 3rd Conference in 1931 that in Turkey there were no class divisions but only occupational differences. A corporatist imaginary in which society was viewed as a harmonious whole of complementary occupational divisions presented as the new 'national-popular will'. Populism, which meant corporatism and solidarism, and some degree of Kemalist obsession with authenticity and 'national character' described below, became another active principle of the RPP.[439]

Turkish experience, as a 'perverted' model, due to 'uneven development', of Marx's notion of 'primitive capital accumulation', as outlined in *Das Capital* Volume I. Etatism of the 1930s, as in the practices of Mexico under Cardenas, Brazil under Vargas and Chile under the Popular Front, was the prelude to the passage to industrial capitalism. In the lack of the commercial bourgeoisie's ability to convert its capital into industrial capital and foreign capital having remained indifferent to Turkish overtures, the state had to act as the *collective entrepreneur* and invest heavily in order to build national economy around the logic of the modern factory system (Taylan 9-10). The state capitalism of the 1930s was therefore essentially programmed for increasing the public sector assistance to the private sector. Private companies were encouraged to become subcontractors to the state enterprises while the state remained to be the primary customer of the goods and services provided by the leading private companies (Insel 1996).

[438] Weiker 1973:171.

[439] In fact, a corporatist-solidarist monoparty program, based on a detailed analysis of 'objective conditions', had been articulated by Mustafa Kemal as early as 1923:
'This nation suffered a lot from political parties. In other countries, parties are formed on the basis of economic aims, because, in those countries there are various social classes. As the counterpart of one party, which supports the interests of one class, another party is formed to defend the interests of another class. This is very natural. The results of the formation of various parties, as if there were class divisions in our country, are well known. On the other hand, when we say People's Party, not only a certain sector, but the whole nation is included in this. First of all, let us view our people:
'As you know, our country is a country of farmers, therefore the majority of our people are farmers. When it is so, the landowners come to the mind. How many landowners own large plots of land in our country? What is the quantity of this land? If analysed it would be seen that in comparison to the capacity of our country no one owns large plots of land. Therefore the landowners need protection, too.
'Then come the artisans and small traders of the province. Naturally, we need to protect their interests, status and future. (...) There are no owners of large capital situated against these traders. How many millionaires do

A number of peculiarly Kemalist or monoparty-republican discursive practices emerged at this juncture. They included the purification of Turkish language; formulation and dissemination of Turkish History Thesis and Sun Language Theory; the formation of the republican Turkish academia around these 'theories' to carry out research in linguistics, historiography, sociology and anthropology; the formulation and dissemination of discourses of populism, villageism, authenticity and national character, all of which were related to grand-narratives of development and progress of the 'nation' to catch up with the contemporary civilisation. The formation of specifically republican institutions marked the turning point of this new orientation of the republican regime.

The ideological reservoir of these apparatuses and practices leading to the consolidation of republican power was the Turkish History Thesis, which was formulated with the primary aim to scientifically prove that Turks were not aliens to Anatolia and Europe, in geographical and cultural regards. In the next section, I will consider in detail this ideological plan of republican governmentality.

II.1. The Republican Ideological Plan: Turkish History Thesis

we have? None. Consequently, we would not be the enemy of those who have some wealth. On the contrary, we will work for the emergence of many millionaires and in fact billionaires in our country.
'Then comes the worker. In our country, institutions like factories and manufactures are very few. There are no more than twenty thousand workers at present. We however need many factories in order to raise our country, and for this we need workers. Therefore, it is necessary to protect the workers, like the farmers.
'Then come the intelligentsia and that layer called the *ulema*. This intelligentsia and *ulema* cannot gather together to become the enemies of the people. Their duty is to enter among the people and enlighten them, by showing them the way of progress.

The ideological reservoir of the consolidation of republican power, Turkish History Thesis, was formulated with the primary aim of scientifically proving that Turks were not aliens to Anatolia and Europe, in geographical and cultural regards. Kemal's following statement on history and reality is revealing of the core of the Kemalist program of 'civilisation':

The Turkish people, which has founded the Turkish republic, is civilised. Civilised in history, civilised in reality. (...) The people of Turkey, which calls itself civilised, and is civilised, must show by its outward appearance from head to toe that it is comprised of civilised and advanced individuals.[440]

For Lacan, desire and reality are intimately connected and the nature of their link can only be revealed in fantasy.[441] The Kemalist desire to 'civilise' is manifestly linked with 'reality' in the above statement and the fantasmatic nature of this link, 'history', is also stated. At this point, we are inevitably in the field of fantasy or the 'Turkish History Thesis'.

Afet Inan, a close associate of Kemal, recalls showing a French antropology book to Kemal in 1928, in which it is said that Turks belonged to the yellow race and are, therefore, inferior people. Upset with what she had learnt she asked Kemal, 'is it so?' to which he replied: 'No, it cannot be so. Let us get busy on this'.[442] Kemal immediately set up a small library with appropriate books and ordered a number of teachers and important members of the new state apparatus to begin historical research on the subject and make reports to him at the appropriate time. There followed in quick succession a number of events, which marked the turn toward an official state pronouncement on theories of Turkish history and eventually of

---

'This is how I see our nation. Because the interests of various occupations are complementary to the others it is not possible to divide them into classes and as a whole they are the people' (Atatürk 1989: 97-8).
[440] Yerasimos 1987:85.
[441] Stavrakakis 1999: 62.

206

Turkish language. In 1931, a Turkish historical research committee (Turk Tarih Tetkik Heyeti) was founded under Mustafa Kemal's command. The movement culminated in the holding of the first Turkish History Congress in Ankara in 1932, where the 'Turkish History Thesis' was formally and officially proclaimed, declared to be the possession of the Turkish nation and turned into an official state dogma. The basic assertion-conclusion of the First Turkish History Congress was threefold:

1. The history of the Turkish nation as it has, up to today, been known does not consist merely of Ottoman history. Turkish history is much older, and the nation which dispersed culture to all nations is the Turkish nation.

2. The Turkish race ... is not yellow. The Turks are white men and brachycephalic.. today masters of our homeland and founders of the oldest culture we are their children acknowledging the same name.

3. The Turks, bringing civilisation to the places in which they settled, and first founders of the civilisations of Mesopothamia, Anatolia, Egypt and the Aegean, are from the Central Asia. We, today's Turks, are the offsprings of Central Asiatics.[443]

This thesis is based on a crude articulation, in racial terms, of the Orientalist *a priori* that the East is 'an otherness of an essentialist character',[444] and hoped to prove that in their essence, Turks were not different from the West. This *a priori* would in fact continue to constitute the primary dilemma of the Turks' search for identity: if we assume an ontological difference between the Orient and Occident, Turks are, at least geographically, located at the very margin separating the two, the inevitable consequence of which is that Turkish identity remains partially Oriental and partially Occidental, or, to rephrase in terms of the 'history

---

[442] Inan & Karal 1946: 59.
[443] Inan & Karal 1946: 59-64.

thesis', the Turkish race is partially yellow and partially white, and the thesis itself is a symptom of this ambiguity.

A consequence of the civilisation program was the radically changed meaning of the encounter with the West and the resulting ambiguity regarding the boundaries of the new discursive territory. The question was simple enough: 'if the Turks are now part of the western civilisation, what is then the outside of the Turkish identity against which the Turkishness could be defined?' The thesis' response to this question consists of the claim that Turkish history is much older than Ottoman history, which is traced back to a 'golden age' in Central Asia, by referring to the second thesis of Gokalp - what is Ottoman is in fact, alien to the Turks' essence, and leaving the Ottoman legacy means the emancipation of Turkish nation from the culture of the oppressor.[445] Republican discourse was thus critically located at the moment of a denial of the Islamic-Ottoman past, in fact, its rearticulation as a 'negativity' to become the republic's constitutive outside.

The lacking hegemony of early Kemalism meant that for the majority of the citizens of the new republic, the real alienation consisted in the forcible introduction of western norms into a Muslim society.[446] The republican response to this view was to present westernisation as claiming back of a lost essence which was not only the essence of the authentic Turkishness but also the source of all civilisation. Consequently, the thesis reads:

---

[444] Malek 1981: 107.
[445] See Chapter 3.
[446] Peyami Safa's 1931 novel *Fatih Harbiye* (Safa 1995) is an example of this line of criticism.

Only the Turks had the original power of creativity and power to create civilisations. (...)
Other racial types were not able to create civilisations before they came into contact with the
Father-Turks.[447]

The thesis thus asserts that at an imaginary point in history, the Turks, after leaving their
homeland in Central Asia, encountered other 'racial types' which they transformed into
civilised races, and this is how the first known civilisations of Mesopotamia, Ancient Greece,
Anatolia and Egypt emerged.[448] The Turkish Language Institute supported the history thesis
by providing 'scientific proof' through the 'Sun Language Theory' that Turkish was the origin
of all world languages.

Although the Kemalist leadership liquidated and silenced through a wave of terror both the
Islamists and the leading cadres of the nationalist Ottoman bureaucracy[449], i.e. the
representatives of the 'imperial vision', Turkish History Thesis was not born in a vacuum. It
drew from certain elements of all the 'three modes of politics'[450], particularly from Turkism,
the source and an organic component of Turkish nationalism from the outset.[451] But the
relationship between Kemalism and Turkism did also involve some tension, particularly on
the definition of the Turkish homeland. Thesis reiterates to a large extent the ideas asserted
by the Turkist thinkers when assuming a continuity of Turkishness from Central Asia to
Anatolia, Hungary, Finland and Estonia. However, this imagined continuity had a logical

---

[447] TTK 1977.
[448] Two state-owned banks, Sümerbank and Etibank, were named after Sumerian and Hittite civilisations.
[449] Independence Courts, Takriri Sukun Law, the closure of the Progressive Republican Party, assassination attempt to Mustafa Kemal, Menemen Incident and the Free Republican Party experiment are the apparatuses and events of this liquidation between 1925 and 1930.
[450] Turkism, Ottomanism and Islamism as described and discussed by Yusuf Akçura (1976). For a recent study on Three Modes of Politics see Yörük 1997.
[451] In fact a prominent figure of the Turkist thought, Yusuf Akçura, was one of the architects of the thesis (See Chapter 5 & Georgeon 1996).

consequence in Turkism, that is, the goal to liberate *Turan,* the Turkish homeland in Central Asia, and unite the 'greater Turkish nation' in this homeland as in their glorious past, Kemalism had to abandon this utopian irredentialist element in favour of the pragmatic motto of 'peace at home, peace on earth', and to concentrate instead on the Turkification of Anatolia, while preserving in its discursive body the rest of the Turkist assumptions. Consequently, Kemalism was born with an inherent logical inconsistency and the 'Turkish History Thesis' represents in this sense, a 'supplement' to the Kemalist discourse, addressing precisely to this inconsistency. When Turks are escalated to the status of the source of all civilisations, there remains no need to return to the original homeland; hence the official claims that prior to the Greeks, civilisations of Turkish origin had existed in Anatolia.

Turkish History Thesis is the constitutive discourse of modern Turkish academia and Turkish 'human sciences' of history, anthropology, archaeology and linguistics. It has produced and reproduced modern political power and academy, and their primary condition of existence, that is, the Turkish national identity.[452] The production and dissemination of the Thesis has

---

[452] I can confirm that majority of the university graduates in Turkey still believe that Hitites and Sumerians were the Turks' ancestors. I also meet archaeology graduates, who read at the university that the antique Aegean civilisation of Lydians had no connection with the modern Greeks. The importance of this assumption is twofold: Firstly, Mustafa Kemal said in an interview in 1930 that 'we are in the process of scientifically proving that we were a nation settled around Izmir before the Greeks'. Secondly, the late President of Turkey, Turgut Ozal, argued in a book titled *La Turquie en Europe* (1988) that Greeks did not originate western civilisation; to the contrary, the first important civilisation was founded in Anatolia and the Anatolian peoples, including the Turks, are the originators and repository of this western civilisation:
  'We have been living in this territory (Anatolia) since the origins of Anatolian civilisations. (…) It is we who have created neolithic revolution. The Sumerians were, moreover, Turanians (Turks from central Asia). (…) At Troy it is we who made war, in alliance with peoples who had come from all corners of Anatolia and who spoke different languages' (Ozal quoted in Vryonis 1991: 20).
There are two conclusions to be derived from above comments: Firstly, Turkish History Thesis is not a phenomenon of the past but it has been the constitutive elements of both the Turkish state and modern Turkish identity, official and popular alike, through decades and many generations. Secondly, Kemalism has been the hegemonic discourse of modern Turkish history. The fact that someone like Ozal, the primal enemy of Kemalism for the neo-Kemalists of the present, deploy abundantly the Kemalist arguments derived from the Thesis in the only book that he ever wrote demonstrates this hegemonic character. A discourse becomes

represented an exceptional case of a modern discursive practice, not merely with its conditions of emergence but with its functioning in the legitimation of the techniques of externalisation, assimilation and repression since the formative years of the republic. Through this functioning, not only the Turkish academia of 'human sciences' was constituted but also specific republican discursive practices were carried out by specifically formed republican institutions, I will consider these institutions and practices in the next subsection.

II.2. Psychoanalytic Excavation: between the Search for Authenticity and Building the National Character

The headquarters where the Turkish History Thesis, the constitutive ideology of the Kemalist 'culture revolution', was produced and propagated was the Turkish History Research Organisation, which was founded in 1931 and assumed later the name Turkish History Institute (TTK). In 1932, a sister organisation, Turkish Language Institute (TDK), was founded with the aims of the purification of language, and later the production of the 'Sun Language Theory' (see below). In 1932 all the historians and history teachers around the country were called to Ankara for the First History Congress, the aim of which was declared as teacher training according to the Thesis. Four volumes of school textbooks had been prepared prior to the Congress, which constituted the backbone of republican 'national education'. Three further 'republican apparatuses' provided the classical Kemalist era its specific character, with the mission of spreading the republican reforms and goals, including national identity, economic development and westernisation, among people. In 1931, the

---

hegemonic to overdetermine the discursive formation only through dispersion, that is, when it is able to provide the grammar of all discourse, including the discourse of dissent.

RPP took over the Turkish Hearths to operate as the People's Houses. In 1939, People's Rooms were also introduced to extend the scope of 'cultural revolution' to the villages. In 1940, Village Institutes were launched by the RPP for teacher training in the rural areas.[453]

Kemalist 'culture revolution', or 'passive revolution', was carried out by these institutions with a range of discursive practices from ethnic nationalism to populism and from the encouragement of participation at economic-corporate level to authoritarian and coercive westernisation. These operations were broadly linked with the Thesis' main tenets of nationalism and 'civilisation'. In these practices a two-way operation can be observed: one of 'excavation' towards the deep inside the 'essence' of Turkishness in the Anatolian population and another of 'construction' which moves from the current popular state to building of a modern man with a 'national character'.

The 'passive revolution's aim of 'excavation' of the Turks' essence was accompanied by an overtly psychoanalytic discourse: ' (Atatürk) is the only statesman who achieved the creation of the regime that was most suitable for the national spirit *that had been forced to sleep in the unconscious* for centuries'.[454] A similar definition was made by Yakup Kadri: 'The main quality that distinguished Mustafa Kemal from the former eminent Turkish characters was his intuitive power. With this power, he *discovered* and *resurfaced* those wills, longings, expectations, abilities and possibilities that lived in his nation's *unconscious*. He was the first to be inspired by the treasures of enlightenment (…) lying in the *depths of Anatolian people's*

---

[453] See Appendix 8 for a detailed account of these republican apparatuses.
[454] Tekin Alp 1988: 38 - my italics.

212

psyche.[455] The relationship between Mustafa Kemal and the nation is therefore analogous to the relationship between the psychotherapist and the patient: to surface the repressed wish that had been pushed to the unconscious. There is however a difference between the analyst and Kemal, which is that Kemalism already knows what is to be surfaced: a 'national character' and 'will to civilise', which had been repressed during the Islamic past.

The concept of 'national character'[456], which has been the subject of an inflation of sublimating definitions, and the concepts of collective psyche and unconscious in Tekin Alp and Yakup Kadri above have striking parallels with Carl Gustav Jung's notions of 'collective unconscious' and 'racial archetype'. Jung claims that evolution and genetic transmission leave traces in human psyche as in human body and therefore that in addition to the conscious and unconscious dimensions of individual psyche, a dimension of collective unconscious formed by particular racial archetypes has to be a central concept of 'analytic psychology'.[457] Not Jung but Gustav Lebon's *Psychologie Politique* is known to have been a source of inspiration for the Turkist intelligentsia since Ömer Seyfettin. Seyfettin referred to Lebon particularly in his argumentation against humanism. One frequent quote of Seyfettin from Lebon is as follows: 'The spirit of a nation consists of traditions, beliefs, collective emotions and even superstitions, which have been determined and reproduced through ancestry. It is because of this spirit that nations think and act in such a way that corresponds to the essential conditions of their existence'.[458] Later in the nationalist thought, references to Jungian notions became

---

[455] Karaosmanoglu 1956: 531-7 - my italics.
[456] For the concept of 'national character', see Bora 1997: 61 and Yildiz 2001: 171-9.
[457] See, Jung 1959.
[458] Seyfettin 1993: 23.

more manifest: '(Ataturk) is the incarnation of an archetype that live in Turk's collective unconscious'.[459]

The Kemalist search for 'national character' and the 'will to civilisation' hidden in the unconscious of this character began with the purification of language and continued with a variety of discursive operations all of which linked closely with the 'Turkish History Thesis'. Therefore, the 'language revolution' and the 'Turkish History Thesis' cannot be understood merely as an isolated elite's fantasies, which operated to compensate for their impossible desires, that is, not *becoming* Turkish but *being* already Turkish; not becoming western but already being western. These practices had important practical consequences: 'This situation is identical to the metamorphosis of a creature, be it an animal or a plant, at a certain stage of evolution. (...) The question is nothing other than the natural development of *biological* properties that *covertly existed* inside that animal. (...) The greatest superiority of Him is His understanding of the *real thoughts* of the *national spirit* and at the same time those elements that consisted of *alien penetrations*'.[460] This statement goes beyond Kemal as psychotherapist and comes very close to introducing Kemal as 'the exorcist'.

This psychotherapeutic and exorcistic desire of discovering the 'essence' of the Turk by peeling off the 'alien shell' covering over particularly the Anatolian peasant led to discursive practices grounded upon authentism and national character determining the course of the 'passive revolution'.

---

[459] Kaplan et. al. 1992: 179.
[460] Tekin Alp 1998: 35 - my italics.

II.3. Anthropology, Language Purification and Villageism

Mustafa Kemal initiated the founding of an Anthropology Research Centre in 1925 as an institute of the Istanbul University with the aim of 'studying the Turk and the Turkish social collective'.[461] Founding members of the institute included the prominent names of the republican nomenclature such as Semseddin Gunaltay and Kopruluzade Fuad, while the associates of the centre included prominent names of the state apparatus such as Hamdullah Suphi, Mustafa Necati and Dr. Refik (Saydam). This implies that anthropologic studies were viewed from the outset as an important state affair.

The emphasis on anthropological research increased in early 1930s, along with growing official inclination towards an ethnic definition of Turkishness. In 1937, an anthropometric research was conducted under Afet Inan's (historian and Ataturk's adopted daughter) supervision. This research analysed 64,000 people around the country regarding 'height, skeleton, weight, head structure, including the wideness of forehead, length of the head-sculpt, facial features, nose length and nose shapes, eye holes, skin, eye and hair colours'.[462] Inan concluded this research by declaring that a 'racial homogeneity' existed in Anatolia', which she called 'the unity of the Turkish race'.[463] There are a number of other researches of the time which all prove that everyone living in Anatolia belongs to the Turkish race.[464]

---

[461] Kansu 1983: 3-4.
[462] Afet Inan 1947: 78-9.
[463] Afet Inan 1947: 181.
[464] Kansu 1940, Atasayan 1939 and Irmak 1939.

Blood groups and fingerprints of the people were also subject to anthropologic research with the same aim.[465]

In 1936, Faculty of Language, History and Geography was founded as the first institution of Ankara University. This faculty collected human skeletons discovered in archaeological excavations in a laboratory and conducted measurements to prove that people who had lived in Anatolia from prehistoric times onwards belonged to the Turkish 'Homo Alpinus' race.[466]

The hypotheses/conclusions of these researches were closely linked to the Turkish History Thesis: 1- There is an ethnic/racial homogeneity in Anatolia; everyone belonged to the Turkish race 2- If all the Anatolian peoples had been ethnic Turks from prehistory to date, then Turks were the origin of all civilisations. 3- Turkish race was not Mongoloit but white Alpine – ' the most perfect race'[467] – like the Europeans. 4- The Turkish people that currently reside in Anatolia are racially descendants of peoples who had founded the prehistoric Anatolian civilisations. 5- Therefore, Anatolia was historically the Turks' homeland.[468]

The continuity of Turkish language was viewed as a significant proof of ethnic continuity of Turkishness, while the purification of language was essential for the future maintenance of the Turkish race.[469] In fact, Turkish language as an essential component of Turkish identity had been a subject of intellectual activity since mid 19th Century. On 3 November 1928, Latin Alphabet was adopted, which Mustafa Kemal announced as a change from Arabic to

---

[465] Onur 1943, Irmak 1943.
[466] Aydin 2001: 362.
[467] Dilacar 1940: 7-8.
[468] For a discussion on Turkish History Thesis, see Appendix 9.

'Turkish letters'.[470] In 1930, Kemal made a further statement in support of the 'purification of language': 'The Turkish nation, which has proved its ability to defend its country and its full independence, should also free its language from the yoke of foreign languages'.[471] These 'foreign languages' were primarily Arabic and Persian, two main components of Ottoman Turkish. The Turkish Language Institution was founded in 1932 with the aim of simplifying and purifying the language by bringing written Turkish closer to the spoken tongue and by trawling dictionaries of various Turkic languages for 'pure' Turkish words. In addition, researchers were asked by Mustafa Kemal to travel the length and breadth of the country to record Turkish words, which had survived only in provincial usage. A 'pure' Turkish vocabulary emerged through the revival of old-fashioned and provincial words and quarrying central Asian Turkic languages, which led to the generation of a private, highly incomprehensible language, remote from everyday usage. Realising the obvious artificial outcomes of their search for naturality, the republican leadership slowed down the purification movement and introduced the 'Sun Language Theory' in 1935, which asserted that the origin of all languages was Turkish. Promoted personally by Ataturk, the efforts of the linguists were now directed to 'proving' that particularly words from European languages had Turkish roots.

The search for authenticity is also evident in the 1930s movement of 'villageism'. This movement, propagated by the periodical *Ulku* and carried out by People's Houses and Village Rooms, was based on a sublimation of the village life and peasants as the essential

---

[469] Yildiz 2002: 229.
[470] Mango 1999: 465.
[471] Perincek 1996: 55.

elements of Turkish nation.[472] Peasants were portrayed as the incarnation of the 'pure',
authentic, noble and smart Turkish prototype. The primary aim of the Turkification and
westernisation program was consequently *'peupleism'*, that is, turning towards the people to
expose their Turkish 'essence' lying underneath that alien (Ottoman/Oriental/Muslim) shell.
'The peasant is the lord of the nation' (Atatürk), not simply because the corporatist state politics
of the 1930s required such a rhetoric but, at the same time, because of this 'Narodnik'
dimension of Kemalism. The Turkish Hearths and later People's Houses, People's Rooms and
Village Institutes operated, on the one hand, like the 'dervish lodges and convents of the
western culture'[473] with the mission of carrying civilisation to the people, and, on the other,
with the determination of discovering 'the Turk' in the essence of the peasant: that 'pure'
kernel, which was the father of all civilisations.[474] The sublimation of the people and the
peasant sometimes breached the 'progressive' aims of the villagist turn, sublimating peasant
conservatism. The 1940s journal *Kopuz* declared: 'Turkish peasant protected the Turkish
culture through their mores and traditions, which remained unchanged'.[475]

A degree of disappointment of this optimistic desire of psychotherapeutic and exorcistic
excavation was the inevitable outcome of these practices. The constructive discourse of
'national character', which was designed as the adjustment of the authentic Turk's essence
with the values of contemporary civilisation which were very suitable for his essence, quilted
over this disappointment. The course that the Kemalist 'passive revolution' had to take while
being fought out by the 'organic intellectuals' of the republic over the battlefield of the

---

[472] Karaomerlioglu 2002: 287.
[473] Belge 1996: 1299.
[474] See, Toprak 1998: 52-64.
[475] Toprak 1998: 56.

social, consisted of a journey commencing with a hope to discover the character that slept in the unconscious and ended in an attempt to build a 'national character' through neurotic-authoritarian interventions into the people's unconscious. The whole affair of Kemalist 'passive revolution' arguably ended in its best with the cultural 'colonisation' of the periphery, that is, the invasion of the nation's psyche by the functionaries of the 'conscious' core:

> It was assumed that by means of theatre, which People's Houses and People's Rooms took to the remotest corners of the country, people would identify with the invented past that had been constructed in accordance with the official ideology's project for the future. The pro-western elites believe that people are unable to separate the fact from fiction and will therefore accept whatever is staged in the theatre as reality.[476]

There were therefore two simultaneous dramas staged in the halls of People's Houses and People's Rooms: on the one side, the drama that was performed on the stage and, on the other, the drama entitled 'modernised subjects watching theatre' that the whole audience performed for a smaller audience of overlooking 'pro-western elites'.

There is a general consensus among the narrators of Kemalist Turkey that despite all its efforts in its 'classical Kemalist era' the republican regime failed to expand its cultural appeal to the periphery (province). Kemalism was essentially a doctrine of the new rulers in urban centres; while the education process and the army were seen as the primary modes of

---

[476] Ayvazoglu 1996: 836.

transmission for the new identity, much of the countryside continued to live according to traditional, usually VolkIslam values [477]

III. Casualties of the Turkish Passive Revolution

An immediate symptom of the failure of 'passive revolution' was the intensification of the ethnic nationalist tone of the republican discourse, while Turkification of those not of 'pure Turkish stock' was also a frequently emphasised task:

> In this unified nationality, alien cultures have to be melted. (...) We offer openly to those who view themselves belonging to communities other than the civilisation of the Turkish nation: come together with the Turkish nation; not as an aggregate of different cultures, not as confederated civilisations; but as one culture and one civilisation. (...) If we are to live, we will live as an indivisible mass of nation.[478]

The alien cultures, communities and civilisations were those who would be subjected to an official campaign for the Turkification of Turkey. The purification of language movement was accompanied by a 'Citizen Speak Turkish!' campaign, which pressurised the minorities. In 1938, the British Ambassador reported that 'local Greeks and Jews were fired or blamed for speaking a non-Turkish language'.[479] Following the outbreak of the World War II, the government mobilised all Jewish, Greek and Armenian males between 18 and 45 years old to be sent to special camps in the Anatolian interior where there were reports of harsh treatment

---

[477] In villages, the arrival of the personnel of the people's houses usually caused the children run away screaming, 'mommy, the state is coming!' (Arman 1969.)

[478] Inonu's 1925 speech to teachers cited in Yucel 1994: 25.

[479] Poulton 1997: 116.

and high mortality rates.[480] In 1942, a Capital Tax was introduced mainly on non-Muslim businesses. Defaulters were deported to labour camps in east Anatolia. This episode of Nazi-like treatment of the minorities, including a bitter anti-Jewish campaign, ended in 1944, obviously due to the changing course of war.

The non-Turkish Muslim minorities, who had no international protection, were also among the above-referred 'other cultures, communities and civilisations'. In fact, Inonu's above speech can be read to a large extent a programmatic statement for the Kurds' assimilation. The intensification of policies of assimilation of the Kurds, the accumulation of ethnicity based nationalist discourses and the authoritarian inclination of the republican government were synchronised events. If the primary dispositif of the Kurdish assimilation was the punitive/corrective military operation, the headquarters of the ethnicity based discourses of assimilation was the Turkish History and Turkish Language Institutions.

III.1. Thesis and the Kurds

The violent annexation of Kurdistan and the subsequent policies of assimilation were the new Turkish state's experiences of living through the fantasy of the Turkish History Thesis, that is, the practice of dealing with the double lack, of a 'de-Islamised' nation and of 'civilisation' both gesturing further towards the primary trauma: *Anatolia* was neither 'Ana' nor 'dolu', that is neither 'mother' nor 'full'. There are no ancient political borders separating Anatolia from Mesopotamia and the Turkish History Thesis declares forcefully that the Mesopotamian and Anatolian nations of Sumerians and Hitites were of Turkish origin. North Kurdistan, which

---

[480] Okte 1964: x.

221

remained within the borders of the republican state, was therefore part of the original Turkish land, although it was currently inhabited by an alienated group (Kurds) of originally Turkish ethnicity. It was therefore the mission of the state to integrate this portion of Anatolia into the 'motherland' and to Turkify the Kurds by introducing them into civilisation. This introduction usually began with the military products imported from the Soviet Union and fascist mentalities imported from Europe. Turkish History Thesis and the Sun Language Theory thus matured a theoretical toolbox on Kurdish question and offered it to the political/military authorities' use. It is remarkable that all these theoretical gains were achieved in compliance with the Father's abolition of the signifier Kurd in the symbolic order. Consequently, most of the discussion on new findings of the Thesis and new scientific proofs of Sun Language Theory went without the pronunciation of the Kurds. Celal Sahir, an executive of the Turkish Language Institution (TDK), declared in the First Language Congress held in September/October 1932 :

> There is no doubt that the languages spoken by those uncivilised tribes are not desired.[481]

After the departure of Real Father to the eternity (Atatürk was posthumously declared the 'Eternal Chief' by Inönü), the prohibited signifier could find limited expression under the supervision of the Symbolic Father (Inönü declared himself the 'National Chief' after Atatürk's death). In the fourth congress of the TDK, S. Fethi Gökçaylı made the following statement:

> If the Kurds, Laz and the Cyrcassians, who are originally Turkish, and who had been given linguistic liberty under the Ottoman State, were allowed the same liberty in our time, this would mean a retreat from the unity of our language. The dialects of

---

[481] Cited in Besikçi 1977b: 183.

Karadeniz, East, South, Kastamonu and Central Anatolia, which have certain nuances, should be replaced by the Istanbul accent.[482]

In the same discourse, the Kurds exist but Kurdish does not occur; all we can have instead is an 'East' accent of Turkish. The 1936 edition of the Turkish Dictionary of the Turkish Language Institute (TDK) reads on the subject of the Kurd:

A group of people and the individual who belongs to this group living in Turkey, Iraq and Iran, consisting of the Turks most of who changed their language and speak a defect Farsi.[483]

If the ideological apparatuses of the state went so far then the military would naturally be expected to interpret it in colloquial terms. So, the super-Governor of Tunceli, General Abdullah Alpdogan, asserted in 1936 that, 'the people of the Eastern Turkey are mountain Turks and Kurdish is the mountain accent of Ottoman Turkish'.[484] Alpdogan's bold statement was not treated as an embarrassing accident, but became the blueprint of military indoctrination. A 'white book' published by the General Staff in the 1980s attempts the same description to read like pastoral lyrics:

There was snow on the peak of the mountains, which did not melt in the summer. When sun shined, the surface of snow became a glass-like radiant layer. Hard on the surface, soft underneath.

When one walked on this snow, the point where the foot stepped on the snow would collapse making a noise like 'kırt-kürt'. This was the reason why the Turkomans of the East were called the Kurds. What the separatists refer to as the Kurd, was in fact the

---

[482] Cited in Besikçi 1977b: 183
[483] TDK 1936: 481.
[484] Mumcu 1995: 155-6.

223

name of this noise of the footsteps of the Turks lived on the high and snowy plateaux on the mountains.[485]

What can be observed in the formation and the practices of the TTK and TDK is a theoretical preparation on the basis of the retrospective reflections on the republic's decade long campaign to annex north Kurdistan. This theoretical preparation was no doubt a long-term project of production of discourses of human sciences, including archaeology, linguistics, anthropology and history to be translated into geography, demography, medicine, economy and sociology, as the precondition of politics, that is, to assist the consolidation of a specifically republican governmentality.

III.2. Annexation and Assimilation

With the break of the Sheikh Said rebellion Kurdish provinces were immediately put under martial law. Two subsequent laws of deportation in 1925 and 1927 were resolved in the parliament and the members of the Kurdish clans which participated in the rebellion and the potential rebels were forcibly deported to the western provinces.[486] On 26 June 1927, a special law for the formation of 'General Inspectorate' which would govern the Kurdish provinces was put in effect. According to Colonel Resat Halli, thirteen large scale counter-insurgency operations were conducted in the region between the suppression of the Sheikh Said rebellion of 1925 and the break of the Ararat rebellion of 1930.

---

[485] Cited in Tusalp 1988: 365.
[486] Tunçay 1981: 174.

224

The Ararat rebellion was organised and coordinated by *Hoybun*, a Kurdish political party founded in exile following the suppression of the Sheikh Said rebellion. The rebels proclaimed Agri 'a province of independent Kurdistan' and assigned their own provincial governor. Agri was located on the Iranian border and until 1930, the rebels were able to cross the border during Turkish army's operations. In order to control the situation, Turkish authorities managed to strike a deal with the Iranian state and closed the passage to Iran. In September 1930, the rebels, including their leaders, were surrounded and then 'destroyed' by 40,000 strong Turkish forces.

After each counter-insurgency operation, villages in the area were torched and captured male villagers 'of suitable age for using firearms' would be summarily executed.[487] The rarely conducted bodycounts show the number of the killed villagers, pronounced in the reports as 'rebels captured dead' were much (six-fold or seven-fold) higher than the number of the firearms captured and in some reports it was overtly stated that 'unarmed rebels' were killed.[488] The excessive killings were encouraged by a special law no. 1850 of 1930 legalising the murder of the Kurds:

> Murders and other actions committed individually or collectively between 20 June
> 1930 and 10 December 1930 by the representatives of the state or the province, by
> the military or civil authorities, by the local guards and militiamen, or by any civilian

---

[487] Halli 1972: 196.

[488] 1935 Sason operation: '155 rebels were killed, 24 rebels injured and 52 weapons were captured.' (Halli 1972: 159)

1937 Correction of Sason: '273 rebels were killed, 52 rebels injured and 39 rifles were captured' (Simsir 1991: 91).

1927 Bican operation: '6 armed and 39 unarmed rebels of Omer Faro gang, 4 armed and 12 unarmed bandits of Emin Miko gang were captured and killed' (Halli 1972: 240-1). According to the reports of commanding officers, 280 villages were torched, and more than 2,000 villagers were killed in the Bican operation (Halli 1972: 108).

having helped the above or acted on their behalf, during the pursuit and extermination of the revolts which broke out in Erciş, Zilan, Agri and the surrounding areas, including Pulumur and Erzincan province and the area of the First Inspectorate, will not be considered as crimes.[489]

A wave of deportations would follow each 'correction' operation. These deportations were initially reprisals against rebellious tribes, a consequence of the operation. In later years, deportations became the priory aim of the operations, as part of a concerted effort to assimilate the Kurds. Massive population resettlement was applied through the deportation of the Kurds to western Turkey and the settlement of the Turks in their place. Law of Resettlement of 1934, the document of assimilation policy, officially proclaimed its aim as the dispersal of the Kurds. The law defined three categories of settlement zones:

- consisting of those districts 'whose evacuation is desirable for health, economic, cultural, political and security reasons and where the settlement has been forbidden,

- designated for transfer and resettlement of the population whose assimilation to Turkish culture is desired,

- consists of 'places where an increase of population of Turkish culture is desired.[490]

The law therefore implied that Kurdish districts included in the zone one would be completely depopulated, whose population would be dispersed in the zone two (west and central Anatolia), while in zone three, the remaining Kurdish districts, the Kurdish element was to be diluted by partial deportation and the resettlement there of Turks.[491] Van Bruinessen reflects on the consequences of these assimilation policies:

---

[489] Kendal 1980: 65.
[490] Bruinessen 1994.
[491] Article 11 of the same law prohibits attempts by non-Turkish people to preserve their cultures by sticking together in ethnically homogenous villages or trade guilds:

Following the major Kurdish nationalist uprisings (...) a systematic policy of the abolition of tribes and the assimilation of the Kurds was adopted. (...) Everything that symbolised a separate Kurdish identity would be destroyed: language, outfit, names.[492]

III.3. Dersim becomes Tunceli

The policy objectives of the consolidation program shifted in the 1930s from the annexation of Kurdistan to the general maintenance of territorial integrity and national homogeneity. The Dersim campaign of the late 1930s emerged as an extensive and systematic consequence of this republican desire to colonise the national sphere.

Michel Foucault defines the condition of governmentality as 'the fixation, control and rational distribution of populations built on statistical knowledge'. The man hence as much as being a liberal humanistic category, becomes a figure of the 'science of the state'. The aggregate of men is 'population', the object of the practices of governmentality, which, deep under the man as rational subject, aim primarily to mould the body into docility. The Dersim plan was a declaration of power to punish, which literally fabricated delinquency and managed to organise a field of objectivity in which punishment would be able to function as treatment. Dersim was, like the French prisons in Foucault's *Discipline and Punish,* a laboratory of modern power.

Those whose mother tongue is not Turkish will not be allowed to establish as a group in new villages or neighbourhoods, workers' or artisans' organisations, nor will such persons be allowed to reserve an existing village, ward, enterprice or workshop for members of the same race' (Besikçi 1977a: 142).
[492] Bruinessen 1978: 242.

The Dersim plan with its application illustrates a straightforward example of transition to modern governmentality. The relationship between population and territory, the relations of men with things, and the proposed adjustments in these relationships for the achievement of governmentality: all these can be observed as the main objectives of the Dersim plan. The Dersim of the late 1930s, with its clearly defined geographical territory (6600 square metres) and a population of 70000 to 100000, which became the subject of detailed analysis of various human sciences, was also the laboratory of these human sciences. Below is an attempt towards an analysis of Kemalism on a field consisting of that laboratory where Kemalist governmentality carried out its experiments on Dersim Kurds in 1937-1938.

Silence on the experience of the 'civilisation of Dersim' is not peculiar to the Turkish State's practices, but is an academic and political tradition of both national and international character.[493] The surviving Dersim generations' approach to the question is understandably overdetermined with 'mourning and melancholia' while monitoring the rather rare dissident literature on the question requires *übermensch* skills to separate exaggerations from valuable data.[494] In these conditions, I shall refer mainly to official documents, legislation and the

---

[493] In the two standard international texts on Turkey, Bernard Lewis (1968) and Stanford J. Shaw and Ezel Kural Shaw (1977), there is not a single word about the Dersim events. Turkish authors usually refer to the incident as one in many security issues that the republic dealt with at the time (see Van Bruinessen 1994: 141), while some others like Mumcu (1995) and Akgul (2000) clumsely slander that it was a continuation of the Armenian problem.
[494] The rarity of the dissident literature is also due to the religious peculiarity of the Dersim Kurds, who practiced a form of Alevi faith and who still keep a critical distance from the mainstream Kurdish politics. Consequently, their case is tend to be overlooked by the Kurdish and pro-Islamist authors, who are usually very sensitive for instance on the Sheikh Said rebellion. Turkish left, on the other hand, views the experience as part of the 'abolition of a pre-capitalist modes of production' at the historical stage of 'national-democratic revolution'. For the examples of the rare dissident literature see, Dersimi (1952), Dr S¸ıvan (1975) and Kalman (1995).

newspaper articles of the period regarding Dersim and a publicly unavailable book,[495] published and subsequently requested back and destroyed by the publishers, the War History Department of Turkish General Staff, which gives a detailed, day-by-day account of the military operations, including atrocities.[496]

From 1926 onwards, Dersim became the subject of nine systematic reports prepared by the important members of the state apparatus.[497] These reports derived from the historical, linguistic and anthropologic theories produced around the Turkish History Thesis and extended the research to reach demographic, geographical, sociological, medical and politico/military conclusions. Following a decade of programmatic preparation, a special law for Dersim region, Tunceli Law, passed the Parliament on 25 December 1935. The law changed the name of the region from Dersim to Tunceli[498] and put the province under the administration of a military governor. The extraordinary powers of the governor included the arrest and deportation of individuals and families and the decision to perform executions.

Minister of Interior Sükrü Kaya in his presentation of Tunceli Law to the National Assembly outlined the findings of the research to date, the plan of the reform operation and the aims of the reform. He began with geographical definition of the field of operation, including the size and the location of the area and its environmental features, and moved to outline the demographic findings. Kaya then outlined the sociological structure including the details of 91 tribes in the region. After referring to the region's economic backwardness and proposing

---

[495] Halli 1972.

[496] There are two previous academic works based on the same data, Ismail Beş,ikçi (1990) and Martin Van Bruinessen (1994), which I have frequently referred to in the preparation of this section, in addition to the memoirs of the late Kurdish intellectual Musa Anter (1990)

229

the anthropologic thesis that the people of the region were authentic Turks, Kaya made a brief pedagogic analysis to conclude that people of Dersim were 'ignorant'. Kaya's presentation continued with a strategic critical account of the 11 previous military operations to the region between 1903 and 1935. He said that after the partial aims of each operation achieved the army returned to their bases, but this time the state intended to stay in Dersim, in order to end banditry and maintain security. Although the matter was defined in terms of a security problem, Kaya also stated that an extraordinary situation did not exist in Dersim: 'I would like to state to the people that there is no extraordinary situation in our country'. Deriving from the medical discourse, Kaya concluded his presentation by terming the situation a disease. A radical treatment was needed, he said, and the law was part of a reform program that would bring civilisation to the people.[499]

An obviously impressed Prime Minister, called the Tunceli law 'a law based on scientific research'. Indeed, Kaya's presentation of the law deployed all the 'human sciences' in the analysis of the situation, through extensive use of statistics to outline a scientific program for long-term treatment, that is to impose a rational rearrangement of men and things within a given territory, which was currently in total chaos. Kaya's argument is an elegant demonstration in political practice of the Foucauldian notion of governmentality, or, rather 'the will to government'.

Following the legislative preparation, a three-year military plan of pacification/correction and 'civilisation' was also detailed in 1936 in a booklet titled DERSIM of which 'one hundred

---

[497] See Appendix 10.
[498] Literally the 'Land of Bronze' referring to an invented myth that Turks lived in the region in the Bronze Age.

230

copies are printed under record' by the General Command of Gendarmary of the Ministry of Interior of Republic of Turkey.[500] The first year of the operation was devoted to the disarmament of people and the deportation of the tribal chiefs. A list of 347 families to be deported to the west was detailed in the booklet's appendix. North Dersim, consisting of Ovacik and Nazimiye districts, 'total population of which is around 11742', was to be evacuated and its population deported to the west.[501] The disorderly settlements were to be prohibited and torched. With the commencement of the 'punitive operation', civil servants of 'local' origin were to be sacked from the government offices. In the second year, the plan suggested, the disarmament was to continue and state institutions were to be planted in the region. Military and police posts, highways and primary schools are stated among these institutions. Tribal families, after being separated from their chiefs, were to be gathered around empty plots of land suitable for cultivation; people would be promoted to involve in farming and other trades. The third year would be the conclusion of the institutionalisation of the state in the region, with more road construction and further measures to improve commercial activities. The booklet, which includes a business plan like budget for the first year of the operation, concludes with detailing the military preparations, including the modernisation of the existing bridges and highways, necessary for the plan's implementation.

The arrival of 'civilisation' in the form of troop deployments, new military posts, modernisation of main roads and the reinforcement of bridges annoyed the tribes.[502] Seyid

---

[499] Kaya's speech before the Grand National Assembly, 25 December 1935, quoted in Beş,ikçi 1990: 10.
[500] For the publication details of this booklet see Göktas 1991: 123-5.
[501] Turkiye Cumhuriyeti Dahiliye Vekaleti Jandarma Umum Kumandanlığı (1936), *Dersim*. Ankara.
[502] For the left's anti-feudal arguments for rallying behind the Dersim operation see Appendix 11.

231

Riza, who had regional authority over the tribes, managed to ally five tribes in resistance.[503] In a symbolic act of resistance, a group of rebels burnt down a wooden bridge and cut the telephone lines. The date of the incident 21 March 1937, coincided with the Kurdish festival *Newroz*. Military moved in full force and began implementing its plan, and continued its operations to subdue until the end of summer. In September 1937, Seyid Riza and his closest associates surrendered. They were summarily tried and executed. The next spring, operations were resumed with even greater force. On 1 November 1938, Atatürk's opening speech of the parliament read by PM Celal Bayar due to Atatürk's illness, stated:

The collective banditry in Tunceli, which continued for decades and caused tension from time to time, was annihilated in a short time as a result of the activities carried out according to a certain program. Such activities are now a thing of the past, since they cannot be repeated again.[504]

We understand from Atatürk's account above that whatever happened there had been scientifically and rationally planned in advance to be conducted systematically 'according to a certain program'. The outcome of the application of this 'program' was, according to Ismail Besikci (1990), a genocide. A report by the British Consul in Trabzon is affirmative of Besikçi's claims by comparing the 'brutal and indiscriminate violence' used in Dersim to the Armenian genocide of 1915:

Thousand of Kurds, including women and children were slain; others, mostly children, were thrown into the Euphrates; while thousands of others in less hostile areas, who had first been deprived of their cattle and other belongings were deported

---

[503] Other tribes either remained neutral initially or took the government's side.
[504] TBMM 1920-1950.

to provinces in central Anatolia. It is now stated that the Kurdish question no longer exists in Turkey.[505]

The official military history of the campaign[506] is affirmative of many of the brutalities reported by Dersimi (1952) and other dissident accounts of the event. A document dated 4 May 1937 entitled 'Secret Decision of the Council of Ministers on the Punitive Expedition to Dersim' envisages a final solution to the perpetual rebellions in Dersim: 'This time the people in the rebellious districts will be rounded up and deported', instructs the government and goes on to order the army to 'render those who have used arms or are still using them once and for all harmless on the spot, to completely destroy their villages and to remove their families'.[507] This reads like an order to kill all men in the area, given that the Dersim reports above had already repeatedly claimed that every men in Dersim was known to carry arms. The Chief of Staff's only figure of rebel casualties, including killed or captured alive, is an ambiguous 7954 for the seventeen days of the 1938 offensive alone.[508] Other reports of individual clashes are impossible to add up to obtain a consistent number. Kurdish sources speak of tens of thousands including women, children and the elderly. We probably will never learn the full dimensions of atrocities of the 'civilisation' of Dersim. Martin van Bruinessen, following Besikçi, argues that what we know from government communiqué, orders and reports in addition to witness accounts and the fact that the official number of deaths above is more than ten percent of the official record of population are sufficient to describe the Dersim

---

[505] Report from the Consul in Trabzon, 27 September 1938. Public Record Office, London, FO 371 files, document E5961/69/44.
[506] Halli 1972.
[507] Published in Besikçi 1990: 67.
[508] Halli 1972: 478.

233

operation, if not a genocide as such, an act of ethnocide, with the manifest aim of 'the destruction of Kurdish ethnic identity'.[509]

IV. Conclusion

Guarded by the Ataturk myth and the military, the republic improved its techniques of governmentality along with a positive ethnic based notion of nation. The advance of republican governmentality also involved the consolidation of the republican power through the institutionalisation of peculiar republican apparatuses. The violent consequences of this model have been observed in the Republic's conquest of Dersim. I have demonstrated in the above sections the points of failure of the attempted 'culture revolution' or 'passive revolution' and argued that despite these efforts a duality was maintained regarding the social objectivity and its discursive articulations including perceptions of political identity. On one side of this duality rests an identity based upon the repression of the conventional Islamic/Ottoman/Oriental identifications in favour of modernisation and the goals of modernity – including particularly secularism – the boundaries of which are guarded by the myth of Ataturk. The field of this level can be called the official Turkish identity, or the 'conscious' identity of the 'centre', the ideology of the nation. The other side of the duality consists of a national territory defined through the exclusion of the non-Muslim identity, the absolute psychic boundaries of which are marked with foreclosure and guarded by the military. The field of this level is that of national-popular which includes the repressed 'unconscious' identity of the 'periphery', that is, 'common sense' level of the nation. The hegemonic expansion of the conscious field over the filed of common sense, through the

---

[509] Bruinessen 1994. See also Chapter 2 and Appendix 12.

234

operation of the republican discursive apparatuses and practices of governmentality, was partially motivated by an ethnic nationalist argument, based on the imagery of a hierarchical ethnic pyramid of the Turkish 'super family'. This argument included an appeal to the Muslim ethnicities for assimilation within the imagined community of the Turks within which the conscious and unconscious levels would be welded onto each other.

The two fields of the split social have been linked together in practice through the long-term operation of education and the military service. It is therefore legitimate to assert that the army is the precise republican space where the popular perceptions of identity have been sutured to the Kemalist notions:

> The republican revolution surfaced as a radical change for many institutions of society, but in this transformation and social rupture, the only institution that did not break with its Ottoman roots was the military. (...) The Republic is the work of the military and its central concept is not change and revolution but the salvation and the maintenance of the state.[510]

The Turkish military astonishingly maintained a religious face unlike any of the state institutions. Symbols of 'Mehmedcik', 'gazi' and 'sehid' are abundantly employed religious signifiers in military. Every private is *Mehmedcik* in the popular and military discourses. The name Mehmed is the Turkish version of the name of the Prophet Muhammad. In fact, the army is often referred to as 'Prophet's Hearth', in both discourses above. All the soldiers who participate in a war are called 'gazi' (veteran/warrior) in the military/popular discourse. The word *Gazi* comes from the Arabic word *Gaza*, which means a battle of the *jihad*, religious war. Similarly, all those that die in military action are called *sehid*, 'a martyr of Islam'. In the military exercises, soldiers are asked to charge on the enemy by chanting 'Allah Allah'.

Moreover, this gesture towards the repressed periphery is not unilateral but mutual. In the popular discourse, a boy cannot be considered a 'proper man'[511] before serving in the army. The educational role of the military is popularly accepted as the ultimate stage of transition to adult life.[512] Mahmut Makal's 'Our Village' demonstrates this point well. Makal writes that the only way in which he managed to convince villagers to send their children to school was to explain that they would need reading and writing skills as conscripts in the army. This loyalty to the nation did not contradict with strong religious feelings. 'The contradiction between republicanism and Islam was a problem for the educated elite, not the common people'.[513]

This interaction between the Kemalist and Volkislam discourses can be called as 'return of the repressed', since the repressed Volkislam constitutes the repressed unconscious of the Kemalist psyche. The equilibrium of the field in which this return is possible is based on a shared definition of the Other, that is, the non-Muslim identity.[514] This open nature of Kemalism towards 'common sense' discourses of religion and nationalism also explains its continuity as a primary component of modern Turkish identity. It as much this 'psychological validity' as Kemalism's flexibility that has made it possible for Kemalism to hover over and above the Turkish symbolic order through the republican history.

---

[510] Celik 2002: 146.
[511] He cannot get a permanent job and cannot marry.
[512] Boys with terminal illnesses or bodily defects, often try to deceive military health authorities in order to be admitted to the military, because refusal on any of these grounds leads to life-long shame and embarrassment.
[513] Ozdalga 1998: 31.

236

I have argued in the previous chapter that Kemalism's value lies in its function as the framework of republican discursive horizon in which a number of discourses and subject positions have been sutured. In this chapter, I have demonstrated the constitutive discursive practices that have operated within the Kemalist framework. Turkish political identity has been built and maintained by these discursive practices which provided Kemalism's main tenets of civilisation and nationalisation with specific discursive contents, such as militarism, ethnic Turkism, authenticism, assimilation and peasantism, along with corporatism, authoritarianism, development and progress. The features of republican power that emerged from this process include the materialisation of the Kemalist regime of truth in the form of republican governmentality, which has been demarcated by a militarist discourse and Ataturk's personality cult as the guardians of the republic.

---

[514] In Chapter 2, I have already considered the crucial role of the 'Borromean Knot' that tie the conscious and unconscious dimensions of Turkish identity 'when necessary', in the analysis of a specifically Kemalist practice, the Dersim operation, as one of the constitutive events of republican governmentality.

CHAPTER 5

AFTER "SALVATION": THE SEARCH FOR IDENTITY UNDER REPUBLICAN HORIZON

The main thesis of this research is threefold: First, Turkey's centre-periphery cleavage is analogous to consciousness-unconscious cleavage of the human psyche, and therefore the functioning of Turkish politics demonstrates many features of neurosis. Second, like every national identity, the structure of Turkish identity contains a great deal of features analogous to psychosis, when the Turkish traumatic perception of the absolute outside or the 'foreclosed' other is taken into account.[515] Third, the contemporary crisis in Turkey is primarily a consequence of the need to redesign Turkey's politico-discursive order for the 21st Century. Due to this character and because it involves the recurrence of the unsolved identity questions, with the symptomatic return and traumatic reappearance of what had been excluded from Turkish identity at the turn of the 20th Century, the current crisis is to a large extent a recurrence of the Ottoman identity crisis. In the preceding chapters I have demonstrated that a crucial point of the construction of modern Turkish identity and the Turkish political order was the formation and operation of mechanisms of exclusion and therefore that the other and the outside have been constitutive of the Turkish identity.

---

[515] What I have observed above is therefore the coexistence of different psychic structures in the same identity. Both neurosis and psychosis can be observed in the discourses that shape modern Turkish identity, which is an obvious inconsistency in strict psychoanalytic terms. However, the concern of this research is not the psychoanalytic treatment of an analysand but understanding a political identity, that is, a particular mode of political subjectivity by applying the methods developed by the psychoanalytic theory. As the juncture of various discourses with groups of people, political identities are arguably suitable for accommodating various psychic structures, and if one is forced to make an analogy, it would be legitimate to view political identities as typical cases of a 'borderline personality'.

In this chapter, I will move further in time through modern history to broaden my analysis towards the search for identity under Kemalist hegemony. I shall concentrate mainly on three discourses – Turkism, Anatolianism and Turk-Islam Synthesis – which have contested until the 1990s to hegemonise Turkey's discursive horizon with different comprehensive designs of Turkish identity. I shall assess each identity claim regarding its responses to the three questions - the problem of the west, the others of identity, the legitimation of the ownership of the 'homeland' – each emerging from the main faultlines of modern Turkishness. I shall then dwell on the intellectual and scholarly discussion, particularly around the problem of the past, which continued in the background of these contesting discourses throughout republican history.

Before beginning the analysis and discussion of this chapter, it has to be pointed out that the intertwined character of cultural identity discourses and political discourses and practices has been a distinguishing character of Turkish politics since at least the late 19th Century. The 'Three Modes of Politics' which constituted the political horizon of the late Ottoman social order were at the same time three modes of culture, or 'three forms of life with family resemblances' in Witgensteinian terms. The republican authorities invested most of their energy and resources on the construction of a national identity through a cultural transformation and culture has always been a primary subject of official politics of modern Turkey. Consequently, all the resistances to the official level have not only included discourses of cultural identity but prioritised cultural identity. Turkey's social order has been constructed and interpreted as the field of conflicting social imaginaries, consisting of conflicting perceptions of political/cultural subjectivity. The study in this chapter is

239

consequently an attempt to explicate these conflicting perceptions, with an additional attempt to establish their limitations which correspond to the 'natural' boundaries of nationhood, that is, a shared set of limitations constituting the absolute borders of the Turkish political psyche. These borderlines which were drawn by a number of traumatic experiences during the formation of identity can be legitimately identified as the absolute boundaries of Turkish nationalism and Turkish political psyche.

I. Kemalist Variations: Influences and Discursive Articulations

I have argued in Chapter 3 that Kemalism emerged through the adoption of a series of definite responses in equilibrium between nationalism and westernisation to the problems that the Ottoman identity crisis had brought to the fore. As a nationalist discourse, Kemalism was influenced to a great extent by Turkism; in turn Kemalism would influence a variety of discourses that emerged through republican history around the questions of national identity, modernisation and the problem of 'civilisation'. In this section, I will provide a general outline of these mutual influences and further questions of identity emerging from these interrelations, which will be followed in the next section with a detailed introduction of these interrelations leading to the emergence of a variety of discourses in republican history.

I.1. Genesis: the Turkist Turkish Revolution

The ways in which the Turkist thought of the late Ottoman Empire[516] influenced republican nationalism include the definition of the 'motherland', the perspective of assimilation of the non-Turkish Muslim population and the formulation of the main tenets of the Turkish History Thesis.

Although they never abandoned their Turanist ideal as the ultimate goal, the Turkists were the founders of territorial nationalism, which would become the distinguishing feature of Kemalist nationalism.[517] The first proposal of assimilation of the non-Turkish Muslim population of the new Turkey also came from a Turkist thinker, Yusuf Akcura:

> Those united by religion who were essentially not Turks but who to a certain extent had become Turks would become more assimilated by the Turks, and even those who had never identified themselves as such could themselves be made into Turks.[518]

Akcura had also written in an article titled 'We Should Learn and Teach Turkishhood' as early as 1908 that 'the oldest civilisation – older than even the Egyptian civilisation – was created by the Sumerians and Achaeans, a *Turanian* people'.[519] This statement is arguably the first manifestation of the 'Turkish History Thesis'. In fact, Akcura played an active role in the formulation of the Thesis as one of the founding members of the Turkish History Research Association. He was elected to the chairmanship of the Association in 1932 and

---

[516] See Appendix 13 and Appendix 14
[517] The 1918 Congress of the Turkish Hearths debated the matter where an amendment to the organisation's constitution was proposed, reading, 'the field of activity of the Hearths is particularly *Turkiya*:' The reasoning of this proposal was that since the Turkish Hearths did not have the strength to work for both the Anatolian Turks and the 'outer Turks' at the same time, 'although the great *Turan* dream was hailed with hope', they needed to concentrate all of the activities in the short term exclusively on Turkey (Ustel 2002: 264). The 'particularly *Turkiya*' phrase was not adopted by the Congress, but the proposal was still a manifestation of a strong Kemalism-like pragmatic tendency within the Hearths.
[518] Akcura 1976: 73.
[519] Arai 2002: 182.

241

chaired the first Turkish History Congress, and participated in the board of authors of 'An Outline of Turkish History',[520] the backbone text of the Turkish History Thesis.

The Turkish History Thesis is the first comprehensive manifesto of Turkish national identity. Its main stance is westernism, which to a large extent is driven by a desire for recognition by the West. The complementary problems of 'the lack in the Other' that were firmly articulated to this main desire are as follows:

- De-Orientalisation: Jettisoning the Ottoman/Islamic past in order to prove that Turkish culture belonged to Western civilisation and not to the Orient, and through this historiographic bypass, linking the Turks' present to their ancient history in Central Asia.

- Civilisation: Proving that Turks were a historically civilised nation by demonstrating that the ancient Anatolian-Mesopotamian civilisations, the cradle of all civilisations, were created by Turkic (Turanian) ethnicities.

- Assimilation: In addition to historical ownership, claiming contemporary identification of the Turks with Anatolia as their 'motherland' by proving that the population currently residing in Turkey were exclusively Turkish in racial/anthropologic terms.

Given the universal bankruptcy of the racial case, the final problematique was bound from the outset to be experienced in terms of a call to the ethnically plural Muslim population of Anatolia for assimilation as Turks within the 'nation'. This, Kemalists hoped, would take place through the 'national' compliance with their appeal to the simultaneous forgetting (de-Orientalisation) and remembering (civilisation). What was asked to be forgotten was not

---

[520] Georgeon 2002: 514.

242

merely the recent Islamic past but, given the task of assimilation, also the memory of the ethnic affiliations, in favour of a long-forgotten - or more likely an invented/imaginary – origin. This was in effect a call for a primal repression and hence a primal split, given the impossibility of immediate amnesia regarding the recent past and ethnicity, along with the impossibility of a sudden recollection of an imaginary ancient past and origin. Moreover, the already split modern Turkish subject would then face a further logical inconsistency originating from the double claim of the Thesis of belonging both to Central Asia and Anatolia at the same time. There have been painstaking attempts to link the two historical origins since the proclamation of the Thesis, but they failed to prevent splits in discourses of identity in the republican era over this essential inconsistency. The question that inevitably led to a further split in the modern Turk, who complied with the call for 'national recollection', was thus: when the nation woke up from their Ottoman/Islamic sleep with the Kemalists' kiss, which of the imagined origins were they supposed to remember; the civilised origins (Sumerians, Hittites, Ionians, etc.) in Anatolia or the nomadic/warrior tribal origins (Huns, Kokturks, etc.) in Central Asia? This question was largely responsible for the proliferation of the discourses of identity through republican history.

1.2. The Problem of 'Motherland': Nationalist Anatolianism

Frank Tachau, in his pioneering work on the Turkish search for national identity[521] compared Anatolianism with pan-Turkism. The particular line of Anatolianism that Tachau analysed was that circle of university students around the journal *Anadolu* of 1919-1923, and the subsequent Anatolianist movement that operated within the Turkist/nationalist paradigm until

243

1925. One of the founders of the movement, Hilmi Ziya (Ulken), argued that Anatolianism was developed as a concrete viewpoint as opposed to the abstract ideals of Ottomanism, Turanism and Islamism.[522] This was because the definition of a nation could only be made with geographical reference and the Turkish nation's reference had to be Anatolia. Neither Turanism nor Islamism were able to provide a clear definition of homeland, while Ottomanism was doomed from the outset with the ill fate of the Empire. In 1923, a new group led by Mukrimin Halil published ten issues of a new journal with the same name. The contributors of this journal fiercely criticised the pan-Turkist ideas and asserted that the source of Turkish culture was Anatolia and that Turkish history began with the Seljuks arrival in Anatolia in 1071. They drew a difference between the homeland and colonies, and argued that the homeland was Anatolia whereas the lost Ottoman lands in Balkans and the Middle East were the colonies. Another journal, *Anadolu Mecmuasi*, published until 1925 by Mehmet Halit (Bayri), made one of the boldest statements on national identity:

When questioned about their nationality, some answer to this 'Turkish'. This is wrong. (...) Although we are of Turkish lineage, because our land is Anatolia our nation is the Anatolian nation.[523]

Another line of Anatolianism, which also represents an early articulation of the Turkish-Islamic synthesis, emerged in 1939 under Nurettin Topcu's leadership around his journal *Hareket*. Topcu argued in an article entitled 'Our Identity' that an Anatolian Renaissance had begun with the Muslim Seljuks' occupation of Anatolia.[524] 'The sources of our nation's

---

[521] Tachau 1962.
[522] Ulken 1966: 800.
[523] Deren 2002: 535.
[524] Topcu 1939.

244

strength are Islam, which gave a new spirit and life to the Oguzes arriving in Anatolia, and the agricultural technique that had been maintained in this continent since the Hittites and was inherited by the newcomers.'[525] According to Topcu, the search for identity could end best by the Turks' turning to their essence. Topcu believed that if the Turks managed to reclaim this Islamic/Anatolian essence, they would initiate the birth of a new age, a new Renaissance for the world.[526] Topcu and his disciples played an important role in the Islamisation of the Turkist movement particularly during the Cold War era (see above).

Tachau asserts that Anatolianist ideas were largely adopted by the 'Turkish History Thesis' and points out that one of the founders of the Anatolianist current, Semseddin Gunaltay, was also an architect of the Thesis.[527] Unlike the early Anatolianists, however, the Central Asian origins were also emphasised in the Thesis. Moreover, the Thesis' Anatolianism differs from the early Anatolianism, in its double claim on Anatolia, in terms of historical time, by relating not only the history since the 11th century, but also the ancient history of Anatolia, to Turkish history.

I.3. Perceptions of the West: Turkish Humanism

The era of 'humanist culture' in Turkey opened up in 1939 with the appointment of Hasan Ali Yucel as the Minister of Education. One of Yucel's first educational policies was to launch a campaign for the translation and publication of the western classics into Turkish:

---

[525] Topcu 1943.
[526] Topcu 1939a.
[527] Tachau 1963: 176.

Republican Turkey, which is determined to become a distinguished part of the western cultural and philosophical community, needs to translate the old and new cultural products of the civilised world and thus strengthen her identity with a universal sense of feeling and thought. This necessity invites us to an extensive translation campaign.[528]

In the first three years of the campaign, 109 translated books, mainly from classical Greek, were published.[529] Yucel also included the classical western languages and the translations from classics in the secondary school curricula for the first time. During the humanist era, the *Encyclopaedia of Islam* was also translated and published with some original entries in the Turkish edition, and an *Encyclopaedia Turk* was also prepared and published.

The importance of the humanistic stance can be realised if Yucel's practice is read against the background of Turkism/nationalism above. In Chapter 3, I have identified the main desire of Kemalist nationalism to repair the damage inflicted on the national pride by the failure to gain recognition from the West (Bihruz Bey syndrome). Ataturk seemed to have put the question of westernisation to a decisive end by formulating the main task of the republican nation as to rise to the level of contemporary civilisations. This statement was however qualified by a strong anti-imperialist stand. Consequently, the republican discourse continued to conceptualise the West as a split Other: the West was the Ego-Ideal that needed to be introjected, but this introjection was linked to the nationalist project, that is, westernisation was presented not only as an ideal but as a necessity at the same time, for Turkey's eventual challenge to the West. In this second sense, the west as the imperialist Other, which

---

[528] Cikar 1997: 81.

246

threatened the integrity of the motherland, led to the reign of a paranoid mentality over modern Turkishness. The fact that Seyfettin's sado-masochistic motto of 'those who do not oppress are condemned to be oppressed' repeated by several Turkist ideologues along with similar statements by men of high governmental positions of the republican era signifies the continuation of this mentality. However, this anxiety and the state of alert against the 'others', besides its ability of mobilising national-popular energies, could well be self damaging if sustained forever as the dominant policy. A literary theorist, Erich Auerbach, who lectured at Istanbul University between 1934 and 1940, commented on this hopeless state of anxiety in a letter addressed to Walter Benjamin in 1937:

> [Ataturk] did everything that he did in a struggle against the European democracies, on the one side, and the panislamist Sultan's economy, on the other. The result is a fanatically anti-tradition nationalism: the denial of the whole (Islamic) cultural heritage, forging a phantasmatic relationship with a primitive Turkish identity, a Europeanised technologic modernisation for the aim of achieving a victory against a simultaneously hated and admired Europe. (...) Result: an extreme nationalism but the destruction of national character at the same time.[530]

In his critique of Gokalp's trilogy 'To Turkisize, To Islamise, To Civilise', Yucel stated that 'we do not need to Turkisise ourselves'; instead, a national self-confidence ('being already Turkish') was needed in the process of integration with humanity.[531] 'I do not see the East and West as different' said Yucel, 'although human works, the longings, concerns and fears of human spirit, differ according to the temporal and spatial context, this is because of the chosen methods and forms. If we did not feel with a western mentality, we would not be able

---

[529] 39 of these were translated from classical Greek, 38 from French, 10 from German, 8 from English, 6 from Latin, 5 from Oriental and Islamic classics, 2 from Russian and one from the Scandinavian literature.
[530] Barck 1992: 82.
[531] Kocak 2001: 394.

to find his substance in the East.'[532] Yucel was thus proposing a restoration through which the second meaning of the encounter with the west –the threatening Other – would be superseded, in favour of adopting the western mentality as the 'form' of reaching the 'substance' of the east.

Yucel's translation renaissance managed to mould the mentalities of a number of generations.[533] However, the spirit of the times, the international climate that was fully determined by 'the logic of equivalence', and its domestic reflections, did not allow Yucel's project to live long. His ministry was the sole target of the Turkists' 1944 McCarthyist campaign led by Atsiz (above). In 1946, when the government decided to follow Atsiz's advice and purged a number of 'leftist' academics particularly from the Ankara University, and began to close the Village Institutes, 'in accordance with the requirements of the multiparty system', Yucel resigned from his post in disappointment. The humanist episode thus ended, though with significant long-term results.

Kemalism, which emerged with an immediate success in responding to the identity questions of the Ottoman crisis, produced further identity questions through time including the problem of the past, the problem of the 'motherland' and the problem of the 'West'. In the following sections, I will consider three major discursive currents of republican history, which have generated comprehensive responses to these further questions of identity within the republican discursive horizon.

---

[532] Cikar 1997: 62.
[533] Yavuz 1987: 147-8.

II. Turkism and the republican Turkey

1971: In the notorious mansion of the Counter-guerrilla in Ziverbey a colonel lectured us about our geopolitical situation: 'You can be socialists somewhere like Austria but here with this geopolitics you are not allowed'. He then considered each of our neighbours. In the north, our traditional archenemy 'communist' Russia; in the west their poker and our old enemy Bulgaria; next to them our worst enemy Greece; in the south two anti-Turkish Arab countries, Iraq and Syria. Then it was the east's turn. The Shah was in power and there were no problems between Turkey and Iran. Our borders had remained the same since 1639. The colonel said, 'I never liked these Farsis'. There had to be a way of being surrounded by the enemies. But maybe the colonel did not want us to be friends. The excess of enemies was legitimising his power.

(Murat Belge 1992.)

4 May 1941

Yagmur My Son!

(...) Follow my advice, be a good Turk.

Communism is our enemy's profession. Know this very well. The Jews are the covert enemy of all nations. The Russians, Chinese, Farsis and Greeks are our historical enemies.

Bulgarians, Germans, Italians, English, French, Arabs, Serbians, Croatians, Spannish, Portugese, Romanians are our new enemies.

The Japanese, Afghans and Americans are our future enemies.

Armenians, Kurds, Cyrcassians, Abkhazians, Bosnians, Albanians, Pomaks, Lazes, Lezgies, Georgians, Chechens are our internal enemies.

It is essential to be prepared very well in order to fight so many enemies.

God be with you!

Nihal Atsiz.

I have demonstrated above that the republican discourse emerged from the Turkist argument. Consequently, there are important historical links between the two discourses and there are common features of nationalist discursive construct developed by Turkism which have been appropriated by the republican discourse. If the 'social Darwinist' paranoid anxiety that rules the mentalities of the two texts above is one of these features, the policy of assimilation, and even territorial nationalism at the expense of the *Turanist* irredentism were other significant ones. The republican identity on the other hand was overdetermined particularly by the necessity to 'civilise', which I have held responsible for the main paradox of the Thesis regarding the plurality of the past to be remembered in the above outline of the Turkist influences on Kemalism. This paradox along with a number of inconsistencies in the Kemalist discourse created a new autonomous space of activity for Turkism under the republican discursive horizon.

Turkism found suitable conditions in the formative years of the republic to be reborn as a complementary discourse to Kemalism. In this section in addition to 'this special relationship', I shall also demonstrate the tensions that this symbiosis involved, which led to a gradual separation. I shall then consider the shifts in the Turkist discourse to accommodate the Islamic identity perceptions within the context of an anti-communist orientation in the Cold War conditions. Although the collapse of communism deprived Turkism of its major enemy, due to the plurality of the enemies as listed in the above quotes, Turkism managed to survive with new internal and external enemies and new aspirations regarding the 'outside

Turks'. I shall conclude this section with an attempt to map out the main features of the Turkist discourse of identity.

II.1. Turkism Under Kemalism

There has been a symbiotic relationship between the modern Turkish state and the Turkist movement, particularly in the formative years of the republic. The Turkist project was largely adopted by Kemalism with the essential alteration that discarded the *Turanist* aspirations in favour of Kemal's realistic motto, 'Peace at home, peace in the world'; and the Turkist cadres enjoyed top governmental positions. Grassroots Turkists of the Turkish Hearths were recruited after 1931 to the RPP's new organisations of People's Houses and Village Rooms. Turkists were particularly active among the republican youth organised in the MTTB (National Turkish Students Union). MTTB was the only organisation that maintained its formally autonomous existence after the 1931 decision to close down all organisations except the RPP. Its emblem was a grey wolf, one of the many names given to Atatürk after a legend of Turkic mythology.[534] The MTTB youth, being extensively influenced by the Turkist discourse of the time[535] organised demonstrations during the 1930s in support of the 'Outside Turks', a term referring particularly to the Turkic ethnicities of the central Asia "oppressed under the Russian (= communist) yoke", and for the annexation of Hatay.[536]

---

[534] The grey wolf would re-emerge in the early 1970s to become the symbol of ultra-nationalist rightwing militancy.
[535] Landau 1995: 93-4.
[536] For the fields of juncture between Kemalism and Turkism, see Appendix 15.

The relationship between Turkism and Kemalism was not always unproblematic, since it involved tensions emerging mainly from the prohibited *Turanist* irredentism. Turanism, however, helped the Turkists to develop a more consistent grandnarrative of Turkish history in which the Thesis' claims to the civilised origins were excluded in favour of nomadic/warrior origins and a different notion of ownership of Anatolia.[537]

II.2. From Nazi Turkism to Cold-War Anti-Communism

As the Nazi sympathies of the Kemalist regime under 'the national chief', Inonu, grew in parallel to the German advance in Europe, Turkist publications began to reappear one after the other in 1941. The Turkist influence on the government was manifested by prime minister Sukru Saracoglu in 1942:

We are Turks and Turkists, and will remain Turkists. For us, Turkism is a matter of conscience and culture as much as being a matter of blood.[538]

However, from 1943 onwards, Turkists began to fall out of favour, in parallel to the reversal of the course of War, leading to the imprisonment of the Turkists for a short period.[539] When the jailed Turkists were acquitted with an official proclamation in 1947 of Turkism as a 'national ideology', a number of 'communists' listed by the Turkists' leader Nihal Atsiz were expelled particularly

---

[537] See Appendix 16 for tensions between Kemalism and Turkism.
[538] Ertekin 2002: 366).
[539] See Appendix 17.

from university posts. The Turkists and the Kemalist government were once again united, this time under the banner of anti-communism.

The majority of the Turkists of the late Ottoman era were Russian émigrés, who developed the pan-Turkist ideal in opposition to the Tzarist policies of expansion and assimilation. The popular image of the Russian (*Moskoff*), on the other hand, had been shaped by the images of 1877/8 Turco-Russian war which ended in a catastrophic defeat and claimed thousands of lives military and civilian alike in addition to causing massive migration from Russian lands to Anatolia. The anti-Russian sentiment was still popular when the republican elite decided to side with the anti-communist camp in the Cold War, and this made a smooth transition from anti-Russian Turkism to anti-communism possible. In this new imaginary, communism was equalled to Russian expansionism: 'Communism means only Moskoffism today'.[540] 'It is impossible to distinguish the communist from the Russian'.[541]

The Turkists formed 'Associations to Struggle Against Communism' around the country and held 'Demonstrations to Curse Communism' in the 1950s and 1960s. These demonstrations put a strong emphasis on the cause of the 'outer Turks', who were oppressed under the 'communist yoke', in addition to the domestic communist threat. Turkist militants began their systematic assaults on workers' organisations as early as the founding meeting of DISK, the first non-

---

[540] Atsiz 1950: 3.
[541] TumTurk 1950: 4.

governmental trade union confederation, in 1962. In fact, given the helpless circumstances regarding the perspectives of liberating their 'outer Turk' brothers, the whole movement, which grew to form their own political party, MHP (Nationalist Action Party), in 1969 with a youth section, Ulku Ocaklari (Idealist Hearths), would base itself upon an exclusive specialisation in assaulting the workers organisations and the socialist left, throughout the two decades that followed the Kemalist coup of 1960. This orientation of activity was based on a mutual understanding between the state apparatuses and the ultranationalist movement over the Turkists' main duty as the protection and maintenance of the Turkish State. The MHP's constituency grew in the 1970s, particularly in the periphery, i.e. 'deep Anatolia', parallel to the deepening economic crisis and the consequent escalation of social and political antagonism, carrying the party leadership twice to government positions as the junior coalition partner

The anti-communist orientation led by the US required national/popular mobilisations around the world.[542] The Islamised requirements of the anti-communist orientation moved the ultranationalist discourse further away from the 'mythological origins' in favour of Anatolian nationalism and Turk-Islam synthesis as proclaimed in the famous motto of the MHP identity: 'Turk as the

---

[542] It was however clear from the outset that the Turkists' shamanistic/atheistic iconography of Central-Asian origins, which arguably served well to popularise Kemalist secularism among the second generation of republican Turkey, would fall short of achieving popular support among both the Turkey's Turks and 'outer Turks', given that both of these peoples were overwhelmingly Muslim. Consequently, a controlled rehabilitation of Islam and Islamism went hand in hand with the sharpening of the discourse of anti-communism of the conservative/liberal governments of the 1950s and 1960s. In this discourse, communism (the Russian – *Moskoff*) was not merely the enemy of the Turks but of morals, religion and primarily Islam, too. As I have argued in Chapter

Tengri Mountain and Muslim as the Hira Mountain'.[543] This discursive transition, which was completed in the early seventies, under the leadership of the retired colonel Alpaslan Turkes led to the expulsion of Atsiz and his supporters – 'shamanists' – from the movement. The MHP adopted the three crescents of the Ottoman flag as its emblem to coexist with the greywolf[544], the emblem of its paramilitary youth wing, the Ulku Hearths.

II.3. Turkism after Communism – the far-right discourse of identity

The 1980 coup d'etat, escalated the MHP's discourse to the status of the main grammar of the Turkish state, while putting the party's leadership in jail. As Alpaslan Turkes stated during their trial, they were in jail while their ideas were in power. Following the mid-1980s return to the multiparty system, the MHP found a new impetus in the Kurdish conflict and developed an aggressive discourse interpreting the Kurdish question in terms of racial antagonism, which provided a subtext for the state's discourse on the Kurdish question. Although the collapse of the communist camp was a blow for the MHP discourse, ripping its constitutive outside off, it opened up new possibilities for the unification of the Turkists left and right. The dynamics of the Kurdish conflict and the overexposed corruption of the centre right DYP (True Path Party) carried the MHP in 1999 to the centre-left DSP (Democratic Left Party) led cabinet as the junior coalition

---

3, repressed Islamism found channels of symptomatic expression in this climate in the form of an anti-communist conservative nationalism.

[543] Ozdogan 2001: 281-7.

[544]But the greywolf was now embraced by Islam's crescent on the Hearths' banner.

partner.[545] Although this coalition was wiped out in the November 2002 elections, it still symbolised the opening of a new era regarding political alliances based on a recourse to the co-operation between the Kemalists and Turkists, through which the foundations of modern Turkey was first laid. Their common ground is a peculiar reading of the post-Soviet globalisation, in which nation-states are viewed as the pockets of resistance to the imperialist expansion, through the global flow of capital.[546]

The outline in this section of the history of Turkist/ultranationalist/extreme-rightwing discourse and movement includes a number of shifts in its orientation, from the symbiotic relationship with Kemalism to the representation of conservative anti-communist paratroopers and from a pagan mythology to the sublimation of Islam. What survives unchanged is the grandnarrative of the nation's history, which firmly refuses to wake up to the ancient Anatolian origins and favours instead a myth of genesis in Central Asia. In this historical journey from the Central Asian steps to the Middle East and Europe through centuries the travelling subject, the Turk, remains unchanged as an essential and essentialist category. The main expression of the Turks' essence is his strength

---

[545] It is also important to note that Turkist movement's and in particular the MHP's influence on the Turkish State does not solely arise from the movement's popularity or growth in constituency, and is therefore not limited to the three episodes of coalition partnership in republican history. Since Nihal Atsiz's demand for communist purge in 1944, the Turkist movement and later the MHP have emphasised the importance of acquiring top positions within the state bureaucracy, the Turkish Academia and particularly the police force. As a result, Turkism *a-la-MHP* has been a key component of the Turkish State discourses and political practices.
[546] A peaceful settlement in Cyprus, improving the Kurdish rights domestically and the prospects of Turkey's entry in the European Union are, in this discourse, the current foreign impositions to be resisted. Moreover, the integration of Turkey into Europe is seen as a conspiracy to liquidate the Turkish nation state, the main 'fetish', through which the Turkist 'reality' is maintained.

(heroism, warriorship, conquest, etc.) as materialised in the tradition of the strong state. The Turkish state, which is one and the same state since the Huns and Kokturks to Seljuks and Ottomans and from them to the republic of Turkey, is the only guarantee of the continuity of this essence and the maintenance of identity. Whatever the conjunctural tensions and disagreements between the Turkists and the State might have been, the Turkist discourse has always experienced a 'determination in the last instance' by this 'State Fetishism'.

In addition to a grandnarrative of history, there are three burning questions to be asked in the assessment of any discourse on Turkish national identity: firstly, the perception of and the proposed relationship with the west; secondly, demarcation, that is, the definition of the 'outside' of the nation; and thirdly, the arguments of legitimisation of the ownership of the contemporary 'motherland'.

1. The second meaning of the West, the imperialist Other, and a consequent paranoid mentality dominates Turkist discourse. In this imperialist West, Russia had an exceptional place as one of the immediate enemies of Turkishness and Islam, and one of the main actors in the Ottoman disintegration. These conventional connotations of 'the Russian' helped a smooth transition from the threat of the imperialist west to an 'imperialist Russian threat' during the Cold War era. The outside of the Turkish identity included particularly Russia as the 'oppressors' of the 'outside Turks'. Hostility towards the 'Jewish' capital, the Christian elements and enemies surrounding the country - Greeks, Bulgarians,

Arabs and Iranians alike – and a strong anti-left sentiment defining them as the agents of Russian interests accompanied this discourse. It maintained the ideal of *Turan*, that is, the eventual reunification of the Turks in their imaginary homeland in Central Asia, the immediate programmatic aim towards this end being the liberation of the 'Outer Turk' cousins. With the collapse of the communist camp, the 'imperialist west' has reappeared as the whole West, the concrete incarnations of which since the 1990s are 'global capitalism', the European Union and particularly the international pressures on Turkey to improve her human rights record, which was interpreted as a conspiracy 'to paralyse the security forces in their fight against separatist terror'.

2. The outside of Turkish identity included the non-Muslim minorities (Armenians, Jews and Greeks) and the non-Turkish Muslims who the Turkists viewed as unsuitable for assimilation (Gypsies, Negroes and the Kurds) from the outset. Given their emphasis on pagan origins, Islam as symbolised in the 'Arab betrayal' was also deployed by the Turkist discourse as the Other of Turkish identity. The first republican Turkist generation opposed the policy of assimilation and instead proposed a double strategy: liquidation of the minorities and when a 'zero solution' was not possible establish the Turks as the indisputable masters of the others. This line of Turkism was best articulated by a Kemalist notable, Mahmut Esat Bozkurt, in 1930, which is also telling of the symbiosis between Kemalism and Turkist racism: 'My personal opinion is that the lords and masters of this country are the Turks. Those who are not of pure

Turkish stock have only one right in the Turkish land, it is the right to be servants and slaves'.[547]

'The communist' became the main enemy of 'the Turk' during the Cold War, when the definition of the Turk was Islamised by the Turkists. Islamisation required the symbolic repression of racism towards non-Turkish Muslims but the distinction between the 'pure Turkish stock' and the 'others' always survived in the Turkist identity as a deep current. This deep current found a golden opportunity in the 1990s to return to the symbolic order of Turkism in the form of a symptomatic anti-Kurdish racism, when the PKK, the synonym for the Kurd, replaced the communist as the main enemy. Imperialism, the European Union and global capitalism have also (re)entered this list of periodical enemies during the 1990s. The problem is that with these shifts in the main enemy, the enemies of the previous periods are not forgotten but piled up and condensed as the 'collective memory traces' of the Turkist identity to lead to metonymic uses of different signifiers, a recent example being the wide selection of attributes to Abdullah Ocalan, the captured leader of the Kurdish movement, from the 'terrorist Kurd' to 'communist', 'religious fanatic', 'an agent of imperialism' and most effectively 'Armenian'.

3. The Turkist position on the legitimacy of the ownership of Anatolia is clear enough: 'Turkey belongs to the Turks' because the Turks have had the strength and power to occupy it since the 11th Century. The sense of belonging to the 'motherland' is reduced to a masculinist perception of a 'right' to 'have it' by force. Since the land is 'mother' in the nationalist literature, this 'right to have it'

---

[547] Bozkurt 1930: 3.

is open to a psychoanalytic reading as an incestuous drive. Here, the constitutive trauma is obviously the simultaneous acceptance and denial of the mother's being the others' mother rather than the Turks'. What is admitted by the Turkist discourse is that the Turk is not the favoured child of 'the mother', in fact the 'real mother' (Asena – the she-wolf) is in Central Asia, but nevertheless it is the Turkists' task to force Anatolia to become their mother. The symbolic articulation of this lack of the desire in the (m)Other, is an irreconcilable certainty on the name of the mother: 'Anadolu', which turns the ancient name Anatolia into 'mother' and 'full', or 'the motherland'. But the simultaneous acceptance of the lack is evident in the fetishistic sublimation of power and the State, the only instruments to 'fill' the 'mother' with, or to 'force' the mother to an incestious intercourse, as a way of coming to terms with the traumatic lack of desire in the Other. The 'favoured children' of the mother, Armenians, Greeks and the Kurds in particular, should either be eliminated or turned into the 'slaves' of the 'dominant nation' (their victorious step-brother). This structure of manifest perversion is probably responsible for the constant production and maintenance by the Turkist discourse of a state of nationalist anxiety, alert and aggression against the others, in addition to the State Fetishism.

III. Blue Anatolianism

The Blue Anatolia movement, which emerged in late 1950s to propose some important solutions to the Turkish search for identity in modern times, was one of the long-term consequences of the Kemalist humanism.[548] It is also a product of the Turkish History Thesis and the early nationalist Anatolianism. In this section, the main tenets of the Blue Anatolianist argument on identity will be examined and Turkism and Anatolianism will be compared in conclusion as two inevitable poles of the Thesis' inconsistent grandnarrative regarding the origins of the Turks.

III.1. Blue Anatolianism: Neo-Kemalist Renaissance

The main programatic stance of Blue Anatolianism can be found in the following statement by one of their prominent figures regarding the problem of the West. Ataturk, he said, was the 'irreconcilable enemy of western colonialism but an obedient servant of western culture'[549], and condemned anyone right and left alike as reactionaries, who failed to understand this distinction. One leg of the Blue Anatolianist project was therefore integration into humanity through cultural westernisation, in which the Anatolianists followed the 1940s' humanist current. The Blue Anatolia movement also built further on the tracks of the early Anatolianism in its attempt to derive a national identity from belonging to a geographically defined homeland. The third leg of Blue Anatolianism corresponds to the Thesis' claim on Anatolian civilisations, through a rather refined rephrasing of the claim that Turks existed in their ancient history in Anatolia.

---

[548] For the nationalist-Anatolianist and Kemalist-humanist origins of Blue Anatolianism see Appendix 18.
[549] Eyuboglu 1974: 168-70.

Following the discarding of the humanist Kemalists during the dissolution of the monoparty regime from 1946 onwards, the humanist Anatolianist writers, in particular, Sabahattin Eyuboglu, Azra Erhat and Cevat Sakir Kabaagac (The Fisherman of Halicarnasus), continued to translate and publish particularly from classical Greek, participated in archaeological research especially in the Aegean region and emphasised in their texts the pre-Islamic Anatolian culture and the surviving traditions in modern times. They imagined modern Turkishness as an Anatolian identity, which was a melting pot of ethnic, linguistic and religious differences. They thus rigorously proposed to jettison the nomadic/warrior origins (Turanism) and to situate the Islamic (Seljuk and Ottoman) heritage within a perspective of temporality as a temporary stage of Anatolian history:

> We were pagans once; then we became Christians and then Muslims. It was this people who built ... both the churches and the mosques. We were the people who filled in those radiant-white [ancient] coliseums and dark caravansarays.[550]

This was a radical relativisation of the Islamic past as opposed to early nationalist Anatolianist assertions and Turk-Islam synthesis, both of which put an essentialist emphasis on Islam in the definition of the 'essence of the Turk'. Instead of essentialism, the Anatolian humanists seem to be advocating an eclectic approach in which various historical stages of the Anatolian geography have been articulated to form a contemporary synthesis:

> Why is this country ours? Is it because we came from the Central Asia as four hundred men in horseback and conquered this country? Those who

say so do not identify with this land, they do not feel it as their homeland. (…) This country is ours, because it is ours, not because we conquered it. (…) We are both the subject and the object of the conquest. We melt the others and were melted by them at the same time. (…) We moulded these lands and were moulded by them. Because of this, whatever there is in our country, from the ancient to the modern, is our property. Our people's history is Anatolia's history.[551]

If not Turkish or Muslim as such, a different 'essence', 'the Anatolian', still operates in this journey through time. The influences and contributions to this essence do modify and improve this essential subject, but some modifications are interpreted as 'contamination' and 'alienation' of this humanistic essence.[552] Consequently, the neurosis that the early Kemalist subject experienced in his search for the pure Turk among the Anatolian population reoccurs in the Blue Anatolianists' encounter with the 'reactionaries and religious fanatics' (softa and yobaz). The Aegean and Mediterranean peasants evidently watched the Anatolianists' admiration of the ancient remains from a distance, saying, 'they are looking for stones'[553] and when Eyuboglu claims that there could be an organic link between the current Black Sea coast folk dances ('horon') and Dyonisos' dance, his interlocutor objected: 'You are the grandson of a proper Turk; how could you say such a thing? If 'horon' were not our ancestors' dance would we

---

[550] Eyuboglu 1961:9.
[551] Eyuboglu 1961: 9.
[552] Belge 1998: 284-5.
[553] Belge 1998: 285.

allow anyone to perform it in Trabzon?'[554] In this context, the name that Eyuboglu chose for his seminal work on the Blue Anatolia philosophy, 'Blue and Black', and the choice of the shades of light as the attributes of the ancient heritage (above), 'radiant-white coliseums' and the Islamic heritage, 'dark caravansarays', cannot be seen arbitrary. This discourse is certainly linked to the Kemalist invitation to national amnesia regarding the Ottoman-Islamic past, and the call to wake up from the Oriental sleep to one of the origins that was proposed by the History Thesis, the ancient Anatolia.

Another Kemalist connection could be identified in one of the strategic tasks of the Blue Anatolian activity. In order to grasp this connection, we need to return to the History Thesis, which declared that Sumerians and Hittites were of Turanian origin, and therefore the first civilisations in Mesopotamia and Anatolia were linked to the Turks. One of the desires that shaped the claims of the History Thesis was to counter the then popular discourse of the 'Greek Miracle' among the European intelligentsia:

> Classical Greek civilisation is not an independent civilisation. For Greek
> civilisation is Ionian civilisation which was born of Aegean civilisation.[555]

Ataturk himself stated as early as 1930 that 'we are currently working to scientifically prove that we were an ancient nation settled around Izmir before the Greeks'.[556]

---

[554] Belge 1998: 285.
[555] Hasan Cemil 1932: 199.

The guru of the Blue Anatolia movement, the Fisherman of Halikarnasus, had a great love of classical Aegean civilisations, which was linked to his particular aim to demonstrate that Greece, the supposed origin of the Western civilisation, was a failed immitation of the Anatolian civilisitation:

> Regarding historians, philosophers and poets, Anatolia is undoubtedly ahead of Hellenistan, in every respect. The whole 'reactionary mind' began with the Greeks' blockage of the 'enlightened' Anatolian thought. It was what emerged from the Greeks that opened the way for Europe's descent into centuries of dark ages.[557]

The Fisherman's disciple, Eyuboglu, firmly relates the case of Ion Anatolia vs. Greece with Ataturk's nationalism:

> Ataturk's ideas on language and history should not be misunderstood: they were driven with his will to identify with all the values on these lands. When he said that Greeks were Turks, he meant that we had been the owners of this country before the Greeks and in fact the Greeks had split from Anatolia.[558]

The proposal to counter the 'Greek miracle' with an 'Anatolian miracle' was thus submitted mainly to the West, the 'Big Other'.

III.2. Considerations on Turkism and Anatolianism: Sibling Rivalry

---

[556] Ataturk 1930: 88.
[557] Halikarnas Balikcisi 1994: 80-1.
[558] Eyuboglu 1961: 9.

Although the Blue Anatolian movement could be listed as a Kemalist activity, prominent figures of this movement remained outside the state's cultural discourse and institutions.[559] In a Turkey governed frequently by centre right cabinets and coalitions, the hegemonic discourse of which consisted of early manifestations of 'Turk-Islam Synthesis', there was more hostility than encouragement for the humanistic Blue Anatolian project.[560] In spite of this embargo, the results of the Blue Anatolia movement cannot be reduced to the 'Blue Journey' of the Aegean coast – a popular cultural tourism activity that was initiated by the Fisherman and has continued since the 1960s. The Anatolianist movement did not have immediate political reflections but its influence on the left's perceptions of Turkish identity, along with the cultural policies of the centre-left cabinets particularly in the 1970s cannot be denied.[561] According to Copeaux, the humanist influence on history textbooks, which began in the 1940s, continued despite all the ruptures until the year 1986.[562] Moreover, the conservative opposition to the Anatolianist movement resulted in the birth of Turk-Islam Synthesis, which formed itself largely on an antagonistic exaggeration of the humanist influence on the state's cultural and educational policies.

---

[559] Among the Anatolianists, archeologist Azra Erhat had been expelled from her post at Ankara University during the 1946 purge of leftist academics. The Fisherman of Halicarnassus, who came from a family of Ottoman aristocracy, lived as a folk philosopher in voluntary exile in Bodrum and Izmir. Sabahattin Eyuboglu was a senior inspector of Ministry of Education and he was the only figure with some influence to integrate the Anatolianist views onto the State's cultural and educational policies, the backbone of which still consisted of humanistic period's products.

[560] In the 1950s' and 1960s' Turkey, where cultural production was largely a state enterprise, Anatolianists' works were not published by the Ministry of Culture. Consequently, Anatolianists published a journal (*Ufuklar* and *Yeni Ufuklar*) beginning from 1951 and in late 1950s they founded a private publishing house (Çan Yayinlari) directed by Vedat Gunyol.

[561] For an interpretation of the Anatolianist movement as the sole reason for the influence of Kemalism over the left, see Kucuk 1985. For the influence of the Anatolianist current on the history textbooks see Copeaux 1998: 262-84.

[562] Copeaux 1998: 56.

The Anatolianist grandnarrative of history is both an essentialist and eclectic one. While the eclectic side opens this discourse to the possibilities of enrichment through further language games, the 'essence', the Anatolian subject as 'us', which comes very close to the Kemalist Turk, closes the gate to these possibilities. I shall conclude this section by reassessing the Anatolianist current regarding the three questions of firstly, the perception of and the proposed relationship with the west; secondly, demarcation, that is, the definition of the 'outside' of the nation; and thirdly, the arguments of legitimation of the ownership of the contemporary 'motherland'.

1. Regarding the relationship with the West, the humanist Anatolianist current takes a clear stand to confront the Turkist orientations. Cultural integration with humanity, i.e. the perception of the West as the Ego-Ideal to be introjected, reemerges as a powerful argument pursued by this line of 'neo-Kemalist renaissance'.

2. Blue Anatolianists also come very close to Kemalism in their perceptions of the 'outside' of the nation, consisting of 'reactionaries and religious fanatics'. Their proposal was to enlighten the 'alienated' people of Anatolia in order to expose their civilised kernel.[563] Moreover, there is a different, 'foreclosed Other' of Anatolianism. As Etienne Copeaux (1998: 304-5) powerfully argues, the

---

[563] On the other hand, Anatolian humanism adopted a peaceful tone and grammar, hence softening the Kemalist exclusion of the Islamic identity, in that, instead of viewing these 'reactionaries' as the antagonistic Other or the 'ontological enemy', they believed that these 'others' could be transformed into 'us' through enlightenment.

267

Fisherman of Halikarnassus, Sabahattin Eyuboglu and Azra Erhat, who were so eager to identify with the heritage of the Anatolian cultures, were totally silent on the heritage of two millennia of Armenian history in Anatolia. The Anatolianist 'us' was prohibited from including the Armenian 'them'. This prohibition signifies that Anatolianists' humanity has its absolute limits where the boundaries between Turkish common sense and its others had once been drawn.

3. Unlike the Turkists, Blue Anatolianists' claim to the ownership of the homeland was not through conquest but through identification with historical traditions of Anatolia. They therefore can be viewed as proposing a French style patriotic nationalism as opposed to 'ethnic nationalism'.

Turkism and Anatolian humanism seem to be the two main opposing discourses of the modern Turkish search for identity. They however share a common ground, that is, that they emerged in republican history from the two poles of the Turkish History Thesis. The first pole consists of the assertion that all civilisations and particularly the Anatolian civilisations were of Turkish origin and the second pole consists of the emphasis on the Central Asian roots of the Turks' history. The inherent split in the assertion of the Thesis that 'the Turks are Central Asian, Anatolian and Western all at one and the same time' was materialised through time in that discursive split between the Turkist and Anatolianist identity proposals. One observation to be made here is that both discourses advanced so far away from their original aims that they often breached the reasons of their enunciation within the Thesis' context, in fact to such positions where these aims were countered. While the original purpose of Turkism within the Kemalist viewpoint was to supply the nation with a non-Ottoman and non-Muslim historical identity, the emblem of the MHP, the representative of this movement since late 1960s, is the Ottoman flag with three crescents, symbolising the Turkists' recourse to Islam. The main purpose of the Anatolianist argument, on the other hand, to demonstrate that the origin of all civilisations was Turkish/Anatolian, was popularly perceived, due partly to the Anatolianists' discursive slips, as a call for the formation of a Greko-Turkish identity, around a sublimed identification with the Mediterranean civilisation. The resulting 'perversion' comes very close to state that although the Turks are not the source of all civilisation, they could still become civilised through the cultural inoculation of the ancient Anatolian and Mediterranean civilisations.

IV. Turk-Islam Synthesis, or 'Ataturkism'

Turk-Islam Synthesis which has determined the cultural policies of the Turkish State since the early 1980s will be considered in this section. I will begin with considering the Synthesis' formation in its difference from and resentment towards the humanistic cultural philosophy of the 1940s, and then move on to analyse the main assertions that the Synthesis articulated to propose an alternative perception of national identity. The Synthesis also assisted to a conservative Ataturkist revision of Kemalism, the making and consequences of which I will consider in this section. I will conclude by identifying what has been preserved and what has been negated in Turk-Islam Synthesis from the discursive bodies of Turkism and Kemalism in order to reach to a clear description of the Synthesis' proposal of Turkish national identity.

IV.1. Nation vs. Humanism

The Turk-Islam Synthesis began in the 1930s with Necip Fazil's journal *Buyuk Dogu* and Nurettin Topcu's journal *Hareket*.[564] But the movement gained proper shape after 1961 as a reaction against Turkish humanism (above) arising from among a number of Turkist academics organised in the 'Club of the Enlightened' and TKAE (The Institute for Research of Turkish Culture) and the subsequent launch in 1970 of the 'Hearth of the Enlightened' by a Turkology professor, Ibrahim Kafesoglu. The anti-humanist stand was constitutive of this new political movement with important implications regarding cultural, educational, security and foreign policies of the Turkish State. The nationalism vs. humanism case was put thus:

> Beyond the nation lies not humanity but other nations. When you leave our east, west, north or south borders you will not find the sublime humanity described by the poets, but other nations, who are foreign to us and may be hostile to us. The term humanity is abstract, while the concrete reality is the nations.[565]

---

[564] See Chapter 6.
[565] Kaplan 1967: 28.

According to the Hearth, the humanist movement was a weapon of western imperialism, which aimed to damage both the Turkish nation and Islam, through its perception of history and its secularist stand.[566] Members of the Hearth believe that the westernisation of the Turkish culture has been carried out by the major cultural institutions such as the Ministry of Education, the Institute of Radio and Television (TRT) and the Turkish Language Institute (TDK), and therefore the strict control of these key institutions by the nationalist governments is viewed as of essential importance.[567]

Among the vast Synthesis literature, two programatic texts could be identified: *Turk Islam Sentezi* (Turk Islam Synthesis – 1985) by Ibrahim Kafesoglu and *Milli Kultur Raporu* (National Culture Report – 1983) by the Hearth of the Enlightened.[568]

IV.2. Rethinking National Identity

The main premise of the Synthesis is a clear statement on the problem of identity and culture: there is an identity crisis in Turkey, due to the defected 'national

---

[566] The resentment towards the humanists, which can be observed in the writings of all the prominent names of the movement, continued a decade after the dominance of Turk-Islam synthesis over state institutions. A leading member of the Hearth stated in 1990: 'Humanism is a Western conspiracy over Turkey. Humanists are those who want to destroy our national culture. Communism failed to destroy Turkishhood, but I am afraid that humanism will cause more damage on the Turkish people. (…) Humanists are those who try to link our ancestors and cultural heritage to the Romans and Greeks. (…) They do not teach us our history. They teach us the west's history. Turkish youth is being brought up by learning the Roman and Greek civilisations (Donuk, A. 1990).
[567] Copeaux 1998: 59.

culture'.[569] The 'humanist degeneration' was responsible for 'over-westernisation' and the subsequent alienation of the Turkish subject to his cultural heritage consisting of Central Asian 'essential values' and Islam. The prescription to repair this defection lies, according to the Synthesis, in that historical moment when the Turks became Muslims. The Turks' transition from pagan clans to Islam was a smooth and miraculous occasion: 'The Turks took Islam and spread it around the world, while losing nothing from their essential values'.[570] Kafesoglu teleologically narrates the Turks' history, in which Islam is viewed as the inevitable fate of the Turks, where the Turks found their true selves. Turk-Islam synthesis had occurred at this historical moment, which was so influential and deeply rooted that

> it succeeded in standing against all the defective-subversive currents
> including the Crusaders (…) and led to the formation and maintenance of
> two great Empires of the Seljuks and Ottomans.[571]

There are three assertions in these statements, which help to decode the Synthesis' contemporary message. Firstly, Kafesoglu's assertion rigorously insinuates that Turk-Islam synthesis is not something that is being generated but is the 'natural state' of the Turk. What is proposed is nothing more than 'natural' cultural policies to go along with this natural essence, instead of breaching it as in the humanistic period. Secondly, the reference to the Crusaders lays the premises for the Synthesis' perceptions of the West as the imperialist Other, the constitutive

---

[568] This report was adapted in 1986 as an official policy document by the AKDTYK (The Supreme Board of Ataturkist Culture, Language and History), an institute formed by the military junta of the 1980 to replace the Turkish Language Institute and Turkish History Institute.
[569] Gulec 1992: 50.

outside of Turkishhood. Thirdly, the West (Crusaders) is referred to as the 'defective-subversive currents', a contemporary reference to the leftist and separatist movements. What we obtain from this reading is therefore an international conspiracy with indigenous collaborators to alienate the nation from its harmoniously integrated natural essence and cultural identity.

The Synthesis declares in the Report that 'cultural policies have to be seen as a component of the state's national security policy'[572] and states that the implementation of national cultural policies among the duties of the National Security Council. The Report makes a comprehensive list of state institutions, including the Ministry of Culture and Tourism, the Ministry of National Education, National Security Council, State Planning Organisation, the Radio and Television Institution, the Higher Education Institute and the AKDTYK, assigning each specific duties regarding the conservation, improvement and dissemination of the national Islamic culture.[573]

If the rehabilitation of Islam against subversive influences of the imperialist West constitutes one leg of the Synthesis' proposals, another is on one of the constitutive problematics of modern Turkish identity, that is, that 'incurable feeling of inferiority'[574] vis-à-vis the West. Kemalism, as we have seen in previous chapters, attempted this cure by referring to the imagined 'civilised'

---

[570] Kafesoglu 1985: 169.
[571] Kafesoglu 1985: 208.
[572] The complete text of this report was published by Ataturk Yuksek Kurulu (1987).
[573] Copeaux 1998: 60-1.
[574] Atay 1980: 468.

roots along with the national task of rising to the level of contemporary civilisations. The partial bankruptcy of this attempt led the Synthesis to develop a different line of rehabilitation: 'the Ideal of World Domination'. Osman Turan (1969) argued in the 1950s that world domination has been one of the essential ideals of the Turks through history, and therefore to bring the world in an order (Nizami Alem) was one of the missions of the Turks. Within this perspective, Muslim Turks, who founded the Seljuk and Ottoman Empires, come closest to fulfilling this mission. The world domination ideal also helps the Synthesis to distinguish its anti-west imperialism from the leftwing Third Worldism, by relating itself to an imperial past and an imperial ideal. Kafesoglu argues that Turkey is different from and superior to the Third World nations, because of the historical weakness of the latter. On the other hand, the Turkish nation, 'needs neither to fabricate a history nor to search for a culture to support itself, because it has already been integrated in consciousness and spirit'.[575] Although the Synthesis opens the cultural orientation towards Islam, Arabs are clearly seen among these 'inferior' nations.[576] This apparent inconsistency can become intelligible as part of a consistent discourse when read together with another apparent inconsistency: the 'sigh of the oppressed', which dominates the Synthesis' discourse on the 'Outer Turks'. The consistent story therefore reads as follows: the Turks are a first class nation, who will achieve world dominance, and two immediate moments of this ideal are the liberation of the 'Outer Turks' and achieving 'hegemony over the Muslim world'.

---

[575] Kafesoglu 1964.
[576] Cay 1983.

IV.3. Conclusions: Superseding the sibling rivalry

The Synthesis is a success story, since it managed to assist a significant revision in the core of the republican discourse, that is, the Ataturkist revision of Kemalism.[577] The Synthesists achieved this by stepping outside the Thesis' paradoxes at the outset and working out a comprehensive alternative to the current cultural policies suitable for the future of the Republic of Turkey. Although their influence over the far-right/Turkist current cannot be denied, they differ from both the Turkists and Blue Anatolianists in this initial orientation outside the Thesis' paradigm. This move outside is observable in their practice, too: Instead of infiltrating into the Republican Institutions of Turkish History Institute (TTK) and the Turkish Language Institute (TDK),[578] the Synthesists chose to challenge the cultural products of these institutions through rigorous criticism and alternative cultural products. They thus worked out an alternative grandnarrative of the Turks' history, in which the Islamic past was clearly rehabilitated, and linked this narrative to a nationalist utopia (world domination).

In this section, I have mainly considered the Synthesis' perceptions of history, which in fact went hand in hand with a policy of language. The Synthesists objected to the ongoing purification of language as 'linguistic liquidationism',

---

[577] See Appendix 19.
[578] Others, including the Peoples' Houses and Village Institutes, had already stopped functioning when the Synthesis emerged in early 1960s.

which 'impoverished' the language and deprived the generations of the means to communicate with each other [579] As opposed to 'forced and absurd purification by the TDK', the Synthesists developed a notion of a 'living language', which is assumed to be enriched through the assimilation of new words from the interacted cultures, particularly from Farsi and Arabic.[580] The Synthesists, therefore, developed a well-embroidered comprehensive alternative to the products of both the Turkish History Institute and Turkish Language Institute.

Regarding the three identity questions (the perception of and the proposed relationship with the west; the definition of the 'outside' of the nation; legitimisation of the ownership of the contemporary 'motherland'), the Synthesis seems in the first glance as not adding much to the Turkist positions. However, by placing itself outside the Thesis' habitus, the Synthesis successfully avoids the red-herrings and paradoxes of the Kemalist discursive territory, and while preserving Turkism as its core, it manages to supersede it by softening the Turkism's rigid perceptions on the three questions of identity. In this 'dialectic' movement, a holistic reconceptualisation of nationalism through a recourse to the Gokalpian grounds is observable. The Synthesis brought Gokalp's programmatic

---

[579] Kaplan (1982: 200-1) interestingly relates the pure-language movement in Turkey with Roland Barthes' programmatic proposal of 'permanent revolution in language' by disturbing the linguistic conventions through language games.

'Why do they violate our language?

'See what French communist Roland Barthes, who (…) influences our purification extremists has to say: " (…) language is fascism. (,,,)" The likes of Roland Barthes are very few in France. Because of this, they are unable to destroy French language and literature. In Turkey, however, the recent incidents demonstrate that there are state institutions which bring up and protect the anarchists; if they are not put under control, the existing order will suddenly collapse.' Here, the 'Barhesian communist' targets shown to the military junta are certainly the TDK, TTK and TRT which were full of personnel unaware in their crashing majority of the name Roland Barthes.

trilogy of Turkish nationalism, 'To Turkisize, To Islamise, To Civilise', to a new equilibrium by not negating but pruning 'civilisation' (overwesternisation) and reintroducing the formerly neglected task of Islamisation. A further consequence of the recourse to Gokalp is Ataturkism, that is, the emphasis on 'national security', which consists of a reorientation on authoritarian corporatism, with the primary concern of denying class conflict and social stratification, guided by the Gokalpian/Comtean principle of 'progress in unity and harmony'.[581]

Although the Synthesis developed mainly a critique of humanistic 'overwesternisation', its end product in the form of a self-confident nationalism crowned with a utopia of world domination, includes a revision of the Turkist resentment towards the West. Mehmet Kaplan views westernisation as a vital task. If there was a nationalist, who refuses the task of westernisation, 'if there is such a person, he deserves to be called a reactionary'.[582] But this does not prevent the criticism of the westernisation that was carried out by the first republican generation:

> [Westernisation] is not imitating the West like a monkey, but to understand the West, to choose the useful elements for our development and to melt these into our body.[583]

This viewpoint is an obvious recourse to the position of Al-Afgani and the Islamic intellectuals of the Constitutional era (see chapter 1), that is, taking the technology

---

[580] Kaplan 1982.
[581] Parla 1992: 324.
[582] Kaplan 1992: 23.
[583] Kaplan 1997: 43.

of the West and not its culture. Gokalp's split discourse between culture and civilisation is also evident in the Synthesis literature:

In the Ataturkist cultural politics, 'to develop our culture according to international cultural values' is as important as the principle of 'protection of our national culture'.[584]

Another Turkist resentment, that towards the non-Muslim and non-Turkish population, is also superseded in the Synthesis discourse. According to Kafesoglu, the Turks are neither racists nor religious fanatics, because tolerance and secularism[585] are the main features of Turkish history. The Turkish nation, which exists primarily with its language, religion and historical consciousness, protects the weak, respects the elderly, loves justice and freedom, and respects women and family honour.[586] It is important to note here that the precondition of the expression of these good manners is the existence of the Turkish nation as a historical, linguistic and religious unity. When this unity is threatened, the Turk is prepared to have recourse to the Turkist externalisation:

I am not disturbed by a citizen being Kurdish, Laz, Greek, Armenian or Jewish. But if that citizen attempts to pursue Kurdism, lazism, Greekism, Armenianism or Jewishness, that is, if he is involved in actions with separatist aims, I cannot stay idle.[587]

---

[584] *Report* quoted by Guvenc, et al. 1991.
[585] This 'natural' national secularism has to be read as tolerance towards other religions rather than the Kemalist secularist principle.
[586] Kafesoglu 1970.
[587] Kaplan 1992: 104.

Consequently, the anxious and alarmist discourse of Turkism was maintained by the Synthesis:

> **Enemies of Our Country:** Turkey is a paradise on which many enemies have an eye. The fact that Turkey is situated in a very important location where two continents meet, increase the number of those who have aspirations on our country. Her underground and overground treasures, climate and historical richness cause envy in many. In fact, there are many enemies, who claim land from our country, on the basis of a subjective interpretation of history according to their interests.[588]

Like the above example, current history textbooks by Synthesis authors refer frequently to external enemies and their indigenous collaborators, 'who try every method to destroy our state from inside and particularly to damage our unity',[589] and relate these conspiracies to the Crusaders' attempts to expel the Turks from Anatolia.[590] Here, we are already in the field of the third identity question, i.e. the legitimation of Anatolia as the Turks' homeland, which the Synthesis relates to the question of defending Islam. Anatolia became the Turks' homeland through their resistance against the Crusaders in order to defend Islam. It is also the 'last fortress' left from the larger Turkish world and has been owned by the Turks for 900 years. Synthesists emphasise this temporal length of Turkish settlement in

---

[588] Sumer-Turhal 1986: 11.

[589] Aksit 1987: 1.

[590] Anatolia, which has been the Turks' homeland for 900 years has been the target of many states because of her natural riches and strategic importance. The attempts to expel the Turks from Anatolia, which began with the Crusaders and was decisively defeated by the National Struggle, currently continue under the disguise of political forms. Movements that aim to divide our country, their support and the prevention of our economic development are all continuations of a mentality began with the Crusaders (Yildiz 1991: 12).

Anatolia and assert that it is equal to that of the majority of the European states founded in the Medieval Age.[591]

Turk-Islam Synthesis was declared the state's official ideology after 1980,[592] with the founding of the AKDTYK, which officially assimilated the TDK and TTK, and remained officially in power until the anti-Islamist coup of 28 February 1997, which silenced temporarily the Synthesis cadres.[593] These cadres however are expected to remain in key positions of conservative and pro-Islamic governments, given the increasing weight of civilian politicians and elected cabinets in political life in parallel to EU integration. This, however, is of secondary importance when compared to the fact that the Synthesis achieved a path-breaking shift in the state's discourse. The Islamisation of the centre through Synthesis which continued under Ozal meant the weakening of the Kemalist core and resulted in a symptomatic explosion of Islamic identity politics, which had not been foreseen. This symptomatic return of the repressed constitutes one of the sources of the contemporary crisis in Turkey, which I shall consider in the next chapter.

V. The Intelligentsia, the Left and Identity Crisis

Ever since Said Halim Pasha wrote *Buhranlarimiz* ('Our Crises'), identity crisis has been a major theme of discussion among Turkey's intelligentsia. Pasha made

---

[591] Copeaux 1998: 105-6.
[592] For the rationale of the State's presentation of Turk-Islam Synthesis as 'Ataturkism' see Appendix 19.

in this seminal work the case for nationalisation in order to balance westernisation:

> In order to ascend as a nation, we were obliged to derive from western civilisation. (...) This led to that false contemplation that 'for salvation, we are bound to imitate the western nations'. (...) [We need to] derive from the term 'Turk', a social and political entity, as strong as the connotation of the terms French, English and German.[594]

The primary matter of this ongoing discussion on identity, enriched with conjunctural problematisations of current particular issues, has been the split nature of Turkish identity between East and West, or, how to achieve westernisation, while preserving cultural values. The three frontiers above that have emerged in modern history around various perceptions of political identity have largely been influenced by this cultural discussion. In this section, I will consider this cultural discussion in order to expose further the background of contemporary identity politics in Turkey.

V.1. The Problem of the Past

> Why does the past pull us like a well? I know very well that I am not after the personalities of these people; nor am I longing for the time that they lived in (...) No, we certainly love these things not for what they were:

---

[593] Cadres of the Synthesis were not expelled from the bureaucracy after this coup presumably because there was nobody to replace them, after the elimination of all the left-Kemalist cadres in two subsequent coups of 1971 and 1980.
[594] Said Halim Pasha in Alkan 2002: 462-4.

what pulls us towards them is the very void that they left behind. Whether there are visible traces or not, we search in them a part of ourselves, which we believe to have lost in that quarrel within ourselves.[595]

The void that pulls Tanpinar (1901-1962) like a well is the lacking past, the past that was amputated, externalised and re-presented as the Other of the present. The different grandnarratives of history that determined various notions of identity considered in the above sections owe their emergence primarily to this constitutive lack and the subsequent desire that it produced. But Tanpinar's metaphor is a well, and consequently the emerging desire involves a movement down towards the depth, of sinking or digging, as opposed to viewing this lack merely as a hole in the symbolic universe of republican reality to be 'patched' or 'quilted over' with grandnarratives. Given his knowledge and interest in psychoanalysis, Tanpinar seems to be calling for a journey towards the nation's unconscious to 'that quarrel within ourselves' or to the constitutive moments of those repressed, foreclosed or disavowed traumas,[596] in which we have lost 'a part of ourselves'.

In spite of these rich connotations, the limits of Tanpinar's archaeological desire were determined by his manifest nationalism,[597] which led him to propose not a radical but 'restorationist' program concerned primarily with how to incorporate Anatolia's Muslim cultural heritage and the treasures of the imperial high culture

---

[595] Tanpinar 2001: 256-8.
[596] The programmatic stand that these metaphoric assertions implies is precisely what constitutes the aims of my study in this doctoral thesis: a radical query to the sediments of those repressed,

in the modern republic's universe. Tanpinar searched for and reproduced in literary form traces of these riches within his extensive scope of interest ranging from popular traditions and folklore to monumental architecture of both Seljuks and Ottomans, classical palace music, Ottoman 'Divan' poetry, and so on.[598]

Poet Yahya Kemal Beyatli (1884-1958), whom Tanpinar always referred to as his mentor, had prepared Tanpinar's grounds on questions of identity upon a perception of nation with its history primarily as an aesthetic reality. Kocak (2002: 395) defines this as the 'hermeneutic' position and compares it with Gokalp's positivism in which culture and aesthetic were seen merely as tools of nation building. One of the practical implications of Beyatli's position was to avoid the exaggeration of the actual political dimension of nationalism and the illusion of the possibility of resuscitation of a glorious past. Instead, Beyatli invited the nationalists to see that the desired integral and authentic nation could not be that unified and pure, but despite its hybridity, a relatively unproblematic local culture does live on. Kocak (2002: 395) sees this self-confident nationalist view as constitutive of the humanist program of Hasan Ali Yucel.

Tanpinar's concern has been a manifest theme of Turkey's conservative right, the MHP discourse and Turk-Islam synthesists, but his self-confident hermeneutic approach, which resembles the humanists (above), and his political stand seeing

foreclosed or disavowed traumas, that constitute the grounds of symptomatic identity politics of contemporary Turkey.
[597] Kaplan 1970: 8-9.
[598] Tanpinar 2001 and Tanpinar 1970.

the republican rupture a historical necessity[599], distinguishes Tanpinar as an original thinker, whose concerns have been shared by many thinkers on the right and left of Turkey's political spectrum, both inside the nationalist paradigm and outside.

V.2. Histories of the present outside the nationalist horizon

Philosopher Hilmi Yavuz, following Tanpinar's footsteps, sees the problem of the past significant for understanding and tackling the contemporary identity crisis. However, he points out that the effects of Ottoman and republican westernisation built on an already existing social duality between the elite and the public and therefore the main problem is not the westernisation per se but the fact that this program was implemented from above[600] on an inappropriate social structure:

In the 18th Century, when western societies had completed their industrial revolutions to acquire the form of bourgeois societies, the feudalisation of Ottoman society had only begun, through the collapse of the conventional fiefdom. (...) The incompatibility of westernisation with the Ottoman social structure can only be understood from this perspective, that is, in the attempt to introduce the bourgeois culture over a structure in transition to feudalism.[601]

---

[599] Tanpinar's support for the republican transformation led him in 1932 to sign a proposal by secondary school teachers to discard the teaching of Ottoman 'Divan' literature from national curriculum. He also participated in the Education Ministry cadres that carried out the humanist program in 1940s (Kocak 2002: 399).
[600] Yavuz 1975: 78.
[601] Yavuz 1975: 82.

Yavuz campaigned in the 1970s, for the reintroduction of instruction in Ottoman language in secondary schools as a part of his general call for reconciliation with the past.[602] In a recent article, Yavuz dwelled on the problem of westernisation to argue that the Ottoman and republican import of the Enlightenment included the import of the Orientalist mentality, which corresponded to the elite's social position. 'I believe, we failed to Europeanise but managed to Orientalise.'[603]

Yavuz's engagement from primarily a Marxist perspective with Turkey's two centuries long adventure of westernisation achieved the problematisation of various levels of this process, thus opening up an intellectual space for the proposing solutions.

Murat Belge introduces the problem of obstructed civil society to the discussions on identity crisis. After listing the failures regarding a just distribution of income despite economic development, the cultural-spiritual failure including the lack of aesthetics in over-urbanisation and the lack of any scientific or artistic contribution at the international level, the failure in education, democratisation, human rights, and so on,[604] Belge describes Turkey as 'a society dragged to its failure by the state'.

On the problem of the past, Belge pursues two lines of argument. Firstly, he argues that the problem of the past does not merely consist of that *coupure*

---

[602] Yavuz 1996: 45.
[603] Yavuz 1998: 101-2.

epistemologic with the past but on the contrary most of this problem has to be seen in the failure of a real rupture between the Ottoman and republican political/ideological structures. The continuity was particularly in the state tradition and the state's absolute superiority over society and the individual. Secondly, instead of cultural westernisation, Belge problematises the transition to a monolithic nationalist polity from a pluralistic Empire. The nationalist political structure has been too rigid to accommodate the plural structure of society, including the Kurdish identity. Belge proposes a transition to 'a new state' which has to transcend the perception of society based on a discourse of 'minority rights', since the very concept of 'minority' presupposes a 'dominant nation':

> This new state has to be perceived as a partnership based on the participation of all the existing groups in the formation and responsibilities of the state (...) Then the main weight of life needs to be shifted towards the notion of 'citizen'.[605]

Belge also observes 'fundamentalism' not as a position specific to the Islamic movement but as a state of mentality applicable to the Turkish State with its official ideology and society as a whole. In these circumstances, Belge argues, rather than a secularist regime, Turkey has practised a system in which members of society were allowed to choose from among various 'fundamentalisms'.[606] Belge has combined these political diagnoses with sociological research particularly into the cultural change in parallel to modernisation and over-

---

[604] Belge 1992: 107-8.
[605] Belge 1992: 180.
[606] Belge 1992: 98.

urbanisation.[607] Belge's works thus represent a comprehensive study of Turkey's identity crisis with its various dimensions including the Kurdish rebellion and the crisis of secularism in parallel to the Islamic revival, which are linked to the problems of modernisation including the cultural consequences of rural-urban migration and the emergence of an 'arabesque' mass culture. The solution that he proposes is an overall shift in political culture towards the primacy of civil society and citizenship over the state.

Fikret Baskaya's study (1991), which analyses the contemporary identity crisis as a 'paradigmatic crisis' with special reference to the Kurdish question, preceded the recent proliferation of discourses on ethnic, religious and political plurality of the social structure, and the consequent need for a new political structure to correspond to the social. Taner Akcam's study (1992) on the constitutive role of the elimination of the Armenian population in the historical formation of the Turkish national identity also proposed an alternative to the perceptions of the past, beyond the question of westernisation.

V.3. Conclusions: The Past as present

This section has been an attempt to outline the scholarly and intellectual discussion, which influenced immediately or belatedly the three hegemonic discourses of identity politics. The discussion was shaped around the problem of the past particularly on the consequences of westernisation and secularisation.

---

[607] See, Belge 1983 and Belge 1992: 119-141.

287

Tanpinar's introduction of the problem was followed by a proliferation of language games under the nationalist discursive horizon, which mainly led to the production of rightwing and leftwing versions of the Turk-Islam synthesis.[608] Yavuz's approach moves beyond this horizon to problematise various dimensions of the problem of westernisation. Belge, on the other hand, deals with the problem of the past not merely as revealing of the roots of the present split between East and West but of the necessity of rethinking the political system as a whole. Belge also situates the Kurdish question within a perspective of democratisation through the ascending power of civil society at the expense of monolithic state power. Baskaya's and Akcam's works also approach the past from outside the nationalist habitus and reach significant conclusions on Turkish identity by concentrating on the exclusion of the Kurdish identity and the elimination of the Armenian population.

VI. Results and Prospects

Psychoanalytic discourse has rarely been a source to derive from in the discussion that shaped the Turkish search for identity. When such discourse was deployed, it was either affirmative of the shared conscious and unconscious transference and projection which shaped the popular mentalities of externalisation, that is, the perceptions of the other and 'outside', or of the form of the relationship between state and society – the therapist/patient relationship – that has determined the

---

[608] See Appendix 20.

288

Kemalist mentality.[609] My argument in this chapter is primarily concerned with the demonstration that the main characteristic of these discourses, and most of the others taken into account above, on identity, although they accuse each other of being respectively 'communist' and 'reactionary', is the fact that they speak from inside the identity that they claim to be problematising. This inside consists of a discursive field provided by nationalism, dominated by the concern of protection and maintenance of the nation and the state, as 'ordered' by Ataturk in his 'greatest hit', the 'address to the youth' in the closing paragraphs of his six-day Speech:

> Your first duty is to protect and defend the Turkish independence and the Turkish Republic. (…) In achieving this duty you will have to face many internal and external enemies.

Ataturk does not order in this programmatic speech progress or secularism or any other principles but 'protection' and 'defence' as the primary duty of the republican generations. The contesting political identity designs and most of the cultural discussion considered in this chapter are in compliance with this constitutive command to protect the State and Nation and be in a state of constant anxiety against internal and external enemies. The problem, illuminated particularly by Belge's, Baskaya's and Akcam's contributions to the identity discussion, in this statement is twofold: firstly the glued existence of the state and nation (Turkish independence and the Turkish Republic), and secondly the perception of the 'outside' of this nationalist field, as internal or external enemies, who threaten the accomplishment of the command to protect and defend. This

---

[609] See Appendix 21.

rigidly demarcated nationalist field also determined the boundaries of most of the

scholarly and intellectual discussion considered in the previous section. I shall

conclude this chapter by referring again to Tanpinar, who deserves an exceptional

place in any study on identity crisis for he courageously opened up a space for

cultural, intellectual and scholarly discussion:

> The past is always present.

This statement can be followed by asserting that the past is always present, both as

a symbolised reality, that is a reality that could be assimilated and articulated by

the language and, as the Real, which resists symbolisation and escapes the

language – or is externalised, disavowed, foreclosed – after symbolisation as a

surplus. Tanpinar continues:

> In order for us to be able to live as ourselves, we are obliged all the time to
> quarrel, reconcile and make peace with our past.[610]

But this quarrel and reconciliation have some absolute limits, the subject of taboo

and disavowal even for Tanpinar himself. In his *Bes Sehir,* while the Ottoman and

Seljuk heritage is being excavated, the only trace of the foreclosed/disavowed past

is mentioned in Erzurum in the form of the word 'Armenian', in a sentence aiming

to prove that 'Turks have always existed here as a *crashing* majority'.[611]

'Crashing' indeed.[612]

---

[610] Tanpinar 2001: iv.

[611] Tanpinar 2001: 38-9.

[612] Bozkurt Guvenc (1992: 268) claims that in *Bes Sehir* Tanpinar observes 'Anatolia's cultural plurality and continuity that challenge the central (unitary) state ideology', without any quotes or evidence to this effect.

The above comments enable us to make a statement as the overall conclusion of this chapter: The primary reason of the deepening of the identity crisis in spite of all the political and scholarly queries outlined in this chapter is the fact that the absolute psychic boundaries that constitute the roots of this crisis are identical to the boundaries of the discursive surface on which these politico-cultural discourses operate with the aim of overcoming this crisis.

These boundaries which had been drawn by a number of subsequent traumatic experiences during the formation of identity can be legitimately identified as the absolute boundaries of Turkish nationalism. Most of the Turkish search for identity considered in this chapter has consisted of proposals of reconceptualisation of the interactive relations between the conscious and unconscious components of Turkish identity, while most of the causes of the identity crisis has originated from what was left outside of the 'Turkish nation' and therefore required courageous interventions to 'touch the real', as in the overall aim of this research.

CHAPTER 6

GENEALOGIES OF THE OTHER: PRELUDE TO THE CONTEMPORARY IDENTITY CRISIS

I have argued in the first two chapters of this research that modern Turkish identity was made out of a proto-national material which had emerged through the exclusion of non-Muslim identity. The modern nationalist operations on this fabric consisted of further exclusion, including the repression of the popular Islamic identity and a reinforcement of the mechanism of foreclosure for the exclusion of heterogeneous identity perceptions within this proto-nation. In chapters 3 and 4, I have inquired into the territory of the emerging discursive constructs of modern Turkish identity and the republican polity, which was defined primarily in its difference from the excluded others, including the non-Muslim identities, national identity claims other than Turkish and the Islamic identity. The features of republican power that emerged from this process include the materialisation of the Kemalist regime of truth in the form of republican governmentality, which has been demarcated by a militarist discourse and Ataturk's personality cult as the guardians of the republic. Inside this territory, operate discourses attached to the episteme of modernity, that is, cultural westernisation, economic development and progress, in addition to discourses of nationalism and secularism. Kemalism, I have argued, has provided a surface of inscription for a plurality of discourses of power, identity and difference, and a nodal point that has sutured a variety of subject positions to a model of modern and national political subjectivity. To demonstrate this range of proliferation, I have presented in chapter 5 the debate among the contesting perceptions of identity, which have primarily problematised the notions of the past and the meanings of the west within the republican discursive territory.

In this chapter, the political developments that accompanied this debate through republican history will be considered in terms of a series of crises. This outline will help to explicate the peculiarity of the contemporary crisis, which will be considered in the context of the global erosion of the episteme of modernity, in comparison to the previous crises: it is distinguished as an identity crisis accompanying the organic crisis of republican governmentality. I will demonstrate the nodal points at which the republican order has been eroded and destabilised in parallel to the intensification of the current crisis. This nature of the contemporary crises arises primarily from the connection between the challenging discourses of Kurdish national liberation and political Islam on the one hand, and the identities that had been excluded from the process of formation of republican Turkey and the constitution of modern Turkish identity, on the other. The Turkish experience of the 1980s and 1990s is in this sense a process of the return of the repressed.[613] It is therefore necessary to focus on the returning identities in order to establish the nature of the link between these and what had been repressed. Consequently, I will conduct genealogical inquiries into the spaces beneath and outside the discursive surfaces of the Turkish symbolic order where the excluded Islamic and Kurdish identities have survived and accumulated

metaphorical criticisms of the deficiencies of the social order throughout the
republican history

I. Crises and Identity Politics in Republican History

I have described the modern Turkish polity as a specific form of governmentality
existing under the referential horizon of a Kemalist regime of truth, which in turn
is a specific 'objectivication' of the episteme of modernity and modernisation.
This model has produced economic, political and institutional crises in each
decade since its emergence, the trajectories of which I will outline below.

I.1. Crisis of the Populist-Corporatism

Following the Kemalist cut over the proto-national 'historic bloc', the republican
grammar tended to interpret all resistence to the centre with a convenient label:
the challenge of the remnants of the ancien regime against revolution.[614]
Kemalists chose to recognise exclusively the repressed and externalised Islam as
the official signifier of any dissident mobilisation against their political authority.
This logic was largely shared by the popular masses and resentment of the state
was expressed in the vocabulary of religious conservatism – the only language
commonly available to the majority of the people.

---

[613] Yegen's objections. 75-6
[614] This label was introduced by Kemal to apply to the Kurdish rebellion of 1925. Kemal labelled
the Progressive Republican Party similarly and closed it the same year. When the second multi-

The Kemalist grammar also brought about the logic of populism as the hegemonic perception of the political contest. Kemalist populism argued that the people of Turkey were a homogenous mass, without class divisions, who had been politically dominated, socially oppressed and economically exploited by the *ancien regime,* and the Kemalists viewed themselves as a nationalist-populist vanguard, whose mission was to initiate a 'revolution from above' at the common sense level, which would eventually eliminate the mass-elite cleavage through the mobilisation of 'national-popular will', consisting of national unity, economic development and cultural modernisation. The Kemalist logic was consequently based on an interpretation of reformism in terms of a 'passive revolution' to be carried out through a 'war of position' by the 'organic intellectuals' of the republic, whose mission was to disseminate the Kemalist message and initiate social change through the transformation of the 'economic-corporate level' into a corporatist variant of capitalism.[615]

The oppositon would adopt the same populist grammar based on a mass-elite dichotomy when the republican polity was antagonised at the destabilised nodal points where the failure of the Kemalist hegemonic attempt was exposed. During the transition to multi-party system in 1946, the opposition Democrat Party (DP) managed to mould a populist alliance among the social classes based on resentment against bureaucracy's political and ideological obtrusion of the

---

party experience was put to sleep in 1930, Kemal alleged that this party had become open to counterrevolutionary influences.

universal principles of economic and religious freedom. A new historic bloc thus emerged under the DP's leadership consisting of the same economic-corporate popular elements with the significant addition of a 'matured bourgeoisie' as the 'politically most conscious participant of the populist mobilisation'.[616]

Populism, therefore, was the form of political process for government and opposition alike during the 'classical Kemalist era', while political contest was primarily over the meaning of Islam, a sediment of the *ancien regime* to be overcome or the metaphor of political and economic freedom denied by the state elite.

Keyder (1987: 123) observes that in the following three decades the elements of this populist model of mobilisation remained an important dimension of Turkish politics even when class-based interests came to be much more fully articulated. This observation needs to be qualified by an emphasis on 'a dimension' since the very crisis of 1946 was a crisis of this simplistic populist model, which failed to correspond to the progressive sophistication of republican polity, particularly the emergence of the bourgeoisie as a significant actor in Turkish politics. The fact that economic freedom, in addition to religious freedom, against bureaucratic obstruction was a motto of the '1946 spirit' was an early sign of this sophistication.

---

[615] See, Chapter 4.
[616] Keyder 1987: 124.

I.2. 1950s: Sophistication of the Republican Order

The transition to multi-party system in 1946 and the subsequent success of the DP in the 1950 elections brought about a controlled relaxation of Kemalist secularism in favour of the repressed Islamic identity. Under a decade of liberal/conservative DP rule, Islam-State relations reached an equilibrium, where Islamic cadres, rather than aspiring to political power, were satisfied with limited influence on state affairs and the relaxation of the state intervention in religious affairs. As a result, the 1950s did not witness the emergence of a distinct Islamist movement with the aim of gaining a decisive weight in politics; instead, the religious communities seemed to have been satisfied with limited representation at the political level via their partial influence on centre-right political parties. The growing weight of the market economy, urban life and industry in the Turkish political economy as a consequence of capitalist development resulted in the transcendence of the secularism/Islam dichotomy of the classical Kemalist era. The foreclosed 'Kurdish Question' remained unpronounced, while being tackled through the entry of a number of tribal leaders to the Parliament as deputies of the Kurdish provinces.[617]

The 1960 coup had the immediate profile of a symptom of a Kemalist crisis, that is, a bid by the military to reinstall the 'classical' republican regime. This manifest aim, however, soon proved to be anachronistic, and the over-Kemalised colonels, inspired by Nasserism and Ba'thism, were soon expelled from the ruling junta, after the decision to hold elections. The 1960 coup, instead of restoring a 'pure' Kemalist regime, served to reform Turkey's judicio-political structure with a new constitution in line with the requirements of industrial capitalism. The new 'model of accumulation', as Keyder puts it, was a transition from a naïve market economy of the 1950s to the import substitution model of industrial capitalism with economic regulation, in which the state assumed a significant role, including, in particular, the planning of the economic activity through a constitutional body named the State Planning Organisation.[618] The republican governmentality was neither problematised nor abolished nor restored before and after the 1960 coup, despite its immediate profile of a bureaucratic intervention by the Kemalist cadres.

I.3. The Rise and Ideological Annihilation of the logic of the Labour/Capital Dichotomy

The emergence of working class organisations and student militancy armed with new discourses based on Labour/Capital and Independence/Imperialism dichotomies, with visions of a common socialist-social democratic future dominated the political agenda through the 1960s and 1970s. In those two decades, the questions of democratisation, state/citizenship, and national-religious identities began to enter the vocabulary of political discussion, in parallel

---

[617] This issue will be considered in detail in the subsequent sections of this chapter.
[618] See Keyder 1987: 144-150. The state's role was summed up by Keyder (1987: 147) as follows: 'First, the political allocation of scarce economic resources – especially foreign exchange and

particularly to the rise of the labour movement, but as merely complimentary to the main body of the political discourses. This can be observed in the 'Eastern Demonstrations' of the Workers Party of Turkey (TIP) in the 1960s, which primarily aimed to expand the party's constituency by emphasising the social and economic backwardness of the region, and proposing equal development for the Kurdish citizens. In the 4th Congress of TIP in 1969, a resolution was passed to declare that 'the Party views the Kurdish question from the angle of the realities of the working class struggle for socialist revolution'.[619] Another observation of the manifest entry of identity into the political process can be made about the ruling bureaucracy-bourgeoisie alliance, which preached an Islamised nationalist identity when pressed by the leftwing opposition for democratisation and demands for redefinition of state/citizenship relations. Consequently, there have been a series of official concessions to the Islamic identity, and not exclusively by the rightwing coalition governments[620], in order to counter the ascending opposition articulated by the discourses of political and economic rights and freedom.

In the right/left polarisation of the 1970s' political spectrum, Islam became increasingly identified with anti-communism and the nationalist right, while pallid articulations of the Kurdish identity claims in the leftwing discourses of development could be observed.

---

credit- and second, the assurance of a redistribution of income with the multiple aims of purchasing social and industrial *detante* and creating and sustaining an internal market.
[619] Noktali 1996: 851.

The economic crisis of the late 1970s triggered by the traumatic impact of the global 'oil crisis' on the Turkish economy, literally dragged Turkey's two decade long import substitution model to a situation where 'the economy could no longer be reproduced'.[621] The late-Kemalist dreams of salvation in progress and development were rapidly replaced by a dispute among various classes on the question of the distribution of the burden of the economic crisis. The growing Capital/Labour antagonism, which primarily emerged from the successful resistance of industrial workers against sharing the burden of the crisis, was violently reflected on the streets as armed conflict between far-right paramilitary groups and leftwing youth. The mass massacre on May Day of 1977 in Istanbul, the massacre of the Alevi Kurds in K.Maras in December 1978, and the escalating intra-left violence led to the alienation of the trade union movement and left inclined intelligentsia from the radical left. The streets were deserted to the rule of arms and the coalition cabinets of right[622] and left[623] alike were hopeless spectators, and sometimes provocateurs, of the growing violence and the underlying economic crisis.

---

[620] The 1960 military junta, for instance, who strongly claimed to have toppled the DP government in order to protect secularism, initiated the building of 6,000 new mosques around the country (Landau 1974: 176).

[621] 'The local crisis, like the boom before it, was the refracted appearance of the world economic cycle in the mirror of import substitution industrialisation. In this mirror, the effective constraint on the economy took the shape of the availability of imports. Without imported inputs and technology the economy could no longer be reproduced. Problems in securing inputs translated into obstacles in maintaining the material conditions of production. Through a chain of causation from reduced use of capacity to declining profits, and declining investment in manufacturing, economic growth stopped, unveiling various shades of social conflict' (Keyder 1987: 196).

[622] Nationalist Front – MC, consisting of the centre-right Justice Party [AP], Islamist National Salvation Party [MSP] and the ultra-nationalist Nationalist Action Party [MHP].

I.4. Crises and Identity Politics

I have outlined three major crises of modern Turkish history, each of which was resolved by significant transformations regarding economic and political organisation. If they are to be rephrased in terms of identity politics, each of these crises did involve struggles for recognition by emergent social identities, which pressed the conventional networks of identity/difference to be recognised as new subject positions within the symbolic order. The major actors of the 1946 crisis mobilised the masses in line with the populist logic of elite-mass dichotomy but effectively abolished this simplistic structure by initiating the addition of the bourgeoisie to the republican political process to reflect the sophisticated map of socio-political stratification. Similarly, although the manifest content of the 1960 crisis was Kemalist restoration, it was resolved with the recognition at the symbolic level of the further fragmentation of the social, particularly the addition of the working class identity, which effectively abolished the 'people' as a political category.[624]

---

[623] CHP, which had adopted a social democrat stance since early 1970s.

[624] Sina Aksin's map (1977) of social structure below illustrates what is involved in this point:

1950-1960	**1960-1980**
I. Bourgeoisie	I. Bourgeoisie
A. Agrarian and provincial bourgeoisie	A. Urban industrial and commercial bourgeoisie
B. Urban Commercial bourgeoisie	B. Agrarian and provincial bourgeoisie
II. Rulers	II. Rulers
III. Rulers of the periphery (notables)	III. Workers
IV. Religious notables	IV. Rulers of the Periphery
V. People	V. Merchants
A. Workers	VI. Religious notables
B. Merchants	VII. Peasants
C. Peasants	

The partial coup of 12 March 1971 and the complete coup of 12 September 1980 both aimed to curb the rights and liberties of the 1961 Constitution – ironically made by the generals, which the next generation of generals overtly criticised for being 'extra-large' for Turkish society. The generals' aim, especially in the 1980, could therefore be interpreted as a desire to bring the proliferation of social identities to an end by fortifying the rigidity of the boundaries of the republican symbolic order.

The crises of republican history and their resolutions can therefore be analysed in terms of identity politics, as the consequences of struggles of recognition. None of these crises however problematised the premises of Turkish identity by attacking the territorial boundaries of the republican discursive formation. Because of this, they were crises *within* republican order and not crises *of* the republican order. The major faultlines that split the imaginary integrity of Turkish identity have not been the primary cause of any of these crises.[625] All the discourses that were attached to the emergent identities, including liberalism, conservatism, social democracy and socialism, were sharing a horizon of modern Turkish identity grounded upon the episteme of modernisation. They represented the proliferation of language games and antagonisms within this horizon rather than presenting fundamental challenges to the republican governmentality and the Kemalist 'regime of truth'. The metanarrative of emancipation through progress and

---

[625] Although the bureaucracy usually presented them in these terms (the Islamic threat or the 'separatist' threat) for the legitimation of their heavy-handed interventions in the political process at the moments of crisis. In fact, the official referral to these faultlines as a source of legitimation

modernisation, with the complementary grand-narrative of economic developmentalism and productivism leading to the nation's salvation either as a wealthy partner of the 'free world' or as an ally of the 'socialist world', was the benchmark of the shared late-Kemalist horizon. Republican history until the 1980s was a history of disputes on an extensive list of issues except for the 'republican subject' defined as a modern surface of inscription over which a variety of subject positions was able to proliferate. Beyond this 'republican subjectivity' lay the denied Islamist and Kurdish political subjectivities. Before reviewing their histories, I will outline below the conditions of their revival as an organic crisis of the republican order.

II. The Crack of Doom: The Organic Crisis of the Republican Order

The military regime that took over the government on 12 September 1980 concentrated primarily on the suppression of leftist politics, by breaking down working class organisations and the trade union movement in order to eliminate the 'communist threat' and to implement an IMF prescribed 'structural adjustment' program in the economy. The immediate advantage of the economic restructuring was the suppression of the capital accumulation crisis through declining agricultural prices, lower wages and decreased social expenditure.[626]

---

in the description of crises is further revealing of the popular and naturalised legitimacy of the exclusion of Islamic and Kurdish identities for the republican polity.
[626] Keyder 1987: 223-228

This structural maintenance of the damaged economy was accompanied by an 'Ataturkist' politico-ideological closure under the military regime. The junta's first declaration was summed up in the headlines of the Turkish dailies as 'The Aim is Ataturkism'. Until 1980, the ideology of national development had borrowed freely from a certain strand of socialist discourse, especially in its etatist developmentalism and populism, which contributed to the proliferation of the language games under the Kemalist horizon. However, Ataturkism was designed as a specifically state security discourse signifying the nation in its difference from the 'threat of communism'. This externalisation of the socialist discourse against the background of the growing class conflict and the manifestly threatened social peace from late 1960s to 1980 occurred in parallel to a revision in the perception of Kemalism. The revision emerged from the emphasis on national security and tranquillity and the need to fill in the ideological vacuum that was left from the physical elimination of the socialist influence on social and political life of the late-Kemalist Turkey, for which the Ataturk cult proved to be too unsophisticated. In these circumstances, the 'Turk-Islam Synthesis', which was produced by conservative-religious intellectuals organised in the 'Hearth of the Enlightened' provided the perfect ideological content for the junta's Ataturkism, with its emphasis on authoritarian politics and social control through the use of cultural and religious codes.[627] In other words, if religion was 'the opium of the people', then it could be administered in an appropriate dose to tranquillise the social. This pharmacological transition from Kemalism to Ataturkism, escalated the Turk-Islam Sythesis to the status of the ideological roof of the Ataturkist

---

[627] See Chapter 5.

revisionism of Kemalism. The Ataturkist Islamisation of the centre brought the conservative-religious political elements to key positions in the state bureaucracy, particularly in the educational apparatus where the left had previously been influential.[628]

The structural adjustment of the economic organisation therefore necessitated a 'discursive adjustment' of the Kemalist horizon, consisting of an attempt to fix the empty signifier Kemalism through the inoculation of its discursive obverse, Islamism, with a authoritarian-conservative myth of 'depoliticisation and tranquillity in national security'. This military discursive manoeuvre would produce effects beyond its purposes of suppression of the symptoms of crisis. Firstly the politicisation of religion under the official banner of a Turk-Islam Synthesis opened the politico-discursive structure to the challenge of discourses, based on the articulation of the repressed Islamic identity. This would lead to a process of the 'explosion of the repressed' in the 1990s. Secondly, the attempt to fix the empty signifier Kemalism in terms of an Islamic argument, that is, its constitutive outside, meant stretching it beyond the limits of signification, where the radically blurred Kemalism would no longer have any value. In this sense, Ataturkism operated as the 'gravedigger' of Kemalism. The post-1980 erosion of Kemalist/republican discourse with its 'will to civilisation' was progressively revealing the insufficiency of the republican model to confine the imagination of the political community within the horizon of republican modernism. This erosion was an ironic consequence of the achievement of the Kemalist goal of full

---

[628] See Appendix 19 and Akin and Karasapan 1988: 18.

integration with 'civilisation', the contemporary horizon of which was marked by globalisation, neo-liberalism and the New Right.

The economic architect and minister of economy of the military junta, Turgut Ozal, won the first post-1980 elections in November 1983 to form a cabinet consisting of his Motherland Party (ANAP). Under ANAP, the structural adjustment that commenced under the junta was furthered by a neo-liberal globalist economic orientation, accompanied by a discourse grounded in a liberal criticism of Kemalism and the bureaucracy as the main fetters of Turkey's free development. A technocratic vision of society was favoured in contrast to the bureaucratic view through which Kemalism was equated by a number of terms, namely, etatism, dogmatism, authoritarianism, territorial nationalism and communism, all of which Ozal believed were being superseded by a 'new world order', in the wake of the collapse of the Eastern Bloc.

This overtly anti-Kemalist stance corresponded to a new perception of the State, fundamentally different from the 'corporatist vanguard state' of the republican perception. The neo-liberal trend of globalisation tailored a new role for the State as the engine of liberalisation and privatisation, as the inventor of a new free trade regime and as the actor of new modes of foreign policy in search of foreign markets for export. Consequently, the State had to initiate its own retreat from the social by imposing its own limitations. The neo-liberal transformation consisted of the opening up of the field of the social to allow its participation directly in the flow of capital, human resources, knowledge, technology, communications and cultural expression. The goal was the integration of the social to the supra-national space of a global system, without the mediation of the State, which effectively meant the bypassing of the 'moderniser State'.[629] Ironically, the engine of this transition was the State itself. The emergence of the neo-liberal minimal State over a number of shifts in economic policies from import substitution to export promotion, from the logic of productivism to consumerism and the revolution in communications technology, without a comprehensive recomposition of the ideological, institutional and judicial structures of the conventionally bureaucratic-authoritarian State, brought about the inevitable erosion of its legitimacy.

The weakening and decreasing legitimacy of the centre was accompanied by increasing claims of politico-economic corruption. Although etatism had been abandoned, the retreat of the State from the economy was only a myth, given that the precarious interconnection of the bureaucratic, political and economic élite of the country did not end with the new policy of economic liberalisation. The state continued to play an essential role in the allocation and distribution of public resources. Besides high rates of growth, the liberalisation of the Turkish economy also resulted in widespread tax evasion, the growth of the underground economy

---

[629] As Keyder (2000: 223-4.) argues, the Turkish crisis developed within the context of 'globalisation', which has replaced from 1980s onwards 'modernisation' as the episteme of social change in those countries, called by the globalist jargon 'emerging markets', that had been formerly referred to as the 'developing countries' or the Third World. In the modernisation paradigm, social transition was viewed as a consequence of interaction between the State, which was perceived as the representative of modernity and an essentially traditional and stagnant society. In the logic of

and rising instances of bribery, corruption and embezzlement. The legitimation crisis thus intensified parallel to the changing perception of the state in the neo-liberalised Turkish economy. The process of liberalisation was associated with a 'loss of confidence and a decline in the moral authority of the state'.[630]

Ozal attempted to tackle the challenge of legitimation through a rather ambiguous reform program. He believed that the contemporary problems that his government was facing, particularly the Kurdish and the Islamist challenges were the consequences of the rigid First Republic structure, which needed a thorough reform. In his reformist perspective, the terms associated with the First Republic would be replaced by the logic of the Second Republic favouring market forces, liberties, tolerance, liberalism and an 'imperial vision', with a prospect of devolution of power to local administrations at the expense of central authority. However, this equivocal reform program, which was referred to as Second Republicanism and Neo-Ottomanism and uttered partially by Ozal and a circle of journalists and scholars around him[631], was never formulated in a consistent programmatic format.

The Ozalist debate that entered the symbolic order from the authoritarian core of the republican state demonstrated 'a touch to the real' for the first time by the centre, including a shed of hope to end the exclusion of the Muslim and Kurdish

---

globalisation, this field of social transformation is dominated by international flows, in the expense of the geographical and societal limitations of the nation states.
[630] Onis 1997: 752.

identities from the republican reality. This move was however immediately countered by the conventional cultural elite with a strong Kemalist rhetoric. This 'First Republicanist' core, consisting mainly of left-Kemalist intelligentsia, who had fallen out of favour since the 1980 coup, and the conventional bureaucracy, progressively politicised Kemalism in order to forge a discursive frontier of the dislocated 'modern forces' upon nationalist and secularist premises to counter Islamism and Kurdish separatism.[632] The republican core was splitting around an antagonistic struggle among its various wings, which further vindicated the impression of a weakened, ambivalent centre, and was received by the Islamic and Kurdish movements as encouragement to press their demands of recognition harder, thus destabilising further the republican symbolic order.

The legitimation crisis would deepen further as a consequence of the search for legitimacy in Islam under Turgut Özal's ANAP government, which launched an overall Islamisation/peripherialisation of the centre. The economistic stance was stretched further to include consumerism to the conventional republican discourse of 'national development'. In the emerging symbolic order, identities were reorganised according to their position vis-à-vis the code 'consumption' as much as 'production'. Consequently, religious communities, who had been perceived in the old mode as 'fetters of progress and modernisation' were now able to claim an equal 'subject position' with other identities as consumers and contributors to

---

[631] Prof. Mehmet Altan, Mehmet Barlas and one time leftist journalists Cengiz Candar and Hadi Uluengin were the prominent names among these 'advisers'.
[632] This counter-reformist discourse tried to hegemonise the 'deep state' structure, consisting of a wing of military and civilian bureaucracy, who opposed any solution to the Kurdish question apart

economic activity. Muslim identity was thus rehabilitated in the social imaginary of an emergent consumerist society, ANAP continued the policy of the Islamisation of the state and society over an authoritarian judicio-discursive structure laid down by the military regime's 1982 Constitution, without having to recourse to the mask of Ataturkism. The Islamisation of the centre included unprecedented concessions to the formally banned Islamic orders.[633] Islamists constituted an important wing of ANAP,[634] including primarily Ozal himself.[635] The budget of the *Diyanet,* the number of religious personnel, the number of Imam-Hatip graduates, mosques and Koran courses increased dramatically in the 1980s, according to a 1989 report by the *Diyanet.*[636] In addition to the state measures, the 1980s also witnessed increasing economic activity blended with a discourse of Islamic principles. Islamic financial institutions emerged rapidly to increase the share in national economy of small investors and traders in conformity with Islamic values, including non-interest banking.[637] Al-Baraka and two more Gulf-based Islamic banks introduced the Islamic non-interest banking system in order to serve Islamic capital and small investors. In such a favourable

---

from the suppression of the PKK revolt and had been previously allied with the MHP cadres, centre-right and the religious identity.

[633] Cakir 1990: 277. An example of this concessionary attitude, detailed in Cakir's narration of the Islamic movement of the 1980s is that in 1983, when there were heavy restrictions even on the centrist politics, the *Nakshibendi* order decided to publish its first ever journal in history, *Islam,* in order to maintain the community's communication in modern conditions. The second example is even more striking: Fethullah Gulen, the leader of the largest section of the Nurcu movement was in the junta's list of wanted after the 1980 military coup. 'For some reason Gulen could never be captured. It was known that he had not fled the country and continued his community activities particularly in the Aegean region. At one stage, he was captured in Burdur (South West Turkey) but the city's police chief was 'appointed the police chief of Erzurum (East Turkey) the next day' (Cakir 1990: 104). Gulen remained officially wanted until the charges dropped in his absence.

[634] ANAP was claiming to have brought 'four tendencies' (centre-right, centre-left, Turkist right and religious right) together.

[635] Ozal was a member of the Nakshibendi order as his Minister of Education Vehbi Dincerler, who banned the teaching of Darwin in primary and secondary schools.

economic, political and ideological atmosphere Islamist publications along with radical Islamist groups and circles proliferated. The Islamisation of the republican core, like the liberalisation of economy, also had a global dimension. It was to a large extent a part of the global 'revival' of Islam as a mode of political subjectivity in the midst of fundamental changes in the international arena.[638]

The Islamisation of the centre and the revival of Islamic identity need to be read further as the consequences of the global opening up. Until 1980, the territory of modern Turkey was marked by literal closure. The ultimate aims of the republic were pronounced in terms of modernisation, economic development and productivity, in which the state assumed a guiding role. This closure was further reinforced by an import substitution economy and the State's monopoly on cultural life.[639] In the 1980s, the end of economic closure through neo-liberal economic policies was accompanied by a sudden invasion of cultural life by diverse images and traditions through the explosion in communications.[640] This 'media revolution' meant that the Turks were, for the first time, becoming aware of the existence of a world beyond Turkey in a 'real' sense.

---

[636] Poulton 1997: 185-6.

[637] Al-Omar & Abdel Haq 1996: 63-83.

[638] The cold war strategy of partial rehabilitation of Islam developed into a global promotion of Islamic fanaticism in the second half of the 1970s in order to counter the increasing Soviet influence in the Middle East and Asia, particularly in Afghanistan. Iranian Revolution of 1979 vindicated further the Islamist revival around the world.

[639] The 'republican closure' was symbolised by the Turkish TV and radio broadcasting monopoly: the only TV channel in 1980 was a black and white state channel, while the only radio broadcasting institution was the Turkish state radio.

[640] By the year 1990, people were able choose from among over 20 national TV channels in addition to hundreds of foreign channels received through cable TV and satellite anthens. Dozens of privately owned FM radio stations broadcasting various programs engaged in a fierce competition to attract listeners. Printed press, particularly coloured, glossy magazines with

Moreover, the time of this opening up of the republican horizon coincided with a global epistemic crisis of modernism in parallel to growing 'incredulity towards metanarratives'. This crisis of late-modernity, which for many marked – along with the revolution in communications technology and the post-fordist shift in the logic of (post)industrial organisation – the transition to a post-modern age, implied a radical erosion of the universal referential horizon of the republican regime's rationale, which had conventionally provided its positive norms of modernisation, civilisation, enlightenment and progress.

The politics of the 1980s, which commenced with an authoritarian intervention to repair the damaged structure therefore led to a crisis, which effectively damaged the republican structure further at its constitutive axes of modernisation, nationalisation and secularisation. The consequent erosion of the republic's discursive formation (the Kemalist regime of truth), institutional logic (nation-state and militarism) and the logic of economic organisation (national development, industrialisation, productivism) has radically destabilised the identity perceptions and social configurations leading to a state of ambivalence and uncertainty.

1980s, which commenced with and authoritarian regime's attempt of closure therefore concluded with an unintended and unprecedented crisis and the opening

---

specialized readers, has also experienced a boom. Foreign newspapers and magazines are also sold extensively.

up of the republican order. As Gurbilek argues, it would be irrelevant to perceive the 80s solely through the concept of oppression:

On the one hand, the 1980s represent by and large the harshest decade of oppression that this society has ever experienced; it is a period when the State's violence became tangible in its most naked presence. But, on the other hand, it brought about a cultural proliferation, that is, the unleashing of those cultural identities, which had up until then remained the prisoners of holistic ideologies. Cultural demands that could exist within political designs as the subordinate elements of their discourses were able to find opportunities of self-expression for the first time in the 1980s.[641]

The prelude to Turkey's identity crisis was thus performed by an authoritarian State, which paved the way for the problematisation of the legitimacy and efficiency of the republican governmentality. In other words, the State's attempts to overcome a crisis in the system resulted in the emergence of a crisis of the system. This new crisis was further triggered by challenges against the republican social order and subjectivity particularly by political Islam and the Kurdish national liberation movement. The novelty of these challenges lie in that the identity perceptions enveloped in these discourses are as much contingent upon the new dislocations of the social order as 'revivals' of the politico-discursive challenges to Kemalist nationalisation, that had been externalised in the formative years of the republic. The structures of republican governmentality with the accompanying perceptions of national identity and political subjectivity had been largely grounded upon their externalisation and potential threat. Consequently, their articulation subverts the discursive boundaries of the republican order: the language games that have pressurised the republican order have not been assimilible with the available signifiers of the existing symbolic order. This combined 'revival' or 'return' of the 'others' of modern Turkish identity has radically dislocated the existing social order and national identity, leading to traumatised perceptions.

III. Islam from Repression to Repolitisation

This section will present an analytic outline of the history of the Islamic identity from its exclusion during the construction of the republican order to its gradual repoliticisation to lead to its recent powerful revival. It will narrate a long upward march from the level of the unconscious of the Turkish political psyche to eventually strike the surface at the very centre of the conscious core, that is the Turkish symbolic order to disturb radically the modern designs of identity grounded heavily on a notion of rational political subjectivity.

III.1. Spaces of the Repressed

I have argued in Chapter 1 that the republicans imagined Turkish identity as a split identity and postulated a dialectical 'aufhebung' regarding the relationship between the opposing sides of this split. The conscious core, or the

---

[641] Gurbilek 1992: 109.

314

Kemalist/republican centre[642], with its 'regime of truth' consisting of the task to civilise and the cult of Ataturk, would win over the unconscious periphery of the 'popular religion' or common sense nationalism of Muslim Anatolia, where the the sediments of the repressed, including non-western elements, the Ottoman past and Islamic identity, remain to flow as 'a diminishing deep current'.[643] However, this 'deep current' has continued to flow as the repressed dimension of the Kemalist psyche, as the unconscious component of modern Turkish identity: the inescapable sediments of the *ancien regime,* mainly because the Kemalist discourse has reproduced this dual structure. This inconsistency was partly because without this dualism the Kemalist discourse would lose an essential rationale of its existence, as evident in abundant references to 'the threat of Sharia'. The location of the unconscious – or 'insane' – deep current varied from state institutions to the outlawed tarikats and the modern ecoles Islamique. Below, I will outline the formation and operation of each of these three spaces of the 'repressed', where Islamic identity has reproduced itself in various forms beneath the discursive surfaces of the republican order. The analysis in this section will demonstrate that the modernist 'core' and the repressed 'periphery' have reached equilibrium during the decades that followed the Kemalist exclusion to constitute the totality of national identity. This has however been an inherently split totality bringing together radically different discursive formations, each having hostile perceptions of the other.

---

[642] Mardin 1975.
[643] Ayvazoglu 2002: 545.

Kemalists had to allow the 'deep current' to continue to flow around the country, hoping that Kemalist generations inoculated by their 'nationalised divine' would inherit the young republic from the 'old guard'. Military service, a national education network, 'village institutes', the People's Houses and the Village Rooms would overtake in time the functions of dervish lodges, with military officers, schoolteachers and agricultural specialists preaching around the country a Kemalist 'common sense'.[644] Although Atatürk's chronologist Falih Rıfkı Atay described Kemalism as the reform of Islam, for the republican regime, religion was mostly a phenomenon to be kept under check, the influence of which was hoped to diminish with the advance of 'civilisation'. *Diyanet Isleri Baskanligi* (The Religious Affairs Administration) was formed with this philosophy, but in order to maintain the functioning of religious affairs under state control it had to recruit from among the generations trained by the former *ulema* and Sufi orders, due to the lack of appropriate religious education run by the state.[645] Although the religious personnel consisting mostly of the provincial *ulema* of the *ancien regime* were put under strict police and gendarme control, they remained in positions to run the republic's religious affairs. The lives of two leading Nakshibendi notables of the republican era, Mehmed Zahid Kotku and Süleyman Hilmi Tunahan, are

---

[644] See Chapter 4.
[645] Abdurrahman Dilipak (1989: 100) complains about the shortage of religious personnel in the formative years of the republic by citing anecdotes from the 1930s when people could not find imams to conduct funerals.

two examples.[646] Consequently, *Diyanet* began to fulfil two contradictory functions: it served the republican state in maintaining control over religious affairs, while it facilitated grounds for the religious groups to operate with 'entryist' tactics and Islamist strategies to infiltrate the bureaucracy and expand their influence among the state cadres.[647]

Tarikats

The existence of the *tarikats* was the guarantee of peace and order within the communities that they operated.[648] Their influence, however, inevitably reproduced authoritarian communal structures in which the communal norms always preceded the individual. Pre-capitalist tribes, rural villages and urban neighbourhoods were the typical units of such structures. Modernisation was expected to liquidate these closed communities through time. The primary target of the Kemalist reforms in Turkey was, according to Serif Mardin (1991:72) these conservative structures.[649] Kemalists expected that with the diminishing influence

---

[646] See Appendix 22.

[647] Tarhanli (no date): 34-5.

[648] See Appendix 23.

[649] Mardin argues that Mustafa Kemal's personal distaste of *tarikats* was related to a vision of the liberation of individual from these traditional structures such as the *Gemeinschaft* of 'neighbourhood': 'Neighbourhood was usually something more than an administrative unit; it was a cumulative *Gemeinschaft* within the borders protected by neighbourhood braves and loyal dogs. It was the environment in which an ordinary Ottoman subject was expected to spend most of his life. The neighbourhood was the place where primary education was given, births were celebrated, marriages were arranged and funerals were held. This was where the mosques operated like an institution mobilising the dwellers of the entire neighbourhood in order to make sure that the things that needed to be heard were actually heard. (...) The neighbourhood was where compensation for the blood that had been spilt was fixed, where the Islamic institution of the moral inspection was secretly countered in drinking parties and gambling sessions in gloomy rooms. Nightwatchmen patrolled the neighbourhoods in order to raid shattered lovers. Cafés operated as communication centres. The first seal was stamped by the neighbourhood's imam on

of the *tarikats,* the traditional structures would be available for liquidation and transformation by being included in the process of modernisation. Once such modernisation was achieved, the *tarikats* with all the attached 'superstitions' and irrationalities would lose their conditions of existence and whither away.

The *Tarikats'* survival was partly due to the lack of Kemalist hegemony, which mainly transformed the centre and was only tangible as police measures in the periphery.[650] While modernisation and de-Islamisation (secularisation) were partially successful in shaking the traditional units and conventions, modern values and institutions were falling short of providing alternatives to reabsorb the scattered individuals. Neither Kemalist nationalism, which lacked a convincing divine dimension, nor the new horizon of 'civilisation' were able to 'reoccupy' the place of Islam. Modern notions of citizenship and civic identification with modern polity, on the other hand, lacked an accompanying political will and practice within the new state elite, who largely inherited the Ottoman state mentality based on state class/people (Askeriye/Reaya) division. The republican state elite, who viewed the notion of citizenship as an obligation guaranteeing loyalty to the state[651] rather than a right as such, treated from the outset any 'civil society'

---

the petitions before being submitted to higher authorities. The shrines of local saints were visited regularly by the whole neighbourhood. Local holy men distributed justice through self-styled decisions and sentences. (…) Any contact between opposite sexes was prohibited' (Mardin 1991: 72-4).

[650] Paul Sterling notes that in 1950, 95% of the population were still engaged in traditional occupations, and 75% still lived in villages. He also observes that the Kemalist elites charged with enforcing the new rules were not keen on their ruthless application. (Stirling 1981: 583-8.)

[651] The slogan of the Citizenship Week in Turkish Army in April 2001: 'The best citizen is the one who fulfils his duty'. Belge (1992: 108-112) argues that unlike the European bourgeois-democratic revolution, Turkey experienced a bourgeois-anti democratic revolution. See also Chapter 4 on the lack of Kemalist hegemony in the periphery.

initiative with suspicion, hostility and disciplinary suppression. In these circumstances, republican power, after expelling Islam from its exceptional place in the symbolic order and prohibiting folk Islam practices, continued to reproduce and rely on conventional clientalist networks as the primary form of socialisation and legitimacy.

Given these failures of Kemalist modernisation, Islam prevailed as the primary ideological source of identification, particularly in the periphery. *Tarikats*, which lacked a physical structure to attack, beyond shrines and dervish lodges, managed to survive the 'waves of Kemalist terror' with moderate losses and continued to provide sanctuary for many Muslims, deep under the discursive surfaces of the republican order. Moreover, the results of modernisation, particularly the rural-urban migration, rather than securing the supersession of the *Tarikat* structures, brought about new problems, new crises and hence a new vacuum to be filled by the *tarikats*, and thus provided them with new ideological spaces of activity. In a sense, economic development and modernisation served to bring the *Tarikat* structures from the periphery to the urban centres, with the migrating rural population.

The results of modernisation thus provided a new space of activity for the *tarikats*. The relaxation in the secularist practices, on the other hand, provided new surfaces of organisation and expression for these formally underground networks. The 15,000 mosques, built in the 1950s according to the prime minister, were mostly the work of charity associations which mobilised their localities in raising funds. Associations for assisting the Koran schools, solidarity with the Imam Hatip schools, religious staff solidarity associations and associations for the promotion of the Islamic faith also proliferated from 1946 onwards.[652] Most of these associations were linked somehow to the *tarikat* networks.

Ecoles Islamique

Nurcu and *Suleymanci écoles Islamique* developed and proposed modern tactics of survival under Kemalism for pious communities, such as propaganda through modern means of communication, organising Koran courses and infiltration into the *Diyanet* as religious personnel. A detailed account of the development of the *Nurcu* school is given in Appendix 24. It is important to emphasise here that Said-i Nursi's various practices presented to Muslims a strategy of modernisation of Islamic subjects under the disciplinary social conditions of modern Turkey. This strategy consisted of a transformation of the traditional *tarikat* structures into modern *écoles Islamique*, or Muslim communities that reproduce communal identities using modern communication methods, and a political style, which can be called 'doing politics without a political statement'. Said's stand proved to be effective in a society, where the primary aim of the sustained repression of religious signification was to eliminate the Islamic subject. The sociological profile of Said's followers' corresponded to the Kemalist image of the ideal middle class family, rather than the image of 'ignorant' rural conservatism. They

---

[652] Yucekok 1971: 119-122.

were mostly middle-income level urban civil servants, professionals and tradesmen, usually received a reasonable level of secular education, who wanted to lead a modern life but as conservative families, rather than engage in modernisation *in toto*. The modern Islamic subject in the form of *Nurcu* disturbed the new regime of truth, which tried to constitute itself around the logic of the modernity/tradition dichotomy. *Nurcu* was not pure tradition or pure modernity, he was split: modern but Muslim, modern but refusing to be secularist, 'inside' but 'outside', and was therefore the chaotic 'undecidable' of the republican order.[653] With this character, *Nurcu* was the exact mirror image of the Kemalist Turk: the split subject of the 'torn country'.[654]

The style of struggle through ecoles islamique continued along the traditional *tarikat* structures and modern Islamist parties (from 1970s onwards). The current influence of the largest *Nurcu* community led by Fethullah Guven is believed to be extensive both in Turkey and abroad.

---

[653] Deconstructive research shows how symbolic orders are constructed through the categorisation and fixation of differences. Symbolic borders are determined through taking sides in the dichotomies fixed by difference. Order and hierarchy are determined through purity. Those entities, which are not pure because they cannot be categorised and are ambiguous, would connote danger, contamination and the annihilation of the order, due to their subversive orientation breaching the borders. Their existence erodes the claims to purity and wholeness, leading to destabilisation and tension. They therefore represent the rule's outside, by being situated between inside and outside, order and chaos, friend and the enemy. They constitute the category of "undecidables" (Derrida 1981). Derrida includes in this category *pharmakon, hymen* and *supplement*. The Greek word *pharmakon* can mean both cure and poison at the same time. And *hymen,* another Greek word, signifies both virginity (the separation between inside and outside) and marriage, that is, the breach of this separation through the unification of the self with the other (Yumul 2003:20-1).

[654] See Chapter 4.

III. 2. Partial Reconciliation in Multi-Party Period

By the year 1946, when a decision was taken for transition to a multi-party system, Kemalist modernisation had transformed mainly the centre and was only tangible as police measures in the periphery. The fruits of the 'passive revolution' attempt in the form of village institutes, people's houses and village rooms had not yet been matured to build hegemony in the periphery.[655]

The decade of DP rule saw a carefully balanced relaxation of the secularist measures.[656] DP government lifted the ban on call for prayers in Arabic and in

---

[655] An example of this lack of hegemony in the periphery is a book entitled *A Village in Anatolia* consisting of the memoirs of Mahmut Makal (Makal 1965), a village teacher from the 1940s. Makal repeatedly narrates in this book the villagers' hostility towards him. He hardly gets a place to stay for himself, and the villagers are very reluctant to set aside space for a schoolroom. So, for some time he has to gather children in the mosque, which leads to lots of complaints and a state of near-tumult. One day a young man arrives in the village. He is in his twenties, has studied to become a *hafiz*, and he brings news and greetings from a venerated religious leader in a village not too far away. The villagers give this man all the best that they have to eat and drink, they rejoice and gather around him with great curiosity and sincerity. The contrast between how the man of religion and the man of secular education are received by the villagers speaks for itself. Makal, with his enlightened ideals, was left feeling crushed and puzzled (Makal 1965: 94).
Makal also sums up the points raised in the above paragraphs regarding the maintenance of the place of *tarikats* in people's lives during a period when secularist reforms and the prohibitions were still in full force:
In our part of the world there is a veritable epidemic of Sheikhs; and the Sheikhs themselves don't know what Order they belong to. In September 1947, among eleven villages which I visited, and yet another twenty nearby villages not visited but known to me, the village that I found to have fewest Sheikhs was H. And that had more than fifty! The village consists of one hundred and fifty households: children are keen about the *tarikat* and they join it. Everyone who joins the *tarikat* is called 'Sheikh'. He lets his beard grow; to all appearances he has no use for this word. His task is to attain sainthood. In all these villages the Sheikh's duty seems to consist of playing the tambourine till the small hours of the morning, and reciting until they are hoarse (Makal 1965: 86).
[656] Tunaya asserts that the Islamic current in the post-1946 era was unable to contribute to the Constitutional era Islamism with any novel theses, apart from the critique of the secularist experience by labelling it atheism. The positions on Islam, westernisation/modernisation, spiritual values etc., remained as they were (Tunaya 2003: 189). Tunaya bases this observation mainly on the scanning of three pro-Islamic journals of the era, including *Sebilürreşad, Selamet* and later *Hür Adam*. Tunaya continues: 'These ideas and opinions that emerged between 1945 and 1950 prepared the grounds for the future developments, by forming a suitable environment for the

October 1950 religious lessons in school became the norm and those who did not want this had to opt out by parental letter. The government increased funding for religious education in Imam Hatip schools. In 1957, prime minister Menderes claimed that some 15,000 mosques had been built in Turkey in the previous seven years.[657] By the late 1950s, the consequences of the restoration regarding the relations between the State and Islam were observable by the way in which the Islamic communities seemed to enjoy a limited influence on government controlled religious affairs, without a perspective of a 'return' to *Sharia*.[658] The poor signs of Islamic revival and the lack of a discursive practice aiming at the formation of 'Islamist' subjects can be interpreted as a consequence of the strictly secular legal structure that the DP had to maintain when in power. This judicio-discursive view needs to be enriched by two further observations: First, the growing weight of urban life and industry in the Turkish economy as a consequence of rapid capitalist development. With the emergence of working

---

revival of Islamist ideas and events resulting from these ideas, with full force. They demonstrated their influence particulary on the political group that seized the power' (Tunaya 2003: 189).
It is difficult to see how these comments, 'revival' and 'full force' in particular, could follow the above observations. Nor do the scholar's list of examples of this revival - *Ticani* attacks on Ataturk statues, which were promptly suppressed, the development of *Nurcus* and an incident in the main mosque of Bursa in 1957, involving a man with a sword, who proclaimed himself Mahdi and attacked the imam (Tunaya 2003: 204 & 248) - support his emphasis on the Islamic threat. Tunaya's overemphasis on the image of 'Islamist revival' is intelligible if read against the background of the difficulties that the Kemalist junta was facing in legitimising the execution of the prime minister and two top cabinet ministers in the wake of the 1960 coup
[657] Poulton 1997: 175.
[658] DP declared that they would not pursue the implementation of some of the Kemalist reforms, which, they believed, had failed to take root in society, such as the call for prayers in Turkish. There was a proliferation of pro-Islamic publications, criticising the three decades of one-party rule. DP attempted to amend the Penal Code article 163 in order to clarify the 'religious crimes', but withdrew the proposal after facing a fierce opposition in the parliament. In the annual budget discussions, a higher share for *Diyanet* was demanded by DP deputies, which, together with a motion for the protection of Islam against verbal abuse, faced fierce opposition from the RPP and sent back to the sub-commission. Another motion in 1959 to reinstall Islam as the official religion of the state was not even put on the assembly's agenda for discussion (Tunaya 2003: 195-201).

class organisations signifying the construction of modern class identities, Turkish politics seemed by the 1960s to have had transcended the Islam/Secularism dichotomy of the unsophisticated social structure of the 1920s and 1930s.

Increasing working class and student militancy, armed with new discourses based on the new dualisms of Labour/Capital and economic independence/imperialism with visions of a socialist future would dominate the political agenda from the late 1960s until the anticommunist coup of 1980. Second, the increasing weight of the anticommunist discourse among the determinants of the conservative identity. In this new line of identity formation, discourses of nationalism, economic liberalism and Islam went though a re-composition under the global hegemony of anti-communism to be rearticulated in their opposition to étatist economy, atheist secularism and the Russian threat.

This evolution will be traced below, since it has a significant impact on the nature of the Islamic subject's formation during the 'Islamic revival' from 1980s onwards.

III.3. Early Symptoms of a Holy Articulation[659]

The decision to make the transition to a multi-party system in 1946, mainly under international pressure[660], provided a new opportunity for the pro-Islamist ideas to

---

This data of 'Islamist activities under DP rule' provided by Tunaya fall fairly short to sustain the charge of 'threatening the secularist grounds of the State', which Tunaya places on the DP.

[659] Açıkel baptised the Turkish Islamic Synthesis as 'Holy Articulation' (See Açıkel 2000).

[660] In the wake of the World War II, Turkey had to choose between the two camps of the Cold War. The choice, in fact, had been made as early as 1923 with the manifestation in Izmir Economy Congress of their will to implement the 'National Economy' policies of the CUP. Kemalists were the heirs of the Young Turks and they most significantly inherited a 'bourgeois' mentality from

be expressed through new means of communication. Veteran Islamist Esref Edip recommenced to publish *Sebilurresad* in 1948 to continue his criticism of the government's religion and secularist policies. The RPP government made a number of significant concessions from secularist policies between 1946 and 1950, including the legalisation of Koran courses, reopening the holy shrines and the formation of a Faculty of Theology in Ankara. The village institutes, which underwent a silent popular opposition through the years of World War II, were gradually liquidated from 1945 onwards. The newly formed DP, on the other hand, chose to secure the support of a number of religious communities, most importantly the *Nurcus* and Nakshibendis, with a promise to end the state pressure over religious practice. One of the first resolutions of the DP government in 1950 would be to lift the ban on the call for prayers in Arabic.

It was as much the climate of the Cold War as the above reconciliation that contributed a great deal to the nationalisation of Islam in Turkey, which can also be viewed as a 'symptom' of the 'deep current'. The threat of communism in the

---

them. They wanted to build a capitalist Turkey, in which private but national entrepreneurs would generate wealth. The *Tesvik-i Sanayi* (Promotion of Industry) Law of 1927 was another manifestation of the same policy, which guaranteed state support for national entrepreneours. Given this ideological orientation of the Kemalists, etatism of the 1930s (see Chapter 4) can be bracketed out as a form of 'primitive accummulation' or 'war economy'. On the other hand, Kemalists did certainly want to remain in power as a monoparty regime to 'nurse' Turkey's transition from state capitalism to 'capitalism proper' in the post-war period, but their choice to integrate into the 'liberal camp' in the cold war required a minimum level of political liberalisation. Political liberalisation was also necessary for the damage of the war economy of the first half of the 1940s, particularly inflicted on the peasantry, to be healed. Most importantly, though, the economy was ripe for private enterprise to initiate a transition to 'capitalism proper'. In these

paranoiac climate of the Cold War brought religion and the State closer, and a conservative identity emerged as an amalgam of nationalism, economic liberalism and Islam under the global hegemony of anti-communism in its opposition to étatism, 'atheist secularism' and the 'Russian menace'. Early expressions of this synthesis were observable in the journals *Hareket* and *Buyuk Dogu* of the 1940s.[661] The editors of these two journals Nurettin Topcu and Necip Fazil Kısakurek met on a shared anti-Semitic and anticommunist stance[662] and expressed in every opportunity their loyalty to the state. The founder of the *Nurcu* sect, Said-i Nursi, enthusiastically supported Turkey's entry into NATO and the government decision to send Turkish troops to join the anticommunist war in Korea.[663]

This Turk-Islam-NATO Synthesis discourse was deployed in the mobilisation of the pious citizens in 'Associations to Struggle Against Communism' in the 1960s. A horrific symptom of the alliance between the US and Turkey's Islamists was the 'Bloody Sunday' on 16 February 1969, when Islamist militants countered a

---

conditions, Democrat Party would secure a controlled transition to a multi-party model within the republican limitations rather than a 'counter-revolution' of the religious reaction.
[661] See Appendix 25.
[662] Akgün & Calıs 2002: 596.
[663] Said wrote letters in 1948 to members of the government of the time explaining the nature and seriousness of the dangers facing the country from communism and freemasonry. He enthusiastically supported Turkey's entry into NATO, arguing that after the Second World War, Britain, France, and America were no longer opposed to Islamic Unity, rather, in the face of the anarchy arising from communism and atheism, they were now in need of it. Particularly America, which he saw as working for religion in a serious manner, Said regarded in friendly terms: 'In addition to continuing the struggle against communism and irreligion within Turkey, Bediuzzaman supported the decision to send Turkish troops to Korea to fight the communist invasion from the north, and was delighted when his close student Bayram Yüksel was to be sent there in 1951 during his military service, saying; 'I wanted to send a Risale-i Nur Student to Korea, and was thinking of either you or Ceylan. It is necessary to go to Korea to fight against atheism there' (Dogan 2003).

demonstration in Istanbul by workers and students, killing two demonstrators and injuring hundreds. The interesting aspect of this incident was that the demonstration which was attacked was held to protest a visit by the American Navy's 6th Fleet to Bosphorus.[664] Bloody Sunday took place against the background of the 1960s, when the Islamist militants, consisting usually of politicised Imam-Hatip students, along with Turkist militants, who ran the MTTB as a Turk-Islam alliance,[665] were encouraged by the centre-right governments of the 1960s to attack on leftist and working class organisations.[666]

The Islamist subject, more than four decades after being repressed by the Kemalists in the pro-western turn of the formative years of the Republic, was able to reappear in the form of violent rightwing militant.[667]

The nationalisation and 'anti-communisation' of Islam could also be seen as signifying the hegemony of the Kemalist psyche over the republican discursive formation. Islam, as the other of this psyche, had no opportunity to enter the signifying chain 'as it was'. Such entry from 'outside' the symbolic order had to be unintelligible and traumatic like the lunatic's discourse, as in the Menemen

---

[664] For two rather shy self-critical accounts of this affair see Duman 1997: 59- 61 and Dilipak 1991: 171-3.
[665] Duman 1997: 63
[666] See, Poulton 1997: 174
[667] The first manifestation of the Islamist subject's re-emergence is the national convention of *Mukaddesatçılar* ('those revering sacred things') that was held in Bursa in early 1968, which declared that sovereignty belonged to Islam not to the nation. This convention called for the return of the *Sharia* and a sustained effort to infiltrate education system, the press, judicial system and the military. (Landau cited by Poulton 1997: 175).

affair[668] and the *Ticani* assaults on Atatürk statues.[669] Instead, the repressed desire of 'Islamisation' had to attach itself onto the signifiers of conservative nationalism and anti-communism, the major contents of which were Turkism and extreme rightwing racism.

It is not so surprising that a powerful return of the repressed, in the form of the making of specifically Islamist political subjects, had to wait the collapse of the communist bloc before appearing in Turkish politics.

III.4. The Islamist Party

In Chapter 1 of this research, I have considered the moments of exclusion of the Islamic identity each of which corresponded to the formative moments of a specifically Kemalist psyche, the constitutive backbone of the republican order. I have further described in two subsequent chapters the structure of this Kemalist psyche in its relation to the Islamic identity as analogous to a split neurotic structure, frequently disturbed by the symptomatic returns of the repressed. In this structure, Islam was more a discursive construct imagined as the Other of Kemalism than a religious identity. I have dwelled above on spaces of identity in which Islam found pockets of survival and maintenance during the 'classical Kemalist era', namely, the *Tarikats, écoles Islamique*, and the *Diyanet* and later the Cold-War symbiosis between the Turkists and Islamists, which began with the

---

[668] See, Chapter 3.
[669] See, Appendix 1.

328

conclusion of the World War II continued until late 1960s. In 1969, Turkists founded the Nationalist Action Party (MHP) with an intensively Islamised discourse. The fellow travellers in the anticommunist fight, the Islamists, had to break with the Turkist movement decisively in these years when pressed by the question, 'Are you primarily a Muslim or a Turk?'[670] This split was finalised by the founding of the National Order Party (MNP) in January 1970, with the profile of an Islamist party, under the leadership of Necmettin Erbakan.

In addition to being an alliance between the *Nakshibendi* order and the *Nurcu* cadres[671] and building on the anti-communist Muslim militancy of the 1960s, MNP had its social base in the growth of 'petty-bourgeois' trade and artisan associations with a religious bias. Consequently the MNP program advocated measures to disperse capital accumulation geographically and to reverse the tendency toward economic concentration. By identifying large industrial capital with a 'Western-Jewish masonic' alliance against Islam, the MNP defended a state directed industrialisation whose benefits would accrue to the small businessmen of the province.[672] The goal of heavy industrialisation through state investment was synchronised with vital demands of the petty producers. The opposition to the principle of secularism and the aspirations of the revival of the *Sharia* order did constitute a platform that brought together all the religious elements under the MNP banner, although they were never articulated in the

---

[670] Duman 1997: 62.
[671] Cakir 1990: 217
[672] Keyder 1987: 213. Erbakan promised from the outset that he would introduce zero-interest rate credit for small businesses, a promise with both economic-corporate and religious meanings.

party's discourse. In spite of this cautious attitude, the militarily instructed government of 1971 closed the MNP within a year of its launch.

The significance of the short-lived MNP experience lied in its revival of the repressed Islamism for the first time as a distinct political discourse in republican history and in being the prelude to the Islamic identity politics of the following decades. MNP's reincarnation in the 1970s as the MSP (National Salvation Party) managed to participate in most of the coalition governments of the decade as the 'key party'. Although the MSP never had any opportunity in these coalitions to implement their program consisting of Islamisation of the State and society, swifter industrialisation and a redistributive populist economy, they did manage to locate religious elements in the state bureaucracy.[673] But the main achievement of the MSP was the reclamation of the legitimacy of Islamic politics in defiance of the constitutional ban. The popular affirmation of this legitimacy in the ballot box heralded the development of a specifically 'Islamist political subject' as a modern identity that would stamp Turkey's political process of the 1990s.

III.5. Welfare Party: Islamisation through Globalisation

The ascending pro-Islamic tendency met its political representative shortly after the transition back to multi-party system from 1983 onwards in the Welfare Party

---

Economically, petty producers would enjoy the privilege given by the state in a patrimonial fashion, while religiously this would mean to obey the Koran's prohibition of usury.
[673] Mardin 1977: 292.

(RP), which was founded by the former cadres of the MNP/MSP movement, also known as *Milli Gorus* (National Outlook).

The RP emerged in the 1980s as the (re)surfacing of the repressed Islamic identity by building on the MNP/MSP heritage and the new trends in the re-politicisation of Islam. The best illustration of the RP's difference from its predecessors is its unprecedented success in the urban centres of modern Turkey, that is, the fact that it won the municipalities of the two largest cities of Turkey, Istanbul and Ankara, in the 27 March 1994 local elections and kept most of these positions to date.[674]

Islamic politics after RP no longer consisted in the political expression of the disadvantaged provincial merchants and businessmen combined with the demands for recognition of an Islamic identity, which had not only been repressed and degraded but had also acquired an increasingly anachronistic profile in a progressively modernising country. In order to achieve an appropriate picture of the RP, the new trends that constitute the social and political composition of political Islam need to be considered in comparison to the conventional perception of Islamic politics in republican history.

The RP derived its constituency in addition to the known 'conservative forces of tradition', consisting of the *Tarikats* and the disadvantaged conservative merchants of the province, from a number of new elements, including the radical

---

[674] After the closure of the RP, most of these municipalities were won by the Islamist parties of FP, SP and AKP, which took over the RP tradition.

Islamist youth and intelligentsia, non-government organisations, such as the businessmen associations and labour unions, a growing conservative urban middle class and the urban poor. I shall consider each of these elements below.

The 1980s Islamist youth radicalism inherited a pro-Islamist political tradition, which formed the *Akincilar* (Raiders) Association in 1976 with a program aimed at 'the overthrow of the westernist-secularist republican order and its replacement with the order of an Islamic State in which the rules of the divine order (would) reign'.[675] Under the political environment of the 1980s, which favoured Islam as a component of the state ideology, an unprecedented proliferation of Islamist publications was experienced.[676] The 1980s' Islamist youth also had an increasingly urban profile, the majority (over 72%) being in higher education. A new layer of Islamic intellectuals emerged from this process. Islamic intellectuals are mostly the products of the Kemalist modern education system, mostly university graduates and well versed in essentially secular modes of discourse. They are not 'backward, ignorant' elements of society, but mostly of urban origin university graduates, the very people whom Kemalists originally saw as the harbingers of secularism. Radical Islamists compare the Western model as adopted by the secularist Kemalist elite with the fundamentals of an Islamic society, and they find the Western model wanting. They further attack the basis of the Western ideals of modernisation and development, which they see as

---

[675] Duman 1997: 63.

[676] In addition to translations from Islamic scholars and radical Islamist leaders of the Muslim world, a proliferation of Islamist magazines published by various intellectual circles was also observed in the 1980s. These magazines, which discussed a variety of issues from Bosnia and

obliterating the true values of Islamic civilisation by imposing the consumer values and materialism. The Western ideal promises 'paradise on earth' but fails to deliver. Inherent in this criticism, which derives to a certain extent from Western environmentalist and communitarian criticisms[677], is an attack on the drive for incessant economic growth, which is seen as leading to an increase in the individual's narrow self-interest at the expense of the communal values.[678]

The MUSIAD (Independent Industrialists and Businessmen Association) is the national organisation of the small and medium businesses with pro-Islamic sympathies, which has traditionally represented the provincial capital's interests against big business. In the 1980s, the weight of the MUSIAD in economic and political fields increased in parallel to the growing importance of the small and medium businesses under the global hegemony of the post-Fordist logic.[679] In addition to the small business base, the emerging corporations of Islamic capital, such as Ihlas Holding, Kombassan, Yimpas, known as the 'Anatolian Tigers', operating particularly in the sectors of textile, food processing and machinery spare parts manufacturing, are also allied with the MUSIAD. On the other side of Capital, the Islamic movement had a trades union confederation, HAK-IS, whose membership also grew in the 1980s.

Chechnia to family and women, from ecology to the 'mysteries of the universe', and from the problems of the university students to the Kurdish question (See, Cakir 1990).
[677] In 1997, Rudolf Bahro visited Istanbul upon an invitation by the then RP led Istanbul municipality. In an interview that I conducted on behalf of a national newspaper, Bahro emphasised enthusiastically these parallels between the Green argument and the radical Islam's anti-developmentalist stance.
[678] See Bulac (1991), Ozel (1992 and 1987) Tabakoglu (1987), Toprak (1999), Gundogan (1991) and Hamitogullari (1987).
[679] Gulalp 2002: 70-2.

The unprecedented success of the RP in cities is usually related to the rural-urban migration. In this interpretation, the migrants bring their conventional life styles to the poor suburbs of major cities and stick to their traditions and belief systems when struck by poverty and alienation in the cities. Therefore, the RP is the party of the rural population living in the cities.[680] This is only a partially correct interpretation, which fails to take into account the fact that the Islamist RP, by emphasising 'social inequalities' more than any of its contestants, managed to articulate in the 1990s a defensive blue-collar working class critique of the neo-liberal authoritarianism of the 1980s. The RP's discourse of 'Just Order' aimed to fill a gap emerged from the descent of modernist ideologies, including etatism, developmentalism and socialism, through communitarian solidarity and religious charity, and thus represented an alternative notion of ' social justice'. With this discourse at hand, the RP of the 1990s successfully played the role of the 1970s' social democrat CHP, and grew rapidly in the poor suburbs, formerly referred to as the 'fortress of social democrats'.[681]

The MNP and MSP programmes had emphasised the need for 'heavy industry' under the state's leadership, as the precondition of Turkey's march towards economic and political independence. Heavy industry, a popular dogma of the

---

[680] See, Salt 1995: 23-4.

[681] The RP miracle was also due to its emphasis on grassroots political organising. Passionately committed party volunteers, many of them veiled women, did not simply arrive on doorsteps to ask for votes at election time. They made it their business to know the needs of their neighbours all year long, and to ensure that no one who sought the party's aid went unsatisfied. Through their efforts thousands of hungry urban poor were fed, the homeless sheltered and the sick given medicine. In big cities, party workers waited at bus stations to greet arriving migrants, found them places to sleep and, in many cases, jobs at factories owned by pious businessmen. 'Naturally, their

1960s and 1970s particularly in the post-colonial Third World, was advocated by the MSP in the 1970s as a project in which the small capitalists would join together under the state's leadership to initiate a leap forward towards heavy industrialisation.[682] The MSP's inheritor in the 1980s, the RP, amended this corporatist view significantly. In the 1980s, the tables were turning globally towards environmentalism, anti-etatism, civil society and private enterprise. Erbakan stated in 1993 that the 'Just Order' aimed at spiritual development, protection of the environment, ending corruption, decentralisation of government, supporting individual development and the retreat of the state from all economic activity.[683] He demanded that the state's role be limited to the maintenance of infrastructure and social order.[684]

The RP defended civil society against the state according to the resolutions of the 1993 Congress. This position reflected the views of the pro-Islamic intellectuals who argued that the modern state centralised power, law, education and culture and aims to achieve a uniform society. The modern state is totalitarian,[685] while in Islam community comes before the state. The Islamist thinkers propose a multi-legal system as a proper form of pluralism against modern democracies and the western models of multi-culturalism, which they see as doomed to be bureaucratic and hierarchical. In the multi-legal system, the sole duty of the state is to

---

gratitude was limitless; many became not simply RP voters but enthusiastic organisers' (Kinzer 2002: 66).
[682] Saribay 1985: 125.
[683] Erbakan 1993: 48
[684] Erbakan (1993: 69) declares on these neo-liberal grounds, 'Welfare Party is the proper private sector party'.

guarantee the autonomy of each community, while the laws and rules of each community is only binding for the members of that community.[686]

The RP relied, as much as the dislocated lower middle classes, on the rising expectations of a new urban middle class, who demand both a life-style determined by Islamic values and to live in a technologically advanced welfare society. The Islamic technocrats, who came to power during Ozal's reign and who rose to the leadership of the RP, emerged from among these upwardly mobile layers. They had been marginalised in a country dominated by the secular elite, although they sharde with the secular elite the desire to exploit the material benefits of a modern country. However, unlike the secular elite, while appreciating western technology, they do not accept the westernisation of the social values.[687]

The specific features of the RP, in its difference from the preceding Islamic movements in Turkey are outlined by Gulalp (2002: 66-7) as follows:

> RP is not conservative but radical. Its ideology has post-nationalist and post-etatist elements. RP does not solely rely on the *Tarikat* support. Its ideologues are graduates of secular universities, who are well-versed in Marxist and post-modernist theories. Its constituency includes middle class professionals and marginal workers of major cities in addition to the small businessmen.

---

[685] Bulac 1995: 43-8; Dilipak 1991: 66.
[686] Bulac 1993: 34-42.

In these circumstances, the modern definitions of the 'Islamic identity', 'Islamist subject' and their political parties have undergone a 'semantic' crisis, where the discursive 'order of the things' was radically changing:

> The profile of the Islamist, which had been represented within a certain typology, did change. In other words, it is no longer possible to define and label the Islamist political currents and those persons who stand for an Islamic political order within the semantics of the conventional term 'yobaz'.[688]

Classified as ordinary traditionalism in the republican discourse, religiosity represented a familiar phenomenon, something that was intelligible according to the scheme of thinking that sees religion as a natural part of traditional society, but an anachronism in modern society. However, when social groups that had emerged from the modernising process also turned to Islam, this was viewed as symptomatic of something that had gone wrong in the development process. It was looked upon as an anomaly, a dislocationary attack on the symbolic order, and consequently as something that would need to be combated.

In this section, I have conducted a genealogical inquiry into the trajectory of Islamic identity from repression to repoliticisation. I have first inquired into the spaces of the repressed Islam, including the *Diyanet, Tarikats* and *Ecoles*

---

[687] White 2000: 111.
[688] Saylan quoted by Duman 1997: 68.

Islamique, which survived beneath the discursive surfaces of the republican symbolic order, returning in various symptomatic forms to this surface through republican history. The limited influence on political process via centre-right parties and the ultra-nationalisation of Islamism in Cold War conditions were two such symptoms of significance. From 1970 onwards, Islamist elements organised in MNP and later MSP primarily with the profile of a provincial middle class party. The RP's profile was different due to the politico-cultural climate in which it emerged. The Islamist subjectivity, which has emerged as the material form of a contemporary Islamist political identity from the decades long cycles of return and repression, differs largely from the republican portrayal of the 'fanatic Islamist' in that it is an ambivalent subjectivity situated neither in tradition nor modernity. The power of the Islamist discourse lies mostly in its success in providing a language for modern Turkish identity's repressed unconscious, which disturbs the republican perceptions of modern and traditional.

I will comment in the conclusion of this research on those aspects of Turkish identity that Turkey's decades of experience with political Islam led to problematise and the attempts to arrest this process of return of the repressed including the symptomatic rise of neo-Kemalist identity from a process of second secularisation. It is however necessary to consider the reappearance of the Kurdish identity in order to complete the setting of the crisis at hand, which I shall attempt in what follows in this chapter.

IV. The Kurds from Exclusion to Return

In this section, I will consider the background to the contemporary Turkish encounter with Kurdish political identity, which has led in recent decades to the triggering of an already structured psychosis and added above all an important human tragedy to modern history by claiming over thirty thousand lives and creating over a million refugees both inside and outside Turkey. The difficulties of writing a history of a 'completely silenced Other' (by being penalised for speaking their language) are, as it to be expected, immense. I therefore had to limit my attempt in this section to an outline of what is archaeologically discoverable from this history of silence. I will investigate below the fields of survival of the Kurdish identity both inside and outside the symbolic order of modern Turkish identity. This will mainly be the narrative of a movement of accumulation 'outside' the Turkish political psyche. But this 'outside', is as much connected to the nodal point that has been welding together the perceptions of Turkishness as being radically alien to Turkish identity: it is the order of the real. It is because of this nature of the Kurdish identity for Turkishness that the impact of its reappearance in the real on the Turkish identity has been traumatic.

IV.1. The Politics of Silence

In Chapter 3, I have reflected on the Kemalist policies of coercive assimilation through which the state's nationalist discourse gained an increasingly ethno-cultural character. Kurdish provinces were turned effectively into a land under colonial administration governed by a 'special inspector' under the shadow of the

gendarmes' arms with grave human rights violations[689] Until the 1950s the

Kemalist administration appointed deputies of the Kurdish provinces, who were

mostly of Turkish origin, even excluding those *Kurdish Turks,* who denied their

Kurdish identity'.[690] The denial of the Kurdish identity was in fact perversely

related to its recognition and the potential threat of the formation of the 'real

horrific Kurdistan' as Inonu stated in a 'secret East report'.[691] This fear also

implied that there were concrete limits to the policies of assimilation: the

modernised and educated Kurd could in the future present an even more articulate

and dangerous challenge to the Republic's integrity.[692] Government investment,

the sole source of economic and social development under the predominantly

etatist economy of Turkey has remained poor in the Kurdish provinces throughout

the 20th Century. The foreclosed Kurd was therefore recognised by the republican

reality in addition to its paranoid perception as a security threat, as an inferior

entity perceived within a project of assimilation aiming towards a racial hierarchy,

as overtly formulated by Kemalist notable Mahmut Esat Bozkurt in terms of a

---

[689] The most publicised among these atrocities is the '33 bullets affair'. On 28 July 1943, 33 Kurdish villagers were stopped and summarily executed by the gendarmes in Van near the Iranian border by the order of the Regional Military Inspector General Mustafa Muglali. After the transition to multi-party regime, the opposition Democrat Party brought this event to the Parliament, which led to the trial and conviction of the then former Regional Inspector (Besikci 1991a).

[690] Kutlay 1997: 188.

[691] See, Chapter 4.

[692] Turkish Chief of Staff Fevzi Cakmak held this opinion and opposed the extension of the educational facilities to the Kurdish region. (Kutaly 1997: 295-6).

master-slave relationship.[693] This 'recognition' required the backwardness of the Kurd and Kurdistan to prevail as a phenomenon of modern Turkey, which could invite the 'uncivilised and primitive' Kurds to become 'good servants' as the sole route to assimilation or to 'melting' in the supreme pot of Turkish identity.[694]

The decade that followed the suppression of Kurdish uprisings and the consolidation of the Kemalist power in Kurdish provinces is referred to by the Kurds as 'a great disaster', particularly for the damage that the one-party rule inflicted on the Kurdish identity.[695] With the transition to multi-party system, the relaxation of circumstances opened channels for the participation of the Kurds in the political process in various ways and allowed the gradual development of a specifically Kurdish political subjectivity. There were two spaces in which the (re)emergence of a specifically Kurdish political movement were preluded – the clientalist structures of centre-right political parties and radical left politics – both of which I shall consider below.

e)   Tribal Representation

The Kemalist discourse presented the annexation of North Kurdistan in terms of progress and modernisation and associated the Kurdish resistance with 'religious reaction' or 'regional backwardness'. However, the feudal-tribal structure of the

---

[693] 'My personal opinion is that the lords and masters of this country are the Turks. Those who are not of pure Turkish stock have only one right in the Turkish land, it is the right to be servants and slaves' (Bozkurt 1930: 3).
[694] Kutlay 1997: 267.

Kurdish provinces was not touched by the republican regime through a land reform or an attack on the conventional mentalities through the introduction of civic liberties and individual rights into the Kurds' social life.

The multi-party era, which brought the DP to power in 1950, began to articulate the tribal structures of the Kurdish region into Turkey's clientalist party politics. The DP promised the reinstatement of the exiled tribal leaders and the return of their property and swept through most of the southeast in the 1950 elections. This triumph of the 'periphery' over the Kemalist 'centre' brought many Kurdish tribal leaders to the Parliament as deputies of the Kurdish provinces. 'However, they failed to state overtly *I am Kurdish*, and failed to stand properly against injustices'.[696] The Kurdish tribal chiefs resumed their positions mainly as brokers in the patronage system, whereby they delivered votes for government in exchange for state favours for them and their 'clients'. Kurdish tribes, like the Muslim *tarikats*, assumed the role of 'vote depots' for the centre-right DP.[697]

The DP decade also brought about a relative improvement in freedom of expression that allowed all, including the Kurds, to articulate their grievances. A new philosophy called 'Eastism' advocating economic development of the east sprang up, in parallel to the increasing Kurdish activism in Iraq and the exposure of the eastern region to Kurdish language radio broadcasts from neighbouring

[695] Kutlay 1997: 269.
[696] Kutlay 1997: 189.
[697] Agri deputies Halis Ozturk and Celal Yardimci, Bingol deputy Sait Goker (Agha), Mus deputy (Sheikh) Giyasettin Emre, Kars deputy Sirri Atalay, Erzurum deputy Serafettin Elci, Bitlis deputy

countries. There were however absolute limits to this democratisation and the DP proved to have no intention of allowing activities that could have encouraged the renewal of 'separatist' feelings. Although the 'Eastists' carefully avoided any reference to Kurds or Kurdistan, forty-nine prominent Kurdish intellectuals leading this movement were arrested in 1959 and tried for sedition.[698] The 49's affair signified the emergence of a potential new leadership of the Kurdish cause consisting of the Kurdish intelligentsia, which was progressively alienated from the centre-right politics towards the left of the political spectrum.

It is against this background that the Kemalist leaders of the 1960 coup that overthrew the DP in May 1960 referred to 'separatism' as an essential threat along with 'reactionarism' and quickly arrested some 484 Kurds and banished 55 tribal leaders to western provinces. They were also concerned with the 'outside': the return to Iraq of the legendary Kurdish leader Molla Mustafa Barzani had rekindled the dormant hopes of Kurdish nationalism there and was no doubt being watched closely by Turkey's Kurds. Consequently, the military regime reinforced the uncompromising Kemalist stance grounded upon the foreclosure of Kurdishness.[699] The coup leader General Cemal Gursel warned that 'the army would not hesitate to bombard towns and villages' in the event of unrest among the 'mountain Turks'.[700]

Kamuran Inan are some prominent tribal deputies of centre-right tradition, some of whom held top positions in the Turkish state.
[698] Barkey and Fuller 1998: 14; Poulton 1997: 209.
[699] Gursel's address to the people of Diyarbakir: 'Spit on the face of those who call you Kurds' (Oran 2002: 876). The junta initiated a campaign to rename Kurdish villages in Turkish, and Kurdish folksongs were rewritten in Turkish to be broadcast by the state radio.
[700] McDowall 1996: 404 & Oran 2002: 876.

The tribal chiefs' centre-right representation in the Parliament continued through 1960s and 1970s and the tribal integration into the state apparatus gained a new significance under the military regime's Islamist turn. The Ataturkist junta of the 1980s and the Ozal government that followed it appealed strongly to the Islamic conservatism of the Kurdish traditional structures to counter socialism and growing secular Kurdish nationalism. In a sense, a 'Kurd-Islam synthesis' was aimed alongside the dominant ideological turn towards 'Turk-Islam synthesis', grounded particularly upon the 'Kurdish origins of Islamic identity in Turkey' and included a re-promotion of the *Nakshibendi* order in a fashion similar to Abdulhamid II's policies.[701] This move was increasingly translated from the mid-1980s onwards into rising electoral support among the Kurds – particularly those living in major cities of West and Central Anatolia - for Islamist parties,[702] particularly in those elections where Kurdish parties (HEP, DEP, HADEP or DEHAP) were prohibited from standing.[703]

---

[701] See, Chapter 1.

[702] The rising popularity of the Islamist parties (RP, FP and currently SP and AKP) among the Kurdish electorate has also been due to these parties' anti-systemic and anti-Kemalist stance at a time when the mainstream politics as a whole turned against Kurdish political existence within the sharpening climate of political polarisation around the Kurdish question.

[703] Hamit Bozarslan (2002: 866) asserts that the Sunni/Zaza section of the Kurdish population have voted for the Islamist parties. From this anthropologic insight of electoral behaviour, we can move on to reach the following scheme of Turkey's Kurdish population's political tendencies:
Sunni Zaza: Islamist parties (pro-Islamist tendency)
Sunni Kurd: Kurdish parties (nationalist tendency)
Alevi Kurd/Zaza: Radical Left (youth), CHP (mature) and Kurdish parties (post-nationalist tendency).

The Kurds and the Radical Left

> 'If you call me brother now
>
> Forgive me if I inquire: according to whose plan?'
>
> (Leonard Cohen, *The Story of Isaac*.)

The leaders of the Kemalist coup, who toppled the DP government in 1960, while reinforcing pressures on Kurdish identity, legislated at the same time a liberal constitution that set the groundwork for the emergence of trade unions and other civil society organisations. In these organisations, the Kurdish intelligentsia would find important channels of political expression. The charged political atmosphere of the 1960s was dominated by leftist discourses championed by the Workers Party of Turkey (TIP) and the Revolutionary Workers Unions Confederation (DISK). The 'Eastern Question' entered the leftist discourse as an emphasis on the growing difference and distance between the underdeveloped 'East' and those of the western provinces, which increasingly won over the educated layers of the Kurdish population to left-wing activism. Many leading Kurdish intellectuals looked to the TIP, which welcomed them into its ranks, took up the 'Eastern cause' and established branches throughout the Kurdish provinces. The Justice Party (AP) led government replied by prohibiting pro-Kurdish journals and arresting their editors. These measures led to further political protest and most remarkably the first Kurdish mass demonstrations in republican history in seven Kurdish cities, including Silvan and Diyarbakir, on 3

August 1967.[704] These demonstrations were supported by TIP but the party's pro-'East' stand did not turn into electoral support in the Kurdish provinces. Kurdish voters were not willing to breach the preferences of their traditional leaders in favour of the leftist proposals of the emerging Kurdish intelligentsia. In fact the Kurdish intellectuals were soon frustrated by the Turkish left's less than committed attitude to the Kurds and began to contemplate on forming autonomous Kurdish organisations.

The Kurdish split took place in parallel to the radical-left youth movement's split from the TIP under the influence of new doctrines of guerrilla warfare and with an aim of 'anti-imperialist democratic revolution'.[705] Although the Kurdish radicals began in the late 1960s to form spaces of political activity separate from, but parallel to the Turkish left habitus, this did not mean that the radical left had lost all their appeal for the Kurdish intelligentsia. Because, on the one side, the Kurdish question began to find greater reflection in radical left discourse, as an ally of 'democratic revolution' with increasing references to the Leninist (or Wilsonian) principle of 'self determination'. The terms of 'oppressing nation' and 'oppressed nation'[706] soon led to the first formulations of Kurdistan as a 'colony' within the radical left literature.[707] On the other side, through urbanisation and education the emerging Kurdish intelligentsia had increasingly been integrated

---

[704] McDowall 1992: 40.

[705] Aydinoglu 1992: 149-166.

[706] Dr Hikmet Kivilcimli, a dissident of the Communist Party (TKP) criticised Kemalist practices in these terms during the suppression of the Ararat Rebellion in 1931 (Kivilcimli 1978). His views were however overridden by the TKP's pro-Kemalist stance, leading to his expulsion from the party, which supported the Kemalist regime's war against 'tribal feudalism' and 'religious reaction' as a progressive act of Turkey's 'bourgeois democratic revolution'. (Tuncay 1981)

into Turkey's social order, by being mostly sutured to the subject position of socialist opposition. Consequently, the radical Kurdish intelligentsia found a surface of inscription for the national question in Marxist discourse, the hegemony of which over the national liberation movements around the world was in the ascendant, which tried to situate the 'national question' within the framework of capitalist injustice, world imperialism and dependency. The solution to the national question could therefore be indexed to a project of revolutionary transformation of Turkey's social order as a whole. There was an additional element of religious identity for an important sector of Kurdish radicals' preference of remaining part of the Turkish left. Alevi Kurds, bearing the 'memory traces' of a centuries-long history of systematic Sunni attempts on their existence, supported the secular republic as an historical gain. They had fought against the Kemalist annexation of north Kurdistan in Kocgiri[708] and Dersim[709] but separately from the Shafi-Nakshibendi Kurdish resistance, which extensively appealed to the Muslim identity of Kurdish masses during the Sheikh Said uprising.[710] This religious split is partially responsible for the fact that Alevi Kurdish intelligentsia, rather than participating in the pro-Kurdistan tendency, have manned in their thousands the rank and file of the radical Turkish left, which

---

[707] This was first formulated by Ibrahim Kaypakkaya, the founder of the Maoist TKP-ML in 1972.
[708] See Chapter 2.
[709] see Chapters 2 and 4.
[710] A leader of the Dersim rebellion, Aliser, emphasised Kurdishness and Alevi identity together in his agitative poems written in a mixed Kurdish-Turkish language (See, Bozarslan 2002: 868). In his declaration to the French authorities in Syria in 1941, Nuri Dersimi, another rebellious leader, defined his 'race' as 'Kurd-Alevi'. (Dersimi 1992: 209). See also Chapters 1 and 2.

they have viewed as aiming to supersede the Kemalist order in a progressive project of social justice.[711]

The Turkish left-Kurdish cause relationship always had two faces. On the one side, the Kurdish existence within the left has been fruitful: the left discourse provided a form of supra-national legitimacy for the 'national question' and linked the Kurdish cause with the broader social issues of Turkey and the world. This way, the Kurdish movement, which perceived itself as part of the workers-peasants movement as one of many oppressed peoples fighting imperialism around the world, assumed from the outset a post-nationalist character.

On the other side, however, the radical left's support for the Kurdish cause has been extensively conditional. 'The Kurd' was called to participate in the left's struggle with conditions more or less identical with the Kemalist call to 'the Kurd' to participate in the Turkish nation. The difference was merely the lifting of the prohibition on the taboo terms Kurd and Kurdistan. 'Right to self-determination' was declared but with a subtext 'this does not necessarily imply separation' attached to it, since nationalism was a regressive ideology.[712] Leftwing groups have consistently suppressed any assertion among themselves of a separate identity, including the demands of organising 'Kurdish sections' inside

---

[711] The ascendance of the PKK in recent decades with a discourse refusing the influence of Kurdish religious notables on national liberation movement and attacking the Kurdish cadres of the Turkish left as 'assimilated characters' turned these tables, leading many Alevi Kurdish activists to revise and eventually change their position. This destabilisation of the sources of recruitment is arguably one of the factors of the Turkish left's popular anti-PKK stance.
[712] For these points and more on the problems between the Turkish left and the Kurdish identity see Yasar 1988: 2115.

the organisation's structure.[713] Moreover, the Turkish left also approached to the emerging Kurdish organisations of the 1970s not with a view of internationalist solidarity but as rivals of the same contest, and consequently mostly with hostility.

The problem of the Turkish left's encounter with the Kurdish cause, if not the denial of Kurdish identity, is the narcissistic lack of a perception of the boundaries separating the self from the other, that is, the Turk from the Kurd. This lack of separation is further related to the left's incomplete Oedipal process: the Turkish left was born within the discursive body of Kemalism and has never perceived self-separation from this 'patriarchal origin' as a vital question to be engaged in. Consequently, as Riza Tura (1998) asserts, the naturalised reproduction of many Kemalist tenets in a Stalinist envelope has been characteristic of the leftwing discourse.[714] In this envelope of 'the iron law of historical stages', the Kemalist 'bourgeois-national revolution', including its destruction of 'the remnants of feudalism',[715] corresponds to an historically necessary moment of progress

---

[713] The same suppression applied to the demands of forming 'women sections' within the left groups, which have been viewed by suspicion as a bourgeois-feminist plot to divide the proletarian struggle. (In such climate, one can only fantasise what the demands for a 'gay and lesbian section' could have led to!) This authoritarian monolithism, popularly known as 'Stalinism', rather than Kemalism or nationalism as such, could be held responsible for the Turkish left's attitudes towards the Kurdish identity. However, its Kemalist and nationalist origins, which have never been subject to serious (self) criticism, have certainly vindicated the Stalinist monolithism. As Fikret Baskaya said in a recent interview, the Turkish left has to a large extent represented an amalgam of Stalinism and Kemalism (Baskaya 2004).

[714] I have argued elsewhere (Yoruk 1996) that during her entry into the 21st Century, there were only two Kemalist institutions remaining in Turkey: the military and the left.

[715] Annexation of North Kurdistan, the massacre of the Kurdish population and the destruction of Kurdish culture found its perception in terms of an attack on Feudalism as a moment of historical progress in the leftwing jargon.

towards socialism. Claims to a separate Kurdish identity would mean the expression of a 'desire of regression' to an already superseded stage of development to result in the disturbance and dislocation of the clear and certain progressive march through historical stages and were therefore suitable for the labels of 'nationalist' or 'regressive'.[716] This line of argument can be read as demonstrating that the inability or unwillingness of the recognition of boundaries with and separation from 'the Kurd' could become intelligible as a consequence of the failure of the paternal function, which led to the left's incapability of an Oedipal separation from Kemalism. In a sense, the Turkish left failed to achieve coexistence at the expense of a symbiotic and ambiguous existence vis-a-vis the Kurd, as a consequence of a similar failure of coexistence – in a balanced separation and connection – with the 'father'. Furthermore, this father, no matter

---

[716] Below is a stark articulation of the Turkish left's resentment towards the Kurdish movement addressed to the captured PKK leader Abdullah Ocalan:
'Are you an Idiot or are you very Smart?
What does national liberation mean?
Its definition used to be easy: "the Kuvayi Milliye fought to liberate Turkey from the imperialism of capitalism."
(…)
Do the ethnic conflicts in the "New World Order" have any meaning other than serving the ends of imperialism and capitalism?
Whose ends the Turkish-Kurdish war in Anatolia will serve?
Have you ever thought of it, you idiot?'
Is socialist theory not based on class conflict rather than the ethnic conflict?
What is the method that imperialism applies to the idiots in the underdeveloped countries: "Divide and Rule!"
(…)
Isn't taking the ethnic conflict instead of the class conflict to the front an act of archaism?
(…)
have you ever thought you idiot?
(…)
Did they teach you this as Marxism at the Ankara University's café?
Did they tell you, "prioritise the ethnic conflict over class contradictions"?
Did they say to you, "Leave the essential contradictions away and create Turkish-Kurdish hostility?"
Are you not aware that you have become a bloody puppet in the hands of imperialism?'
Ilhan Selcuk, *Cumhuriyet*, 4 June 1999.

what his ethnic origin might have been, is the 'Fatherturk'. The pathologically narcissist Turkish left, despite its novel openings towards internationalism and 'recognition of the oppressed nation', has inevitably betrayed its perception of nationalism as a regressive ideology by operating within the 'iron cage of Turkish nationalism'. In this cage, the much feared 'Kurdish regression' in history was bearing the danger of extending as far back as the repressed and foreclosed birth trauma of Turkish identity. The Turkish left has consciously and unconsciously shared with the rest of the 'nation' that primordial fear of facing the 'roots of the nation' where this constitutive trauma of the horror of separation and disintegration lay.[717]

IV.2. Separation: The emergence of the Kurdish political subject

There is a tendency particularly among the European academics, and those Turkish writers who aim to introduce the problem to the European reader, to view the Kurdish question in terms of 'conflict resolution'. In this view, 'Kurdish nationalism' emerges in 1984 from two major factors: the state violence over the Kurds and its 'counterpart', the PKK, particularly the personality of Abdullah

---

[717] When the Kurdish struggle reached its peak in the 1990s, the best slogan the Turkish left could produce emphasised the 'fraternity of the peoples'. A Germany based Turkish band, 'Kartel', was rapping in mid 1990s, 'The Turk and the Kurd are brothers/Those who separate them are traitors'. A Kurdish leftist intellectual, Dursun Buyukbas, pointed to me the ambiguity in these slogans. It could mean empathy for the Kurds but it could also be read as a statement against the Kurdish demands of separation. He powerfully questioned the absence of the Kurdish demands, and the terms 'Kurd' and 'Kurdistan' (such as 'freedom to Kurdistan'), in the Turkish left's slogans. His conclusion was that these terms remained 'a hot potato', not for security fears, since the Turkish left had proved to be sufficiently courageous to face persecution for what they believed, but as a matter of political will and belief. The lyrics of Cohen on hostile brothers quoted above should therefore be read as the Kurdish response to the Turkish left's calls for fraternity and 'brotherhood'.

Ocalan.[718] The Kurdish question thus becomes a security or 'terror' issue and 'resolution' becomes not the solution of the Kurdish question but a pharmacological intervention to 'tranquillise the antagonistic social'. This way, the 'conflict resolutionists' seem to be convinced that the 'problem can be cured', while in reality their proposals amount at their best to 'symptomatic treatment' leaving the roots of the problem untouched and repressed. Among many other inconsistencies, naturalisation of the Turkish state-sponsored 'criminalisation through terrorisation' of the Kurdish question in the personality of Ocalan being the primary one, this line of treatment considers the PKK and the contemporary Kurdish revival as a sudden reaction to decades long state oppression. I have demonstrated in the previous chapters that exclusionary practices against the Kurdish identity, including repression and foreclosure, have been a constitutive feature of the republican discursive formation since its emergence in the 1920s and therefore they are not recent phenomena. Moreover, moments and discourses of Kurdish resistance, political protest and organisation stubbornly accompanied these exclusionary practices.

The trajectory of the emergence of modern Kurdish political subjectivity can be identified as beginning with the 1950s 'Eastism' and the 49's movement led by an urbanised Kurdish intelligentsia situating themselves as much in opposition to the

---

[718] See, Imset (1991), Barkey and Fuller (1998), Kinzer (2002) and Poulton (1997). Poulton exaggerates Ocalan's 'terrorist personality' by referring to the fact that his name means 'an avenger' in Turkish.

'backward' tribal structures of Kurdistan as against the official denial.[719] The transition to a multi-party system was quickly followed by the launch of five Kurdish journals in 1962 and 1963, in which gendarme violence and regional underdevelopment were criticised. In 1965, the Kurdistan Democratic Party (KDP) was founded as a clandestine group parallel to the Iraqi KDP led by Barzani but despite its strong communal roots among the inhabitants of Turkish Kurdistan, the KDP was doomed to remain a small organisation violently paralysed by faction-fighting.[720]

The leftwing Kurdish activists, who split from the TIP along with the radical Turkish left, formed in 1969 the Revolutionary Eastern Cultural Hearths (DDKO). The formation of the DDKO, which provided the kernel of a large number of revolutionary Kurdish groups including the PKK of the following decades, was a turning point in Turkey's Kurdish movement. This move manifested the new generation of Kurdish activists' tendency to break with the traditional ties, moving closer to the radical left movement. Yet this move also included a separation from the Turkish left towards the formation of a specifically Kurdish space of political activity. The contemporary Kurdish political subject, who would 'suddenly' appear in 1984 to challenge the imagined integrity of the republican order, has emerged within this space of identity. This autonomous space was in

---

[719] In fact, this movement was also preceded by the launch in 1948 of a periodical *Dicle Kaynagi* by a group of young Kurdish intellectuals in Diyarbakir (Oran 2002: 876).

[720] On 4 July 1966, the first secretary general of the KDP, Lawyer Faik Bucak, became the victim of an 'unresolved murder' in Urfa (Balli 1991: 73). Dr Sait Elci, the new secretary general, was killed in 1971 by a splinter group leader, Dr. Sivan (Sait Kirmizitoprak). Dr Sivan would in turn be executed by the order of Barzani (Bozarslan 2002: 856). These turbulent moments of the T-

turn formed at a 'nodal point' of condensation of a range of tendencies and influences. In this range, the legacy of the 1920s and 1930s suppressed Kurdish rebellions and the traditional communal mentalities and bonds (feudalism) were in manifest decline.[721] On the other hand, the ascending influences consisted primarily of the Kurdish revival in northern Iraq under the KDP leadership and the rising hegemony of radical socialist discourses over leftwing activism in Turkey. DDKO's political defence against an indictment produced by military prosecutors in early 1970s represented these ascending influences, by formulating the Kurdish cause in terms of a skilfully embroidered synthesis of Marxist and nationalist discourses.[722] Consequently, the proliferating Kurdish discourses of the 1970s reflected on the one side the world-wide fragmentation of the socialist/Marxist movement between pro-Soviet[723], Maoist[724], and Latin American style guerrilla lines,[725] and, on the other, the division between the KDP[726] and

---

KDP reflected to a large extent the same within the I-KDP, shaped around the escalating conflict between Mesud Barzani and Celal Talabani.

[721] The DDKO considered the Sheikh Said rebellion as a reactionary and feudal movement. 'It is ironic that the logic of Kurdish activists of the 1970s and the Turkish state were the same. According to this logic, the Sheikh Said rebellion was the resistance of political reactionaries, for the rebellious Kurds demanded the Sharia, by means of opposing the removal of the Caliphate' (Yegen 200?: 224).

[722] The DDKO defence emphasised the 'progressive' role of the anti-imperialist warfare carried out by the Vietnamese people and drew parallels between the Kurdish cause and the Basque liberation movement (Oran 2002: 877).

[723] Socialist Party of Turkish Kurdistan (TKSP), also known as *Ozgurluk Yolu* (the Path of Liberation) and recently as PSK (Kurdistan Socialist Party), split from TIP in 1975 under Kemal Burkay's leadership employing a pro-Soviet socialist discourse. A smaller pro-Soviet group, DDKD (Revolutionary Eastern Cultural Association), also operated through 1970s.

[724] Kawa, a splinter group of DDKD, achieved the Maoisation of the Kurdish discourse adding the Russian Social Imperialism to the enemies of the Kurdish cause along with Turkish colonialism and the US imperialism.

[725] *Tekosin* split from the radical Turkish left group Kurtulus in 1978 to start guerrilla warfare with an aim to form a socialist Kurdistan.

[726] KDP of Turkey supported the KDP line from the outset but it suffered from a further split in 1978 leading to the formation of the KUK (Kurdistan National Liberationists) as a group standing for 'scientific socialism' and armed struggle with a perspective of the formation of 'a united, independent and socialist Kurdistan' (Balli 1991:163).

PUK in south Kurdistan, following the 1975 defeat of the Kurdish revival led by Barzani.[727] The Kurdish radical discourse developed unique theoretical concepts of 'internal colonialism' and 'nationalism of the oppressed nation' that managed to incorporate a number of essentially nationalist aims in the hegemonic discursive body of Marxism.[728] The hegemony of the radical Kurdish discourse over the Kurdish population was materialised in municipality elections of 1977, when independent candidates supported mainly by TKSP won the local government seats of Agri and Diyarbakir.

The PKK, long before its spectacular appearance on 15 August 1984 in which the gendarme stations of Eruh and Semdinli on the southeast borders of Turkey were targeted in heavy guerrilla assaults, emerged from within the 1970s' political climate as one of many Kurdish groups, which stood for separation from the Turkish left with an aim of founding a united, independent and socialist Kurdistan through armed struggle.[729]

IV.3. 'The Kurd' or the Real

The 12 September coup caught the PKK along with the rest of the Kurdish and Turkish left groups unprepared. Hundreds of Kurdish militants and intellectuals were arrested and dozens of them were killed in prisons. The military junta, which

---

[727] Another major group of Kurdish socialists, *Rizgari*, refused to take a position in this multilateral fragmentation.
[728] Oran 2002: 877.

put most of the blame for the late 1970s' episode of political polarisation on Kurdish secessionism was particularly heavy handed in Kurdistan. Turkish troops were deployed abundantly in rural areas and terrorised ordinary Kurds, which was officially called the policy of 'disarming the east and southeast regions'. While the written use of Kurdish was extensively prosecuted, the oral use of it was also banned and penalised.[730] Diyarbakir prison, where most of the Kurdish activists were held, became the synonym for unprecedented torture and ill-treatment.[731] In these circumstances, PKK attacks on military targets, which escalated in the second half of the 1980s, were silently and sometimes vocally welcomed as the only language available for dissidence.

The PKK retreated to Lebanon and northern Iraq following the 1980 coup and reorganised itself on military grounds. The majority of activists of other Kurdish groups, on the other hand, fled to Europe along with the Turkish radical left, to launch a diasporic Kurdish renaissance.[732] This movement in exile proliferated in total contrast with the deteriorating conditions in north Kurdistan and did not find

---

[729] PKK declared these aims in its 1978 founding congress with a *Manifesto* titled 'The Road of the Kurdistan Revolution' (*Kurdistan Devriminin Yolu*). See Ocalan 1993 .

[730] Diyarbakir mayor Mehdi Zana's is the most illustrious example: he defended himself in Kurdish at the court and was penalised further for 'using a language prohibited by law' (Oran 2000: 153).

[731] The conditions of Diyarbakir prison, which was worse than the Mamak (Ankara) and Metris (Istanbul) prisons both of which operated as concentration camps, where the Turkish radical left activists were held and systematically tortured, were protested by hunger strikes and other forms of resistance. Three leaders of the PKK set themselves alight in prison to protest 'inhuman treatment of Kurdish prisoners'. This method of protest through self harm, taken after Vietnamese Budist monks (Oran 2002: 878), would popularise among the Kurdish movement particularly in the aftermath of Ocalan's capture in February 1999.

[732] The Kurdish Institute in Paris, which was founded in 1983 has been the initial headquarters of this renaissance, which was later proliferated around Europe with the formation of Kurdish associations and cultural centres, leading to the launch of the Kurdish Parliament in Exile in 1995 and a PKK controlled TV station, Med TV.

any immediate reflection. The Kurdish soil seemed to have been evacuated by the Kurdish leadership to face its fate of naked state violence and coercion. It is in this vacuum that the PKK guerrillas returning from training camps 'outside' swiftly filled in by deploying the only available language of violence. Ocalan stated in 1991: 'Our military methods do work. Every military action opens up a new space for politics ... our actions will lead to the malfunctioning of the Turkish army's stick in Kurdistan and this will increase the opportunities for a solution'.[733] This tactic of opening up politico-discursive spaces ('the symbolic') through military confrontation ('the real') did yield some important returns. The PKK, which opened its ranks to the to the Kurdish peasant youth along with the usual reservoir of educated layers, enjoyed an unprecedented popularity both in the Kurdish provinces and major cities, particularly among the younger generations. The escalation of state terror in the Kurdish region in parallel to the expanding PKK activity also played a role by coercing people to choose between government militia (village guards) or being treated as PKK supporters.[734] The PKK used the politico-discursive space opened up through military conflict mainly to attack the tribal structures and criticise the 'assimilated character', formulating their primal aim as to initiate a 'Kurdish renaissance', through 'moral and intellectual independence'.[735] This powerful call to 'separation', not so much a physical separation through land claims but a separation in mentality, has been received enthusiastically by the Kurds of Turkey leading to an assertion of irreversible

---

[733] Ocalan 1991: 252.
[734] Ocalan admitted that their popularity is due more to the government terror than their own activities (Ocalan 1991: 252).
[735] Ocalan 1991:232.

boundaries with the imposed Turkish identity. While the PKK's manifest aims and military and political tactics have shifted through time from a 'socialist Kurdistan'[736] to the recognition of cultural rightsand from there to the recent stance of 'democratic republic',[737] this call for separation in identity has remained unchanged as the backbone of PKK discourse.

It is arguably the same politico-discursive space where HEP (People's Labour Party) was formed in 1991 with the profile of a Kurdish party and entered the parliament with 22 deputies. The Kurdish representation in the parliament was put to an end with a military-sponsored putsch on 2 March 1994 when Kurdish deputies were arrested in the parliament to be charged with treason. However, the activities of a legally recognised Kurdish party have continued despite a series of constitutional court decisions to ban HEP, OZDEP, DEP and HADEP[738], and a sustained campaign to assassinate its leading activists.[739] DEHAP and its predecessors have not been able to beat the 10% threshold to enter the parliament since 1994, but their undeniable electoral success in Kurdish provinces has paid off by DEHAP's occupation of the mayoral positions of the major Kurdish cities becoming a custom. Although the DEHAP and its predecessors have denied the

---

[736] See, Ocalan 1978. The 5th Congress of the PKK (1995) was arguably the turning point in the PKK discourse's shift in emphasis from socialism to independence. See PKK 1995.

[737] Ocalan proposed during his trial in 1999 the slogan of democratic republic as a reform program for the Turkish political system. In March 2005, a new programmatic slogan, 'confederation', emerged as the official aim of the PKK movement. Ocalan defended the case for confederation as an anarcho-Marxist or 'post-Marxist' stance during the interviews with his lawyers. (See Ocalan 2005.)

[738] The Kurdish party had to reform with a different name after each prosecution leading to its closure. Currently, the same party is operating under the name DEHAP (Democratic People's Party) and is being prosecuted by the constitutional court.

[739] 57 HEP members, 24 DEP members and 16 HADEP members have been the victim of 'unsolved murders' so far.

existence of any organic links with the PKK, it is a well known secret that their relationship has been analogous in many ways to that between the IRA and Sinn Fein.

In this section, I have considered the contemporary Turkish encounter with Kurdish identity, including the moments of the decades long Kurdish struggle for recognition. I have observed that after going through the stages of tribal representation within the republican order and finding channels of articulation within the radical left discourse, a modern Kurdish political subjectivity has been decisively shaped in the 1980s to radically challenge the conventional networks of identity/difference of republican symbolic order. The PKK led Kurdish struggle of the 1980s and 1990s has been a crucial stage of Turkish and Kurdish history, which, in spite of a military defeat symbolised by the capture of its leader, Ocalan, in February 1999, has managed to place decisively a radical Kurdish political subjectivity at the centre of Kurdish politics, which led the Kurdish identity to become visible from the centre of Turkish politics, with its traumatic consequences, at a time when radical discourses particularly among the Turkish left have beeen increasingly marginalised.

V. Conclusion

In this chapter, I have considered the crises that occurred through the republican history to identify the peculiarities of the contemporary crisis, which is distinguished with its character of an organic crisis of the republican order. I have demonstrated the nodal points at which the republican order has been eroded and destabilised in parallel with the intensification of the current crisis. The organic nature of the contemporary crises has lead to the vulnerability of the republican order to the challenging discourses of political Islam and Kurdish national liberation which are connected with the identities that had been excluded from the process of the formation of republican Turkey and the construction of modern Turkish identity. The Turkish experience of the 1980s and 1990s is in this sense a process of the return of the repressed. I have consequently focused on the returning identities in order to establish the nature of the link between these and what had been repressed. I have conducted in two subsequent sections genealogical inquiries into the spaces beneath and outside the discursive surfaces of the Turkish symbolic order where the excluded Islamic and Kurdish identities have not only survived but accumulated metaphorical criticisms of the deficiencies of the social order throughout the republican history leading to the formation of Islamist and Kurdish political subjectivities. In the next chapter I will conclude this study with an analysis of the consequences of their recurrence as an identity crisis, that has been progressively compelling Turkey to redesign its political order and reality for the 21st Century.

CONCLUSION

In this research, I have argued that modern Turkish identity was born through a process of nationalisation accompanied by a process of secularisation. I have considered in detail how these processes were realised through the exclusion of Oriental/Islamic/traditional elements of Turkishness and of ethnic heterogeneity of Anatolia. The hegemonic discourse of these processes of exclusion and the consequent formation of contemporary Turkishness as a modern identity was Kemalism. Kemalist discourse provided Turkishness above all with a clear demarcation that separated the nation from its outside and led to the emergence of a discursive formation which, in addition to its demarcating function, provided a surface of inscription for a variety of perceptions of identity. In the previous chapter I have demonstrated how this republican discursive space managed to accommodate a series of crises on this surface until the 1980s. I have then outlined the distinguishing features of the contemporary crisis as an organic crisis of the republican order in its difference from the previous series of crises of republican history. The genealogical inquiry into the spaces of the excluded has demonstrated that the histories of the survival of Islamic and Kurdish identities outside the republican symbolic order have also been the histories of the formation of modern Islamist and Kurdish political subjectivities. In this concluding chapter I will provide an analytic description of the scene of the contemporary identity crisis as a process of two major attempts by the centre to repeat the originary exclusion of the returning identities. The concluding argument of this thesis is therefore that the organic crisis of the republican order has triggered the psychic defence mechanisms of the 'centre', including the revival of the exclusionary mechanisms of repression and foreclosure, which, instead of achieving the intended maintenance of the damaged order, has led to the intensification of the crisis. I will conclude this chapter by presenting the main thesis of this study that the organic crisis of the republican order, which disperses through the social as a deepening identity crisis, necessitates progressively a redesign of the Turkish reality, including the political order and political identity, for the 21st Century.

I. The Second Secularisation

The second half of the 1990s witnessed a painful process of accommodation of the Islamic identity by the traumatised republican centre, through a reactivation of the repressive mechanisms. The process of second secularisation reached its peak in 1997 when the ruling Islamist party (RP) was forced out of office, under severe criticism from the military. Although the military appeared to be the main actor in this 'post-modern coup', the secular public actively participated in the process of second secularisation through anti-Sharia demonstrations and aggressive lobbying activities of the purpose-built non-government organisations. For the 'establishment' this repressive process of second secularisation yielded positive results by forcing Islamist politics to reorganise as a systemic centre-right party. It was, however, bound to failure regarding the problem of identity: the whole process was based on the mobilisation of one side (the conscious centre) of the split identity against the other (unconscious periphery), thus deepening rather than suturing this cleavage. I will outline below the moments of the second secularisation experience following the chronological order of its appearance.

I.1. The Explosion of the Repressed

The RP won the 1995 elections with 21 per cent of the vote and less than a third of the seats in a hung parliament. The two centre right parties tried to prevent an RP led coalition and formed a coalition government, which however collapsed dramatically. In June 1996, Erbakan managed to form a coalition with the centre right True Path Party (DYP) and became Turkey's first overtly Islamist Prime Minister. In the pre-election rallies, Erbakan had promised to create an Islamic currency, an Islamic United Nations, an Islamic NATO and an Islamic version of the European Union,[740] and on the day he declared the formation of his cabinet, Erbakan said that he 'reinvented Turkey'.[741] Erbakan visited Iran a few weeks after taking office and declared on his return that a campaign for worldwide Muslim solidarity had been launched. He then decided to visit Libya in October 1996, where he received in silence a scandalous 'welcome' speech by Muammar al-Qaddafi, criticising Turkey's alignment with the US and Israel and the repression of the Kurds. 'A barefoot Bedouin stood in front of the Turkey's premier last night and hurled insults at Turkey', reported the daily *Sabah* the next

---

[740] Kinzer 2002: 68.
[741] Kinzer 2002: 70.

morning.[742] But Erbakan ignored secular criticism, notably from Mesut Yilmaz, the centre right ANAP's leader, who stated that 'A party that won only twenty-one percent of the vote has no right to change Turkish foreign policy', and began to talk of a Muslim M-8 to counter the influence of Western group of wealthy nations known as the G-7.

The RP's moves that would easily outrage the Kemalist establishment were not limited to foreign politics. A prospect of domestic pro-Islamic transformation could also be detected in Erbakan's proposals that female civil servants be allowed to wear headscarves and the readjustment of office hours according to the prayer times. Erbakan was also making speeches encouraging the youth to attend *Imam Hatip* schools instead of public schools and urging that *Imam Hatip* graduates be made eligible for placement in the officer corps. The Islamist cadres' infiltration into state bureaucracy also gained momentum under the RP-led government.[743] Erbakan looked determined to attack the long-established conventions of Turkey's public space and revealed his plans to build a grand new mosque overlooking the Taksim Square of Istanbul, the celebrated 'shopwindow' of Turkey's western lifestyle, and another in Cankaya, the 'Kaabe of the

---

[742] Kinzer 2002: 71.

[743] Years before the RP coalition. by 1994, the RP reportedly had 700 of the 1,500 key administrators in the country, such as provincial and county governors or inspectors (Poulton 1997: 192). Kinzer states that the RP government 'removed almost everyday some Kemalist or other from a post in the bureaucracy and appointed an RP follower to fill the vacancy (Kinzer 2002: 72). Several RP held municipalities began to recruit men who had been expelled from the army for fundamentalist leanings (Kinzer 2002: 72).

secularists'[744] of Ankara. On a religious holiday, he held a reception at his official residents for the *Tarikat* leaders, most of them dressed in traditional robes and turbans. The nightmare of the secularist was thus coming true: The precise thing, the Other of Kemalism, that had been repressed some seven decades ago during the emergence of the republican order was hitting the surface at the very centre of the symbolic order from where it had been expelled.

Navaro-Yashin (2002: 40-43) demonstrates how the secularist notions of Islam generated self-fulfilling prophecies within the context of the post-1994 municipal election victory of the RP in Istanbul and Ankara. The local election success of the RP was followed by reports of attacks on women in western dress in a number of places including Istanbul's social centre, Beyoglu. One report told of Islamists stopping an inner city train and ordering all the women to sit in a separate compartment.[745] Navaro-Yashin argues that 'it is in no way 'essential' to Islamism ... to segregate men and women by gender or to impose veiling on women'. What happened was a peculiar case of 'projective identification':

Secularists in Turkey have projected this onto Islamism as part of their own expectations of an Islamic order. In the process of cross-political relations, Welfarists came to understand themselves in these terms, as well. (...) To a certain extent, Welfarists began to know themselves and to take action upon the world assuming, internalising, reversing and upholding what secularists had demonised. Islamists were working within the conditions of possibility of

---

[744] See Chapter 3.
[745] *Turkey Briefing*, 8/1, 1994.

a secularist discourse and structure of feeling in Turkey's predominant

public culture.[746]

Navaro-Yashin's argument is applicable to the RP's practice outlined above when in power, which was related more to the secularist nightmare of an Islamic take-over than to the RP's programmatic aims of a 'just order' and democratisation. This nightmare scenario included a comprehensive reversal of the country's decades long efforts of becoming part of the 'civilised world' and a fanatical campaign against the decades old republican conventions. More significantly, it turned out to be including a fundamentalist assault on the everyday lives of the majority of the urban population, which had long been styled and naturalised along secular and Westernised fashions.[747] The discursive space that had been allocated for the Islamist identity to operate in the secularist imaginary, or the 'prophecy of the secularists', was being fulfilled by the RP led coalition government and the RP-held urban administrations around the country. The rise of political Islam in Turkey was not limited to electoral politics, and the experience of the 'return of the repressed' was even more traumatic on the street, at the grassroots level of politico-social life.

On 2 July 1993, a fanatic Islamist mob attacked and set on fire a hotel in Sivas in which 37 delegates for a conference on folk poet Pir Sultan Abdal were burnt to

---

[746] Navaro-Yashin 2002: 42.

[747] Islamist mayors around the country worked well to make the 'Islamic threat' on modern lifestyle come true in their localities. One closed cinemas on the grounds that they were places where unholy ideas were propagated. Another banned the selling of turkeys, saying they were being eaten at dinners whose purpose was to celebrate Christian holidays. A third shut down a lingerie market because he found its display offensive. Others terrorised merchants into shutting

death. The main target of the mob was reportedly the writer Aziz Nesin for publishing at the time extracts from Salman Rushdie's controversial novel *Satanic Verses* in a national newspaper. The scenes of this incident immediately evoked memories of the 31 March and Menemen incidents of modern history, as if the much feared re-staging of the same scenario was being realised: the repressed Islam was returning.[748] If not the full scenario, what was referred to as Islamic terror was obviously escalating through increasing attacks on women in western dress, people who did not observe fasting during Ramadan and the political assassinations of leading secularist intellectuals. These assassinations were no doubt the work of organised violent groups, and were blamed mainly on two major radical Islamic groups, IBDA-C and Hizbullah.[749]

---

their shops at prayer time and ordered restaurants to close every day during Ramadan (Kinzer 2002: 72).

[748] This fear, however, was not immediately universalised, since Pir Sultan Abdal was an Alevi rebel and the murdered intellectuals were predominantly leftists. Even the deputy prime minister Erdal Inonu of the Social Democratic People's Party (SHP) blamed the massacre on Nesin for 'provoking the mob' (Poulton 1997: 256). There was after all a tradition of Sunni attacks on the Alevi communities in republican history. As I have argued in chapter V, the worst massacre was carried out by the republican state on the Alevi Kurds of Dersim in 1938. In December 1978, a Sunni mob attacked on the Alevi community of K.Maras in east Turkey killing thousands which led to the escalation of violence between the left and the right prior to the 1980 coup. The tradition of attacking on Alevis continued on 12 March 1995 after Sunni Islamists shelled cafes in Istanbul's Gazi neighbourhood killing fifteen Alevis. In the riots around the country that followed, the police opened fire on Alevi crowds killing a further 30 people.

[749] IBDA-C (The Islamic Great Eastern Raiders Front) appeals in its publications to the Islamist youth with a stance consisting of 'armed struggle' to overthrow the 'secularist oligarchy'. Some 20 political assassinations of prominent secularist intellectuals, among them Bahriye Ucok, Cetin Emec and Ugur Mumcu, in the 1990s were blamed on IBDA-C. The group itself denied involvement in these assassinations but by 1995 claimed responsibility for some ninety violent incidents, including bombings in various cities. The group deployed in their publications a radical activist discourse based on a secularist oligarchy/people antagonism, deriving as much from the discourse of Islamist radicals, such as Ali Sheraiti and Seyyid Qutb as from the leftist guerrilla movements' discourse as articulated by Che Guevara and adapted to Turkey's conditions by Mahir Cayan in the early 1970s (Cakir 1990: 166-7). *Tavir, Ofke, Son Karar, Olus, Elif, Kararli Genc Adam, Ak-Dogus* are the name of the periodicals published by the group's symphatisers. The translation into English of some of these names would hint the radical contents of these publications: 'Anger', 'The Final Decision', 'The Determined Young Man'. IBDA-C supporters also published the works of Necip Fazil Kisakurek and the writings of their leader Mirzabeyoglu

I.2. Reflections on the Return of the Repressed

I have argued, particularly in Chapter 3, that Islamic identity constituted the repressed unconscious of the modern Turkish identity. Consequently, the Islamist explosion of the 1980s and 1990s was primarily a return to the surface of the sediments of what had been repressed during the primordial split that had given birth to modern Turkishness. It was in a broad sense the return of those popular practices that could be named 'provincial' or 'peripherial', which have been able to survive until 1980s only in a repressed form within the modern identities and were subordinated by modern discourses. Freud made the process of repression

---

in book form. IBDA-C militants and their leader, Salih Mirzabeyoglu, were captured and imprisoned after the 28 February 1997 coup.

Hizbullah was launched in the Kurdish province Batman in 1987 as an organisation committed to establishing a Sunni Turkish state. They declared themselves a section of an International Islamic Movement as advocated by Ayatollah Homeini, despite the fact that Homeini was a Shiite, while the Turkish Hizbullah was Sunni. Following the purge of a number of pro-Islamic police officers from their posts in July 1991, an escalating wave of political assassinations of Kurdish activists occurred in the Kurdish provinces like Diyarbakir and Batman, which were blamed on Hizbullah. There were 20 such killings in 1991, over 400 in 1993 and 380 in 1994 (Amnesty International 1995: 14). In turn, Hizbullah's activities were largely blamed on the state, which allegedly utilised the group as its 'hit squads' as part of the 'dirty war' against the Kurds. This charge of Turk/Kurd/Islam synthesis is vindicated by the fact that any arrests or prosecutions stemming from the actions of the Hizbullah occurred after 1995, following a reported accommodation in 1993 between Hizullah and the PKK to cease assassinations (Barkey and Fuller 1998: 73). The anti-Hizbullah operations of the state forces intensified after February 1997 coup, where some blood was spilt between the state and the Islamists for the first time since the reign of 'Kemalist terror'. In February 2000, Turkish security forces raided the Hizbullah safehouses around the country shooting and capturing important leaders of the group and charged 440 people with Hizbullah involvement. The horrific dark side of the 'return of the repressed' a la Hizbullah was revealed during these operations, when the police discovered 57 corpses of tortured and strangled victims in the group's safehouses. Most of the corpses were of former Islamists militants who had been punished by Hizbullah for leaving the ranks of the group. After a latent stage, in November 2003, two 11 September-like concerted bombings in Istanbul claimed over a hundred lives, injured hundreds and destroyed two synagogues, the tower bloc which served as the HSBC bank Turkey headquarters and half of the British Consulate General building. The persons charged with these terrorist attacks were reportedly Hizbullah militants, who have allied themselves with the international Al-Qaida network since September the 11th 2001.

intelligible by observing that the repressed is a representation or the 'idea' of a drive rather than the 'crude drive' as such.[750] On these grounds, Lacan argued further that the repressed was always a signifier. If, therefore, we are to talk about a process of 'return of the repressed' in understanding the 'Islamic revival' in Turkey, we need to look at the repressed signifier 'Islam' and how it had been discursively constructed in the symbolic order at the moment of its repression. In chapter 3 of this research, I have argued that the Kemalist 'revolution' consisted in the confinement of the signifier Islam to a discursive space to signify the 'dark', superstitious, primitive, irrational and even the insane side of the 'civilised' modern subject. The emphasised symbol of these attributes was the 'fanatical mullah' (yobaz), who would exploit the innocent feelings of pious public for his 'counterrevolutionary ends' at every opportunity: a primarily discursive construct, which the republican subject has built through decades by projecting his fantasmatic fears and self-suspicions.[751] Navaro-Yashin's above argument suggests that it is this imaginary discursive space that was the available form for the Islamic identity for its return to be perceived, when it found an opportunity in the 1990s to form itself as Islam qua Islam.

It also needs to be noted that given the nature of repression and the consequent radical otherness of the unconscious, what returns can never be what had been repressed but a symptom of it. The formation of the symptom, as in the

---

[750] Evans 1996: 165.
[751] The Kemalist self-suspicion or 'fear' is twofold: the possibility of not being of 'national character' and the possibility of not being western. The repression that Kemalism experienced was not limited to the suppression of revolts, that is, the suppression of Islamic resistance to Kemalist

369

dreamwork, includes processes of condensation and displacement, and therefore in addition to the sediments of the repressed it is a contingent and metaphoric articulation of additional elements that have had to be repressed through time. In the Turkish case, in addition to the forms of volk Islam and Islamist discourses repressed by Kemalism and that have survived as a 'deep current' flowing in the *Tarikats, ecoles Islamique,* the religious personnel of the Kemalist *Diyanet* institution and the common sense conservatism, the (re)emergence of the political Islam was shaped by contemporary dislocations, such as the deprivation of the urban poor denied housing and employment, the provincial merchants and businessmen seeking an equal status with their urban counterparts under the horizon of globalisation, and the upwardly mobile urban professionals degraded by secular conventions for leading a conservative lifestyle. The sedimented Islam has inevitably spoken not only for itself but also on behalf of an aggregate of piled up dissatisfactions, deprivations and shattered expectations, and is seeking not merely recognition but also revenge and compensation from the existing order. The consequences have been mostly traumatic, opening the social order not necessarily to democratisation but further to dislocations and antagonisms.

I.3. Political frontiers

The traumatic return of political Islam can be analysed as a metaphorical symptom condensing at least three displaced, distinct but interrelated contents.

---

westernisation reforms. The Kemalist subject had to deny and repress in his unconscious first and foremost his own continuity with the tradition (see chapter 4).

First, a 'struggle for recognition', which includes a promise of democratisation of the existing order, as in the emphasis on civil society and the multiculturalistic interpretation of the *Sharia* by the Islamist intellectuals.[752] Second, a claim that Islam furnishes the 'real' ground of 'political subjectivity', which challenges the discursive horizon of modern Turkey as a whole and dislocates the established subject positions. And third, the compensatory and resentful 'discourse of the oppressed'.

The main codes of this metaphorical structure can be identified in the RP's discourse as anti-imperialism/anti-Zionism, a 'just order' and the ultimate goal of transition to an 'order of prosperity'. These codes are contrasted in much of the Islamist literature to the definition of the existing order as an 'order of slavery', marked by imperialist/Zionist dominance which emphasises 'financial interests', corruption and moral degeneration and is maintained by a centralised authoritarian/totalitarian state. These positive vs. negative elements are articulated within a grandnarrative beginning with an 'age of prosperity' under Prophet Mohammad and the Four Caliphs. Then, a second 'age of *jahilliyya*' began in which the Muslims were forced to forget their 'golden age' under Western influences. With the success of the Crusades in the form of modern imperialism and Zionism, the Muslims' position turned into slavery causing 'constant pains and tears'. Muslims therefore had to reclaim their 'golden age' under the banner of Islam. The first step is the formation of a 'just order', which would reform the financial, economic, moral and political systems through a purge of

---

[752] See chapter 6.

Zionist/imperialist influences. The RP argued that democracy was the essential tool of this transition and therefore the Islamists had to win popular consent in the ballot box, in a country where '99 percent of the population are Muslims' and therefore potential constituency of the RP.[753]

The instrumental perception of democracy as a mere tool of taking power certainly accommodates the possibility of disposing of it in favour of more authoritarian tools once the power is attained. Islamist discourse does not merely promise the democratisation of the existing order but includes an inherent perspective of replacing the existing authoritarian regime with an Islamised authoritarian order, in which the compensatory 'discourse of the oppressed' finds channels of articulation. This is precisely the location where the secular identity's *che vuoi?*, the much feared surplus of the 'real desire' of the Islamist, is materialised. The secularist argument implies that the Islamic tactic of *takiyye* governs the moves of political Islam in Turkey. There is always a fanatical surplus desire, a hidden agenda, behind the Islamists' mask of 'innocent' demands of recognition:

> 'The head scarf is a symbol that represents an ideology. Many people who like to see scarves would also like to see a totalitarian regime like the one in Iran'.[754]

The above statement made to the *New York Times* correspondent Stephen Kinzer by an economics lecturer of the Istanbul University has been abundantly shared in

---

[753] Key elements of this outline of the RP's discourse was first elaborated by Cakir (1994).
[754] Kinzer 2001: 80.

the Turkish media. This bold expression of the fear of the Islamists' surplus desire, is an expression of the secularist mentality that lies behind the symptomatic responses of the dislocated republican 'core' against the 'return of the repressed', no longer from the 'periphery' as conventionally expected but from the very modern centre or the 'republican core' itself, which had long been 'peripheralised' through the 1980s. The symptom of the Kemalist is therefore a reaction by the republican subject, when she is forced to face not so much the 'outside' of her own identity but her own split self. 'We are not Arabs', said Turkan Saylan, a professor at an Istanbul medical school and chair of the Association to Support Civilised Life: 'Fundamentalism wouldn't make us happy. It is a fantasy to think we could ever go backwards'.[755] Saylan made this statement in the wake of the RP's electoral seizure of the Istanbul and Ankara municipalities. Another sample of an identical response by the secularist elite to a foreign journalist is from 1999:

> We turn to ever-pressing issue of veiling. Someone suggests looking at how France deals with it. Someone else invokes a comparison with Israel, where secular establishment's hatred of the ultra-religious is every bit as fierce as in Turkey. 'Why not look at what the Muslim countries are doing, like Jordan or Egypt?' I ask. The question is met with howls of outrage. 'We are not Arabs! How can we possibly compare ourselves with a Muslim country? (...) In the constitution it is clearly stated that Turkey is a secular country.[756]

---

[755] Rugman 1994.
[756] Kristianasen 1999.

In both statements above, the return of the repressed, and with it the disturbing affirmation of split identity, meets the ever disturbing mirror of the Big Other, the West, which boldly reflects not merely the modern/secular conscious subject but a portrait of the 'unfinished secularisation' on which the modern subject also faces her unconscious; the repressed Oriental self. The West's mirror, the Gaze of the Other, thus served as a surface of inscription over which a desire of 'second secularisation', which radically negates the possibilities of recognition or democratisation, would emerge.

The incommensurability of the modern Turkish identity with the Islamist identity led to a new antagonistic polarisation of Turkey's political scene. The secularist panic was not limited to the feelings of state bureaucrats, army personnel and Kemalist intellectuals, but the possibility of an Islamist take-over to prohibit the modern 'lifestyle' was becoming tangible for an increasing number amongst the urban population. In these circumstances, the retreating secularist élite shaken in realising that they had to defend the state that they took for granted, rather than staging yet another military coup, decided to mobilise popular opposition to political Islam. Under fire from the Islamist discourse in which the social was constantly reinvented as the field of a political subjectivity fundamentally different from the conventional republican perceptions, the secular élite came to realise that coming forward as representatives of the state and preaching the principles of Ataturk would no longer be enough. Instead, they had to incorporate 'society' into their discourse to produce an effect or an image of being representatives of society. The republican governmentality could no longer be taken for granted; it had to be fought for and reclaimed. The officially non-govermental organisations of 'Association to Support Civilised Life' and the 'Association for Ataturkist Thought' played a vanguard role in this 'war of position'. The 'Civilised Life' activists, most of them women, particularly countered the RP activists' campaign by calling on the doors of shantytown houses, distributing food and other resources to people in need. They also launched 'houses of learning' in various shantytowns around Istanbul, where local women were taught all sorts of skills, from sewing to embroidery, childcare to hygiene, along with the 'principles of Ataturkism'.[757] The state ceremonies of official holidays were popularised by performance of pop-singers in public squares, and mass visits to Ataturk's mausoleum in Ankara were organised particularly on the anniversaries of Ataturk's death on 10 November each year. Large numbers of people began to wear badges of Ataturk around the country.

The excesses in the rediscovery and repopularisation of the cult of Ataturk appealing most of the time overtly to mystical and religious sentiments[758] heralded the course of events to follow. Turkey's entry into 21st Century would not be marked by a post-Kemalist democratic development but by neo-Kemalism, which involved a symptomatic reaction from the republican core to repress violently its exploding unconscious. The republican core, consisting mainly of left-Kemalist intelligentsia, who had fallen out of favour since the 1980 coup, and

---

[757] Navaro-Yashin 2002: 145.
[758] See, Navaro-Yashin 2002: 188-203.

the conventional bureaucracy, progressively politicised Kemalism in order to forge a discursive frontier of the dislocated 'modern forces' upon nationalist and secularist premises to counter Islamism. The political frontiers were thus elaborated with the stepping in of the neo-Kemalist discourse: the Turkish political scene was antagonised in a secularism/Islam dichotomy.

I.4. The Secularist Coup

In February 1997, the 'Jerusalem Day' event organised by the RP mayor of Sincan, a small town on the outskirts of Ankara, at which the Iranian ambassador addressed the public calling for the establishment of *Sharia* in Turkey, accompanied by slogans in support of Hizbullah and Hamas, triggered the imminent secularist symptom. Army tanks were ordered to parade through Sincan as an unusual route for 'military exercise', during which a brigadier stated that they were 'tuning the balance of democracy'. The mayor was arrested and a 'postmodern coup' consisting of a number of measures to curb the Islamist movement thus began. On 28 February 1997, the National Security Council meeting, at which participated the commanders of the armed forces and certain cabinet members presided over by the Prime Minister Erbakan, adopted a twenty-point program. The program was designed to undermine the influence of political Islam by purging its supporters from the state apparatus and curbing the *Imam Hatip* schools. A law extending compulsory primary education from five to eight years was passed in August aiming to weaken the hold of political Islam on

Turkey's lower middle class youth. The angry demonstrations in protest of the NSC[759] resolutions were handled brutally by the police.

In the spring of 1997, generals began to invite various groups – judges, civil servants, journalists and others – to 'briefings' in the General Staff Headquarters in Ankara at which they issued vivid warnings about the Islamist threat. Generals did not openly demand Erbakan's resignation but their pressure soon became irresistible. Erbakan resigned in June 1997 expecting that President Demirel would appoint Tansu Ciller the leader of his coalition partner as prime minister and he would continue as the deputy premier. But Demirel appointed Mesut Yilmaz, the leader of the opposition ANAP, instead and a new coalition was formed excluding the former coalition partners RP and DYP. Turkey's first postmodern coup was thus staged.

Within a few months after its removal from office, RP was outlawed by the Constitutional Court; Erbakan was banned from politics and subsequently sentenced to one-year imprisonment. A number of leading RP figures, including

---

[759] The legacy of a security focused top-down modernisation against external and internal threats and the leading role of the military-bureaucratic élite in the modernisation process itself, is still clearly visible in Turkey's polity. With regard to the political institutions of the Turkish Republic, the National Security Council (NSC) is one institution representing this tradition. The military junta first introduced the NSC after the 1960-61 coup. Under General Kenan Evren's military rule (1980-1983) the NSC was reactivated and formally established as a legal political institution in article 118 of the constitution from 1982 which was written by the army. Today, considered as the most important decision-making institution in Turkey, the NSC consists of the prime minister, the ministers for defence, interior and foreign affairs, the general chief of staff of the Turkish Armed Forces and the chief commanders of the navy, the air force, the land forces and the paramilitarian gendarmerie. Its function is, chaired by the president of the republic, to formulate and implement a national security policy. Although the decisions of the NSC are not binding, the elected governments have routinely enforced what has been decided in the NSC. See: Heper/Günay (1996: 645).

the mayors of Kayseri, Sukru Karatepe, and Istanbul, Recep Tayyip Erdogan, were convicted of subversion, Islamist bureaucrats in the Interior Ministry and the Ministry of Education were sacked. Governors of more than 40 provinces and 200 districts were listed for pro-Islamist views and warned to comply with 'the Laws of Revolution'. Islamic Holdings were put under investigation with allegations that they were financing fundamentalism.[760] Alleged illegal economic ties between RP municipalities and Islamic holding corporations were revealed. Islamic finance-capital supported by the Saudi Arabia was put under check. Some members of the MUSIAD were arrested and tried. Religious foundations were fiscally and ideologically checked, regarding their budgets, joint ventures and residences. The educational privileges of the Islamic groups and private colleges through which religious education was given to the pupils were placed under strict control. Veiling in public institutions and schools was banned, and universities were invited to implement this measure without tolerance. Private TV channels and newspapers were brought under new controls. These authoritarian measures of de-Islamisation of the republican order managed to obstruct the return of the repressed Islam through a new wave of repression.

The Virtue Party (FP) that was formed after the RP's closure took a moderate stance but it was also outlawed in June 2001. The Islamist politics was soon split between the old guard, who rallied around Erbakan to form the Felicity Party (SP)

---

[760] The shares of the largest of such corporations, Kombassan, were frozen and it was investigated for suspected illicit moneylaundering..

and the moderate wing led by the former radical mayor of Istanbul, Recep Tayyip Erdogan, who formed the Justice and Development Party (AKP).

I.5. AKP and westernised Islam

The main consequence of the repression of the Islamist movement through a wave of 'second secularisation' was therefore a split in the Islamic political organisation. The dispute between the two wings is above all on the appropriate strategy of survival as a political movement under a re-Kemalised establishment. The younger generation gave the impression that they accepted the necessity of becoming part of the political establishment rather than trying to remain legal while preaching a subversive political project. From a more analytical stance, this split, beyond the 'taming' of political Islam, should be seen as a consequence of the built-in ambivalence of the RP's stance between traditionalism and democratic radicalism. The traditionalists of the SP, who remained loyal to the 'National Outlook' line and their leader Erbakan, can be identified as the political representatives of the repressed province. The AKP wing on the other hand emerged as the representative of those layers, who index their outlook to a feasible conservative 'future' rather than an ideological attachment to the project of bringing back a Muslim past. The two wings of the split political Islam can therefore be identified as follows:

Felicity Party (SP)	AKP
The reaction of the provincial merchants and businessmen to the destructive effects of *modernisation*	The voice of the rising Islamic capital to claim their share by exploiting the opportunities of *globalisation.*
State planning and protection of small businesses. economy.	Favouring private capital against the state's role in
A conservative anti-liberal political vision	Emphasis on civil society and political liberalisation
Hostility towards the West A prospect of alignment with the Islamic countries of the Middle East and Asia	Willingness to align with the West in the European Union

The above distinction is a schematic and oversimplified one and constant crossings between the two sides in both parties' discourses have been observed ever since their split. The AKP discourse, rather than a head-on challenge against the republican conventions hopes to supersede the Kemalist horizon through political liberalisation, hence the frequent references to '46 spirit'. The AKP has shown through its time in government that its liberalisation program includes the sincere aim of Turkey's integration into the European Union.

The 'Islamist social imaginary', which includes the sediments of the desire of Islamisation of Turkey by reinstalling *Sharia*, the traditionalist resistance to modernisation and the resentful and compensatory 'discourse of the oppressed', have apparently been jettisoned from the AKP discourse. It is however more appropriate to discern this exclusion in terms of 'repression' given the sediments of 'radical Islamism' observable in the political manoeuvring of Recep Tayyip Erdogan since his escalation to the post of Prime Minister following the AKP victory in the November 2002 elections. Erdogan has demonstrated, particularly in his statements concerning religious liberties, that he and the AKP could not completely dissociate themselves from the frequent returns of the repressed Islamism. These returns included proposals to allow women to wear headscarves in public administration buildings and universities and *Imam Hatip* graduates to be selected by any academic branch in higher education,[761] the abolition of the Higher Education Institute (YOK) and the criminalisation of adultery in the new Turkish Penal Code. Erdogan had to step back each time under fierce reaction of the secularist bloc of forces, including in particular the military, and complained particularly to the foreign press that the Islamic identity in Turkey was treated by

---

[761] The choices of the graduates of these schools are currently limited to a list of faculties of theology.

the establishment like 'the negroes of 1950s America'. These 'returns of the repressed' through Erdogan's 'slips of tongue' can also be read as his gestures towards a broad electoral base consisting of politicised Islamic subjects, aiming to demonstrate that although the AKP currently has the profile of a 'party of the establishment' it still holds on to the original ideals of political Islam. Erdogan's 'slips of tongue' have also served to maintain a constant state of alert, anxiety and awareness among the (neo)-Kemalist bloc.

I will return further in this chapter to the aspects of Turkish identity that Turkey's decades of experience with political Islam managed to problematise. It is however necessary to dwell on the reappearance of the Kurdish identity in order to complete the setting of the crisis at hand, which I shall attempt in what follows in this chapter.

II. Second Nationalisation

The re-secularisation of Turkey's symbolic order did not occur as an isolated affair but the context of organic crisis necessitated an additional process of re-nationalisation. I will outline below the moments of this process which developed through symptomatic encounters with the Kurdish political subjectivity. This outline will include an analysis of the process of second nationalisation as a symptomatic consequence of the Turkish collusion with the inassimilible signifier Kurd.

II.1. Beyond Turkish Névrose: Kurdish Newroz

According to Kurdish mythology, a Kurdish ironmonger, Kawaye Hesinker, rose up against the tyrant Dehaq at the break of the spring 2600 years ago. The Kurds called this 'the new day', *Newroz*, and have celebrated it as the festival of their genesis. Kurdish historians also trace the date back to the demolition of Ninova, the Capital of the Assyrian Empire by the Kurdish Med Empire forces in 612 BC, as 21 March, the day of the Kurdish New Year, Newroz.

Eric Hobsbawm asserts that all nations are usually built through the revitalisation of long-forgotten traditions in modern times. When modernisation, which meant rapid social change and novel industrial relations, came to threaten traditional societies with atomisation and disintegration, the need to set up a new communal nexus through the construction of a sense of common identity became a necessity. This is the momentum where quasi-modern elites decided to 'invent' or 'imagine' nations by employing old practices, which usually have a ritualistic and symbolic character. These practices insinuate a natural continuation with a suitable past and aim at the installation of certain values and behavioural norms through repetition.[762]

Not any more than two decades ago, when things were relatively calm in Turkey's Kurdish provinces and the then small Kurdish quarters of major cities, the date 21 March was not a big deal for most people of Turkey. But since the mid-1980s, with the beginning of what can be defined as Kurdish nation-building, Newroz celebrations as the start of the Kurdish New Year have featured both in these provinces and in the major cities where the Kurds have begun to reside in their masses. The Kurds of Turkey were discovering through Newroz celebrations their 'glorious past', a long-forgotten 'golden age'. Many books were published detailing Kurdish culture and history in which the legend of Newroz played a significant role. A variety of peculiarly Kurdish symbols, including the Kurdish flag and its colours, Kurdish national songs, Sheikh Said and Seyyid Riza as Kurdish martyrs and Abdullah Ocalan as the Kurdish leader, were blossoming around the country. It looked as if everything was working in line with Hobsbawm's assertion detailed above, although not at the outset of the modern times but at a time of transition to what many have agreed to call a post-modern age.

Hobsbawm distinguishes between the adaptation of genuine 'old' traditions to new situations and the conscious invention of essentially 'new' traditions to meet new needs. Celebration of national days with military parades, invention of imaginary national heroes from a 'glorious past' or new national heroes who 'liberate' their nation and the sense of respect for the national symbols are among these inventions which, according to Hobsbawm, all take place in the invention of national identity. A careful look in the Kurdish practice since mid-1980s will also

---

[762] Hobsbawm and Ranger 1983.

reveal a similar process of 'invention of traditions'.[763] But the story does not end here.

In March 1995, the then Prime Minister Tansu Ciller suddenly announced that Newroz – which she now called *Nevruz* – was in fact a Turkish holiday and that the government would organise celebrations in Ankara and the southeast for this 'national' occasion. The Turkish government had suddenly realised that Nevruz had been celebrated for centuries by their 'outer Turk' cousins as the spring holiday and decided to celebrate it with the representatives of the Central Asian 'Turkic Republics' to mark the 'sublime day of the nation'. The Kurdish national colours – red, yellow and green –the wearing of which was one of the reasons for the 1994 indictment of Kurdish deputies, were now declared to be Turkish colours. On 21 March 1995 and 1996, official Nevruz was marked with military parades, official Nevruz fires and ceremonies emphasising how large and sublime the Turkish nation was. Ministry of Culture sponsored the publication of a number of books, including a children's book, which defined Nevruz a centuries old Turkish tradition. In the children's book, the main character is a grandmother who remind her grandchildren that Nevruz used to be celebrated by her generation but then it was almost forgotten. She thus initiates the children to begin celebrating Nevruz again by revoking the old traditions. According to Ayse, the grandmother, Nevruz which used to be celebrated in Sogut, the hometown of the Ottoman State in northwest Anatolia, on 9 March has for the last thirty five years been celebrated in September, because 'it was difficult for so many people to

---

[763] For an example containing both forms of nationalist narrative, see Bender 1991.

travel to Sogut on horseback in winter conditions.' For some reason, the grandchildren do not wonder why for the last thirty five years, those people have not thought of using modern means of transport! The grandmother continues saying 'did you know children, Ataturk used to give great importance to Nevruz ceremonies every year and he always made sure that he participated in the festival?'.[764] Faced with the authority of Ataturk, children are convinced that they had to celebrate Nevruz. There is, however, a further aspect of the official Nevruz, which claims that Nevruz had an exclusively Turkish mythological significance.

According to Turkish mythology, the Turks' 'golden age' in their imaginary homeland, *Ergenekon*, was ended with overcrowding, famine and draught and their imaginary mother, she-wolf *Asena,* led the nation out of this abyss to spread them around the world. The official Turkish view since March 1995 is that not only was Nevruz an old Turkish holiday but that it was in fact the day that Turks were led out of Ergenekon. This claim was most rigorously pressed by Professor Abdulhalik M. Cay in a book titled *Nevruz: Turkish Ergenekon Holiday*. Cay bases his claim on the narration of the Ergenekon legend by Ebulgazi Bahadir Han, in which Han wrote, 'since their escape from Ergenekon, Kok-Turks celebrated the new year as a festival.'[765] Being aware of the weakness of this sole reference, Cay goes on to claim that he has a video tape in his archives which

---

[764] Gulensoy 1995.
[765] Cay 1995: 11.

proves the relationship between Nevruz tradition and Ergenekon legend.[766] Apart

from these two 'references', there is no evidence neither in Cay's book nor in any

of the books published the same year by official backing that would support their

claim to 'scientific' proof of this mythical relationship.[767] Yet the official news

agency Anadolu Ajansi claimed on 15 March 1996 that 'Turks of the Central Asia

recite the Ergenekon legend in Nevruz celebrations', and that Nevruz has always

been celebrated with the names Sultan Nevruz, Ergenekon or Bozkurt (Greywolf)

day, as the 'Turks' liberation day' throughout the Turkic world from Central Asia

to Azerbaijan, Anatolia, Bulgaria, Greece and Cyprus.[768] On 20th of March 1996,

the Ministry of Education also issued a message to be read aloud to the

schoolchildren throughout the country. In this message, the ministry declared,

'Nevruz is a Turkish holiday. Its origin is Ergenekon. Our ancestors celebrated

this day as the day of passage out of Ergenekon for many centuries'.[769]

What is involved here is an aspect of nation-building which Hobsbawm would not

have imagined, that is, 'stealing traditions'.[770] Turkish professors had to work

hard to prove that the millenniums old Kurdish and Persian spring holiday was

exclusively Turkish in its origin and that the 'real' myth that is related to

New(v)ro(u)z was not the Kawa uprising but the Turkish Ergenekon myth and

---

[766] Cay 1995: 13n.

[767] Other books consist of collections of articles by historians and antropologists of the Turkic republics of Central Asia, and have no mention of Ergenekon myth. See, Eker, Suer and Abatoglu, Ahmet (1995), *Nevruz, Ulusun Ulu Gunu,* Ankara: Tum, and Pekcan, Yildiz and Ozturk, Sevinc (1995), *Tarih ve Etnografya Acisindan Nevruz,* Ankara: Tum.

[768] Anatolian News Agency report sheet, 15 March 1996.

[769] Anatolian News Agency report sheet, 20 March 1996.

[770] Imagine the British declaring St. Patrick's Day an originally English festival!

this is where nothing but the use of psychoanalysis becomes relevant in any possible understanding of the official Turkish behaviour

Beyond the rather meaningful coincidence that newroz is the Turkish pronunciation for the term 'neurosis' (from the French word névrose), this event demonstrates all the features of an envious attack; but still, beyond its immediate psychoanalytic interpretation as a symptom of narcissist personality[771], this event needs to be interpreted as a symptomatic attempt to reproduce the constitutive mechanism of 'foreclosure':

> 'Coercion' allows the State to 'face' the 'Kurdish threat' by attacking to its 'roots' or its 'heads' or its 'symbols' that are in competition with those of the 'Unitarian State'.[772]

The moments of traumatic perception of the Kurdish 'awakening' by the Turkish political psyche constituted the moments of a process of 'second nationalisation'.

II.2. Moments of Encounter with the Real

---

[771] Rosenfeld (1987: 20-1) introduces the term 'narcissistic object-relation' to identify a situation where 'the patient simultaneously identifies with the object to the extent that he feels he is the object or the object is himself. In these circumstances, 'the object becomes part of the self to such a degree that any separate identity or boundary between self and object is felt not to exist'.
[772] Bozarslan 2000: 24-5.

'And we will come from the shadows'

(Leonard Cohen, *The Partisan*)

In Chapter 2 and the subsequent chapters, I have considered in detail the moments and the peculiar nature of exclusion of the Kurdish identity during the construction of the modern Turkish identity through the formative years of the republic. I have argued that this exclusion, far from being an historical 'accident', was an 'historical necessity' for the Kemalist project of nation building out of the diverse ethnic mosaic of Anatolia. Yegen (2000) also emphasises this 'necessity' by arguing that contrary to the perceptions of the opposition, the exclusion of Kurdish identity has to be seen as the outcome of the political project of building a modern, central and secular nation-state, the necessary condition of which was the exclusion of religion, tradition and the periphery. We can conclude therefore that the exclusion of Kurdish identity constituted an integral part of the republican nationalist discourse and republican governmentality, and that modern Turkishness and modern republican subjectivity were largely grounded at the outset upon these discursive practices of exclusion.

It is most striking that this crucial discourse of exclusion has operated for almost eight decades without the pronunciation of the excluded object, the signifier 'Kurd', and this is where I believe consulting the tools of psychoanalysis becomes a necessity. This research led me to understand that 'the Kurd', beyond its

389

immediate denotation, is a metaphorical connotation for 'the Turk' of his constitutive/primal trauma, that is that life-and-death struggle of the Ottoman elite and the Muslim masses of the Empire against non-Muslim identity. I have derived from this analysis that the Kurdish exclusion has been executed by a mechanism analogous to the psychotic foreclosure (of the inassmilable signifier Kurd).

Following the tracks of Anderson's *Imagined Communities*, I have argued in Chapter 2 of this research that it would be legitimate on psychoanalytic premises to assert that nationalism is structured like psychosis since the imagination of nations necessitates the construction of 'other nations', as the obverse of the 'nation' in antagonistic terms, or, as 'Hallucinated Communities'. The national identity tailored by Kemalism for republican population had to be based on the denial of Kurdishness, which could not be recognised but nevertheless the shadow of the foreclosed Kurd was visible from 'outside' the 'republican reality' through the corner of the eye. This could but only lead to the effects analogous to those of the entry into psychosis with the onset of hallucinations and delusions, which explains the excessively violent nature of any encounter with the Kurdish identity in republican history.

The Turkish encounter with the 'real' recommenced in August 1984 with the launch of an armed struggle against the Turkish forces in southeast Turkey by a guerrilla group, the Kurdistan Workers Party (PKK). In parallel to the increase in PKK activities throughout the 1980s, the military presence in the region grew dramatically, intensifying state terror over Kurdish civilians, who were forced to choose between joining the government militia or being labelled as PKK supporters. One clear consequence of these oppressive policies was the paradoxical growth of the PKK's popularity, which, as the leader of the PKK, Abdullah Ocalan, admitted, owed more to government terror than their own activities.[773] The PKK gained popular support not only from among the population of southeast Turkey, but also the Kurdish inhabitants of major cities who constitute the largest portion of the alienated urban poor.

With these features, the popularity of Kurdish nationalism has gone well beyond the official claim that the whole movement was simply the work of an isolated group of terrorists. In 1991, the People's Labour Party (HEP) was founded with the profile of a Kurdish party and Kurdish deputies entered the Parliament. The government had to relax its initial hardline approach; top officials and mainstream media would speak of 'Kurdish reality' while the prohibitions on publications in Kurdish language were removed and strict military measures that had been imposed to suppress any Kurdish appearance were relaxed. This 'detante', however, proved to be provisional: On 21 March 1992, in the wake of the Gulf War, large Newroz demonstrations turned into civil uprising in a number of Kurdish towns and cities, which would be suppressed at the expense of the lives of hundreds of civilians. Following these uprisings and the sudden death of President Turgut Ozal, which coincided with the sudden deaths in controversial

---

[773] Quoted by Balli, Rafet (1991), 'Kurdistan Workers Party: Interview with Abdullah Ocalan', in Balli, *Kurt Dosyasi,* Istanbul: Cem, p.252.

391

circumstances of a number of top military officers, who defended a softer approach to the Kurdish question than the 'hardliners', the government seemed to have returned to its original uncompromising position. The 1993 coup that followed Ozal's death consisted of a rigorous reintroduction of the doctrine of the 'unitary state' and 'one nation'.

All Prime Ministers after President Ozal promised improvement and reform concerning the 'southeast problem' when they were sworn in, but never materialised this promise.[774] On 2 March 1994, deputies of DEP were arrested in the Parliament and charged with treason. The prevention of Kurdish participation in the political process was accompanied by an escalation of State violence in the 'southeast' with immense human rights violations[775] committed by the soldiers, police, gendarmes, village guards, 'death squads' and some 23,000 'Special Teams' deployed by the organs such as the 'Prefecture of Zone of Exception' and 'Special War Bureau'. The results were a military victory crowned by the capture of Ocalan in February 1999, the strengthening of a 'core state' bringing together the 'military-bureaucratic complex'[776] with the ultra-nationalist MHP and the Mafia,[777] more than a million Kurdish refugees in Kurdish cities and major cities

---

[774] See Gurbey 2000: 70-2.
[775] For the records of human rights violations see Amnesty International annual reports from 1990 onwards and my interview with Mahmut Sakar, chairman of the Diyarbakir Branch of Human Rights Association in *Turkish Daily News*, 20 April 1996.
[776] Bozarslan 2000: 22.
[777] This 'historic bloc' is what was referred in the Kurdish discourse as the 'war lobby'. It emerged with the commencement of the Kurdish conflict in 1984 and was strengthened with the collapse of the Eastern Bloc in the late 1980s providing the Cold War structures within the State with a new *reason d'etat* and mission. The liquidation of the 'war lobby' under the conditions of 'low intensity conflict' began with the Susurluk Accident of November 1996 but lost pace within a year of legal investigations and parliamentary inquiries.

of the West from the evacuated and torched villages and more than 30,000

deaths, mostly Kurdish civilians, all of which were to be blamed on Ocalan.

Another Kurdish rebellion was thus suppressed, the 'unitary state' and 'one

nation' successfully prevailed as declared in the 1999 indictment of the Kurdish

party HADEP:

> There is only one identity in Turkey, that is, the Turkish identity.
> Demands for recognition of the Kurdish identity are but the first step of a
> devious attempts to divide the country.[778]

II.3. Nationalisation of the 'Popular Religion'

> There is a war
>
> Between those who say 'there is a war'
>
> And those who say 'there isn't'
>
> (Leonard Cohen)

The 1990s Turkey witnessed all the symptoms of an anti-Kurdish collective

hysteria performed at football matches, soldier farewell ceremonies, martyr

funerals and any nationalist gathering of an official or unofficial character. The

escalating war has seen a rise in the racially motivated attacks on the Kurds,

particularly in the West of Turkey.[779] The popular exclusion of the Kurds was

---

[778] Briefing no. 1228, 1 February 1999, p. 10.
[779] In late 1992, two Kurdish youths were rescued from a lynch mob in Alanya and there were attacks on Kurdish property. In Igdir, there were anti-Kurdish riots after HEP gained a seat on the municipal council in Novemer 1992. On 13 July 1993, an anti-Kurdish riot broke out in Ezine,

made possible by coding the Kurds with the signifier 'Armenian'. The Kurdish national movement was linked in the popular psyche to 'the Armenian' which is perceived as the 'ontological enemy', 'the subcontractor of that "master-plan" of the disintegration of Turkey'.[780] The social hysteria reached to its climax during the Ocalan trial with soldier relatives chanting 'Armenian seed Vampire Apo!'[781]

This hysteria was the inevitable result of a 15 year long war in north Kurdistan and haunted the popular masses in spite of the official attempts to present the event in terms of 'state security' as opposed to 'national war'.[782] The Kurdish conflict has been presented officially as an episode of threatened state security. The 'conflict resolutionist school' approached the matter by emphasising violent methods from both sides, while the pro-Kurdish analysts usually emphasised the State violence and the 'core state', 'military' and 'Kemalist doctrine' as the source of conflict. My argument differs from all of these diagnoses by emphasising the popular-national rallying behind the State policies. With the Kurdish conflict, which was popularly perceived as a matter of existence, not merely the State but with it the Turkish identity was at stake. The appearance of 'the Kurd' from the order of the Real was analogous to delusion and hallucination regarding its impact on Turkish identity. The mechanism of foreclosure thus provides an explanation for the use of excessive violence in the encounter with 'the Kurd' and the popular Turkish support behind this violence. What happened

---

Canakkale. In April 1998, ultra-nationalist mob attacked the corpses of the PKK guerrillas in Antalya, protesting their burial in 'Turkish sole'. The corpses were excavated from the graveyards by the local cougovernment to be reburried in an unknown location.
[780] Bora 2002: 918.

with the delusional appearance of the inassimilible signifier, the 'real Kurd' is analogous to the triggering off of psychosis. With the undeniable appearance of the Kurd, the memories of the accumulated traumas that structure Turkish political psyche have been revived and triggered the escalation of state violence against the Kurds and the accompanying popular-national symptoms.

III. Consequences of Identity Crisis

In this concluding chapter I have added the dimension of identity crisis to the analysis of the organic crisis of Turkish political order, which I began in the previous chapter. I have argued that the contemporary re-secularisation and the re-nationalisation of the republican order need to be analysed beyond the elite/people dualism as national-popular affairs representing the symptomatic responses of modern Turkish identity to the threat of split and disintegration. The analysis in this chapter demonstrate that these responses, rather than 'touching the real' of the problem of identity, consist mainly of attempts to suppress the symptomatic appearances of the identity crisis, and due to this nature, they are bound to failure. The failure of re-secularisation is that by reviving the built-in mechanism of repression, the attempt to overcome the identity crisis resulted in the reinforcement of the split nature of Turkish identity,[783] by deepening as opposed to suturing the cleavage between the secular-modern and Islamic identity

---

[781] I have presented an analysis of this symptomatic slogan in chapter 2.
[782] Laciner 1999.
[783] This reinforcement can be immediately observed in the tangible movement towards the constitution of the de facto *Sharia* rule in the province, the geography of Turkey excluding the

perceptions.[784] Re-nationalisation, on the other hand, has proved to be successful in mobilising the nation to rally behind the Turkish flag and national anthem, which symbolise the nodal point that weld together the conscious core to the unconscious periphery around the theme of national security and a strong anti-Kurdish sentiment. This successful reconstitution of political subjectivity however reveals at the same time a major malfunction of political psyche by gesturing towards that primordial hole in the symbolic order, thus affirming the ever presence in the order of the real, of the incompatible idea that had been purged from the symbolic register. Not only that a complete suppression of the 'Kurdish symptom' has proved to be impossible,[785] but through the damaged symbolic order 'the Armenian', the ultimate Other of Turkishness, and with it the religio-ethnic heterogeneity of the Turkish nation, progressively reappear.[786]

The Turkish identity crisis can be understood as a repetition of the late Ottoman identity crisis. In Chapters 2 and 3, Abdulhamid's pan-Islamism was presented as the beginning of nationalisation of the Ottoman system. Abdulhamid II tried to Islamise society – in effect he secularised and nationalised it. The argument in the presentation of the current crisis in this chapter implies that in a similar irony,

---

three major cities, – in fact, including most of the suburbs of these metropols – governmental offices and military barracks.

[784] A caricature of this split can be observed in the fact that the wives of Turkish Prime Minister and most of the cabinet members are not allowed to official receptions because they wear headscarves. Husbands govern the State while wives are confined to the domestic life: this is but a perfect realisation of the dream of Sharia regarding gender divisions through secularist coercion.

[785] Given, for example, that most of the local governments of the Kurdish provinces are run by DEHAP as an affirmation of the ascend of Kurdish political subjectivity

General Evren tried to Kemalise and nationalise society – in effect he Islamised it. The resolution of the Ottoman crisis included a new nationalist design of the political order and the accompanying notion of Turkish identity for the 20th Century; the contemporary republican crisis similarly brings about a discussion over the redesign of the political order and accompanying identity questions for the 21st Century. The Second Secularisation and Second Nationalisation of the 1990s are also comparable to the late Ottoman attempts of consolidation through Islamism and Ottomanism, both of which ended with failure and the third mode of politics, nationalism, prevailed. The failure and instability of the republican attempts of consolidation through nationalism and secularism increasingly point towards the direction of a third 'mode of politics' similar to the Ottomanism of the late 19th Century. Finally, the Ottoman crisis began with the economic integration with the European capitalist networks, and intensified as the country progressively Europeanised and westernised. Similarly, the republican crisis, which emerged within the context of globalisation, has intensified through the Turkish attempts at integration with the European Union. New political frontiers have emerged between supporters and opponents of Europeanisation.[787]

---

[786] The suppression of the Minority Report has been presented in the Introduction as a typical symptom of this appearance in the real.

[787] The forces of pro-European and anti-European alliances shift constantly. It would be however possible to assert that the anti-European alliance consists mainly of the former 'war lobby' (above) and the recent neo-Kemalist bloc, which is in turn an alliance between the military and the left-Kemalists. The most condensed declaration of the anti-European alliance's stance is probably MHP leader Devlet Bahceli's following statement: 'With the adjustment legislation under European Union pressure, Sevres is being resuscitated, Lousanne is being violated. The Minority Report is evidence to this.' (*Cumhuriyet* 18 November 2004).

This research has followed the trajectory of the emergence, development and the crisis of Turkish political identity along with the genealogies of the excluded identities. Chapters 1 and 2 have demonstrated that the Ottoman crisis was resolved through the suppression of ethnic/religious heterogeneity of the 'nation' and the subsequent de-Islamisation of the social accompanied by the suppression of the Islamic identity. Chapters 3 and 4 have demonstrated that this extensive suppression failed to achieve the 'Imperial Salvation' but necessitated the formation of a new political order, the ideological horizon ('civilisation') of which was demarcated rigidly by a new 'regime of truth' (Kemalism) grounded upon sustained mechanisms of exclusion. The emerging governmentality was based upon a radical *rejection* of the Islamic identity and accompanying reconstitution of the social as split between a conscious centre and unconscious periphery, a cleavage that could also be depicted in Gramscian dualities of State-civil society and Ideology-common sense. Chapters 3 and 4 have also demonstrated that the new governmentality was grounded upon a second exclusion: a radical *ejection* of the Kurdish identity, the metaphor of the ethnic/religious heterogeneity of the social, 'outside' the political reality of Turkish identity, which was accompanied by a paternal-pedagogic prohibition of the signifier 'Kurd'. This demarcation included an appeal to the 'natural' field of Turkishness, the Turkish-Muslim identity – and the national psyche and 'psychosis' that is constitutive of it – for the reconceptualisation of its absolute 'psychic' boundaries, by introducing the code 'separatism' to include and broaden the 'natural' code, 'non-Muslim'. The relationship between the core national consciousness and the unconscious periphery of 'common sense' thus involved as much pragmatic interaction when necessary as radical exclusion and otherness. In Chapter 5, the discussion on identity under this horizon and within this reality, which has affirmed above all the inconsistencies of the new order in providing sufficient grounds for an unproblematic identity perception to accompany the new national subjectivity, has been analysed. Chapter 6 has been devoted to the analysis of the determinants of the recent crisis of the republican order as an organic crisis. This analysis has included an observation of the development of the excluded discourses of identity, including the repoliticisation of the Islamic identity as an upward march from the depths of 'unconscious' to strike the surface at the very centre of the symbolic order on the one hand, and on the other, the accumulation of Kurdish identity outside the reality of modern Turkish identity to become visible once again leading to traumatic perceptions of the Turkish subject located 'inside' this reality.

I argued in Chapter 1 that the end of 'Islam' as the episteme of the 'Ottoman Regime of Truth' began with the emergence of Islamism as a political discourse to compete with other discourses of salvation. There is a similar development in the contemporary crisis, affirming the erosion of 'Ataturk' as the empty signifier of the 'Republican Regime of Truth'. In Chapter 3, I outlined the trajectory of the Ataturk myth and Kemalism in the formative years of the republic and demonstrated how Ataturk and Kemalism were escalated to a supra-party position after transition to the multi-party system. 'Ataturk' remained as the empty signifier of the republican order and Turkish identity until the 1980s. The anti-communist coup, by reinforcing this myth began to fix Ataturk to signify two contents: first, 'national security' which radically contracted the power of Kemalist signification. And second, religious conservatism, that is, Kemalism's constitutive outside, which stretched the body of Kemal and Kemalism beyond the limits of signification, where the radically blurred Ataturk was in danger of losing any discursive value. The 1990s neo-Kemalism tried to restore the myth of Ataturk by re-fixing it with the specific content of 'secularism'. These operations eroded further the status of Ataturk and Kemalism, which made this myth vulnerable to question and contest by various liberal democratic discourses. The reactivation of the icons, consisting of the representations of Ataturk's body, head and face, ironically corresponds to a moment when this body has proved to be too narrow to continue to symbolise the progressively sophisticated Turkish social formation.[788]

This research therefore points out the resemblance between the contemporary crisis of Turkish political order and the organic crisis that led to the collapse of the Ottoman Empire and the emergence of modern Turkey. The Ottoman organic

---

[788] In this sense the following verdict by Anderson (1991: 86) for the 'imperial nationalisms' applies to the efforts of neo-Kemalists: 'These 'official nationalisms' can best be understood as a means for combining naturalisation with retention of dynastic power, in particular over the huge polyglot domains accumulated since the Middle Ages, or, to put it another way, for stretching the short, tight skin of the nation over the gigantic body of the empire". For an analysis of the

crisis consisted of a battle, under an ambivalent discursive horizon, radically destabilised by its politically eroded episteme of Islam, fought by a number of political actors[789] on a number of fronts, to redesign the politico-discursive order, including primarily the definition of identity, nation and political subjectivity, for the 20th Century. The contemporary identity crisis also consists of a battle being fought, under the ambivalent republican horizon with its Kemalist regime of truth radically destabilised by its globally eroded episteme of modernity, on a number of fronts to redesign the politico-discursive order, including primarily the redefinition of the 'nation' and political identity to lead to the design of a political subjectivity for the 21st Century.

A sociological literature around the term 'second Istanbul' developed in the 1990s and led within a short time to the generalisation of this approach to declare the existence of a 'second Turkey'. This 'second Turkey', consisting of the poor suburbs of the major cities and in general the 'periphery' outside the major cities, did certainly exist before their discovery by the sociological discourse in the 1990s, but have never been described in such bold terms. What is to be inquired into here therefore is what made the recent decades so special. The observation to be derived from this study is twofold. Firstly, the second Turkey existed before the 1980s in as much as it found articulation with terms provided by the ruling discourse of republican Turkey, such as the 'threat of regression' or 'the

---

reactivation of the Turkish flag as the symbol of 'greater nation', that is, the conscious nation of the centre and repressed nation of the periphery, see Yoruk 1997.

underdevelopment of the East'. What differentiates the recent decades from the rest of the republican history is that the repressed and foreclosed identities forced spaces within the symbolic order for their articulation with their own terms. Secondly, the main impact of this self-symbolisation has led to a further realisation that the 'second Turkey' was not so much physically separated from the centre – 'out there' in poor suburbs and on the 'periphery' – but consisted of the essential elements that had been rejected and ejected from the modern and conscious political subjectivity to form the unconscious and the 'constitutive outside' of this subjectivity. However, it is the totality of all these included and excluded elements which made the Turkish identity, including the discourses of nation, modernity and secularism, and the built-in defence mechanisms of repression and foreclosure. If, therefore, the Islamist discourse represents the threatening return of the modern Turk's repressed Oriental origins, the Kurdish identity similarly forces the Turk to face the fact that his/her identity is also based on a lack and a consequent myth of Turkish identity moulded out of the ethnic and cultural heterogeneity of the Anatolian population. This facing of reality in the mirrors of Islamic revival and Kurdish uprising has produced mostly traumatic consequences, which have been considered in this chapter.

I have analysed the trajectory of the contemporary identity crisis through its three major sources, including the Islamisation and peripherialisation of the centre in

---

[789] The Ottoman bureaucracy, the West, non-Muslim ethnicities and Muslim majority of the Empire.

parallel to the globalisation and neo-liberalisation of the 'national' sphere, the return of the repressed Islamic identity and, the powerful challenge of Kurdish identity from 'outside' the republican symbolic order. I have argued that each of these sources is significant in that they compel the modern Turkish identity to explore for the first time the 'periphery inside', that is, those aspects that the Turk had to reject and eject from his/her conscious self in order to identify with a number of notions that constitute Turkish identity, including above all modernity and national integrity. These forcible encounters with the Other have produced traumatic consequences consisting of the triggering of the psychic defence mechanisms and their reinforcement through an intertwined process of second secularisation and second nationalisation.

The Turkish identity crisis, therefore, makes the reconceptualisation of two things necessary. Firstly, the political order, consisting of republican governmentality as a 'regime of truth' protected by the myth of Ataturk and guarded by the military-bureaucratic establishment, under the episteme of modernisation. Secondly, the social, consisting of some 70 million population identifying with Turkishness in varying degrees, that is, the redefinition of Turkish identity. I have already asserted the reasons for this necessity, which I repeat when concluding as follows:

The combined consequences of the 'return of the repressed' and the 'reappearance of the foreclosed' are that the Turkish political reality cannot reproduce itself. If the crisis of capitalism is marked by the moment when capital, which according to the laws of capitalist economy, has to accumulate in order to survive, becomes unable to reproduce itself, similarly identity crisis is marked with that traumatic

moment when reality becomes incapable of self-reproduction. This is precisely

what the overall argument of this research is: Turkish political identity is in crisis

because it is no longer capable of reproducing reality, that is, the environment in

which Turkishness has been able to exist up to our time.

Appendix 1: The Confinement of the Ticanis

The Great Confinement

The order was given 'to poor scholars and indigents' to leave the city, while *it was forbidden 'henceforth to sing hymns before the images in the streets'*.

(...)

The fifth chained prisoner released by Pinel was a former ecclesiastic whose madness had caused him to be excommunicated; suffering from delusions of grandeur, he believed he was Christ; this was 'the height of human arrogance in delirium.' (...)

A source of strong emotions and terrifying images that it arouses through fears of the Beyond, Catholicism frequently provokes madness; it generates delirious beliefs, entertains hallucinations, leads men to despair and melancholia. We must not be surprised if, 'examining the registers of the insane asylum at Bicetre, we find inscribed there many priests and monks, as well as country people maddened by a frightening picture of the future.'

(...)

The asylum must thus be freed from religion and from all its iconographic connections; 'melancholics by deviation' must not be allowed their pious books; experience 'teaches us that this is the surest means of perpetuating insanity or even of making it incurable, and the more such permission is granted, the less we manage to calm anxiety and scruples'.

(Michel Foucault, *Madness of Civilisation*)[790]

Ticanis and 'Civilisation

'*Ticanis began to chant publicly the Koranic slogan 'God is great'*, in the streets, government buildings and justice halls.

(...)

'An imam was observed in 1946 shouting at the Atatürk's statue in Uzunköprü: 'You hanged all the hodjas. Whores are everywhere... Muslim girls are made to dance on the stage in theatres'. The imam admitted in detention that he was a *Ticani*.

(...)

'Finally, in February 1949, a *Ticani* recited the call for prayers laudly in Arabic from the listeners bench during a parliamentary session in the Grand National Assembly' (Tunaya 2003: 193).

(...)

In 1951, *Ticanis* began to smash Atatürk statues around the country. A 'law of protection of Atatürk's spiritual personality' had to be introduced on 25 July 1951 to penalise this line of action. The leader of the *Ticani* sect, Kemal Pilavoglu, was detained and sentenced to fifteen years according to the Article 163 of Turkish Penal Code. He was subsequently forced to reside on the Aegean island Bozcaada with his followers. 'Pilavoglu formed a *tarikat* commune on this island but this could not prevent the rapid elimination of his sect. In our day, *Ticanis* have no tangible influence in society' (Saylan: 18-9).

---

[790] Extracts from Rabinow 1984: 141-167.

Appendix 2: Islam and Reform

In the late 17th Century, when the West, armed with the knowledge and organisation of modernity, came to challenge the Ottomans, the Empire's lands were covering most of the Middle East, the heartland of Islam. Ottomans' legitimacy for the Muslim-Arab world had rested upon their absolute military might, which secured the superiority of the Muslim world over the Christian West. Muslim thinkers inevitably linked the problem of Ottoman decline to a general defeat of Islam. The long record of military success and assured domination had for the Muslim faith a transcendental significance. It served to prove that Mohammed's message was true, that God prospered those who believed in him and hearkened to his revelation. Political success had vindicated Islam, and the course of world history had proved the truth of the religion. Muslims fought to extend the bounds of Islam and humble the unbelievers; the fight was holy and the reward of those who fell was eternal bliss. Such a belief, which history of Islam itself seemed to establish beyond doubt, inspired Muslims' self-confidence and powerful feelings of superiority. Hence the long series of defeats at the hands of Christian Europe could not but undermine the self-respect of the Muslims and result in far-reaching moral and intellectual crisis. For military defeat was defeat not in a worldly sense, it also brought into doubt the truth of the Muslim revelation itself: If Islam was the true religion, how were the infidels so successful in this world?

The Muslim answer to this question has been shared by the most diverse reformist movements, namely, "Christians are strong because they are not really Christian; Muslims are weak because they are not really Muslim" (Hourani, 1970, 129). In order to become "really Muslim", it was necessary to rid Islam of foreign accretions and folk religiosity which corrupted the original message of the Prophet. Only then it was possible to discover original, pure Islam, which was seen to be completely compatible with the modern scientific world. Pure Islam was based on an ascetic, activist and this-worldly ethic. The enemy of both pure

Islam and modern society was a set of attitudes - fatalism, passivity, and mysticism - which had been introduced into Islam by erratic elements. Sufi mysticism thus received the blame for cultural decay, which the Muslim reformists viewed as lying underneath the general decline of the Muslim world. Paradoxically, the way forward was a return to scriptural, authentic and original Koranic orthodoxy. Active involvement in this world thus became a major theme of Islamic reform directed against Sufi quietism. The cultural response from Islam to Western superiority therefore involved a thorough interpretation of Islam, which was, in principle, to be transformed into a democratic, active and modern ideology. A favourite Koranic text of the reformer Jamal al-Din al-Afghani was "Verily, God does not change the state of a people until they have changed themselves inwardly" (Keddie 1968). Similarly, his disciple Rashid Rida asserted that the first principle of Islam was "positive effort". The parallels between this discourse and Puritanism and Protestant ethics are evident. It is no surprise that al-Afghani saw himself as the Luther of Islam.

Appendix 3: Mutiny vs Revolution - 31 March Affair

Turkish transition to modernity also involves a linguistic shift from 'janissary mutinies' to 'revolutions', 'military interventions' and failed 'coup attempts'. Like the discourse of Ottoman rulers and chronologists, republican discourse does not express a high opinion of military interventions under the Ottoman rule, categorising them as 'mutinies'. Although the exclusive aim of all these mutinies was change of government or even change of Sultan, they would not be called coups d'etat or military interventions. The first of the coups, on the other hand, occurred in 1876, when Midhad Pasha supported by the Navy stormed the palace, dethroned the sultan and declared the Ottoman Empire a constitutional monarchy. The second military intervention – called a 'revolution' by the Young Turks - was in 1908, when the Sultan was forced by young officers loyal to the clandestine Committee of Union and Progress (CUP - of the Young Turks) to reinstate the constitution. In 1909 a curious confrontation between 'revolution' and 'counter-revolution', involving a confrontation between concepts of mutiny and coup, was staged (Appendix 15).

This affair – known as 31st March incident – resulted in the dethroning of Sultan Abdulhamid II to be replaced by his brother Mehmed Reshad. Transition from the 'classical age of mutinies' to the 'modern age of coups and revolutions' was thus completed. After 1909, Ottoman Empire was practically governed by the CUP. The CUP regime, which claimed to have derived its legitimacy from the 'people', initiated a tradition of military interventions as a legitimate method of dethroning sultans and governments. The raid on Sublime Porte on 23 January 1913 is the prototypical model of the future coups d'etat in Turkish politics. On that day, the CUP leader Colonel Enver guarded by a group of gunmen, stormed the principal office of Ottoman government, the council chamber of the Sublime Porte. One of Enver's companions executed the Minister of War Nazim Pasha, whom the CUP held responsible for the defeat in the Balkan War. Enver also forced the Prime Minister to resign and declared Mahmud Pasha the new Prime Minister. This 'blueprint' of 'military revolution' was re-staged in the coups d'etat of 27 May 1960 and 12 September 1980, with the modern difference that instead of an armed mob, army tanks would roar around and the fighter jets would fly low over the government buildings. In each of these modern coups, and the 'postmodern' coup of 28 February 1997, generals always claimed to have derived their authority from the 'nation'.

The 31 March incident, the last battle between mutiny and 'revolution', requires detailed consideration since it is revealing of both the officers' will to power and the discourses of identity that still shape modern Turkish politics. The incident broke out as a military mutiny in Istanbul. The discontent that preceded the mutiny and its subsequent expansion as an all out revolt had a number of elements. The immediate reason was the growing conflict within the ranks of the Ottoman army between officers without military college training, whose careers were threatened by the government, and the graduates of military colleges who manned the ranks of the CUP. The CUP led government also decided to end the Medrese students' exemption from military service and the leading CUP members such as Ahmed Riza gave anti-ulema speeches at the Parliament. On 6/7 April 1909, an opposition journalist, Hasan Fehmi, whose newspaper *Serbesti* had published the claims of a financial scandal involving the CUP, was murdered as he was crossing Galata bridge on the Golden Horn in Istanbul. The assassin escaped, which raised a vocal suspicion that he must have been linked with the CUP. Hasan Fehmi's funeral turned into a large-scale anti-government demonstration.

The mutiny that broke out on 13 April 1909 had built itself up on all these elements of discontent and turned into a popular uprising with the participation of some Sufi sheikhs and a fraction of *ulema*, including some Medrese teachers and students. Demonstrators marched to the Parliament and the Grand Vizier resigned as demanded. Two deputies and a naval officer were killed by the mutineers. Istanbul was "liberated" from the CUP power, but this situation would last no longer than ten days. 31 March incident provided a golden opportunity for the Macedonia based ambitious young officers' bid for power: Troops loyal to CUP were mobilised from bases in Salonika and Edirne towards the Capital and promptly quelled the revolt. The end results of the short lived 'liberation' were dethroning of Abdülhamid II, the execution of eight "counter-revolutionaries", among them the leading figure of the conservative Islamists and the editor of *Volkan* newspaper Dervish Vahdeti (Aksin 1972), closure of the Islamist *Ittihadı Muhammedi* Party and the liberal *Ahrar* Party.[791] The CUP thus began to relinquish the banner of *Liberté* to be replaced with one party dictatorship. Four years later, in 1913, following the Turkish defeat in the Balkans, the military wing of the CUP led by Colonel Enver would take the country under their sole control with a military coup.

The most durable result of this affair, however, was its contribution to the new military elite's psyche with an image of 'the reactionary' as the other. The CUP officers viewed the 31 March incident as a counter-revolutionary attempt carried out mostly by conscripts, who had been deceived by Mullahs to turn against the CUP rule. The image of 'the reactionary', who abuse innocent masses by using religion for his political ends, thus entered the officers' political psyche, as the 'other' of the moderniser's identity.

However, the articulation of this image into the state's discourse had to wait until after the declaration of the republic and the abolition of the Caliphate. We can observe the officers' psyche at work in the political and scientific discourses of republican Turkey. An example of this articulation is the comprehensive academic work on the history of Turkey's Islamic movements, *Islamcılık Cereyanı* (The Islamist Current) by late Professor Tarık Zafer Tunaya. Tunaya, a

---

[4]*Ahrar* Party's leader Prince Sabahaddin, formerly the leader of the liberal wing of the CUP, was briefly detained after the suppression of the revolt, but released without charges. The CUP leadership interpreted the revolt both a Hamidian plot and Prince Sabahaddin's bid for power. With the closure of the *Ahrar* Party, the consequences of the revolt served to the CUP's aim of suppressing the liberals.

professor of law, published this book in 1962,[792] when he was the spokesperson of the Constitutional Commission formed by the military governors in the wake of the Kemalist coup against the centre-right DP government.

The subtitle of the section on 31 March incident is '31 March Incident as an example of exploitation of religion for political ends and a reactionary affair' (Tunaya 2003: 106). Before narrating the incident Tunaya states: 'The conclusion that we aim to reach here is that 31 March incident (...) is a "famous" and fanatical reactionary event of the Ottoman history, which clearly demonstrated the potentially devastating destruction that the exploitation of people's religious and divine feelings could bring about' (Tunaya 2003: 107).

The professor's *a priori*, 'exploitation of religious feelings for political ends', has been one of the primary prohibitions of the Turkish Republic's juridico-discursive practices. In the wake of the Sheikh Said rebellion a new bill passed the Grand National Assembly on 25 February 1925, as an addendum to the 'Law of Treason' stating the use of religion for political ends a crime to be treated as treason (Koçak 1995: 100).

Ataturk, in his autobiographical references, always claimed that he led the 'operation army' to Istanbul to quell the 31 March revolt, which is not true (Mango 1999: 87-9). Similarly, in republican history textbooks, 31 March incident is given great emphasis as a reactionary uprising suppressed by the revolutionary commander Mustafa Kemal. Ataturk's claim on this particular incident is curious when it is read as the constitutional trauma of the officers' psyche. It has constitutive status due to its ability to provide the secularist imaginary with all the elements of a perfect fantasmatic scenario of 'the return of the repressed'. The discursive construction, symbolisation and the practical consequences of this incident, including the manifest fear of a re-staging of the same scenario, that is, of its return, are telling of an act of not merely quelling a

---

[5] I shall refer in this text to the final (2003) edition of this book.

revolt, but of an act of repression, which marks the moment of the formation of the identity of the secularist officer. The narration of the 31 March incident is a gesture towards the repressed dimension of modern Turkish symbolic order. It demonstrates that 'if the people are left unchecked, they will be won over by the forces of reaction and counter-revolution'. It also names the institution capable of maintaining this control over 'people', that is, the military, and by doing so serves to provide the officer with an exceptional mission, leading to the legitimation of the exceptional role of the army in Turkish politics. 31 March incident was therefore the moment when the construction of the self-image of the modern secularist officer was finalised, with a mission to lead the 'nation' to progress, which required above all the repression of the Islamic/Oriental dimension of his own self. With these features, 31 March incident also served to intertwine the discourses of secularism and militarism. With the realisation of the 'military dream of society' through the colonisation of the social by the military model, the militarist/secularist officers' psyche would be promoted to the status of an integral component of modern Turkish identity.

The accounts of the formative years of Turkish republic usually view the discursive construction of Islam as a dangerous counterrevolutionary ideology articulating the hopeless desire of bringing back the *ancien régime*, as merely paving the way for sweeping secularist reforms and the suppression of local resistances to 'revolution'. There are two important features that escape this perception. Firstly, the Kemalist subject itself was a split subject,[793] constituted through a primal repression of the ego's oriental aspects and secondly, the

---

[793] To constitute themselves as western, the Kemalists felt it necessary to deny any traces of the Oriental dimension of Turkishness. In doing so, they placed themselves clearly 'outside' of this 'object' out of which the modern 'subjects' were to be made. They were 'outside' for they imagined themselves within the horizon of modernity, as the 'agents' whose mission was to inoculate modernity into a traditional structure as Gokalp had proposed: Kemalists were the modernisers. But since the very term 'modernisation' is situated by definition at the spatial and temporal margin separating the traditional from the modern, the East from the West, Kemalists also belonged to the Orient. Kemalism itself was ambiguous and 'undecidable', in this regard. It was an impure entity, which threatened the purity of the very symbolic order that it so eagerly desired. Therefore, to be western, one had to reject more than the Orient: the rejection had to involve a certain metaphorical surplus: the rejection of the impossibility of identification with the Other (Sayyid 1994).

Kemalist program contained an appeal to the nation for the repetition and generalisation of the Kemalist neurosis in order to become a modern nation. Therefore, becoming a Turkish subject means splitting, since entry to the Turkish symbolic order preconditions a primal repression.

The moment of formation of Turkish subject contains a primal split: a split along the axis of 'the clash of civilisations', which became evident in the physical split of 'historic bloc' that had existed roughly from the beginning of the Abdulhamid II's reign in 1876 to the declaration of the republic (see Appendix 1). Instead of 'suturing', in a Gokalpian fashion, the building stones of the split Turkishness, the Kemalist subject decided to deepen this East/West cleavage further with their bureaucratic Jacobinism, grounded upon a will to build a new national identity based primarily on a violent repression of the East. Kemalists breached Gokalp's distinction between culture and civilisation with a series of pro-western reforms, which amounted to 'force to civilise' a cultural entity as a whole after reducing it discursively to an object to be civilised. Kemalist discourse consists of a decision of split in its appeal to 'collective amnesia' by inviting the 'nation' to repress its 'Oriental' nature, as well as representing an invitation to collective memory, as a general rule of nationalism set out by Ernest Renan (1990).

Since repression and the return of the repressed are the same thing (Evans 1996: 165), what we observe from the moment of Ataturk's call to repression onwards is a republican history experienced as a series of repressions and subsequent returns of the repressed. The unconscious is the context that accommodates in particular the 'backward' nature of the 'nation' with the Ottoman past and Islamic identity as the 'dreams and shadows' that are attached to it.[794]

Since this moment of split, republican Turkey has demonstrated the features of a 'torn country' as described by Huntington (1993). The same moment was also the

---

[794] 'Away with dreams and shadows! They have cost us dear in the past' (Kemal quoted in Armstrong 1932: 218-9).

moment of emergence of modern Turkish identity. The consequence of this congruence as Tanpinar said, is that the birth of the nation meant the birth of the split subject with an identity crisis.

If the split between East and West is constitutive, then the 'Menemen Affair' is the constitutive myth of modern Turkish psyche (See Appendix 16). Its discursive construction, symbolisation and practical consequences, including the manifest fear of a re-staging of the same scenario, that is, of its return, are telling of an act of not merely suppression or quelling of a revolt, but also an act of repression, which has formed and reproduced through generations the unconscious dimension of Turkish identity. In other words, the Menemen Affair of 1930 is the moment of declaration of the will to colonisation of the 'national common sense' by the 'officers psyche' which had been largely built on a fear of repetition 31 March Affair (Appendix 15). This 'will to colonise' marks the moment of commencement of the dispersal and generalisation of the image of 'the reactionary', who abuse innocent masses by using religion for his political ends, as the 'other' of modern Turkish identity.

The 'nationalised' split between the repressed unconscious and modern consciousness corresponded to an already existing social division between the people and the elite. The politico-cultural name of this cleavage is the centre-periphery division. In Gramsci's terms, the centre corresponded to the field of state and ideology and the periphery to civil society and common sense. Taking the mechanism of repression, which is the form that this politico-cultural and social split found its reflection on modern subject's psyche into account, it would be legitimate to assert that Turkish socio-political entity is structured like neurosis. This structure consisted of a conscious republican subject and his repressed unconscious the popular religion, that is, society's common sense. There are two consequences of this neurotic structure: First, the Kemalist consolidation had to include a 'passive revolution' to be fought as a 'war of position' by the Kemalist functionaries throughout the battlefield of the social including its 'common sense'. Second, the prevailing radical otherness of the two levels to each other, as a manifestation of the failure of this 'passive revolution', led to the experience of each push for a democratic accommodation from the periphery towards the centre as a symptomatic disturbance, like the return of the repressed. The DP decade between 1950 and 1960 and its conclusion with a military coup and the subsequent executions of three top government figures, including the prime minister, and the popularisation of Islamic politics in the 1990s which led to a 'post-modern coup' on 28 February 1997, are two such symptomatic experiences of republican history.

Appendix 4: Three Segments of the Turkish-Muslim 'Historic Bloc'

1- The Ottoman Ruling Class (Askeriye) and Paranoia

The centrifugal tendencies and movements which caused the continuous contraction of particularly the European portions of the imperial land, and the European powers' overt involvement in this process as the protectors of one or the other 'separatist' *millet,* within the rules of the 'Eastern Question' game, were traumatic enough for the Ottoman ruling strata to develop a paranoid discourse of being besieged by 'enemies', meaning the Great Powers, primarily Russia. A hostile discourse and attitude towards Christian elements of the Empire, who had been increasingly seen by this élite as the potential collaborators of the exogenous enemy accompanied this mentality. These factors were vindicated by the disappointing results of the economic integration with Europe: while the Treasury and the peasant masses of Anatolia were suffering from the economic 'peripheralisation' of the Empire, a new class of commercial bourgeoisie, consisting almost exclusively of non-Muslim subjects, was ascending to challenge the dominant status of the central bureaucracy in the Empire's political economy and social structure.[795] In these circumstances, Ottoman élite engaged in a series of intellectual debates usually focused on the topic of salvation the 'Sublime State' (*Devlet-i Ali*).

2- The Scarred Dominant Nation

Empire's Muslim population was similarly traumatised from the beginning of the modernisation onwards. Alongside the economic transformations, which destabilised the conventional order, Muslim masses were finding it increasingly difficult to accommodate the hastily transplanted tenets of equality and

---

[795] For an interpretation of the late Ottoman history as a class struggle between bureaucracy and bourgeoisie see Keyder 1987: 25-48.

416

constitutionality in favour of non-Muslim subjects. The effects of integration with Europe also included the development of an ironic situation in terms of political economy: whilst the Ottoman Empire was based on Islamic dominance of an unpronounced *millet-i hakime* over various religious and ethnic communities, Muslim landowners, provincial merchants and the peasant masses that bonded to them through clientalist networks were increasingly subordinated to a non-Muslim commercial bourgeoisie. The ethnic differentiation of the imperial population was becoming to coincide with the class differentiation in the expense of the Turkish-Muslim majority. As the Ottoman historian Cevdet Pasa put it in 1870s: 'We have lost in our day our sacred national order, which had been achieved through sacrifices of our Muslim ancestors. The nation of Islam, which used to be the dominant nation, has now been deprived of such a sacred right' (Cevdet Pasa, cited in Ogun 1997: 213). This 'injustice' was increasingly associated at the dislocated popular level with a desire to reinstall the Muslim-Turks as the 'dominant nation'.

3- Sublimation of Humiliation: The Oppressed Nation and Ideology

The development of nationalist discourses by the *millet-i mahkume* ('imprisoned nations') of the Empire to challenge the integrity of the Ottoman State became the cause of a further politicisation of the Muslim-Turkish population. Over two million people had been displaced and migrated from Crimea, Caucasus, Balkans and other outlying portions of the periphery of the Empire to the Ottoman hinterland, Anatolia, between 1850s and early 20th Century (Keyder 1987: 80). These refugees contributed above all to the Muslimisation and Turkification of Anatolia, and brought with them the frustrating memoirs of their suffering in the hands of the victorious enemies, consisting primarily of the Russians and the former *milleti mahkume*.[796] Their frustration was open for an articulation in a

---

[796] The first works of Turkist fiction consist of short stories written by Omer Seyfettin which narrate and exaggerate this suffering in a language designed to signify a circular chain of hatred of the 'enemy' and the glorification of the 'Turk'. If Seyfettin's sentiments represent the general

discourse of the oppressed: in fact, a discourse of *mazlum millet* ('oppressed nation') had already emerged in Central Asia, Caucasus, Balkans and Anatolia, narrating the agony of the Muslim-Turkish 'nation' in the hands of the non-Muslim and Russian brutality, encouraged by the imperialist Western policies aiming to destroy this nation. When this discourse of the oppressed subject, this 'sigh of a living creature', appealed to the empathy of the larger fraternity of Muslims and Turks, it would be rearticulated in terms of a pan-Islamist discourse which preached the spiritual and political unity of Muslims. In the years of the second half of the 19th Century, threatened by a frantic policy of Russification, the Muslims of Russia, especially the Tartars in Kazan and Crimea and the Azeris, had come together under the banner of Pan-Islamism.[797] Parties and newspapers were launched, congresses were held, Turkish language was advocated as a cultural bond, and the Turkic peoples of Russia were called upon to unite under the auspices of Ottoman Turkey. Just as Christians oppressed by the Sultan were protected by the Tsar, so Muslims under the Russian yoke placed their hopes on the Ottoman Empire where so many Muslim ethnicities had taken refuge. In this process, emphasis gradually shifted from Islam to Turkishness, and alongside Pan-Islamism, a discourse of Pan-Turkism grounded upon the nostalgic utopia of reincarnation of a lost tranquillity in the land of origin (*Turan*) which would reunite the Turkic world, was born with objectives almost identical to pan-Islamist ones. Both discourses sublimated the scarred Turkish Muslim identity and located their present tragedy within historical grand-narratives of Turkish-Muslim emancipation.

---

mentality of these millions strong Muslim immigrants, some important clues can be obtained in understanding Turkish political psyche and, in particular, the motives of the Armenian massacre.
[797] For the early influence of pan-Islamism among the Ottoman intelligentsia see the section on New Ottomans in Chapter 1.

Appendix 5: Kocgiri: An Untold Massacre

The Kocgiri unrest began with the clan's leader Alisan Bey's questioning of Mustafa Kemal in Sivas (September 1919) regarding the national movement's aims with reference to Kurdistan. Alisan was not impressed with Kemal's agitation on how Cemil Pasha and Captain Noel were plotting against the National Movement and Kemal's personality, and raised instead the demands of education in Kurdish and the assignment of Kurdish officials and governors for Kocgiri and Dersim Kurds (Kutlay 1997: 145-6; Goktas 1991: 36-7). After this meeting Kemal resorted to a classical Ottoman tactic, delagating Alisan Bey as Sivas 'deputy'. This did not impress Alisan either and Kurdish Club (*Teali*) branches were launched in Kocgiri and Dersim regions. The first effective Kurdish awakening against the cynical possibility of Turkish centralisation thus begun among the Alevi Kurds of Kocgiri and Dersim. Instead of a clear statement on the future of Kurdistan, Mustafa Kemal once again tried to win over the Kocgiri clan by declaring Alisan the Governor of Refahiye and his brother Haydar the Director of Umraniye (Göktas 1991: 38). These assignments only assisted the rebellion aims of the Kocgiri Beys. Following a period of preparation, Kocgiri and Dersim notables opened their rebellious flag with a cable message to Ankara dated 25 December 1920:

> To the Grand National Assembly Presidency:
>
> According to the Sevres Treaty, an independent Kurdistan is to be established consisting of the provinces of Diyarbekir, Elaziz, Van and Bitlis. This has to be recognised and established. If not, we hereby declare that we will be forced to achieve this right by resorting to arms.
>
> Signed by West Dersim Leadership Council (Göktas 1991: 40).

Koçgiri rebellion was quelled violently. Out of the 135 villages that homed the Koçgiri clan, 132 villages were torched to the ground; thousands of civilians were killed. Laz militias led by infamous butcher of Armenians, Lame Osman, were deployed along with the national army commanded by notorious Nurettin Pasha. The anti-Alevi and anti-Kurdish sentiments of the Sunni Laz people were appealed by the Kemalist administration to promote a genocide-like massacre of the Alevi Kurds of Kocgiri and Dersim. Survivors were deported to central Anatolia, particularly to the Sariz district of Kayseri. The indifference of the Sunni Kurds towards the Kocgiri tribe's appeal also surfaced another division within the Kurdish identity: that between Sunni and Alevi Kurds. Although the West Dersim declaration was nationalist and not religious by any criteria, in practice the Kocgiri rebellion was limited to the Alevi sector of the Kurdish population. This surfacing division between Alevi and Sunni Kurds would prevail as one of the determinants of the contemporary Kurdish political identity in Turkey.

In spite of its shortcomings, Kocgiri rebellion brought about some political results for the Kurds and the nationalist government. Kemalist leadership came under severe pressure to clarify its position on the status of Kurdistan. On 10 February 1922, 'The Law on the Autonomy of Kurdistan' passed in the Grand National Assembly, against fierce opposition from the Kurdish deputies (Olson 1991: 70).[798] The autonomy law however was never implemented. In fact, the fact that such a law had ever passed in the parliament has been officially denied to date; destroyed minutes of the parliamentary session of 10 February 1922 (a lack) being the sole proof of such a law (Kutlay 1997: 158).

---

[798] The reason for this opposition was the weak and cosmetic character of autonomy proposed by the motion.

420

Appendix 6: Three components of Kurdish identity

As part of the modernisation attempt, the Ottoman government abolished the Kurdish emirates and replaced the Emirs with governors appointed by the central administration. The Kurdish Emirs resisted this intervention into their three centuries long autonomy,[799] and the early 19th Century witnessed a chain of Kurdish rebellions to be suppressed brutally.[800] The practice of exiling Kurdish notables to west began with the suppression of these rebellions, when many Kurdish Beys were exiled to Aegean islands and Balkans with their families. First seeds of potentially anti-imperial sentiments have thus been spread around the Kurds who began to differentiate between the Kurds and Ottomans, which they referred to as Rom.[801] The 1858 Land Decree, which for the first time recognised the private ownership of land was particularly aimed to promote the settlement of nomadic Kurdish tribes. With this legislation, the lost political power of the Kurdish emirs were compensated by economic gains, when nomadic tribal leaders -- aghas and beys -- were escalated to the status of feudal lords. The settlement of the nomadic tribes was hoped to make taxation and conscription possible for the central administration. The Kurds, however, regarded the centrally appointed governors as "foreigners", and did not allow them to maintain a successful administration. In this power vacuum, Kurdish Sheiks, leaders of primarily Nakshibendi and Kadiri religious orders, strengthened their position as the communal leaders. The Time of the Sheikhs thus began in Kurdistan. (Kutlay 1997: 37; Bruinessen 1992.)

---

[799] The Kurds had become Ottomans not through conquest but with a convention in the 16th Century between the Ottoman Sultan and the Sunni Kurdish emirates by which the latters were persuaded to act on behalf of the Ottoman Empire against the Shii Iranian Empire. The Kurds would provide the Sultan with taxes and soldiers and in return they were left autonomous in their internal affairs. (Yegen: 217; Barkey & Fuller: 6-7.)

[800] Among these rebels, Bedirhan Bey was the most famous, since he was the first Kurdish 'sovereign' who would mint money in his own name. On one side of this coin it read "Bedirhan the Emir of Bothan" and the other side read 1258, indicating the year in Islamic calendar that the coin was issued.

Whatever event may be taken as the origins of Kurdish national identity, it is generally accepted that the Kurds experienced a form of national awakening in parallel to the Armenian and the subsequent Turkish awakening from the second half of the 19th Century onwards. The increasing influence of the Kurdish sheikhs in social life contributed to this awakening. Their orthodox views on Islam led them to a cautious and distinct position towards the reformist Ottoman administration.[802] This orthodox Muslim sense of difference, supported by the traditional resistance of the Kurdish aghas and peasants to taxation and conscription, would prevail through decades in the core of the Kurdish identity. This orthodox Sunni component of Kurdish identity would further make it possible for the Kemalists to label the most effective Kurdish uprising in the 1920s as 'a reactionary religious movement'. This religious element of the Kurdish awakening is evident in the Kurdish way of referring to the Ottomans as 'Rom'.

Sultan Abdulhamid, who came to throne in 1876, tried to hail the wounds of earlier modernisation in Kurdistan. He invited Kurdish aristocrats and Kurdish Islamic scholars to Istanbul and provided their children with schooling and opportunity to obtain high positions in the Ottoman administration. He opened two "Tribe Schools" (*Asiret Mektepleri*) in Istanbul and Baghdad, which were specifically designed for the Kurdish youth.[803] The second generation of the Kurdish aristocracy and the graduates of the Tribe Schools would constitute the Istanbul-based Kurdish intelligentsia to play a significant role in Kurdish politics in the coming decades. The first Kurdish periodical, *Kurdistan,* was launched under these conditions in 1898 by Miqdat Mithad Bedirhan and a political association by the name *Kurdistan Azm-i Kavi Cemiyeti* was founded in 1900.

---

[801] Traditionally, the term "Rum", which comes from "Rome" and "Roman", was used by the Ottoman Turks to refer to the Byzantium or to Anatolia. This term still refers to the Greek inhabitants of the Turkish controlled lands.

[802] Ironically, and understandably in many ways, at a time when the role of the Ottoman *ulema* was diminishing at the centre, their influence was increasing in the 'periphery' both in the Arab Middle East, Central Anatolia and Kurdistan.

[803] Abdulhamid wrote in his memoirs that with these measures he expected 'to win over the Kurds to ourselves in time' (Abdulhamid: 73-4).

Kurdish intelligentsia also found representation in the opposition to Abdulhamid regime. In the two congresses of *Ittihad ve Terakki* in 1902 and 1907, Abdurrahman Bedirhan and Hikmet Baban participated as the Kurdish delegation. Another Kurdish figure, the self-styled spiritual leader Said-i Kurdi, also entered the political scene in early 20th Century as part of the Kurdish delegation to the *Ittihad ve Terakki* congress of 1907. He would in the Twentieth Century lead the most popular Islamic opposition to the republican regime (see Chapter 3). Following the declaration of Constitution in 1908, there was a proliferation of Kurdish associations and publications. A Kurdish School was also opened during this period. (Kutlay 1997: 69) Kutlay lists eleven Kurdish periodicals published by various Kurdish circles based in Istanbul and eight organisations including a "Kurdish Women's Association" and "Kurdish National Party". (Kutlay 1997: 92-3 & 97.) A modern Kurdish intelligentsia was born in Istanbul to play its historical role during the collapse of the Ottoman Empire.

Promotion of and Islamic identity by the Sultan also meant the encouragement of Kurdish banditry against the Armenian population and property. In response to the Berlin Treaty, which the Ottoman government was forced to sign after suffering a defeat in 1877-78 Turko-Russian war, and which granted minority rights to the Armenian population, Abdulhamid initiated the Kurdish officered and soldiered *Hamidiye* regiments, with the purpose of protecting Muslim population from Armenian excesses and maintaining law and order in eastern provinces. Thirty six regiments were established in 1891, each consisting of 512 to 1152 troops from thirty six Sunni Kurdish tribes and commanded by the tribal chiefs decorated with the ranks and positions of Pasha, Major or Governor (Göktas 1991: 22). These regiments were engaged in many atrocities against the Armenians and Alevi Zazas and Kurds of the region. They were deployed in the Sassun 'operation' and later in the Russian front during the First World War. The official Turkish position is that Kurdish political identity began with the *Hamidiye* regiments.[804] Kurdish sources also emphasise the *Hamidiye* and later *Asiret* (Tribe) regiments' role in being a source of inspiration for Kurdish organisations (See Göktas 1991: 23 and Kutlay 1997). Leaving aside their aims of maintaining order on behalf of the Sultan, they were the first Kurdish armed forces overtly recognised by the central administration.

The relations between these three actors, religious/tribal/feudal leaders (Sheiks and Agas), Hamidiye regiments and Istanbul-based Kurdish intelligentsia, largely determined the course of Kurdish politics during the transition from Ottoman Empire to Turkish Republic.

---

[804] At the Inspectors General Conference on 7 December 1936, the Third Inspector General Tahsin Uzer pronounced *Hamidiye* regiments as the sole origin of pro-Kurdish activities. (Mumcu 1995:153.) This statement has a racist connotation in the sense that if there were a Kurdish identity, it was only due to a Turkish initiative. Secondly, there is a modernist-Kemalist reference to Ottoman history. In the republican narrative of Ottoman history, Abdulhamid is presented as the brutal tyrant who oppressed the forces of progress, and therefore, Kurdish identity created by Abdulhamid's invention of Hamidiye regiments, was another reactionary, anti-modernist and anti-Kemalist entity.

Appendix 7: The Kurdish Character of Islamism

There is a point missing in the debate over the nature of Sheikh Said rebellion: while the Turkish side emphasises the religious character of the Kurdish movement in order to label it 'reactionary', no one seems to have thought on the *Kurdish character of the Islamic movement* in Turkey. The background to this character was that the 19th century awakening of Kurdistan was accompanied with the increasing social role of religious leaders, predominantly from the Nakshibendi order (Kutlay 1997: 58), in social life. Koranic orthodoxy and pious conservatism against the influences of the west and modernisation were the main tenets of the *Nakshibendi* teaching. Nakshibendism was brought in the Ottoman lands in early 19th Century by Mevlana Khalid, who arrived from India to Kurdistan in 1811. In a very short time, Nakshibendism became the most popular Sufi sect particularly among the Sunni Kurds, who were predominantly Shafi, the most conservative sect of the Sunni faith, while the Ottoman governors belonged to the pragmatic Hanifi sect, which preached subordination to the state. A distant Kurdish identity, which had its initial peculiarity in Shafiism, was now crowned by the teachings of a Sufi order (Kutlay 1997: 193). Of the 67 caliphs that Mevlana Khalid chose, 33 were Kurdish (Kutlay 1997: 193). Nakshibendism had developed among the Indian Muslims as a doctrine of traditional resistance against the effects of modernisation imposed by the British colonialism. Its rapid popularity among the Kurds in the age of Ottoman modernisation, was followed by its expansion through other Muslim groups of the Empire. Abdulhamid II brought this *tarikat* to the centre of the Empire as part of his Panislamist policies by inviting *Nakshibendi* sheikhs to his palace in Istanbul as consultants in imperial decisions. Sultan also promoted the opening of *Nakshibendi* lodges in Istanbul. This practice of the 'centralisation of the periphery' or the 'peripherialisation of the centre' was arguably taken after by Ozal more than a century after Abdulhamid II and followed by Erbakan in a rather stark style by an invitation of *tarikat* sheikhs to a Ramadan dinner at prime ministerial residence, which would provoke a Kemalist coup in 1997 (see Conclusion). Both Ozal and

Erbakan belonged to the Nakshibendi order, which explains the influence of this order in Turkey. The *Nakshibendi* has also been the most popular current of Islamic identity in republican history. Throughout modern Turkish history, Islam managed to find a shelter in the depths of Turkey's periphery and particularly in Kurdistan. As in the 19th Century, most of the religious leaders of the present day *tarikats* are Kurdish, who received their education in the *medreses* (religious schools) which survived the Kemalist "revolutions" by remaining underground in deep Kurdistan for decades. Kutlay refers to a conversation with Sheikh Giyasettin Emre, MP, in the 1950s, which is revealing of Islam-Kurdish relationship: 'If not for the Medreses and mullahs, Kurdish language, literature and identity would vanish as a whole. If these partially survive in our day, it is thanks to these institutions' (Kutlay 1997: 192).

Appendix 8: Republican Apparatuses

.

It was in the context of transition to a monoparty system that the People's Houses took over the Turkish Hearths' organisational structure to operate under the RPP's instructions with the specific mission of disseminating the reforms among people (Saydam 1931: 1). Villages, where traditional life continued within almost self-sufficient and autonomous structures, were the major targets of this 'culture revolution' campaign and People's Rooms were formed in 1939 as the village branches of the People's Houses. Prime Minister pronounced the duty of the People's Rooms as 'the organisation of national days in villages and assisting the realisation of national unity in the rural areas' (Cecen 1990: 208). People's Houses and People's Rooms, the total number of which reached respectively to 478 and 4322 by 1950, were the primal institutions of the dissemination of republican principles around the country. Between 1932 and 1940, 23,750 conferences, 12,350 theatre plays, 9,050 concerts, 7,850 film showings and 970 exhibitions were held in People's Houses (Cavdar 1983: 882). 1930s' Prime Minister Inonu emphasised often the importance of the people's compliance with military service and paying taxes (Inonu 1933: 196) and pointed out the fact that organisations like People's Houses were more convincing than the coercive methods. But the best description of the function of the People's Houses was made by the President Mustafa Kemal:

> If people are left on their own, a progress can never be attained… An interest (in progress) among the people should be awakened by a positive work programme… and it should be serving the aim of the welfare of the nation as a whole (Karpat, 1991:50).

Turkish History Research Organisation, which later assumed the name Turkish History Institute (TTK) was founded in 1931, and was involved in the production and dissemination of the Turkish History Thesis. In 1932, a sister organisation, Turkish Language Institute (TDK), was founded. In addition to the purification of

427

language, TDK produced the 'Sun Language Theory', which aimed to make a linguistic case for the Turkish History Thesis, by 'proving' that the origin of all languages around the world was Turkish. In 1932 all the historians and history teachers around the country were called to Ankara for the First History Congress. The main aim of the Congress was to train teachers according to the Thesis. Four volumes of school textbooks had been prepared prior to the Congress, which constituted the backbone of republican 'national education'.

Teacher training was given special emphasis in republican Turkey, where education, along with the military, was viewed as the main engine of national identity. A peculiar teacher training experience was put in practise in the 1940s: The Village Institutes. In addition to training the rural youth as village-school teachers, village institutes also aimed to serve the objective of improvement of the economic and infrastructural capacities of the rural areas. The architect of the Village institutes, Ismail Hakki Tonguç emphasised the necessity of creating a people loyal to the state and Turkish nationalism.:

> Today we have 16,000 villages whose population is less than 250. If we do not have people loyal to our state, these villagers will be full of criminals and bandits. If the people we educate as the hands of the state go there, our flag could be put there at least in national festivals and weekends (Karaomerlioglu, 1998:64).

When the village institutes are considered with the expansion of People's Rooms, it becomes clear that the aims of this rural cultural movement were far beyond this manifest aim of performing the official rituals. The RPP expected from the joint operations of these two institutions to increase the level of education in the rural areas while bringing up a new generation of party functionaries, consisting of village teachers and agriculturalists who would become the local political-intellectual leaders (Koçak 129). The 21 village institutes around the country were closed by the RPP itself in 1950 for the reason that they would contradict with the multi-party period.

Of the republican institutions above, people's houses and people's rooms lived their heyday in the 1930s and 1940s and with the political liberalisation of the 1950s that followed the conclusion of the monoparty period in 1946 they stopped functioning. Village institutes were formed in 1940 and closed in 1950. The Turkish History Institute and the Turkish Language Institute, however, operated as important state institutions until the anticommunist coup of 1980.

There is a general consensus among the narrators of Kemalist Turkey that despite all its efforts in the 'classical era of the republic' the republican regime failed to expand its cultural appeal to the periphery (province). Kemalism was essentially a doctrine of the new rulers in urban centres; while the education process and the army were seen as the primary modes of transmission for the new identity, much of the countryside continued to live according to traditional, usually folk-Islamic values[805]:

> It was assumed that by means of theatre, which People's Houses and People's Rooms took to the remotest corners of the country, the people would identify with the new past that had been constructed in accordance with the official ideology's project for the future. The pro-western elites believe that people are unable to separate the fact from fiction and will therefore accept whatever is staged in the theatre as reality (Ayvazoglu 836).

There were therefore two simultaneous dramas staged in the halls of People's Houses and People's Rooms: on the one side, the drama that was performed on the stage and, on the other, the drama entitled 'modernised subjects watching theatre' that the whole audience performed for a smaller audience of overlooking 'pro-western elites'.

---

[805] In villages, the arrival of the personnel of the people's houses usually caused the children run away screaming, 'mommy, the state is coming!' (Arman 1969.)

Appendix 9: Critical Defences and Analytic Failures

An elaborate defence of the Thesis, concealed in the popular line of its criticism among the academic circles, is treating it as an accident in Turkish historiography resulting from the inevitable excesses of the revolutionary change:

> To expect the revolutionary stages such as that period of Turkey of 1920s and 1930s to progress in a balanced and moderate style is against the logic of history. Such periods inevitably bring about many excesses and rigidities, which will be rasped through the new order's normal and stabilised functioning. This is a necessary part of the process of sweeping the dirt of the past away (Berktay 1983: 55).

What Berktay attempts to defend is the 'normal' history of this 'new order' as a whole in which Thesis represents an accidental moment of perversion. However, he fails to identify to support this assertion another period of modern Turkish history, against which the period of the production of the Thesis could be measured, simply because the dream of a 'normal and stabilised order' is itself a fantasmatic construct. What any republican historian would notice is that the history of this order, which contains more 'accidents and perversions' than a normality as such, could only be written by 'piling paralogy over paralogy' (Rorty 1991: 166).

This line of critical defence of the Thesis, by emphasising the conditions in which it was produced, is the most popular line among Turkish academics. Two comprehensive studies on this subject, which divert from defence to concentrate on criticism, deserve reflection. *Power and History* by Büsra Ersanlı Behar (1992) and an almost completely ignored study entitled *Turkish History Thesis and the Kurdish Question* by the veteran pro-Kurdish academic Ismail Besikçi (1977b). I have pronounced the two works in the same sentence, because at one level their conclusions are identical, that is, that, the Thesis is an ideological/irrational historical grandnarrative, which cannot be supported by historical data. Behar's conclusion could at its best be read as an appeal to replace this 'nonsense' with scientific historiography. Besikçi's concern, at this level, is limited to demonstrate that Thesis cannot be held in the light of scientific evidence. Behar further clarified her position by stating that the main error of the Thesis lies in the lack of academic ethics in the 1930s Turkey. According to her, the historians, anthropologists and archaeologists of that decade sacrificed the scientific ethics to the political contemplation of the regime, due to their organic links with political power (Behar quoted in Yegen 1996: 23). This definition is correct but is suitable for turning upside down. The Thesis, as much as being the product of a handful of academics siding with political authority, is the constitutive discourse of modern Turkish academia and Turkish 'human sciences' of history, anthropology, archaeology and linguistics. The Thesis produced and reproduced modern political power and academy, and their primary condition of existence, that is, the lacking objectivity, the nation.[806] The consequences of the Thesis were much more extensive and tragic than 'corrupting academy' and this is why Behar's study represents a valuable compilation of empirical data with poor conclusions, the tragedy of any study with a perspective limited to empiricism. The production and dissemination of the Thesis represent an exceptional example of a modern discursive practice, which is open beyond the reach of semantic content analysis,

---

[806] I can confirm that majority of the university graduates in Turkey still believe that Hitites and Sumerians were the Turks' ancestors. I also meet archaeology graduates, who read at the university that the antique Aegean civilisation of Lydians had no connection with the modern Greeks. The importance of this assumption is twofold: Firstly, Mustafa Kemal said in an interview in 1930 that 'we are in the process of scientifically proving that we were a nation settled around Izmir before the Greeks'. Secondly, the late President of Turkey, Turgut Ozal, argued in a book titled *La Turquie en Europe* (1988) that Greeks did not originate western civilisation; to the contrary, the first important civilisation was founded in Anatolia and the Anatolian peoples, including the Turks, are the originators and repository of this western civilisation:

'We have been living in this territory (Anatolia) since the origins of Anatolian civilisations. (...) It is we who have created neolithic revolution. The Sumerians were, moreover, Turanians (Turks from central Asia). (...) At Troy it is we who made war, in alliance with peoples who had come from all corners of Anatolia and who spoke different languages' (Ozal quoted in Vryonis 1991: 20).

There are two conclusions to be derived from above comments: Firstly, Turkish History Thesis is not a phenomenon of the past but it has been the constitutive elements of both the Turkish state and modern Turkish identity, official and popular alike, through decades and many generations. Secondly, Kemalism has been the hegemonic discourse of modern Turkish history. The fact that someone like Ozal, the primal enemy of Kemalism for the neo-Kemalists of the present, deploy abundantly the Kemalist arguments derived from the Thesis in the only book that he ever wrote demonstrates this hegemonic character. A discourse becomes hegemonic to overdetermine the

and which cannot be 'corrected' by rewriting history books according to Behar's criticism.

Thesis as the Constitutive Discursive Practice

This is the point where the concern of Besikçi's study, that is, to demonstrate not only the conditions of emergence of the Thesis but how this discourse has served to legitimate techniques of externalisation, assimilation and repression by the republican regime since the formative years of the republic, is distinguished from Behar's. Mesut Yegen (1999) shares Besikçi's concern in his study entitled *The Kurdish Question in State Discourse* by extending his analysis, based mainly on a fixation at the structuralist stage of Foucauldian premise, to include state legislation of the 1930s and the practices of 'republican institutions' consisting of Turkish Hearths, People's Houses, Turkish History Institute, Turkish Language Institute and Village Institutes.

Yegen's study, when compared to Besikçi's volume, represents both an advance and a retreat. The advance lies in both the theoretical enrichment of the argument, which makes the Thesis intelligible as a text attached to a particular discursive practice, i.e. Kemalism, and the consequent concern of Yegen on the mechanisms of its dispersal. The retreat, on the other hand, is observable in the author's understanding of Kemalism, as a peculiar discourse of a certain era of republican history, that is, the discourse of the monoparty regime of the 1930s and 1940s.

Both Besikci and Yegen emphasise a further function of the 'Thesis', that is, the exclusion of Kurdish identity and the accompanying policies of assimilation. All the Anatolian and Mesopotamian civilisations that the Kurds legitimately claim lineage were turned into Turkish civilisations in their origins, since 'no civilisation is possible without being contacted by the Turks' creative power'.

---

discursive formation only through dispersion, that is, when it is able to provide the grammar of all discourse, including the discourse of dissent.

Only on these grounds it becomes possible to declare that the Kurds were originally Turks, who, as a result of living on the mountains, had been alienated from their real identity (Besikci 1977: 187-92 and 219-37).

Appendix 10: Dersim Reports

From 1926 onwards, Dersim became the subject of systematic reports[807] prepared by the important members of the state apparatus. These reports derived from the historical, linguistic and anthropologic theories produced around the Turkish History Thesis and extended the research to reach demographic, geographical, sociological, medical and politico/military conclusions.[808]

Most of these reports begins with political findings. The 1926 report by the State Inspector Hamdi reads: "Dersim is Kurdified and the threat is growing". The main problems were outlined as banditry and the lack of security for which the tribal chiefs were responsible. Hamdi's report called Dersim 'an abscess that the republican government ... would have to operate upon in order to prevent worse pain.' The proposed solutions, which were generally agreed upon, were the disarmament of the population, the deportation of the tribal chiefs to western Turkey and the dispersal of the families of certain tribes away from Dersim. To achieve these aims and to secure the permanent settlement of the state in the region, a large-scale military operation was required. The governmental structure also needed to be reformed in the region, particularly the replacement of Kurdish civil servants with Turkish ones was necessary. Chief of General Staff, Marshall Fevzi Çakmak, stated openly in his proposals that the provincial government should have colonial powers: 'Dersim needs initially to be considered as a colony. Then Kurdishness should be melted within the Turkish society. Then, gradually the proper Turkish law can apply there.' The precondition of having equal rights in Turkey was to be melted in Turkish culture.

Prime Minister Ismet İnönü analysed in his 1935 secret 'East' Report the ethnic composition of each province with detail. He proposed demographic plans for Turkification, which involved the forcible and voluntary population resettlements.

---

[807] I am aware of nine such reports for the period between 1926 and 1936.
[808] All the quotes below from the reports were taken from Bulut 1991, unless otherwise specified.

Inönü confesses that there had been a discrimination policy regarding education and proposes a reform by agreeing to teach literacy to Kurds. He says primary school education (and nothing more) was better than illiteracy.

Inönü's, Hamdi's and Çakmak's reports touch on a particular development as the source of problem: the Kurdification of the region. The problem is understood as the expansion of the Dersim Kurds through the occupation of empty villages and lands, remnants of the Armenian massacre, where the government originally intended to settle Turkish/Muslim refugees. This tendency of demographic expansion was united with the growing Kurdish awareness through the experiences of Kocgiri, Sheikh Said and Agri rebellions to present a danger. But this problem could only occur as a subtext in public statements through its manifestations such as the proposals to break the influence of local leaders, the disarmament of the people and the need for demographic solutions and cultural assimilation. The boldest statement was made by Inönü in his secret report:

> The total liquidation of the Armenians left the area to the invasion of the Dersim inhabitants, given the weakness of the Turkish villages. The empty villages around Erzincan are being filled in by Dersim's rough and dominant people. (…) These villages also provide shelter for the expansion of Dersim's looting gangs to the inner regions. The major concern is that with Erzincan becoming a major Kurdish city in the short run, the **real horrific Kurdistan** can be formed (quoted in Mumcu 1995: 118).

Report by General Inspector Abidin Özmen (1936) complains that 'Turks increased by 20 thousand while Kurdish population increased by 250 thousand in the region between 1927 and 1935 censuses. The Ottoman devsirme (conversion) sytem should be applied in the region as ethnic conversion through education. For this, state boarding schools needed to be built.'

Researches were carried out in 1930s to analyse each tribe regarding the population, geographical location, and number of arms, sheep, goats, oxen and horses in each tribe's possession. Detailed analysis of ongoing tribal disputes were also elaborated and the potential collaborator tribes were identified (Goktas 1991: 128-9).

Appendix 11

Covering (up) the Kurds: 'Kemalist Marxism' and the Turkish Press

The Turkish press of the time of the Dersim operation was full of official jingoism as expected, and did not care much about the occasional slip of tongue unmasking a directly racist and colonialist rhetoric:

'Hero sergeant conquers an immense mountain on his own'

A region populated by the starved and the naked is being civilised. In the former capital of backwardness the roar of Turkish motors are now heard (Cumhuriyet, 4 July 1937).

The roar that was heard by 'the starved and the naked' was of the bomber planes, and there was good paparazzi material for Turkish press in all this:

'The heroic services of our first female pilot in Dersim'

It is a very important historical occasion that a representative of the Turkish women, who, after being recognised in social life with full potency following centuries of deprivation, has thrown the last bomb to overthrow feudalism. (...) This brave Turkish girl plays a most active role in this action of healing and reform (Tan, 15 July 1937).

This piece is paparazzi because it is about the first and only female pilot, Atatürk's adopted daughter Sabiha Gökçen, and therefore a member of the 'republican royal family'. Consequently, the reports on her bombing sorties always received front page coverage with great deal of sycophancy. Of the harm of these sorties beyond 'overthrowing feudalism' we get complete silence. With no intention to sacrifice this 'complete silence' as a casualty of my discussion, I shall open a bracket here to open up a further discussion on the nature of Kemalism.

The same extract from the newspaper article above on women's rights, feudalism and war can also be read as an excellent example of a quasi-feminist and quasi-marxist portrait of a bomber woman and as such it is revealing of the international dimension of Kemalism. In illustrating the full process of condensation and displacement involved in the production of Kemalist imaginary, Kautsky's (and Lenin's) concepts of *from within* and *from without* as dimensions of gaining consciousness can be useful. Kemalism was above all a nationalist discourse and it emerged from *within* four subtexts, including Ottomanism, Turkism, Islamism and Westernism, the peculiarly Turkish interpretations of nationalism. But the Kemalist 'dreamwork', like the Kautskyan category of working class consciousness, was also determined from *without*, by the three major internationally competing discourses of the period between mid 1920s and mid 1940s, that is, Liberalism, Stalinist marxism and Fascism. Liberalism provided the grounds for the 'rights of men and women', including the individuals' right against their community (rigorously converted into a political program of offence on Volkislam communities) and equal rights for women. Dersim operation can be viewed as an offence carried out by these liberated citizens, including an outstanding representative of women, on the pre-modern tribes, to break the oppressive chains of tribal power. Marxism, in the form of a Bolshevik tendency entered the discursive horizon of new Turkey during the 'national struggle' and firmly suppressed by Mustafa Kemal after a short episode of compulsory honeymoon.[809] The second honeymoon occurred in the early 1930s, when three prominent members of the TKP capitulated to Kemalism arguing that there was no class conflict in Turkey. They were welcomed in and encouraged by both İnönü and Atatürk to publish a theoretical journal, 'Kadro', with the participation of a Kemalist literateur Yakup Kadri Karaosmanoglu, in which theorisation of the Kemalist discourse, with the help of marxist terminology was attempted. Kadro made a great impact on the already Kemalised Turkish communists[810] and the Kemalist cadres of the time, who welcomed the Stalinist campaign for progress

---

[809] Soviet arm shipments to the nationalist movement in Ankara were at stake, and Mustafa Kemal went so far to found the Turkish Communist Party in 1920 which he dissolved within a few months, realising that the Soviet government's help was secure in any case. Mustafa Kemal then invited the entire leadership of the 'outside' Communist Party from Baku to Ankara, who were massacred in Trabzon by a group of armed men loyal to Kemal.

[810] Turkish communists had been Kemalised by the Communtern's line on Kemalism as an anti-imperialist ally of the communist movement, which brought Turkey to the stage of democratic revolution, the next stage being transition to socialism. Turkey's communists rigorously denounced the Sheikh Said rebellion and any resistance to Kemalist reforms as the 'black voices' of reactionary counterrevolution.

and development and the economist and teleological stages of history to explain where Kemalism came from and where it was heading towards. Thus, the Kemalist reforms, in addition to being a transition to 'civilisation', were interpreted as a transition from feudalism to national capitalism, which stood in contradiction with imperialism (Turkes 2002: 464-76). The 'national democratic revolution' halted the imperialist invasion and overthrew feudalism, but there were inevitably some remnants of the superseded stage of history left, including the Kurds, which needed to be 'overthrown'. The brave and enlightened daughter of revolution was thus throwing the 'last bomb' on the fetters of the development of the forces of production to the applause of an amused quasi-marxist audience.

The relationship between fascism and the bureaucratic corporatist stage of Kemalism in the 1930s was discussed above. The influence of fascism on the Kemalist 'dreamwork' is not immediately evident in the terminology and the symbols used in this passage but the meaning of the whole passage reveals a link between the two discourses beyond authoritarianism and corporatism: the fanatical hatred of the other, ready to evolve into a genocidal tendency.

Appendix 12: The Sound of the Silence

Ismail Besikçi (1990) claims that Turkish state committed a genocide in Dersim. A report by the British Consul in Trabzon is affirmative of Besikçi's claims by comparing the 'brutal and indiscriminate violence' used in Dersim to the Armenian genocide of 1915. 'Thousand of Kurds, including women and children were slain; others, mostly children, were thrown into the Euphrates; while thousands of others in less hostile areas, who had first been deprived of their cattle and other belongings were deported to provinces in central Anatolia. It is now stated that the Kurdish question no longer exists in Turkey'.[811] The official military history of the campaign (Halli 1972) is affirmative of many of the brutalities reported by Dersimi (1952) and other dissident accounts of the event. A document dated 4 May 1937 entitled 'Secret Decision of the Council of Ministers on the Punitive Expedition to Dersim' envisages a final solution to the perpetual rebellions in Dersim. 'This time the people in the rebellious districts will be rounded up and deported', instructs the government and goes on to order the army to 'render those who have used arms or are still using them once and for all harmless on the spot, to completely destroy their villages and to remove their families'.[812] This reads like an order to kill all men in the area, given that the Dersim reports above had already repeatedly claimed that every men in Dersim was known to carry arms. The Chief of Staff's only figure of rebel casualties, including killed or captured alive, is an ambiguous 7954 for the seventeen days of the 1938 offensive alone (Halli 1972: 478). Other reports of individual clashes are impossible to add up to obtain a consistent number. Kurdish sources speak of tens of thousands including women, children and the elderly. We probably will never learn the full dimensions of atrocities of the 'civilisation' of Dersim. Martin van Bruinessen, following Besikçi, argues that what we know from government communiqué, orders and reports in addition to witness accounts and the fact that the official number of deaths above is more than ten percent of the official record

---

[811] Report from the Consul in Trabzon, 27 September 1938. Public Record Office, London, FO 371 files, document E5961/69/44.
[812] Published in Besikçi 1990: 67.

of population are sufficient to describe the Dersim operation, if not a genocide as such, an act of ethnocide, with the manifest aim of 'the destruction of Kurdish ethnic identity' (Bruinessen 1994).

Violence, which was officially licensed and excessively used in the quelling of Kurdish revolts and in the subsequent 'punitive operations' of correction and 'civilisation', can be read as the inevitable monster of the republic's scientific and rational regime of truth. However, this monster, this schizoid symptom of modernity, did not occur in such excess in the Kemalist practices against the Islamic identity or the Kurdish counterinsurgency in general. The best the Kemalism could do against the Islamic identity was to repress it and then place it discursively in a perspective of development and progress, hoping that it would inevitably be superseded at a certain stage of development in the future. Kemalism did react against any threats to territorial integrity with inappropriate violence, but the Kemalist practices never included before Dersim such licence to overkill. Nor did the Kemalists ever contemplate in the previous experiences on the deportation of entire tribes and the dispersal of tribal families. The usual practice was to subdue the revolt brutally, hang the leaders and then send to the exile the notables of those tribes that supported the revolt. Dersim experience is different since in the Dersim plan above the very existence of a community becomes punishable. In the Kemalist laboratory of Dersim, there was no call for surrender to save your life. A book dwelling on in particular the tribal conflict during the Dersim incident confirms that the members of those tribes who offered their collaboration to the state were also eliminated (Kalman 1995: 302-3).

Appendix 13: Turkist Origins of Republican Nationalism

The Ottomans' rediscovery of their Turkish origin via the works of European Turkologists[813] can be observed in a group of mid-19th Century Ottoman bureaucrats,[814] who produced Turkish language dictionaries and Turkish history books.[815] This theoretical preparation found its initial reflection in Sultan Abdulhamid II's 1894 legislation requiring the use of Turkish in all the schools of the Empire. Abdulhamid's decree also included a language reform, stipulating the use of clear, simple language, devoid of Arabic and Persian words not commonly used. The second generation of Turkists,[816] consisting mainly of military-bureaucrats and intellectuals, who were born between 1870 and 1890, were the product of this cultural climate and were distinguished from the first generation in that they – in Yusuf Akcura's words – 'politicised Turkism' (Ertekin 2002: 350). The political atmosphere in which this politicisation took place was traumatic as described in chapter 2.

Yusuf Akcura, an ethnic Tartar from Russia[817], worked out the first manifesto of Turkism in its difference from two other discourses of salvation – Ottomanism and Islamism, in his seminal essay titled 'Three Modes of Politics', published in Cairo in 1904. In this manifesto, Akcura declared the bankruptcy of both Ottomanism and Islamism. The common ground that Akcura's Turkism shares with other discourses is the 'salvation of the Sublime State'. He ends the essay by asking which of the policies of Islamism or Turkism is more harmful to the

---

[813] Joseph De Guignes (France); Arminius Vambery (Hungary); Leon Cahun (French); Wilhelm Radloff (Germany); Vasili Barthold (Russia) were the contemporary Turkologists of the first generation Turkists.

[814] Including Ahmed Vefik Pasha, Semseddin Sami and Mustafa Celaleddin Pasha.

[815] Ahmed Vefik Pasha, *Lehce-I Osmani;* Semseddin Sami, *Kamus-u Turki;* Mustafa Celaleddin Pasha, *Eski ve Yeni Turkler;* Suleyman Pasha, *Tarih-i Alem.* Additionally, an eccentric intellectual, Ali Suavi, wrote in his newspaper *Muhbir* that Ottomans were a Turkic nation whose origins were in Central Asia and that their language was not Ottoman but Turkish (Aydin 1998: 104).

[816] Ziya Gokalp, Yusuf Akcora, Hamdullah Suphi, Hasan Ferit (Cansever), Necip Asim, Veled Celebi, Mehmed Emin (Yurdakul) and Omer Seyfettin were the prominent Turkist intellectuals while Mustafa Kemal, Kazim Karabekir and Ismet (Inonu) were the prominent military politicians of this generation of Turkists.

Ottoman Empire and which is more feasible. But this is only a rhetorical question and it is clear that he preferred Turkism among the three modes of politics. The general observation that Keyder makes on the late Ottoman intelligentsia is explanatory of Akcura's and the emerging Turkist generation's state oriented position:

> [Intellectuals] did not represent a humanistic or critical culture. Their primary purpose always remained the reform of the state in order to better cope with internal conflict and external pressure. (…) There was not a single Ottoman intellectual, even in letters, whose immediate concern lay outside this framework; debates and differences were played out within the narrow field of salvaging and strengthening the state (Keyder 1987: 50).

Akcura's early manifesto clearly articulated the main aims of the Turkist thought, that is, the reorganisation of the Ottoman state as a Turkish state to be followed by the salvation of the greater Turkish nation, including those of the Caucasus, Central Asia and Balkans, under a unified state. Although Akcura's assertions looked complementary to each other, inherent to them was the future tension between territorial nationalism and irredentist pan-Turkism.

Following the Young Turk revolution of 1908, Turkism was largely promoted by the state. Publications and organisations proliferated to propagate the Turkification of the Ottoman lands and to oppose the county's disintegration by the activities of non-Muslim groups supported by the Great Powers. The Turkish Hearths (1912), the Turkist literatours' circle around the journal *Genc Kalemler* (Young Pens-1908) and the intellectual circle around the journal *Turk Yurdu* (Turk's Homeland-1911) served to educate a Turkist generation of political activists in an atmosphere of catastrophic collapse of the Empire.

---

[817] For a comprehensive biography and analysis of Akcura's political thought and practice see Georgeon 1986.

Appendix 14: Turkism of the late Empire: Young Pens and Turkish Hearths

Genc Kalemler initiated the 'National Literature' movement and advocated the purification of language through the elimination of Arabic and Farsi words and grammatical structures from the language. Their prominent figure, Omer Seyfettin, wrote the first works of specifically Turkist fiction in the form of short stories. Seyfettin's stories narrate and exaggerate the suffering of the Turks particularly in the outlying portions of the Empire in the Balkans, in a purified language designed to signify a circular chain of hatred from the 'enemy' and the glorification of the 'Turk'. The split 'Turk' of Seyfettin is probably the best illustration of the 'spirit of times': the Turk, the humiliated object of sadistic torture by the enemy (*Beyaz Lale*), is reincarnated with a flash back to the glorious past as the sublime subject of not only heroism, justice and wealth (*Pembe Incili Kaftan, Basini Vermeyen Sehit*) but of sadism, who literally smashes the head of the leader of a Christian group with aspirations of independence from the Ottoman Empire (*Topuz*). Seyfettin clarifies his message that there is no outside of this sadomasochistic habitus in several occasions by stating that 'nations who do not oppress the others are bound to be oppressed': the 'most evident wisdom: those who do not oppress are oppressed'. (Seyfettin 1993: 35, 87).

Seyfettin's sadomasochistic social-Darwinism, associated with anxiety of a sense of delay and insecurity leading to a constant state of alert, constitute the main theme of his non-fiction work too. Seyfettin relates in his articles these anxieties to a project of nation building. Being aware of the need to define the 'other' of the nation prior to its positive definition, Seyfettin clearly distinguishes Turkishness from non-Muslim identities, through a criticism of the Ottomanist ideal of 'the unity of the elements' as 'an empty illusion and a crude dream'. He asserts that while Turkish intellectuals are preoccupied with this dream, Greeks and

Armenians have been stirring conspiracies on behalf of their nationalist ideals.[818]
After their malicious aspirations, the co-ordinates of the location of these
'enemies of religion and blood' are also pointed:

There are very few Greeks along the shores of the Turkish land. They have
been departing anyhow. In the eastern provinces such as Erzurum, Van
and Bitlis, the Armenian *millet* does not reside in large communities and
their number is negligible compared to the Turks (Seyfettin 1993: 83)[819].

Seyfettin's 'will to oppress' the non-Muslim ethnicities of the 'Turkish
Homeland' became the official policy of the CUP regime in 1913, which led to
the elimination of the Armenian and Greek populations of Anatolia, and these
views have been maintained, to a large extent, in the subsequent Turkist
discourses.

The Turkish Hearths were founded during the Balkan War, with the manifest aims
of 'improving the national education and scientific, cultural and economic levels
of the Turks, and working for the perfection of the Turkish race and language'.
Following the Ottoman defeat in the Balkans, the aim of politicisation of Turkism
from a cultural movement to a political project was put in practice. In this
political project, Anatolia was progressively emphasised as the 'Turkish
homeland', although the *Turanist* (pan-Turkist) tendency never lost its appeal.
Ziya Gokalp wrote in 1911: 'The country of the Turks is neither Turkey nor
Turkestan / Their country is a great and eternal land – Turan' (Gokalp 1987: 186).
Gokalp, the undisputed ideologue of Turkish nationalism, differed from the
'grassroots' Turkist movement of the émigré intellectuals, the best representative
of whose is Yusuf Akcura, in that, as an Ottoman, he viewed Turkism as an
instrument to achieve the salvation of the Ottoman State, while Akcura viewed
the Ottomans, 'the firmest and most civilised component of Turkishhood', a

---

[818] Smart, cunning and dauntless Greek militants, such as Bosho and Kosmopolidi are staging their
conspiracies from the Parliament chair and the miserable Turks – unaware of their ideals and aims
– applaud these enemies of religion and blood (Seyfettin 1993: 38-9).

[819] See also pages 43-7 and 55 of the same work.

means to achieve the salvation of the Turks (the Turkist cause).[820] Gokalp was not only 'the Buddha of the Turkish Hearths' (Karaosmanoglu 1983) but also a member of the CUP central committee and the CUP troika's exclusive theoretical referee. The Turkist influence over the CUP government via Gokalp was evident in a series of government led reforms.[821]

---

[820]Suleyman Seyfi Ögün draws a distinction between these two vicissitudes of Turkism and identifies a State (Staatgeist) and Civil Society (Volkgeist), or Cultural and Political nationalisms distinction in this original differentiation, which leads him in conclusion to declare that Kemalism was anything but nationalist. (Ögün, 216-28.) This distinction may be fruitful in serving his ends but can only be sustained by ignoring the ambiguous character of the late Ottoman discursive horizon, and the consequent processes of condensation and displacement between these discourses. First of all, Ögün's conception of *millet-i hakime* discourse based on Sunni Turkish dominance being an exclusively state oriented discourse flaws in the light of historical experience in which I have pointed out the popular possession of this mentality by the Muslim masses of the Empire. What is witnessed in a reading of this history is also an ambiguity between the levels which Ögün so carefully tries to differentiate, that is, the domains of the state/civil society, political/cultural, and also the discourses that are supposed to be corresponding to these differences, e.g. dominant nation's nationalism/oppressed nation's nationalism. In fact, Yusuf Akcura, who Ögün presents as the champion of the *volkgeist* nationalism, wrote one of the most *staatgeist* natured texts of Turkish nationalism ('Three Modes of Politics'). In this 1904 essay, Akcura defends Turkism against Islamism and Ottomanism almost exclusively in terms of its utility for the State and its applicability. Secondly, the ambiguity around the meanings were so extensive that not only the variations of the same discourse but discourses defined as serving completely different projects of emancipation were often intertwined. The CUP's discourse, for instance, can be identified as both Pan-Turkist and Pan-Islamist or none. Similarly, at the level of the 'oppressed nation', separate meanings that were articulated within these two distinct discourses were already subject to disarticulations and rearticulations at the popular level of 'common sense', as I have pointed out in the case of Russian Muslims (see chapter 2).

[821] The CUP developed and implemented projects for all the three stances above. Pan-Turkist propaganda in the Caucasus and Central Asia was promoted, which would be supported by a military campaign to Sarikamis under Enver's command during the First World War, although only to end in disaster. "National Economy" was the material project of "imperial nationalism", by which the CUP introduced government promotion of industrial and commercial ventures by the emergent Muslim bourgeoisie. (Toprak 1995). Additionally, in the first months of the Balkan War, a National Consumption Society was founded to encourage people to buy goods produced in the homeland even if they were more expensive than imports. On 9 September 1914, the Capitulations were abolished with effect from 1 October. And finally, for Anatolian nationalism, a grand project of Turkification of Anatolia was put in practice by the CUP government, which aimed to break down both the economic strength and political orientations of primarily the Greeks and Armenians, which constituted a considerable portion of population (40% in the eve of the First World War, according to Church registries – Yildiz, 112), since such an existence was seen as the greatest threat to the integrity of Anatolia, the 'last shelter' of the Ottoman Turks. At the cultural frontier of the Turkist cause, the CUP program of 1908 declared Turkish the official language of the Empire. Compulsory Turkish classes were introduced in primary schooling, which continued to be in the mother tongue, while in secondary education Turkish was made the language of instruction (Aksin 1987: 103-4). A law was introduced on 23 March 1916 making the use of Turkish compulsory at work. All registers and bills as well as street signs had to be in Turkish (Aksin 1987: 281).

During the War years, the Turkish Hearths membership grew in numbers from 3,000 in 1914 to 30,000 by 1920. The British closed the Hearths in 1920, but they resumed activity in 1924 and by 1930 had 257 branches and 32,000 members. Many Turkist activists of the CUP period including Yusuf Akcura, Mehmed Emin (Yurdakul) and Ahmet Agaoglu, were recruited to the Kemalist ranks. The Turkish Hearths were allowed to operate until 1931 under their chairman since 1913, Hamdullah Suphi (Tanriover). Ziya Gokalp, after returning from exile in Malta, was elected to the Assembly as the Diyarbakir deputy and commissioned by Mustafa Kemal to write a programmatic essay (*Dogru Yol* – The True Path) for the ruling Republican People's Party. Gokalp also wrote *Turkculugun Esaslari*. (Principles of Turkism) before his death in 1924, in which he reduced, in parallel to the Kemalist spirit of times, the question of religion to one and a half pages devoted solely on the advocacy of prayers in Turkish. Although he was not elevated to the status of the exceptional ideologue of the republic in this last year of his life, he was aware that the possibilities of the implication of his ideas were broadened radically with the transition to Kemalist republic.

Turkists, although never abandoned their Turanist ideal as the ultimate goal, were fist to use the name 'Turkey' in defining Anatolia and Rumelia. The 1918 Congress of the Turkish Hearths debated the matter where an amendment to the organisation's constitution was proposed, reading, 'the field of activity of the Hearths is particularly *Turkiya*:' The reasoning of this proposal was that since the Turkish Hearths did not have the strength to work for both the Anatolian Turks and the 'outer Turks' at the same time, 'although the great *Turan* dream was hailed with hope', they needed to concentrate all of the activities in the short term exclusively on Turkey (Ustel 2002: 264). The 'particularly *Turkiya*' phrase was not adopted by the Congress, but the proposal was still a manifestation of a strong Kemalism-like pragmatic tendency within the Hearths.

Territorial Turkism was not the sole tendency of the Turkist movement to be adopted by Kemalism. The Kemalist regime adopted in particular the perspective of assimilation of the non-Turkish Muslim population of the new Turkey, which had been first proposed in Akcura's programmatic texts:

> Those united by religion who were essentially not Turks but who to a certain extent had become Turks would become more assimilated by the Turks, and even those who had never identified themselves as such could themselves be made into Turks (Akcura 1976: 73).

Yusuf Akcura had also written in an article titled 'We Should Learn and Teach Turkishhood' as early as 1908 that 'the oldest civilisation – older than even the Egyptian civilisation – was created by the Sumerians and Achaeans, a *Turanian* people' (Arai 2002: 182). This statement is arguably the first manifestation of the 'Turkish History Thesis'. In fact, Akcura played an active role in the formulation of the Thesis as one of the founding members of the Turkish History Research Association. He was elected to the chairmanship of the Association in 1932 and chaired the first Turkish History Congress. Akcura was one of the authors of 'An Outline of the Turkish History' (Georgeon 2002: 514), the backbone text of the Turkish History Thesis.

Appendix 15: Kemalist-Turkist Symbiosis

The symbiosis of Kemalism and Turkism can further be observed, for the formative years, in the three fields considered below:

1. Assimilation: In the first decade of the republic, Turkish Hearths operated for the manifest aims of assimilation and Turkification of non-Turkish Muslim population of Anatolia. The Turkish Hearths functioned until their closure in 1931 with a manifest assimilation policy, which aimed to Turkify particularly the East Anatolia, where 'non-Turkish elements' were resident and the immigrants and remaining non-Muslim elements who 'spoke languages other than Turkish'. The aims were, as articulated by the leader of the Hearths, Hamdullah Suphi, 'to isolate the linguistic peculiarities' of the said elements and to achieve their 'cultural Turkification' (Ustel 2002: 265-6). The 'Citizen Speak Turkish' campaign, which was launched in 1928 for a short period, and then relaunched in 1931-2 to survive until the mid-1940s, was enthusiastically participated by the Turkists. The Turkist youth organised in the MTTB systematically intimidated the Jews, Christians and non-Turkish Muslim communities, including the Arabs, Cyrcassians, Cretan Muslims and the Kurds, which they viewed as a requirement of this campaign (Cagaptay 2002: 260).[822] The campaign was given new impetus in 1935 with Prime Minister Inonu's address to the RPP: 'We shall not be silenced any more. All the citizens who live with us will speak Turkish from now on' (CHP 1935: 149). Upon this speech, the MTTB's intimidation particularly of the Jews increased, while the municipalities of a number of cities, including in particular Edirne and Izmir, where Jewish communities lived in large numbers, officially prohibited the use of any language other than Turkish in public (Bali 2000: 281-7). 'Citizen Speak Turkish' campaign was successful in forcibly silencing the non-Turkish and non-Muslim communities. It also provided the first

---

[822]In Mersin, where these communities lived in large numbers, the campaign was particularly harsh. In July 1934, at a People's House meeting in Mersin, the Turkist youth proposed a motion for beating up those who do not speak Turkish and force them to speak only Turkish (Cagaptay 2002: 260).

republican generation of Turkists a broad field of activity as the 'storm-troops' of the Kemalist regime.

2. De-Islamisation (Secularism): The first republican generation of Turkists emphasised the Central Asian origins and assisted the development and popularisation of a 'myth of origins', an important assertion of the Turkish History Thesis. The 'myth of origins' discourse, supported by some archeological findings in Mongolia,[823] was certainly related to the 'prohibited' *Turanist* aspirations. However, the dissemination of this discourse through the Turkist literature was helpful for the popularisation of Kemalist secularism, the main assertion of both being that Islam was an alien culture imposed on the shamanist and animist Turks of the 'glorious abyss'. As Ataturk stated;

Herdsmen do not know anything apart from the sun, clouds and stars. Peasants of the world also know only these. Because, the produce is determined by the natural conditions, the Turk only prays to the nature. (21-24 March 1930, in Ataturk 1961: 84-9).

What is more striking than Ataturk's manifest atheism is the parallels between this statement and Atsiz and his collegues' approach to Islam. Atsiz's guru, Riza Nur[824], saw the Turks' conversion to Islam not a glorious occasion but 'a consequence of Arabic imperialism' (Ayvazoglu 2002: 551). Atsiz refused the divinity of monotheist religions and said of the religious assertion that 'various lineage of people originated from Adam and Eve' an unscientific reactionism. Those who pursued the aspirations of Islamic unity or Islamic fraternity were, according to Atsiz, traitors of the nation, because the Islamic equality of the

---

[823] Finnish archaeologists discovered in the 1890s, monuments erected in the 8th Century, on the surface of which the addresses of the Kokturk's chiefs Kul Tigin and Bilge Kagan to their tribes were recorded (Guvenc 1993: 108-9).

[824] Dr Riza Nur was among the delegate that signed the Lousanne Treaty on behalf of the Kemalist government. He wrote in 1924, *Turkish History,* a 14 volume work which was began to be published by the Ministry of Education, but was halted shortly. Riza Nur was also active among the Turkish Hearths in the early years of the republic. Nur had to leave Turkey when the Kemalist purges began in the wake of the discovery of an attempt on Kemal's life in June 1926. Riza Nur returned Turkey in 1938 after Ataturk's death and received the treatment of ideological leader by the Turkists, including Nihal Atsiz, Huseyin Namik Orkun, Fethi Tevetoglu and Nejdet Sancar. He published a weekly Turkist journal *Tanridag* until his death in 1942.

umma was against the nationalist ideal (Bakirezer 2002: 357). Another prominent figure of racist Turkism of the time, Reha Oguz Turkkan, declared, 'I do not know any other religion. My religion is Turkism' (Onen 2002a: 366).

3. Ethnicity/Authenticity: Another field that Turkists were active was the villageist movement. In fact, Kemalist villageism was a continuation of the Turkist 'narodnism' which had emerged among the Turkish Hearths of the 1910s. One of the journals of the Constitutional era was called *Halka Dogru* (To the People), the stance of which was simultaneously pan-Turkist and socialist.[825] The official republican populism of the 1930s and 1940s, on the other hand, aimed the formation of a bureaucratic/corporatist social order in which the peasants would be mobilised for modernisation and more production. The main objective was to keep the peasants in their villages, thus preventing the rural-urban migration. According to the corporatist/populist government, urbanisation was the evil to be avoided, since it meant degeneration through class stratification of society, which was responsible for social problems including class formations and class struggles leading to social disintegration (Toprak 1998: 52).

The villlage and peasantism had an additional importance for the Turkist thought, since the village was the environment in which the pure race was to be searched for, that is, the location where the Turkish stock had been kept uncontaminated. This line had parallels with the Kemalist search for authenticity, propagated by the People's Houses' official periodical *Ulku* which portrayed the peasants as the incarnation of the 'pure', authentic, noble and bright Turkish prototype (Karaomerlioglu 2002: 287). Peasant conservatism was thus sublimated as a positive nature providing the republican regime with a 'pure' reservoir of 'national character'.

---

[825] Gokalp said of the editor of *Halka Dogru* Huseyinzade Ali (Turan): 'Ali Bey was influenced by two currents in Petersburg University: pan-Slavism and socialism. He derived the ideal of pan-Turkism from pan-Slavism while from socialism, he derived the morals of populism.' Niyazi Berkes affirms these influences on Ali Bey, who formed the first clandestine student organisation in Istanbul Medical Faculty, under the name Committee of Union and Progress, bound with strict

A pro-villageist journal, *Atsiz Mecmua*, was launched by Turkist intellectuals in 1931 alongside *Ulku*, linking the ideal of villageism to the 'cause of the outer Turks'. The 1940s Turkist periodical *Kopuz* declared that 'the Turkish peasant protected the Turkish spirit through their mores and traditions, which remained unchanged' (Toprak 1998: 56).

---

narodnik principles. But, argues Berkes, the constitutional era's populism was more inclined to 'sociologism' than 'socialism' as such (see Toprak 1998: 12-3).

Appendix 16: Turkist-Kemalist Tensions

The editor of the *Atsiz Mecmua*, Huseyin Nihal (Atsiz), was a teaching assistant at the Faculty of Literature of Istanbul University, whose name became known with his protest of the intimidation of the Turkology professor Zeki Velidi (Togan) at the first History Congress of 1932. The main reason for this intimidation was Velidi's objection to the claims of double origins, i.e. origins of the Turks being both in Central Asia and Anatolia.

This affair deserves some consideration since it was heralding a split between Kemalists and Turkists regarding the origins to be remembered. Velidi, a veteran émigré Turkist figure from Russia, criticised Resit Galip's assertion of a great draught in Central Asia which had started the supposed ancient migrations and brought civilisation to other lands (TTK 1932: 169). Velidi immediately received harsh accusations of trying to divide the congress (TTK 1932: 400) and backed down. He resigned from the Turkish History Institute, lost his university post and left Turkey. Velidi's colleague from Istanbul University, Professor Kopruluzade Fuad, also held similar views; but after witnessing Velidi's intimidation he capitulated to the Kemalist position and advised his assistant Huseyin Nihal to leave his post at the university. Nihal resisted this advice but was shortly removed from his post, upon Resit Galip's personal request, to be exiled to Malatya as a secondary school teacher. Nihal's opposition continued in his new monthly *Orhun*, which would be closed by the government in 1934 after the publication of Nihal's harsh criticism of the four volume history textbook which had been prepared in accordance with the Turkish History Thesis' main assertions (Ayvazoglu 2002: 544). After the closure of this Turkist journal, the movement evidently experienced a silent period (Fer 1942).

If, the Thesis' claim to the supposedly *Turanian* origins of Anatolian-Mesopotamian civilisations was to be dismissed, then what would be the grandnarrative of the Turks' history? Atsiz begins his response to this question by refusing the assertion that Turks were a local people resident in Anatolia since antiquity and adds: 'No nation is the ancient residents of their current homeland' (Atsiz 1941: 6). Atsiz's notion of history is similar to Hobbes' state of nature with a nationalist twist, in which all nations are in a constant and natural state of war, where strong nations take the upper hand. The Turks did not belong to Anatolia in the antiquity but because they were a strong nation with a strong state they managed to capture Anatolia from the Byzantians. The year 1071, the year when the Byzantian forces were defeated in Manzikert was a turning point in history; the Turks' existence in Turkey began.

The Turkist message was therefore simple enough to find popular reflection: 'We did not historically own Anatolia but we have the right to occupy it as long as we are strong and in a constant state of alert against the external and internal enemies'. What is proposed here is an Omer Seyfettin-like constant state of paranoia and aggressive anxiety: 'For a nation, the greatest danger is to swallow the opium of peace and friendship'. Therefore, the Kemalist motto of 'Peace at Home, Peace in the World' is 'a miserable political motto aiming to extinguish the spiritual energies of this nation' (Atsiz quoted in Bakirezer 2002: 354). War is an activity of vital importance for national solidarity and national progress; it is a fruitful consequence of the law of nature that prevents moral degeneration and individualism (Turkkan 1940: 91). The Turks' motto instead had to be 'Oppress all the non-Turkish nations!' (Turkkan quoted in Onen 2002: 364.)

The Turkists' war, when there was no international military conflict, would inevitably target the 'other races' within the borders of Turkey. Consequently, the racist discourse was accompanied by overt xenophobic activity targeting the 'Jewish capital' and the remnants of the 'eliminated' Christian ethnicities. For Atsiz, those who do not carry Turkish blood, such as Negroes, Jews, Cyrcassians, Albenians, Kurds and Lazes, had to be considered as foreigners, and therefore the policy of assimilation was also condemned. Only those men of Turkish stock can hold administrative positions of the Turkish state. Contrary to the policy of assimilation, Atsiz sees some elements as unsuitable even for being citizens. He contends that Gypsies have to be repatriated to India and if this is impossible they have to be put in forced residence and 'corrected' in the Kurdish province of Hakkari. Atsiz also advised the Kurds to find a place to go, for instance demand a country in Africa from the United Nations, and consult the Armenians for the consequences if they did not comply with this advice (Bakirezer 2002: 354-7).

Another racist of the time, and a close colleague of Atsiz, Fethi Tevetoglu, would formulate these assertions by modifying Ataturk's famous motto of 'How happy he is who says I am a Turk' to 'How happy he is who was created as a Turk' (Onen 2002: 623).

Much of these vulgar racist assertions, of which some were adopted by the Kemalist elite of the 1930s (see Chapter 5), have lived through the republican history and still continue to mould the ultra-nationalist mentalities.

Appendix 17: Turkists jailed by Kemalists

As the Nazi sympathies of the Kemalist regime under 'the national chief', Inonu, grew in parallel to the German advance in Europe, Turkist publications began to reappear one after the other in 1941. The Turkist influence on the government was manifested by prime minister Sukru Saracoglu in 1942:

> We are Tuks and Turkists, and will remain to be Turkists. For us, Turkism is a matter of conscience and culture as much as being a matter of blood (Ertekin 2002: 366).

However, from 1943 onwards, Turkists began to fall out of favour, in parallel to the reversal of the course of War. In these conditions, Nihal Atsiz, who probably sensed the coming of the Cold War and global Mc Carthyism, decided in April 1944 to make a stand by writing two open letters to the prime minister, in which he complained that the government posts, particularly of the Ministry of Education, were full of communists, 'who conspire to spread their poison over Turkist Turkey'. Atsiz attached to his second letter a list of these leftist-communist enemies, most of them being his one time friends. The Turkist youth followed their leader and performed the first book-burning ritual of Turkish history on 3 May 1944 in Istanbul.[826] This demonstration is currently referred to in ultranationalist literature as 'the day of awakening' (Ertekin 2002: 370).

The National Chief, going along with the spirit of times, decided to jail the Turkists rather than purging the 'communists'. 26 Turkist ideologues were arrested, charged with conspiracy to overthrow the government and put to trial. During the course of this trial, however, the Kemalist state had to make significant decisions elsewhere, regarding foreign policy and international orientation. They felt obliged to become part of the 'free world', as opposed to communism, and a decision for transition to multiparty system was taken in 1946.

---

[826] Books of the leftist writers Sabahaddin Ali and Nazim Hikmet were burnt in this demonstration, and slogans condemning communism and the then Minister of Education Hasan Ali Yucel were chanted. The demonstrators hailed president Inonu as 'Basbug' (The Chief) in

A requirement of this new course was a 'structural adjustment' with an anti-communist reorientation rather than democratisation as such. It soon became clear that Turkey's choice of domestic regime was a matter of some indifference to the Americans: Washington proved ready to lend similar assistance to Franco, Rhee, the Shah, Diem, Chiang, Peron and many lesser dictators (Rustow and Penrose 1981: 9).

The jailed Turkists were thus acquitted with an official proclamation in 1947 of Turkism a 'national ideology', while Atsiz's list of 'communists' were expelled particularly from the university posts. The Turkists and the Kemalist government were once again united, this time under the banner of anti-communism.

---

their slogans. These demonstrations were triggered by the leftist writer Sabahattin Ali's decision to take Atsiz to the court to seek compensation for his degrading comments in open letters.

Appendix 18: Origins of Blue Anatolianism: Nationalist Anatolianism and Humanism

1. Nationalist Anatolianism

Frank Tachau, in his pioneering work on the Turkish search for national identity (Tachau 1962) compared Anatolianism with pan-Turkism. The particular line of Anatolianism that Tachau analysed was that circle of university students around the journal *Anadolu* of 1919-1923, and the subsequent Anatolianist movement that operated within the Turkist/nationalist paradigm until 1925. One of the founders of the movement, Hilmi Ziya (Ulken), argued that Anatolianism was developed as a concrete viewpoint as opposed to the abstract ideals of Ottomanism, Turanism and Islamism (Ulken 1966: 800). This was because the definition of a nation could only be made with geographical reference and the Turkish nation's reference had to be Anatolia. Neither Turanism nor Islamism were able to provide a clear definition of homeland, while Ottomanism was doomed from the outset with the ill fate of the Empire. In 1923, a new group led by Mukrimin Halil published ten issues of a new journal with the same name. The contributors of this journal fiercely criticised the pan-Turkist ideas and asserted that the source of Turkish culture was Anatolia and that Turkish history began with the Seljuks arrival in Anatolia in 1071. They drew a difference between the homeland and colonies, and argued that the homeland was Anatolia whereas the lost Ottoman lands in Balkans and the Middle East were the colonies. Another journal, *Anadolu Mecmuasi,* published until 1925 by Mehmet Halit (Bayri), made one of the boldest statements on national identity:

> When questioned about their nationality, some answer to this as 'Turkish'.
> This is wrong. (...) Although we are of Turkish lineage, because our land is
> Anatolia our nation is the Anatolian nation (Deren 2002: 535).

Another line of Anatolianism, which also represents an early articulation of the Turkish-Islamic synthesis, emerged in 1939 under Nurettin Topcu's leadership around his journal *Hareket*. Topcu argued in an article entitled 'Our Identity' that an Anatolian Renaissance had begun with the Muslim Seljuks' occupation of Anatolia (Topcu 1939). 'The sources of our nation's strength are Islam, which gave a new spirit and life to the Oguzes arriving in Anatolia, and the agricultural technique that had been maintained in this continent since the Hittites and was inherited by the newcomers.' (Topcu 1943). According to Topcu, the search for identity could end best by the Turks' turning to their essence. Topcu believed that if the Turks managed to reclaim this Islamic/Anatolian essence, they would initiate the birth of a new age, a new Renaissance for the world (Topcu 1939a). Topcu and his disciples played an important role in the Islamisation of the Turkist movement particularly during the Cold War era (see above).

Tachau asserts that Anatolianist ideas were largely adopted by the 'Turkish History Thesis' and points out that one of the founders of Anatolianist current, Semseddin Gunaltay, was also an architect of the Thesis (Tachau 1963: 176). Unlike the early Anatolianists, however, the Central Asian origins were also emphasised in the Thesis. Moreover, the Thesis' Anatolianism differs from the early Anatolianism, in its double claim on Anatolia, in terms of historical time, by relating not only the history since the 11th century, but also the ancient history of Anatolia to Turkish history.

It is within the context of this second claim of the Thesis on Anatolia, i.e. the claim on the ancient history, that the left inclined 'Blue Anatolianists' situated themselves. The origins of 'Blue Anatolianism' are however more in the humanistic turn in Kemalism than this early Anatolianism.

2. Turkish Humanism

The era of 'humanist culture' in Turkey opened up in 1939 with the appointment of Hasan Ali Yucel as the Minister of Education. Yucel's one of the first educational policies was to launch a campaign for the translation and publication of the western classics in Turkish:

Republican Turkey, which is determined to become a distinguished part of the western cultural and philosophical community, needs to translate the old and new cultural products of the civilised world and thus strengthen her identity with a universal sense of feeling and thought. This necessity invites us to an extensive translation campaign (Cikar 1997: 81).

In the first three years of the campaign, 109 translated books, mainly from classical Greek, were published.[827] Yucel also included the classical western languages and the translations from classics in the secondary school curricula for the first time. During the humanist era, the *Encyclopaedia of Islam* was also translated and published with some original entries in the Turkish edition, and an *Encyclopaedia Turk* was also prepared and published.

The importance of the humanistic stance can be realised if Yucel's practice is read against the background of Turkism/nationalism above. When considering Kemalism, I have identified the main desire of the nationalist discourse as to repair the damage inflicted on the national pride by the failure in recognition by the West (Bihruz Bey syndrome). Ataturk seemed to have put the question of westernisation to a decisive end by formulating the main task of the republican nation as to rise to the level of contemporary civilisations. This statement was however qualified by a strong anti-imperialist stand. Consequently, the republican discourse continued to conceptualise the West as a split Other: the West was the Ego-Ideal that needed to be introjected, but this intojection was linked to the nationalist project, that is, westernisation was presented not only as an ideal but a necessity at the same time, for Turkey's eventual challenge to the West. In this second sense, the west as the imperialist Other, which threatened the integrity of the motherland, led to the reign of a paranoidic mentality over modern Turkishness. The fact that Seyfettin's sado-masochistic motto of 'those who do not oppress are condemned to be oppressed' repeated by several Turkist ideologues along with similar statements by men of high governmental positions

---

[827] 39 of these were translated from classical Greek, 38 from French, 10 from German, 8 from English, 6 from Latin, 5 from Oriental and Islamic classics, 2 from Russian and one from the Scandinavian literature.

of the republican era signifies the continuation of this mentality. However, this anxiety and the state of alert against the 'others', besides its ability of mobilising national-popular energies, could well be self damaging if sustained forever as the dominant policy. A literary theorist, Erich Auerbach, who lectured at Istanbul University between 1934 and 1940, commented on this hopeless state of anxiety in a letter addressed to Walter Benjamin in 1937:

[Ataturk] did everything that he did in a struggle against the European democracies, on the one side, and the panislamist Sultan's economy, on the other; the result is a fanatically anti-tradition nationalism: the denial of the whole (Islamic) cultural heritage, forging a phantasmatic relationship with a primitive Turkish identity, a Europeanised technologic modernisation for the aim of achieving a victory against a simultaneously hated and admired Europe (...) Result: an extreme nationalism but the destruction of national character at the same time (Barck 1992: 82).

In his critique of Gokalp's trilogy 'To Turkisize, To Islamise, To Civilise', Yucel stated that 'we do not need to Turkisise ourselves'; instead, a national self-confidence ('being already Turkish') was needed in the process of integration with humanity (Kocak 2001: 394). 'I do not see the East and West as different' said Yucel, 'although human works, the longings, concerns and fears of human spirit, differ according to the temporal and spatial context, this is because of the chosen methods and forms. If we did not feel with a western mentality, we would not be able to find this substance in the East.' (Cikar 1997: 62.) Yucel was thus proposing a restoration through which the second meaning of the encounter with the west –the threatening Other – would be superseded, in favour of adopting the western mentality as the 'form' of reaching the 'substance' of the east.

Yucel's translation renaissance managed to mould the mentalities of a number of generations (Yavuz 1987: 147-8). However, the spirit of times, the international climate that was fully determined by 'the logic of equivalence', and its domestic reflections, did not allow Yucel's project to live long. His ministry was the sole target of the Turkists' 1944 McChartyist campaign led by Atsiz (above). In 1946, when the government decided to follow Atsiz's advice and purged a number of 'leftist' academics particularly from the Ankara University, and began to close the Village Institutes, 'in accordance with the requirements of the multiparty system', Yucel resigned from his post in disappointment. The humanist episode thus ended, though with significant long-term results.

One of these long-term results was the 'Blue Anatolia' movement, which proposed some important solutions to the Turkish search for identity in modern times.

Appendix 19: Islam and Ataturkist Tranquillity

It will be legitimate to read Kafesoglu's above statement that 'the Turkish nation does not need to fabricate a history or search for a culture' as a covert but bold criticism of Kemalism. The Synthesis also breaches Kemalist prohibition of irredentism by its overt aspirations for the 'outer Turks'. But most importantly, the whole Synthesis could be read as the 'anti-thesis' of the Turkish History Thesis, for what the Thesis views as the source of alienation (Islam) is sublimated by the Synthesis, while the true source of alienation is clearly identified by the Synthesis as westernisation, one of the constitutive aims of the Thesis. In this context, the neo-Kemalist critique of the Synthesis, that it provides the ideological baggage for an 'anti-Kemalist counterrevolution' (Guvenc, et al, 1991 and Guvenc 1993: 230) gains some substance. However, the above quoted Report also states the following:

Ataturkism constitutes the philosophical roots of the Republic of Turkey. The Ataturkist system of thought provides the form and spirit for our Constitution from its introduction to conclusion. In order to maintain the thought system that constitutes the foundation of the Republic of Turkey, measures need to be taken to analyse, improve and disseminate this philosophy' (Guvenc et al. 1991: 101-3).

Kemalists unsurprisingly dismiss the above references to Ataturk as nothing more than lip service, given that the Turk-Islam Synthesists were operating at the time as the advisors of the 12 September's Ataturkist military junta. This, however, is a too naïve explanation, which assumes that the military junta, or the 'Kemalist core', were deceived by some anti-Kemalists' 'counterrevolutionary arguments'. Instead, the historical conjuncture that brought together these two apparently rival discourses (Kemalism and Islamised nationalism) needs to be taken into account. Without going into historical detail (which I will attempt in the next chapter, with an analysis of this holy alliance's unexpected consequences), the Kemalist obsession with 'social tranquillity' and national security need to be dwelled on.

Taha Parla defines Kemalism as a solidarist discourse, a specific form to achieve 'corporate capitalism', in which not precisely the existence of classes but class conflict is denied (Parla 1989: 120-2 and Parla 1992: 322-6). What is to be added to these assertions is that Kemalism is a pragmatic discourse of power, the discourse of the modern Turkish State. If one primal aim of Kemalism is to build a nation with a contemporary identity, another is to achieve this under circumstances of social tranquillity and national security. Moreover, as I have argued in Chapter 4, for the military, the 'guardian' of the Republic, which maintains an astonishingly religious face unlike any other state institutions, what has been essential is not change and revolution but the salvation and the maintenance of the state. The growing class conflict and the manifestly threatened social peace from late 1960s to 1980 inflated Kemalism's circumstantial connotation of 'national security' for the Turkish State, in the expense of its primary constitutive features.[828] In these circumstances, 'Ataturkism' emerged as a specifically state security discourse, which defined the nation primarily in its difference from terrorism and the 'threat of communism'. The ideological vacuum that was left from the physical elimination of the socialist influence on social and political life of late-Kemalist Turkey was however impossible to be filled solely by the cult of Ataturk. In these circumstances, the junta turned towards Islam as a means of ideological control and homogenisation, thus coming very close to view religion as social cement. In other words, if religion was the opium of the people, then it could be administered in an appropriate doze to tranquillise the social. This pharmacological transition from Kemalism to Ataturkism inevitably opened the doors of key institutions of the state apparatus to the Synthesists. Turk-Islam Sythesis thus gained the status of the ideological roof of the Ataturkist revisionism of Kemalism.

---

[828]Others, including the socialist left also found references for an egalitarian society in Kemalism and took largely a left-Kemalist stand. This, however, does not justify an assertion that the generals betrayed Kemalism; instead, affirms once again that Kemalism, an empty signifier from the outset, operated throughout the republican history as the empty signifier that paradoxically furnished modern Turkey's discursive horizon.

Against the background of the above analysis, Turk-Islam Synthesis looks more like a discourse of restoration than 'counterrevolution' as such, aiming primarily to repair the discursive cleavage between the Kemalist State and popular common sense. Given that the origins of this primal split lie in the Kemalists' secularist turn, the Synthesis could also be read as a Kemalist olive branch presented to its repressed periphery, that is, its unconscious.

It is important to note that the common ground that brought together the State and the nation (core and periphery; ideology and common sense; consciousness and unconscious) was not religion itself but nationalism; religion was the means of this reconciliation. The 'communist threat' was the constitutive outside of the Ataturkist restoration, which once again made it necessary for the Kemalists to gesture towards the Real (the paranoidic recollection of catastrophic collapse), the absolute outside of its unconscious. The shared ground was nationalism ('Ataturk nationalism' according to the 1982 Constitution) for which the state's security and social peace were essential. Turkish nationalism operated over a surface defined in terms of a trilogy by Ziya Gokalp: 'To Turkisize, To Islamise, To Civilise'. Kemalist practices did not breach this trilogy but emphasised Turkification and Civilisation in the expense of Islamisation. The same Kemalist State, under the circumstances of 1980s, or under the 'communist threat', was now attempting a rehabilitation of this neglected element of nationalism.

465

Appendix 20: Ottomanism Right and Left

Right Ottomanism

Traditionalists from the right, who shared some of Tanpinar's views include Fuad Koprulu (1890-1966) and Cemil Meric (1916-1987), although Meric denounced rigorously the left/right differences as 'alienation' (Meric 1985: 77-9). Koprulu argued that the main problem was the fact that intellectuals, who predominantly had a 'colonial mentality', created a cultural crisis by 'degrading the past' (Durukan 1991: 359). Meric furthered this view by arguing that the identity crisis was a consequence of the alienation of the intellectuals by replacing the 'sacred space' with profane 'isms' or 'materialism'. 'Wide popular masses', argues Meric have no such problem and they continue to refer 'Islam as a whole' as their guide to overcome difficulties and illuminate the unknown (Meric 1985: 175-6). The secularisation/materialisation of the intellectual space meant the externalisation of the past: 'We deny our ancestors, the Ottomans. Our only enemy: Turk-Islam civilisation' (Meric 1978: 113). Meric also described the Kemalist History Thesis 'a collection of palaeontologic suggestions, fabricated solely for the purpose of the requirements of the time' and listed it among 'alien ideologies' that poisoned the Turkish intelligentsia – others being national-socialism and socialism:

> Because [those palaeontologic suggestions] were fabricated for us, we had to call them national. The distinguishing characteristic of these damaging suggestions was hostility to history. To history, that is, to the sole architect of national unity and national consciousness. Ottomans were Barbarians, we were the sons of Hittites and Sumerians, etc. (Meric 1985: 175.)

Meric is probably 'the most hermeneutic of the rightwing intellectuals', but what is observable in his assertions above is not a perception of nation and history as an aesthetic reality but history as the 'architect' or the 'means' of achieving 'national unity'. Meric thus represents a retreat from Tanpinar's grounds to Gokalpian (Durkheimean) positivism, which goes in parallel to his political reconciliation with nationalist right (Ayvazoglu 2002: 576). The 'imperialist conspiracy' that Meric depicts is essentially a Crusade, but since the crusaders failed to defeat 'us' with sword their expedition turned into cultural imperialism: 'Europe is in pursuit of the same end since Tanzimat reforms: to kill the sacred in Turkish intellectual' (Meric 1985: 174). On these grounds, Meric provided the nationalist and Turkist right with arguments capable of forming the philosophical background of Turk-Islam Synthesis.

Left Ottomanism

With a similarly hostile view of the west, literateur Attila Ilhan imported Turk-Islam synthesis into the habitus of the leftist intelligentsia. Like Kafesoglu, Ilhan (1984: 138) sees Turk-Islam synthesis as the 'natural' state of the 'western Turks'. However, this synthesis had lost its 'infrastructure', because of the colonisation of the Ottoman Empire after Tanzimat reforms. The alternatives left for a new identity politics were either to ground the nation on Central Asian nomadic past or to capitulate to the 'comprador Levantine culture', that is, 'surrender to cultural imperialism'. Ilhan proposes a third way, which consists of grounding the national identity on the 'glorious' Turk-Islam synthesis and then build a contemporary synthesis, which will be secular, democratic, original and national (Ilhan 1984: 139). Ilhan believes that Ataturk initiated this contemporary synthesis but the 'humanist period' under Inonu, which misinterpreted Kemalism (Ilhan 1986: 329-30), reintroduced the 'imitationist' mentality of Tanzimat's comprador culture leading to the alienation of intellectuals from the 'national value system' (Ilhan 1986: 330 & 103). Ilhan's views include some typical left Kemalist (or nationalist left) thesis, in which nationalist assertions are enveloped in a class struggle and anti-imperialism grammar.[829]

---

[829] In this grammar, Kemalism is presented as a progressive moment of 'national democratic revolution' for it eliminated the non-Muslim bourgeoisie, who had turned the Empire into a colony of the foreign powers. The left's immediate task is to defend and complete the Kemalist 'national democratic revolution'. For a comprehensive overview of left Kemalism see Aydin 2002.

Leftwing novelist Kemal Tahir diagnosed the existence of a society with 'two realities' in Turkey, a situation that has existed since the beginning of westernisation with Tanzimat reforms (Tahir 1972). In order to propose a solution to this split identity, Tahir derived from the Marxian notion of 'Asian Mode of Production' not only the peculiarity of the East and the Ottoman Empire, but their superiority to the West. The people of Anatolia have never experienced slavery or other freedom binding phases as in the west, thanks to the 'protective Oriental State' and therefore they did not need a bourgeois revolution to achieve individual freedom (Tahir 1969: 47). The space where this superiority is materialised has been the State tradition with attributes of constructive ability, freedom, justice, etc. These claims of a *sui generis* East do not add up much to the discussion on identity (since the Turkist and Synthesist discourses had already developed the same attributes to the Turks' strong State tradition) but they arguably played a role in the introduction of the problem of identity to the discursive universe of the leftwing intelligentsia.

Appendix 21: Nationalist Psychoanalysis

Psychoanalytic discourse has rarely been a source to derive from in the discussion that shaped the Turkish search for identity (see Appendix 25). One of the exceptions is the Turkist and anti-communist writer Fethi Tevetoglu, who approached the matter from a psychiatric perspective in his article, 'Communism and Mental Illnesses against Religion'. In this piece, Tevetoglu considered communism as a mental disorder and argued that the importance of religion in social life was primarily its preventive power of mental illnesses and communism:

> Religion, contrary to the claims of over-ambitious politicians and the psycho-neurotic sick personalities, whose souls, identities and all existence have been sold, is not a narcotic substance like opium for the people (Onen 624).

Fortunately, Tevetoglu did not have a licence to practice psychiatry but anti-communist psychiatrists, practising as specialists of 'youth psychology', are known to have made some money from the parents of leftist youths particularly in the 1970s and 1980s. [830]

Another 'group psychology' work to explain Turkish society was by a Kemalist schoolteacher Mustafa Costuroglu, entitled *Social Schizophrenia and Ataturk*. Costuroglu bases his diagnosis of split society on the fact that the majority of people have failed to be influenced sufficiently by the 'revolutionary layer' (Kemalist rulers). In this split, the perception of reality of one side produces fear on the other side (Costuroglu 1981: 50). The reason for this split is the counterrevolution of 1950, which degenerated the revolution. (Costuroglu 1981: 59-60). Ataturk, asserts Costuroglu, also pointed the threat of schizophrenic society in his warnings by favouring science against religious superstitions (Costuroglu 1981: 109). Costuroglu argues on these grounds that the opposite of the schizophrenic society is secularist society, in which 'the state relies on reason and cultural power.' (Costuroglu 1981: 125).

---

[830] One of these psychiatrists was Professor Ayhan Songar, who was invited by the 1980s junta to perform 'clinical research' on leftist 'terrorists' in detention centres and prisons.

If Tevetoglu's 'analysis' is revealing of the shared conscious and unconscious transference and projection which shaped the popular mentalities of externalisation, or the perceptions of the other and 'outside', Costuroglu's 'psychoanalysis' of Turkish identity reveals the form of relationship between state and society – therapist/patient relationship – that has determined the Kemalist mentality.

Appendix 22: Diyanet and *Tarikats*

Suleyman Hilmi Tunahan, a former Medrese scholar with Nakshibendi affiliations, lost his job after the abolition of *Medreses* and began to run a small business. In 1930, he was recruited by the *Diyanet* to give sermons in various mosques in Istanbul. Around the same time, Tunahan began to run Koran courses for children and youths. These were underground courses financed by some rich Muslims. In the lack of official religious education, graduates of these courses filled the *Diyanet* posts of religious personnel, but Tunahan was not rewarded for this service. Instead, he, with his circle of followers, suffered detention and trial several times between 1939 and 1957. The 'golden age' of *Suleymancilar* (Tunahan's followers) began when Koran courses were legalised in 1946, since their courses became the main source of recruitment for *Diyanet*. However, state controlled Imam-Hatip high schools were also opened in 1951 for training religious personnel, and from 1958 onwards their graduates began to take up positions in *Diyanet* along with *Suleymancis*. The *Suleymancis* became an école Islamique, similar to *Nurcus*, after Tunahan's death in 1959. Their new leader Kemal Kacar introduced strict discipline in the *Suleymanci* community (Çakır 1990: 130-1). However, they suffered a major blow in 1965, when *Diyanet* declared that they would only recruit from among the graduates of Imam-Hatip schools and Faculty of Theology. The long conflict between *Diyanet* organisation and *Suleymanci* community thus began. *Suleymancis* refused to accept the Imam-Hatip graduates' authority; they went to the mosques to ask public to refuse to pray behind the official imams. In 1971, all the Koran courses were taken over by *Diyanet*. *Suleymancis* were forced to surrender their school buildings and student networks to the state. They have however managed to survive to date as a powerful community through decades after this blow. According to Turkish Secret Service (MIT) reports dated 1989, the *Süleymancı* Community were running a total of 1,900 Koran courses around the country (Saylan: 67).

Mehmed Zahid Kotku was educated in a Nakshibendi lodge in Istanbul and travelled around the country to disseminate his sheikh's message. With the closure of dervish lodges, Kotku returned to his hometown Bursa and worked there as an imam until 1952, when he returned to Istanbul. In Istanbul, Kotku became the sheikh of Turkey's major Nakshibendi convent, the Iskenderpasha Mosque Convent. His position as a sheikh was known to the authorities but Kotku maintained his position as the preacher of the Iskenderpasha Mosque until the end of his life. Kotku and Iskenderpasha Convent played significant roles in the political life of modern Turkey, essentially by mobilising financial resources among the Nakshibendi followers around the country to fund pious youths' higher education. This way, the Lodge managed to mould generations of cadres in state bureaucracy. Kotku owes his ability to keep his community intact and expand their influence through time to his moderate and 'evolutionary' approach (Çakır 1990: 23). The Iskenderpasha Convent never challenged the secularist state's authority; instead they encouraged the formation of the first pro-Islamist political party in Turkey, Milli Nizam Partisi (National Order Party) under the leadership of Necmettin Erbakan in 1969. Kotku died in November 1980, two months after one of the major 'Kemalist' military coups of Turkish history. The junta issued a special permission to authorise his burial in the Süleymaniye Mosque's courtyard, where all the former sheikhs of his lodge rested.

Appendix 23: Tarikats and Islamic identity: bringing God's message down to the earth

The fact that no more monotheist religions have been able to emerge after Islam was probably due to the fact that Islam had exhausted the metaphysical abstraction to its logical limits. Koran repeatedly asserts a very anti-clerical stand that nobody can mediate between the individual and God. Muslims do not need the masses or congregations in order to pray to God. Even building and visiting the mosques are not among the Muslim's obligations. The individual is essentially obliged to obey the Koran's words and link himself/herself with God through the prayers. God, on the other hand, is also extremely abstract in the Islamic belief. He is not the Father of the Prophet Muhammad or Jesus, nor has He shown any signs of existence as He did to Moses (and Abraham, Jacob and others before him). There are no miracles that the God or the Prophet had to demonstrate to convince the Muslims. The only miracle, Muhammad said, was the creation of world and the universe and the miracle that Muhammad did actually reveal the God's words, that is, the Koran. The significance of the metaphysical questions lie in the semantics of the words Islam, the root of which is 'surrender', and Muslim, which means 'the one who surrendered'. Islam therefore is such a discourse that God (Allah) demands an unconditional surrender of humanity in such self-confidence that He even refuses to hint any convincing signs of the existence of the entity that humanity is asked to surrender to.

Islam probably could have survived as it was, if it had remained as the belief of a 'real community' as in the Muhammad's time. However, the 'miraculous' success of the Muslims in fulfilling the Koranic mission of *jihad,* that is, the expansion of God's message through holy war, inevitably led to a series of crises. At the root of these crises, an essential symptom of which prevails in the conflict between the Shiite and the Sunni, lied two essential problems: first, the individuals' hopelessness in grasping in his solitary the extremely abstract universe of Islamic divinity, and second, the difficulty of identification with the progressively populated 'imagined community' of Muslims.[831] The problem of 'imagined community' was partially solved with a Pope-like inflation of the symbol of the Caliph. In response to the first problem, extensive clergies developed as in the Ottoman and Farsi examples. However, the primary purpose of the Muslim clergy's presence was to oversee the implication of the Koranic law, *Sharia*, and with this feature, the Muslim clerics were more the representatives of the officialdom than religion as such. The official structure of Islamic organisation thus left the individual alone in his search for answers to existential and metaphysical questions.

It is this metaphysical vacuum that explains the vital place of the *tarikats* in Islam. Through the face to face relationship between the *mürid* (disciple) and the *mürshid* (the guide) that the *tarikat* structures provided, the individual Muslim's soul was liberated from its solitary confinement. The personal and material touch of God through the tips of the *mürshid's* fingers, which accompanied the metaphysical opening of the individual's soul to the realm of divine through Sufi mysticism and the practical guidance in problems of everyday life, managed to provide a potent remedy to the tortures of physical and spiritual existence in the Orient. *Tarikats* also helped to cure the distress caused by the identity crisis by converting the whole villages and tribes as units of 'real community' to their faith. The travelling dervishes, on the other hand, would fulfil the function of the modern media of our time, through providing a medium of communication among these real communities, and between these communities on the one side and the Sheikh, the symbol that tied them together, on the other. The Sheikh himself was also personally accessible to the visitors in his convent. With these precious networks at hand, *tarikats* were vital for the maintenance of Islamic identity, as for the legitimation of power of any ruler.

---

[831] On the difficulty of imagining the *umma* as a community Namik Kemal had to say as late as the 1860s, 'we were not aware of the existence of Muslims in Kasgar, prior to our interest in pan-Islamism'. Kashgar is a region in the Central Asia, which was under Russian rule at the time (see Çetinsaya 267).

The existence of the *tarikats* was the guarantee of peace and order within the communities that they operated. Their influence, however, inevitably reproduced authoritarian communal structures in which the communal norms always preceded the individual. Nomadic clans, rural villages and urban neighbourhoods were the typical units of such structures. Mardin makes the following observations on the *Gemeinschaft* of 'neighbourhood':

> Neighbourhood was usually something more than an administrative unit; it was a cumulative *Gemeinschaft* within the borders protected by neighbourhood braves and loyal dogs. It was the environment in which an ordinary Ottoman subject was expected to spend most of his life. Neighbourhood was the place where the primary education was given, births were celebrated, marriages were arranged and funerals were held. This was where the mosques operated like an institution mobilising the dwellers of the entire neighbourhood in order to make sure that the things that needed to be heard were actually heard. (...) The neighbourhood was where compensation for the blood that had been spilt was fixed, where the Islamic institution of the moral inspection was secretly countered in drinking parties and gambling sessions in gloomy rooms. Nightwatchmen patrolled the neighbourhoods in order to raid on the shattered lovers. Cafés operated as communication centres. The first seal was stamped by the neighbourhood's imam on the petitions before being submitted to higher authorities. The shrines of local saints were visited regularly by the whole neighbourhood. Local holy men distributed justice through self-styled decisions and sentences. (...) Any contact between opposite sexes was prohibited (Mardin 1991: 72-4).

Modernisation was expected to liquidate these closed communities through time. The primary target of the Kemalist reforms in Turkey was, according to Mardin, the conservative structure described above through the liberation of individual. It is in this context that Mustafa Kemal's personal distaste of *tarikats* becomes intelligible. With the diminishing influence of the *tarikats*, the traditional structures would be available for liquidation and transformation by being included in the process of modernisation. Once such modernisation was achieved, the *tarikats* and all the 'superstitions' and irrationalism that were tied to them would lose their conditions of existence and whither away.

Modernisation, however, would bring about new problems, new crises and hence a new vacuum to be filled by the *tarikats*. The traditional units of community and identity had been shaken by secularisation and modernisation but there were great shortages in values and institutions able to reabsorb the scattered individuals. Neither Kemalist nationalism, which lacked a convincing divine dimension, nor the new horizon of 'civilisation' was able to 'reoccupy' the place of Islam as the imaginary dimension of the people's psyche. In fact, much of the Islamist criticism of the western civilisation had been directed towards an image of this 'civilisation' enjoying material wealth thanks to science and technology but suffering from 'spiritual degeneration'.

The results of modernisation thus provided a new space of activity for the *tarikats*. The relaxation in the secularist practices, on the other hand, provided new surfaces of organisation and expression for these formally underground networks. The 15,000 mosques, built in the 1950s according to the prime minister, were mostly the work of charity associations which mobilised their localities in raising funds for building mosques. Associations of assisting the Koran schools, solidarity with the Imam Hatip schools, religious staff solidarity associations and associations of promotion of Islamic faith also proliferated from 1946 onwards (Yücekök 1971: 119-122). Most of these associations were linked somehow to the *tarikat* networks.

What is more important is that Kemalist modernisation transformed mainly the centre and was only tangible as police measures in the periphery. Both endogenous and exogenous consequences of the conclusion of the World War II forced the Kemalist regime to initiate a premature restoration through transition to a multi-party system. The fruits of the 'passive revolution' attempt in the form of village institutes, people's houses and village lodges had not yet been matured to build hegemony in the periphery.

An example of this lack of hegemony in the periphery is a book entitled *A Village in Anatolia* consisting of the memoirs of Mahmut Makal (Makal 1965), a village teacher from the 1940s. Makal repeatedly narrates in this book the villagers' hostility towards him. He hardly gets a place to stay for himself, and the villagers are very reluctant to set aside space for a schoolroom. So, for some time he has to gather children in the mosque, which leads to lots of complaints and a state of near-tumult. One day a young man arrives in the village. He is in his twenties, has studied to become a *hafiz*, and he brings news and greetings from a venerated religious leader in a village not too far away. The villagers give this man all the best that they have to eat and drink, they rejoice and gather around him with great curiosity and sincerity. The contrast between how the man of religion and the man of secular education are received by the villagers speaks for itself. Makal, with his enlightened ideals, was left feeling crushed and puzzled (Makal 1965: 94).

Makal also sums up the points raised in the above paragraphs regarding the maintenance of the place of *tarikats* in people's lives during a period when secularist reforms and the prohibitions were still in full force:
In our part of the world there is a veritable epidemic of Sheikhs; and the Sheikhs themselves don't know what Order they belong to. In September 1947, among eleven villages which I visited, and yet another twenty nearby villages not visited but known to me, the village that I found to have fewest Sheikhs was H. And that had more than fifty! The village consists of one hundred and fifty households: children are keen to the *tarikat* and they join it. Everyone who joins the *tarikat* is called 'Sheikh'. He lets his beard grow; to all appearances he has no use for this word. His task is to attain sainthood. In all these villages the Sheikh's duty seems to consist of playing the tambourine till the small hours of the morning, and reciting until they are hoarse (Makal 1965: 86).

Appendix 24: Of the Saints: Said-i Nursi and Saint Kemal

The formative years of modern Turkey were stamped by two men, each of whom sincerely believed that he was a saint with a mission, which was the exact opposite of the other's mission:

"Before the Great War, or around the beginning of it, I had a true vision. In it, I was under the Mount Ararat. The mountain suddenly exploded with a terrible blast. Pieces the size of mountains were scattered all over the world. I looked and saw that in that awful situation, my mother was beside me. I said to her: 'don't be frightened. This is happening at God's command, and He is All-Compassionate and All-Wise.' Suddenly, while in that situation, I saw that a person of importance was commanding me: 'Expound the miraculousness of the Koran!' I awoke and I understood that there was going to be a great explosion, and after that explosion and upheaval, the walls surrounding the Koran would be destroyed. The Koran would then defend itself directly. It was going to be attacked and its miraculousness would be its steel armour. And in a way surpassing his ability, someone like me was going to be appointed at this time to reveal a sort of its miraculousness; and I understood that it was me who had been designated." (Said's Dream quoted in Dogan 2003)

This 'dream', which Said-i Nursi decides to remember much later than having it in the first place, summarises his mission: to defend Koran by the word of Koran at a time when Koran was the subject of an unprecedented assault. The second dream is not personally a vision of our second Saint, but no doubt of one of his intellectual gurus, Dr Abdullah Cevdet. Besides, this is not exactly a dream, but 'a very awake sleep':

Sultan will have one wife and no concubines; (...) the fez will be abolished and a new head gear adopted; (...) women will dress as they pleased, though not extravagantly, and will be free from dictation of interference in this matter by *ulema,* policemen, or street riffraff; they will be at liberty to choose their husbands, and the practice of arranged

marriages will be abolished; convents and dervish lodges will be closed
and their revenues added to the education budget; all *Medreses* will be
closed, and new modern literary and technical institutes established; the
turban, cloak etc. will be limited to certified professional men of religion
and forbidden to others; vows and offerings to the saints will be prohibited
and the money saved devoted to national defence; exorcists, witch-doctors
and the like will be suppressed and medical treatment for malaria made
compulsory; popular misconceptions of Islam will be corrected; practical
adult education schools will be opened; a consolidation and purified
Ottoman Turkish dictionary and grammar will be established by a
committee of philosophers and men of letters; Ottomans, without awaiting
anything from their government or from foreigners will, by their own will
and initiative, build roads, bridges, ports, railways, canals, steamships and
factories; starting with the land and Evkaf (the charitable religious
foundations) laws, the whole legal system will be reformed.[832]

Mustafa Kemal rephrased Abdullah Cevdet's dream as to make Turkey catch up
with the West and assume its 'rightful place' within 'civilisation' as a modern state
and society. He sincerely believed that he was the chosen one for this mission:

"There is no claim that the person that was required by the situation at
hand (…) had to be myself. However, one among the sons of this land had
to come to the fore" (Atatürk 1960: 44-5).

St Said had obviously seen in his vision the coming of Kemalism. Kemalism as a
regime of truth was not established by the national struggle or the proclamation of
republic or the abolition of caliphate. It was formed with the consequences of the
1925 Kurdish rebellion. Mount Ararat, where the explosion took place in St Said's
vision is not far from the battleground between Sheikh Said's Kurdish troops and

---

[832] Adbullah Cevdet, 'Pek Uyanik Bir Uyku'. This article was first published in the Young Turks'
journal *Içtihad* in 1912. For full text of the article see Kocabasoglu (ed.), 2002: 593-8. I used the
summary translation in Lewis (1968: 236) with minor modifications.

the Turkish army. And the "person of importance", who appointed St Said to his mission, is certainly not Mustafa Kemal.[833]

Kemalist Hatred

"At the head of the *Nurcu* movement is Saidi Kurdi, one of the actors of the 31 March Incident, a contributor of *Volkan* and a founder of *Ittihad-ı Muhammedi* Party. (…) Saidi Nursi engaged in his articles to the problems of religion and faith, but never supported the Republican regime. (…) The works of illiterate Saidi Nursi based on revelations that he dictated to his secretaries were collected under the title of *Risale-i Nur*" (Tunaya 2003: 205-207).

Tunaya's presentation of Said-i Nursi's life and work demonstrates the typical elements of the republican discourse's charges on political Islam: resembling the reactionary uprising of 31 March, Kurdishness and ignorance (the claim that Said-i Nursi was illiterate).

Tunaya, on the other hand, knew very well a number of critical problems associated with these charges: For the first, the charge of association with the 31 March Affair, Said-i Kurdi was arrested, tried and then acquitted. The second, blended with racism, is a typical example of Kemalist psyche's unconscious association (condensation and displacement) of the 'others' and the third, the fact that Said-i Nursi never learned the Latin script, can probably be interpreted as an act of resistance. Tunaya knew very well that Said-i Nursi read and wrote in Kurdish, Arabic and Turkish in Ottoman script, probably more in number than the languages that Professor Tunaya could speak.

From Said-i Kurdi to Bediuzzaman Said-i Nursi

---

[833] Saidi Nursi was among the Kurdish notables exiled to the west after the Sheikh Said rebellion. The 'official' *Nurcu* interpretation of this dream however is that the explosion beyond Ararat symbolises the Bolshevik revolution in Russia. This was the greatest assault against Islam. In this

Said belonged to the 1890s generation and was born in the Nurs district of the Kurdish province of Bitlis. He graduated from a Sufi Medrese in Kurdistan and studied philosophy and positive sciences after his conventional education. Because of his speed in grasping the new secular sciences, Said was given the title of *Bediüzzaman* (The unprecedented person of our time). He originally belonged to the Nakshibendi order but also had contact with the Kadiri sheikhs. Said was also influenced by Afghani's ideas of a puritan and scriptural reform in Islam. He joined the group of religious advisers to Sultan Abdulhamid 1896 and returned to Van in 1899. In 1907, Said was back in Istanbul, to submit a petition to the Sultan on educational reform. He then went to Salonica to participate in the Young Turk opposition and in 1909, he was a founding member of the *Ittihad-i Islam* Association (See Appendix 15). Said was tried for the charges of participation in the 31 March mutiny and acquitted. In 1914, Said participated in the preparation of the *fatwa* that called for a *jihad* against the Entente Powers. He became a government agent during the World War I and went to Tripoli in 1915 to urge the local Muslim population to rise against the Italian occupying forces. Said then joined the militia forces in Kurdish provinces and was captured by the Russian army in Bitlis. He escaped from a prisoners of war camp in Russia and returned to Istanbul in 1917. Said then became a scholar in the Islamic Academy *Dar-ul Hikmet-il Islamiye* and after retiring to Van for a brief period during the national struggle, he reappeared in 1923, distributing his treatises in the National Assembly building in Ankara. In these leaflets Said argued that although the war was won with the God's consent, nothing was done to secure a more Islamic lifestyle in Turkey. He was warning the deputies with this leaflet that a dangerous wave of secularisation was immanent. After the parliament was dissolved in April 1923, Said returned to Van. In 1925 he was arrested with many Kurdish notables in connection with the Sheikh Said rebellion and was exiled to Isparta in south central Anatolia. Isparta governor then compelled Said to reside in Barla, a remote and inaccessible village.

---

interpretation, Kemalism was not the primary danger, but presented a danger as much as it resembled to communism.

The Saint's Miracle in 'Deep Anatolia'

Said-i Kurdi, who reinvented himself as Said-i Nursi in the changing climate of republican Turkey, demonstrated in this place of exile that it was possible to influence the masses without having at one's disposal any of the modern means of communication. Said lived through the 'reign of terror' of the 1920's and '30's, by holding lectures with a close circle of disciples, who he had to recruit from among the local peasants. He was not able to preach his ideas from the mosque, which was under surveillance. The use of modern means of communication, printing books or producing magazines or newspapers, had also been made impossible. In these conditions, Said invented a method, which turned out to be miraculous, as his 'vision' had revealed to him: He began to write metaphorical, allusive and parabolic letters, which he called *Lahikalar* (Supplements) addressing certain questions by referring to the Koranic essentials. Enveloped in these letters, was a subversive criticism of the Kemalist modernisation.[834] Said's close circle of disciples would duplicate his letters by hand; these duplications were then distributed to the contacts around the country where they were reduplicated and redistributed. It is estimated that some 60,000 copies of *Risale-i Nur* were in circulation by 1940s (Mardin 1992: 157), and it was estimated that by 1950s Said had around a million followers. The Saint was also being circulated around the places of exile. After about a year's imprisonment in 1935, he was forced to reside in Kastamonu in north central Anatolia and then exiled to Denizli in the west. In 1944, he was tried again and exiled to Emirdag district of Afyon.

It is probably a divine coincidence that Said called his letters 'supplements'. Here, the author's intention is certainly providing contemporary commentary to accompany the reading of Koran. However, my deconstructive reading of Said's

---

[834] This criticism was so well enveloped in a religious discourse that Said was usually 'undecidable' for the republican judges on whether to convict or clear him over the charges of the Article 163 of the Turkish Penal Code. Tunaya, however, firmly dismisses such undecidability and

and the Kemalists' discourses is an attempt to demonstrate that Said's letters can also be read as a supplement to Mustafa Kemal's discourse. Deconstructive research shows how symbolic orders are constructed through the categorisation and fixation of differences. Symbolic borders are determined through taking sides in the dichotomies fixed by difference. Order and hierarchy are determined through purity. Those entities, which are not pure because they cannot be categorised and are ambiguous, would connote danger, contamination and the annihilation of the order, due to their subversive orientation breaching the borders. Their existence erodes the claims to purity and wholeness, leading to destabilisation and tension. They therefore represent the rule's outside, by being situated between inside and outside, order and chaos, friend and the enemy. They constitute the category of "undecidables" (Derrida 1981).[835] Supplement means both addenda, that is, an entity completing an incomplete entity by making an addition, and replacement, that is, an entity which substitutes for the original. Said's supplements claim to be a substitute, a replacement of Kemal's discourse, but they, together with the narration of Said's political practice, are deployed here, in this text, as addenda, that complete the incomplete narrative, or the 'darkside', of Kemalism.

St Said owes his miracle, as much as to the peculiar form of communication, to a number of factors, most of which are related to his position, knowledge and political experience. But the most significant factor that can be identified among these is St Said's orientation as a typical 'undecidable entity', a man, who was 'neither ... nor ...', situated at the margins that constituted the borderlines separating modernity from tradition, the West from the Orient, the mind from the soul, reason from religion, science from superstition, the sane from the lunatic,

---

demonstrates with a painstaking discourse analysis that Said had deserved penalty for subversive codes deployed in his 'Suplements' (Tunaya 2003: 206-208).

[835] Derrida includes in this category *pharmakon, hymen* and *supplement.* The Greek word *pharmakon* can mean both cure and poison at the same time. And *hymen,* another Greek word, signifies both virginity (the separation between inside and outside) and marriage, that is, the breach of this separation through the unification of the self with the other (Yumul 2003:20-1).

483

centre from province, city from countryside, the symbolic from the imaginary and the real; and conscious from unconscious.

Said was not a member of the Ottoman *ulema*. He never sought approval from *Sheikhulislam* for his *Icazetname* (letter of consent) obtained from a Kurdish *Nakshibendi* Sheikh. He was not however simply a holy-man of Sufi folk Islam. His *Icazetname* effectively gave him the status of an Islamic scholar. Said was, in this sense, both an Islamic scholar and a Sufi notable, but neither of these at one and the same time. Said was also ambivalent about his Sufi affiliations: he was educated by the Halidi branch of the Nakshibendi order but was also in touch with the *Kadiri* order (Mardin 1992: 99). At another level, Said was affiliated to the scripturalist school, which charged folk Islam with mystification of the Koranic message that was in its origins compatible with progress and modernisation. Following reformist Islamists like Afghani, Said believed that science and technology were advantageous for Islam and stood against the Sufi orders saying, "the time is not the time of *tarikat*, it is the time to salvage faith" (Cakır 1990: 82). But he was an orthodox at the same time since he argued against the call for opening the gate of *Ictihad* by the Islamists of the Constitutional period.

As in the field of religious thought, Said was both a traditionalist and a modernist in politics. He was a dissident Islamist during the formation of the republican regime, but he insistently refrained from making a political statement. His initial appeal was to the conservative people of the countryside, among whom Said was forced to dwell by the Kemalist regime, with a discourse based on the protection of their faith. Said's appeal expanded rapidly to reach to the more educated urban middle classes and developed in its aim from the defence and protection of pious identity to the formation of a modern Islamic identity. His compulsory change of second name from Kurdi to Nursi, after the name of the district he was born in (Nurs), also provided St Said with a linguistic gain. The name Nursi made it possible for him to associate his texts with the signifier *Nur* (divine light or illumination), at a time when Kemalism was working a tough battle to associate the term Islam with the connotations of darkness, dark past, ignorance, etc. Said's form of organisation was also placed at the margin separating the traditional Sufi order from the clandestine freemason lodges[836], being 'contaminated' by both. By introducing novel methods of survival as a community under modern conditions, Said probably saved the Sufi orders, as much as charging them with mystifying the Koran's message. In fact, various Sufi orders would follow his example of using modern means of communication and forms of organisation[837]. Said emphasised the significance of the text over the person, the *mürshid* (the holy guide or guru), echoing a modified version of Mustafa Kemal's motto, "the truest guide in life is science", yet he enjoyed a sheikh like treatment from his followers. Said's texts ('supplements') were also treated with a Koran-like orthodoxy among the *Nurcu*s. A splinter group still devotes their entire activity to duplication of Said's books by hand in Ottoman script (Çakır 1990: 85). Said studied and admired positive sciences and advised his followers the same, and deployed rational tactics to survive and gain strength in modern conditions. Yet his writings, including their form in Ottoman script, mostly reflect a pre-modern style of argumentation based on the truth of Koran, a truth hard to discover among the abundant use of metaphors and connotative signs. To a modern subject, Said's articles would give the impression of the language of unconscious if not (God forgive me) the delirious expressions of a lunatic. Said advised his followers to remain outside politics but he publicly announced his support for the Democrat Party from late 1940s onwards. Said repeatedly stated his respect for law and order, which did not prevent imprisonment and exile. St Said's disobedience, on the other hand, consisting of his resistance to the denial of his Kurdishness and his firm Islamist stand, was enough to enlist him among the 'others' of the image of Mustafa Kemal.

---

[836] Üstad, "master", is Said's title among his followers. He had been involved with the Young Turks and this is probably how he became familiar with the Masonic organisation.
[837] See for instance the account of the *Kadiris* experience under the leadership of Haydar Bas (Chapter 3).

What was unacceptable for the Republican regime was probably the fact that Said also presented to Muslims a strategy of modernisation of Islamic subjects under the disciplinary social conditions of modern Turkey. This strategy consisted of a transformation of the traditional *tarikat* structures into modern *écoles Islamique*, or Muslim communities that reproduce communal identities using modern communication methods, and a political style, which can be called 'doing politics without a political statement'. Said's stand proved to be effective in a society, where the primary aim of the sustained repression of religious signification was to eliminate the Islamic subject. Said's followers' social profile corresponded to the Kemalist image of ideal middle class family, rather than the image of 'ignorant' rural conservatism. They were mostly middle-income level urban civil servants, professionals and tradesmen, usually received a reasonable level of secular education, who wanted to lead a modern life but as conservative families, rather than modernisation *in toto*. The modern Islamic subject in the form of *Nurcu* disturbed the new regime of truth, which tried to constitute itself around the logic of modernity against tradition dichotomy. *Nurcu* was not pure tradition or pure modernity, he was split: modern but Muslim, modern but refused to be secularist, 'inside' but 'outside', and was therefore the chaotic 'undecidable' of the republican order. *Nurcu* was the exact mirror image of the Kemalist Turk: the split subject of the 'torn country'. The undecidable entity of *Nurcu* was so disturbing that Said's unprecedented influence was cited by the Kemalist generals among the major reasons that necessitated the 27 May 1960 coup d'état, and Said's body was exhumed from his tomb in Urfa, three and a half months after his death, to be reburied by the military in an unknown location in central Anatolia.

Appendix 25: Early Turk-Islam Syntheses

Kemalism's success was primarily discursive, and evident in the rearticulation of the hierarchy of signs Islam and nation, or Islamism and nationalism, leading within a few decades to a development, which can be called the nationalisation of the Islamic identity, and immediately observed in *Hareket,* a journal launched in 1939 with Islamist and Turkist participation.

In an article in the first issue of the magazine, entitled 'Renaissance movements', the editor, Nureddin Topcu[838] put forward a critical view of Western civilisation, science and technology. Topcu argued against intellectuals who expected salvation and solutions from Europe that Europe itself was lacking three dynamics, then said we should await from ourselves the rebirth of the age, and the most important condition of this was tied to our remaining outside the West. 'A nation like us who has embraced European civilisation but is outside Europe according to the map, should await from itself the rebirth of the age. The most important condition for this is for us not to be in the map of Europe and to remain aloof from its greed and egotism.' Topcu thus developed a 'Turk-Islam-Kemalism Synthesis', since unlike the classical Islamic criticism of Kemalism, he viewed the westernisation of society as an advantage, and united this angle with a particular mission for the Turks: 'the initiation of the rebirth of a new age'. (Akgun & Calıs 2002: 596).

Topcu's journal was published in the climate of inter-war period, in which Turkist discourse, partially promoted by the Kemalist state, was popularised particularly among the republican youth (see Chapter 6). The discourse of Atsız, among the pan-Turkists of the inter-war era presented a daringly novel articulation of Islam and Turkishness:

---

[838] Topçu had been sent to France by the republican government to study philosophy in 1928, where he had been involved with the French ultra-right. After receiving his doctorate Topçu returned to Istanbul and got involved with a Nakshibendi sheikh. Topçu's influence grew through

'Turks did not ascend as a result of their conversion to Islam but Islam ascended and lived thanks to the Turks' (Atsiz 1992: 471).[839]

In this sentence, we can identify Akif's notion of 'heroic race' (above), but with a shift in emphasis towards this race's particular interests above the general aims of Islam.

Another charismatic figure of ambiguous rapprochement between Turkism and Islamism is the poet and littérateur, Necip Fazil Kisakurek. In the journal *Buyuk Dogu*, which he published with intervals from 1943 onwards, he employed a more popular and provocative style, through which Kisakürek tended to display and develop political attitudes and to form political relations.[840] *Buyuk Dogu* became more inclined to Islam after 1946. Kisakurek, who defended a triple synthesis for Turkishness, including the pre-19th Century Ottoman culture, and the Eastern and the Western cultural heritages prior to 1946, would argue that the main lesson to be derived from the World War II was the necessity to 'return to religion' (Aksin 1997b: 287-8). A striking feature that both Kisakurek and Topcu demonstrate in their writings is their loyalty to the state and the manifestation in their arguments of the 'salvation of the state' as the essential aim. The republican generations thus inherited an essential feature of the 19th Century Ottoman intelligentsia, by volunteering to become 'organic intellectuals of the state'.

---

decades, with his anti-semitic, anti-communist and xenophobic discourse, leading to the formation of an ultra-nationalist Turkish right, on the basis of a Turk-Islam synthesis.

[839] See Bora 1998: 122. Bora also demonstrates how this mentality prevailed in the Kemalist scholars' later discourse of the Turks' contribution to Islam. Niyazi Berkes wrote:
'While the Turks were fulfilling their duties for Islam in the expense of their self identity, self language, self history, the Arab was always aware of his Arabness' (Berkes 1978: 428).
And Bozkurt Güvenç claimed that only the Turks remained loyal to the idea of *umma* and this was against the Turks' interests (Güvenç 1993: 328, in Bora 1998: 122).
[840] Like Topcu, Kisakurek had been sent to France with state bursary but could not complete his studies there. On his return, Kısakurek, too, joined a Nakshibendi order (Dogan 2003). Kısakurek and Topcu also meet on a shared anti-Semitic and anticommunist stand (Akgun & Calıs 2002: 596).

488

Bibliography

Acikel, F. (1996), 'Kutsal Mazlumlugun Psikopatalojisi', *Toplum ve Bilim*. No. 70, Güz 1996.

Acikel, F. (2000), 'Twilight of the Holy Trilogy: Authoritarian Articulation of Capitalism, Nationalism and Islam', unpublished PhD Thesis, University of Essex.

Adivar, H. E. (1963), *Conflict of East and West in Turkey*. Lahore: Sh. Muhammad Ashraf.

Ahiska, M. (2005), *Radyonun Sihirli Kapisi: Garbiyatcilik ve Politik Oznellik*. Istanbul: Metis.

Ahmad, F. (1969), *The Young Turks: The Committee of Union and Progress in Turkish Politics 1908-1914*. Oxford: Clerandon Press.

Ahmad, F. (1977), *The Turkish Experiment in Democracy, 1950-1975*. London: Hurst.

Ahmad, F. (2003), *Turkey: The Quest for Identity*. Oxford: One World.

Ahmad, K. M. (1994), *Kurdistan during the First World War*. London: Saqi Books.

Akcam, T. (1992), *Türk Ulusal Kimlig'i ve Ermeni Sorunu*. Istanbul: Iletisim.

Akcam, T. (1997), 'Hızla Türklesiyoruz', in (ed.) N. Bilgin, *Cumhuriyet, Demokrasi ve Kimlik*. Baglam, Istanbul.

Akcam, T. (2001), 'The Long Denied Armenian Genocide', *Le Monde Diplomatique*, September 2001.

Akcam, T. (2004), *From Empire to Republic: Turkish Nationalism and the Armenian Genocide*. London and New York: Zed Books.

Akcura, Y. (1976), *Uc Tarz-i Siyaset*. Ankara: Turk Tarih Kurumu.

Akgul, S. (2000), *Amerikan ve Ingiliz Raporlari Isiginda Dersim*. Istanbul: Yaba.

Akgün B. And Çalıs, (2002), 'Türk Milliyetçiliginin Terkibinde Islamcı Doz', *Modern Türkiye'de Siyasi Düsünce, Vol. 4, Milliyetçilik*, (ed.) Tanıl Bora, Istanbul, Iletisim.

Akgündüz, A. (1994), Güneydogu Meselesi ve Çözüm Yolları. Istanbul.

Aksin, S. (1972), *31 Mart Olayi*. Istanbul: Sinan.

Aksin, S. (1987), *Jon Turkler ve Ittihad ve Terakki*. Istanbul: Remzi Kitabevi.

Aksin, S. (1997), 'Siyasal Tarih (1789-1908)', *Turkiye Tarihi Vol.III*, (ed.) Sina Aksin. Istanbul: Cem Yayinevi.

Aksin, S. (1997b), 'Düsünce Tarihi (1945 sonrasi)', *Türkiye Tarihi*, Vol. 5, (ed.) Sina Aksin. Istanbul: Cem Yayınevi.

Aksit (1987), *Ortaokullar icin Milli Tarih Ana Ders Kitabi*. Istanbul: Devlet Kitaplari, Milli Egitim Basimevi.

Akyol, T., *Osmanli ve Iran'da Mezhep ve Devlet*. Dogan Kitap: Istanbul, 1999.

Alkan, O., ed. (2002), *Modern Turkiye'de Siyasi Dusunce, Vol.III, Modernlesme ve Baticilik*. Istanbul: Iletisim.

Al-Omar, F. & Abdel-Haq, M. (1996), *Islamic Banking: Theory, Practice and Challenges*. London and New Jersey: Zed Books.

Althusser, L. (1977), 'Ideology and Ideological State Apparatuses', *Lenin and Philosophy*. London: Verso.

Amnesty International (1995), *Turkey: A Policy of Denial*. London, 23 January 1995.

Anderson, B. (1991), *Imagined Communities*. London: Verso.

Andrews, P. A. (1989), *Ethnic Groups in the Republic of Turkey*. Wiesbaden: Dr Ludwig Reichert Verlag.

Anschütz, H. (1992), 'Türkiye'deki Hıristiyan Gruplar' (Christian Groups in Turkey), in Andrews, P. A., *Türkiye'de Etnik Gruplar*, 1992, Ant, Istanbul.

Anter, M. (1990), *Anılarım*. Istanbul: Doz.

Anter, M. (1991), *Hatiralarim*. Istanbul: Yonyayincilik.

Armstrong, H. C. (1932), *Grey Wolf: Mustafa Kemal – An Intimate Study of a Dictator*. London: Arthur Barker.

Arendt, H. (1965), *On Revolution*. New York: Viking Press.

Arikan, E. B. (1993), 'Second Republic Debates in Turkey', unpublished MA Thesis, Cambridge University.

Arman, H. (1969), *Piramidin Tabani: Koy Enstituleri ve Tonguc*. Ankara: Is Matbaacilik.

Aslan, A. (1999), *Sömürülen Atatürk ve Atatürkçülük*. I'stanbul: Toplumsal Dönüs,üm Yayınları.

Atasayan, M. (1939), 'Anadolu'nun Irk Tarihi Uzerine Antropolojik Yeni Bir Tetkik', in *Tebligler Kitabi* (18. Beynelmilel Antropoloji ve Prehistorik Arkeoloji Kongresi) Ankara.

Atatürk, M. K. (1989), *Atatürk'ün Söylev ve Demeçleri, volume II*. Ankara: Atatürk Kültür, Dil ve Tarih Yüksek Aras,tırma Kurumu.

Ataturk, M. K. (1961), *Ataturk'un Soylev ve Demecleri: 1918-1937, volume III*. Ankara: Turk Tarih Kurumu.

Atatürk, M. K. (1960), *Nutuk, vol. 1: 1919-1920*. Istanbul: Maarif Basimevi.

Ataturk, M. K. (1980), *Nutuk*. Ankara: Kultur Bakanligi Yayinlari.

Ataturk, M. K. (1991), *Ataturk'un Tamim, Telgraf ve Beyannameleri, Volume IV*. Ankara: AKDTYK.

Ataturk Yuksek Kurulu (1987), *Turk Kultur Planlama Teskilati Raporu*. Ankara: AKDTYK.

Atay, F. R. (1980), *Çankaya*. Istanbul: Bates,.

Atsiz, N. (1941), *Cinaralti, no.1*. (August 1941).

Atsiz, H. N. (1950), 'Tarihin Barismaz Dusmanlari', *Orkun, no. 2* (November 1950).

Atsiz, N. (1992), *Makaleler 3*. Istanbul: Baysan.

Aydin, S. (1998), *Kimlik Sorunu, Ulusallik ve 'Turk Kimligi'*. Ankara: Oteki Yayinevi.

Aydin, S. (2002), Sosyalizm ve Milliyetcilik: Galiyefizmden Kemalizme Turkiye'de 'Ucuncu Yol' Arayislari', in T. Bora (ed.), *Modern Turkiye'de Siyasi Dusunce, Vol.IV, Milliyetcilik*. Istanbul: Iletisim.

491

Aydin, S. (2002), 'Cumhuriyetin Ideolojik Sekillenmesinde Antropolojinin Rolu: Irkci Paradigmalarin Yukselisi ve Dususu, in (eds.) T. Bora & M. Gultekingil, *Modern Turkiye'de Siyasi Dusunce, Vol.III, Kemalizm*. Istanbul: Iletisim.

Aydinoglu, E. (1992), *Turk Solu 1960-1971: Elestirel Bir Tarih Denemesi*. Istanbul: Belge.

Ayvazoglu, B. (1996), '1980 Sonrası Kültüre Farklı Bir Bakıs', *Cumhuriyet Dönemi Türkiye Ansiklopedisi, Vol. XIII*. Istanbul: Iletisim.

Ayvazoglu, B. (2002), 'Tanridag'dan Hira Dagi'na Uzun Ince Yollar' in T. Bora (ed.), *Modern Turkiye'de Siyasi Dusunce, Vol.IV, Milliyetcilik*. Istanbul: Iletisim.

Bakirezer, G. (2002), 'Nihal Atsiz', in T. Bora (ed.), *Modern Turkiye'de Siyasi Dusunce, Vol.IV, Milliyetcilik*. Istanbul: Iletisim.

Balcioglu, S. (1991), *Gorusler-Gorusmeler*. Istanbul: Yon.

Bali, R. N. (2000), *Cumhuriyet Yillarinda Turkiye Yahudileri: Bir Turklestirme Seruveni (1923-1945)*. Istanbul: Iletisim.

Balli, R. (1991), *Kürt Dosyası*. Istanbul: Cem.

Barck, K. (1992), 'Walter Benjamin and Erich Auerbach, Fragments and Correspondence', *Diacritics*. Fall-Winter, no. 22.

Barkan, Ö. L. (1942), 'Osmanlı Imparatorlugunda bir iskan ve kolonizasyon metodu olarak vakıflar ve temlikler I: Istila devirlerinin kolonizatör Türk dervisleri ve zaviyeleri', *Vakiflar Dergisi*, V, pp. 279-386.

Barkey, H. J. and Fuller, G. E. (1998), *Turkey's Kurdish Question*. Lanham, Boulder, New York, Oxford: Rowman and Littlefield Publishers.

Baskaya, F. (1991), *Paradigmanin Iflasi*. Istanbul: Doz.

Batur, M. (1985), *Anılar ve Görüsler: Üç Dönemin Perde Arkası*. Istanbul: Milliyet Yayınları.

Behar, B. E. (1992), *Iktidar ve Tarih: Turkiye'de Resmi Tarih Tezinin Olusumu (1929-1937)*. Istanbul: Afa Yayinlari.

Belge, M. (1996), 'Yeni Insan, Yeni Kultur', in *Cumhuriyet Donemi Turkiye Ansiklopedisi*. Iletisim: Istanbul.

Belge, M. (1994), *Edebiyat Üstüne Yazılar*. Istanbul: Iletisim.

Bender, C. (1991), *Kurt Tarihi ve Uygarligi*, Istanbul: Kaynak.

Berkes, N. (1964), *Development of Secularism in Turkey*. Montreal: McGill University Press.

Berkes, N. (1978), *Türkiye'de Çagdaslasma*. Istanbul: Dogu-Bati Yayinlari.

Besikçi, I. (1977a), *Kürtlerin Mecburi Iskanı*.Istanbul: Komal.

Besikçi, I. (1977b), *Türk Tarih Tezi, Günes Dil Teorisi ve Kürt Sorunu*. Istanbul: Komal.

Besikçi, I. (1990), *Tunceli Kanunu (1935) ve Dersim Jenosidi*. Istanbul: Belge.

Besikçi, I. (1991), *Cumhuriyet Halk Fırkası'nın Programı (1931) ve Kürt Sorunu*. Istanbul: Belge.

Besikci, I. (1991a), *Muglali Olayi (1943), Otuzuc Kursun*. Istanbul: Belge.

Blumenberg, H. (1987), *The Legitimacy of the Modern Age*. Cambridge: MIT Press.

Bora, T. (1997), 'Cumhuriyetin Ilk Döneminde Milli Kimlik', in N. Bilgin (ed.), *Cumhuriyet, Demokrasi ve Kimlik*, Istanbul: Baglam.

Bora, T. (1998), *Türk Saginin Üç Hali: Milliyetçilik, Muhafazakarlik, Islamcilik*. Istanbul: Birikim.

Bora, T. (2002), '"Ekalliyet Yilanlari..." Turk Milliyetciligi ve Azinliklar', in T. Bora (ed.), *Modern Turkiye'de Siyasi Dusunce, Vol.IV, Milliyetcilik*. Istanbul: Iletisim.

Bora, T. and Gultekingil, M. (2001), 'Sunus', in (eds.) T. Bora & M. Gultekingil, *Modern Turkiye'de Siyasi Dusunce, Vol.II, Kemalizm*. Istanbul: Iletisim.

Bozarslan H. (2000), 'Why Armed Struggle?' Understanding the Violence in Kurdistan of Turkey', in F. Ibrahim and G. Gurbey (eds.), *The Kurdish Conflict in Turkey: Obstacles and Chances for Peace and Democracy*. New York: St Martin's Press.

Bozarslan, H. (2002), 'Kurd Milliyetciligi ve Kurd Hareketi (1898-2000)', in T. Bora (ed.), *Modern Turkiye'de Siyasi Dusunce, Vol.IV, Milliyetcilik*. Istanbul: Iletisim.

Bozdag, I. (1974), 'Ataturk'un Fikir Kaynaklari, *Milliyet*, 15 November 1974.

Bozkurt, M. E. (1930), 'Mahmut Esat Bey'in Odemis Nutku', *Hakimiyet-i Milliye*, 19 September 1930.

Bozkurt, M. E. (1931), 'Mefkure Ihtiyaci', *Milliyet*, 14 Feburay 1931.

Bozkurt, M. E. (1940), *Atatürk Ihtilali*. Istanbul: Istanbul Universitesi Inkilap Enstitusu Yayinlari.

Bruinessen, M. (1978), *Agha, Sheikh and State: On the Social and Political Organisation of Kurdistan*. Utrecht, the Netherlands: Ryksuniversiteit.

Bruinessen, M. (1994), 'Genocide in Kurdistan? The Suppression of the Dersim Rebellion in Turkey (1937-38) and the Chemical War Against the Kurds (1988)', in (ed.) G. J. Andreopoulos, *Conceptual and Historical Dimensions of Genocide*. University of Pensilivania Press.

Bulac, A. (1991), *Din ve Modernizm*. Istanbul.

Bulac, A. (1993), 'Medine Vesikasi Uzerine Tartismalar' (I), *Birikim*, 47.

Bulac, A. (1995), *Modern Ulus Devlet*. Istanbul: Iz.

Bulut, F. (1991), *Belgelerle Dersim Raporları*. Istanbul: Yön.

Butler, J. (1987), *Subjects of Desire: Hegelian Reflections in Twentieth-Century France*. New York: Columbia University Press.

Cagalptay, S. (2002), '1930'larda Turk Milliyetciliginde Irk, Dil ve Etnisite', in (ed.) Bora, *Modern Turkiye'de Siyasi Dusunce, Vol.IV, Milliyetcilik*. Istanbul: Iletisim.

Cakir, R. (1991), *Ayet ve Slogan*. Istanbul: Metis.

Cakir, R. (1995), *Ne Seriat Ne Demokrasi: Refah Partisini Anlamak*. Istanbul: Metis.

Cavdar, T. (1983), 'Halkevleri' in *Cumhuriyet Dönemi Türkiye Ansiklopedisi*. Istanbul: Iletis̜im.

Cay, A. M. (1983), 'Turkiye ve Meseleleri', *Turk Kulturu*. n. 283, February 1983: 105-7.

Cay, A. M. (1995), *Turk Ergenekon Bayrami Nevruz*. Ankara: Turan Kultur Vakfi.

Cecen, A. (1990), *Halkevleri*. Ankara: Gündoğan Yayınevi.

Celik, N. B. (1996), "Kemalist Hegemony from its Constitution to Its Dissolution, unpublished PhD Thesis, University of Essex.

Celik, N. B. (2000), 'The Constitution and Dissolution of Kemalist Imaginary', in (eds.) D. Howarth, et. al., *Discourse Theory and Political Analysis: Identities, Hegemonies and Social Change*. Manchester and New York: Manchester University Press.

Celik, N. B. (2001), 'Kemalizm: Hegemonik Bir Soylem', in in (eds.) T. Bora & M. Gultekingil, *Modern Turkiye'de Siyasi Dusunce, Vol.II, Kemalizm*. Istanbul: Iletisim.

Celik, O. (2002), 'Askeri Guc, Siyasal Teoloji ve Sag', *Birikim no. 160/161*, August-September 2002, Istanbul: Birikim.

Cemal, H. (2003), *Kurtler*. Istanbul: Dogan Kitap.

Çetinsaya, G. (2001), 'Islami Vatanseverlikten Islam Siyasetine', *Modern Türkiye'de Siyasi Düsünce, Vol. 1, Cumhuriyete Devreden Düsünce Mirası: Tanzimat ve Cumhuriyetin Birikimi*, (ed.) Mehmet O. Alkan. Istanbul: Iletisim, pp. 265-272.

Chailand, G. and Ternon, Y. (1983), *The Armenians: From Genocide to Resistance*. Zed Press, London.

Chatterjee, P. (1986), *Nationalist Thought and The Colonial World: A Derivative Discourse*. London: Zed Books.

CHP (1935), *CHP Dorduncu Buyuk Kurultayi Gorusmeleri Tutulgasi*. Ankara: 9-16 May 1935.

Cikar, M. (1997), *Hasan Ali Yucel*. Istanbul: Is Bankasi Yayinlari.

Connolly, W. E. (1991), *Identity/Difference: Democratic Negotiations of Political Paradox*. Ithaca: Cornell University Press.

Connolly, W. E. (1991a), "Democracy and Territoriality', in *Millennium*, v. 20, no. 3.

Copeaux, E. (1998), *Türk Tarih Tezinden Türk Islam Sentezine*. Istanbul: Tarih Vakfı Yurt Yayınları.

Costuroglu, M. (1981), *Sosyal Sizofreni ve Ataturk*. Ankara: Ari Matbaasi.

Dean, K. (1997), 'Introduction: Politics and the Ends of Identity', in K. Dean (ed.), *Politics and the Ends of Identity*. Aldershot: Ashgate.

Demirbas, B. (1995), *Musul Kerkük Olayi*. Istanbul: Arba.

Deringil, S. (1998), *The Well Protected Domains: Ideology and the Legitimation of Power in the Ottoman Empire, 1876-1909*. London: I. B. Tauris.

Derrida, J. (1981), *Disseminations*. Chicago: Chicago University Press.

Dersimi, M. N. (1952), *Kürdistan Tarihinde Dersim*. Aleppo.

Dersimi, N. (1992), *Dersim ve Kurt Mucadelesine Dair Hatiratim*. Ankara: Oz-Ge.

Devecioglu, B. (1995), *Yeni Yuzyil*, 16 November 1995.

Dilacar, A. (1940), 'Alpin Irk, Turk Etnisi ve Hatay Halki', *CHP Konferanslari Serisi, Kitap 19*.

Dilipak, A. (1991), *Ihtilaller Dönemi*. Istanbul: Beyan.

Dilipak, A. (1991a), *Savas, Baris, Iktidar*. Istanbul: Isaret/Fersat.

Dogan, D.M. (2003), 'The Means of Communicating Islam in 20th Century Turkey and Bediuzzaman Said Nursi in the Face of Efforts to Eradicate Islam', *The Reconstruction of Islamic Thought in the Twentieth Century and Bediuzzaman Said Nursi*, www.sozler.com.tr/symposium.

Donuk, A. (1990), *Turkiye*, 17 November 1990.

Dr Sivan (1975), *Kürt Millet Hareketleri ve Irak'ta Kürdistan Ihtilati*. Stockholm.

Duman (1997), 'Islamci Gencligin Seruveni', *Birikim*. No. 95.

Dündar, C. (2003), 'Kefen Sıyrıldı Ve...', *Milliyet*, 10 November 2003, Istanbul.

Duru, K., *Ziya Gökalp*, 1949, Istanbul.

Durukan, H., ed. (1991), *Turkiye Nasil Laiklestirildi*. Istanbul: Cidam.

Eker, Suer and Abatoglu (1995), *Nevruz, Ulusun Ulu Gunu*. Ankara: Tum.

Ellison, G (1928), *Turkey Today*. London: Hutchinson.

Erbakan, N. (1993), *RP 4. Buyuk Kongre Acis Konusmasi*. Ankara.

Erikson, E.H. (1980), *Identity and the Life Cycle*, London and New York: W.W. Norton & Company Inc.

Ersoy, M. A. (1912), *Hakkın Sesi [Voice of God (Justice)]*, 1912, extract taken from Ünlü, M. and Özcan, Ö., 1987.

Ertekin, O. (2002), 'Cumhuriyet Doneminde Turkculugun Catallanan Yollari', in (ed.) T. Bora, *Modern Turkiye'de Siyasi Dusunce, Vol.IV, Milliyetcilik*. Istanbul: Iletisim.

Evans, D. (1996), *An Introductory Dictionary of Lacanian Psychoanalysis*, London & New York: Routledge.

Eyuboglu, S. (1974), *Sanat Uzerine Denemeler*. Istanbul: Cem.

Eyuboglu, S. (1961), *Mavi ve Kara*. Istanbul: Atac.

Fanon, F. (1967), *The Wretched of the Earth*. Harmondsworth: Penguin.

Fer, C. S. (1942), 'Bir fasli kapayip yenisini acarken hesap veriyoruz', *Gok-Boru*. No.1.

Ferro de, C. (1995), 'The Will to Civilisation and Its Encounter with Laissez-Faire', *Alternatives, no. 27*.

Fink, B. (1997), *A Clinical Introduction to Lacanian Psychoanalysis*. Cambridge-Massachusetts-London: Harvard University Press.

Foucault, M. (1973), 'O mundo é um grande hospicio', *Revista Manchete*, 16 June 1973, 146-7.

Foucault, M (1978), *History of Sexuality: An Introduction*, Vol. 1. Harmondsworth: Penguin.

Foucault, M. (1980), 'Body/Power' in Gordon, C. (ed.), *Power/Knowledge*. Hemel Hepstead, Hertfordshire: Harvester Wheatsheaf.

Foucault, M. (1991), *Discipline and Punish*. London: Penguin.

Foucault, M. (1991), 'Governmentality', in (ed.) G. Burchell et. al., *The Foucault Effect*. London: Harvester.

Freud, S. (1939), *Moses and Monotheism*, Penguin/Pelican Freud Library, Vol. 12, Harmondsworth, 1985.

Frey, F. W. (1965), *The Turkish Political Elite*. Cambridge MA: MIT Press.

Gellner, E. (1995), "Kemalism', in E. Gellner, *Encounters with Nationalism*. Oxford: Blackwell.

Georgeon, F. (1986), *Turk Milliyetciliginin Kokenleri: Yusuf Akcura (1876-1935*. Istanbul: Tarih Vakfi Yurt.

Georgeon, F. (2002), 'Yusuf Akcura', in (ed.) T. Bora, *Modern Turkiye'de Siyasi Dusunce, Vol.IV, Milliyetcilik*. Istanbul: Iletisim.

Gökalp, Z. (1958), *Türkçülügün Esasları*. Istanbul: Varlık.

Gökalp, Z. (1976), *Türklesmek, Islamlasmak, Muasırlasmak*. Istanbul: Inkılap ve Aka.

Göktas, H. (1991), *Kürtler: Isyan-Tenkil*. Istanbul: Alan.

Göldas, I (1991), *Kürdistan Teali Cemiyeti*. Istanbul: Doz.

Gole, N. (1996), *The Forbidden Modern: Civilisation and Veiling*. Ann Arbour: University of Michigan Press.

Gramsci, A. (1971), *Selections from Prison Notebooks*. London: Lawrence and Wishart.

Granda, C. (1973), *Atatürk'ün Usagi Idim*. Istanbul: Hürriyet Yayınları.

Guerin, D. (1946), *La lutte de classes, sous la premiere republique, bourgeois et 'bras naus' (1793-1797)*, Paris: Gallimard.

Gulalp, H. (2001), 'Globalisation and Political Islam: The Social Base of Turkey's Welfare Party', *International Journal of Middle East Studies*, Vol. XXXIII, no. 3.

Gulalp, H. (2003), *Kimlikler Siyaseti: Turkiye'de Siyasal Islamin Temelleri*. Istanbul: Metis.

Gulec, C. (1992), *Turkiye'de Kulturel Kimlik Krizi*. Ankara: V Yayinlari.

Gulensoy, H. (1995), *Nevruz*, Ankara: Sevinc.

Guner, A. (1991), *Tarikatlar Ansiklopedisi*. Istanbul: Milliyet.

Gurbey, G. (2000), 'Peaceful Settlement of Turkey's Kurdish Conflict Through Autonomy', in Ibrahim and Gurbey 2000: 57-90.

Gurbilek, N. (1992), *Vitrinde Yasamak*. Istanbul: Metis.

Guvenc, B., et.al., eds. (1991), *Turk Islam Sentezi*. Istanbul: Sarmal Yayinevi.

Guvenc, B. (1993), *Turk Kimligi*. Ankara: Kultur Bakanligi.

Gurbey, G. (2000), 'Peaceful Settlement of Turkey's Kurdish Conflict Through Autonomy', in F. Ibrahim and G. Gurbey (eds.), *The Kurdish Conflict in Turkey: Obstacles and Chances for Peace and Democracy*. New York: St. Martin's Press.

Halli, R. (1972), *Türkiye Cumhuriyeti'nde Ayaklanmalar, 1924-1938*. Ankara: Genelkurmay Harp Dairesi Baskanlığı Yayınları.

Hasan Cemil (1932), 'Ege Medeniyetinin Menseine Umumi Bir Bakis', *Birinci Turk Tarih Kongresi*. Ankara: TTK.

Hegel, G. W. F. (1966), *The Phenomoenology of Mind*. J. Baille, trans. London: George Allan & Unwin.

Hegel, G. W. F. (1977), *Phenomenology of Spirit*. Oxford: Oxford University Press.

Heper, M. (1993), 'Political Culture as a Dimension of Compatibility' in (eds.) M. Heper, et. al., *Turkey and the West: Changing Political and Cultural Identities*. London: I. B. Tauris.

Hobsbawm, E. & Ranger, T., eds. (1983), *The Invention of Tradition*. Cambridge: Cambridge University Press.

Hobsbawm, E. (1990), *Nations and Nationalism since 1870: Program, Myth, Reality*. Cambridge: Cambridge University Press.

Hourani, A. (1970), *Arabic Thought in the Liberal Age*. Oxford & New York: Oxford University Press.

Howarth, D. and Stavrakakis, Y. (2000), 'Introducing Discourse Theory and Political Analysis', in (eds.) D. Howarth, et. al., *Discourse Theory and Political Analysis: Identities, Hegemonies and Social Change*. Manchester and New York: Manchester University Press.

Huntington, S. P. (1993), 'The Clash of Civilisations', *Foreign Affairs*, Summer 1993.

Ibrahim, F. and Gurbey, G., eds. (2000), *The Kurdish Conflict in Turkey: Obstacles and Chances for Peace and Democracy*. New York: St Martin's Press.

Ilhan, A. (1986), *Ulusal Kultur Savasi*. Istanbul: Ozgur.

Inan, A. and Karal, E. Z., eds. (1946), *Atatürk Hakkında Konferanslar*. Ankara: TTK.

Inalcik, H., *The Ottoman Empire X: the Classical Age 1300-1600*. London: Weidenfeld and Nicolson, 1973.

Inan, A. (1947), *Turk Halkinin Antropolojik Karakterleri ve Turkiye Tarihi, Turk Irkinin Vatani Anadolu*. Istanbul: TTK.

Inan, A. (1969), *Medeni Bilgiler ve M. Kemal Atatürk'ün El Yazıları*. Ankara: TTK.

Insel, A. (1996), *Düzen ve Kalkınma Kıskacında Türkiye*. Istanbul: Ayrıntı.

Insel, A. (2001), 'Giris', in (eds.) T. Bora & M. Gultekingil, *Modern Turkiye'de Siyasi Dusunce, Vol.II, Kemalizm*. Istanbul: Iletisim.

Irmak, S. (1939), 'Anadolu Yoruklerinin Antropolojisine Dair Tetkikler', in *Tebligler Kitabi* (18. Beynelmilel Antropoloji ve Prehistorik Arkeoloji Kongresi) Ankara.

Irmak, S. (1943), 'Turk Irkinin Biyolojisine Dair Arastirmalar: Kan Gruplari ve Parmak Izleri', in TTK, *Ikinci Turk Tarih Kongresi Calismalari ve Kongreye Sunulan Tebligler*. Istanbul: TTK.

Jaschke, G. (1972), *Yeni Türkiye'de Islamlık*. Ankara. Bilge Yayinevi.

Jung, C. G. (1959), 'The Archetypes and the Collective Unconscious', *Collected Works, Vol. 9*. Princeton-N.J.: Princeton University Press.

Kafesoglu, I. (1964), 'Bir Turk Kulturu Yok mudur?', *Turk Kulturu*, n. 25, November 1964.

Kafesoglu, I. (1970), 'Turk Milliyetciligi Nedir?', in *Turk Milliyetciliginin Meseleleri*. Ankara: TAKE.

Kafesoglu, I. (1985), *Turk Islam Sentezi*. Istanbul: Aydinlar Ocagi Yayinlari.

Kalman, M. (1995), *Belge ve Taniklariyla Dersim Direnisleri*. Istanbul: Nujen.

Kansu S. A. (1983), 'Ataturk ve Cumhuriyet Doneminde Turk Antropolojisi', *Ataturk Konferanslari,VIII, 1975-1976.* Ankara: TTK.

Kaplan, M. (1982), *Kultur ve Dil.* Istanbul: Dergah.

Kaplan, M. et. al., eds. (1992), *Atatürk Devri Fikir Hayatı -I.* Ankara: Kültür Bakanlıg'ı Yayınları.

Karabekir, K. (1988), *Istiklal Harbimiz.* Istanbul: Merk Yayın.

Karaosmanoglu, Y. K. (1983), *Ataturk.* Istanbul: Iletisim.

Karaosmanoglu, Y.K. (1956), 'Türk Milleti ve Atatürk', *Türk Tarih Kurumu "Belleten",* Cilt 20, no. 80.

Karaosmanoglu, Y. K. (1960), *Yaban.* Istanbul: Remzi Kitabevi.

Karaomerlioglu, A. (2001), 'Turkiye'de Koyculuk', in (eds.) T. Bora & M. Gultekingil, *Modern Turkiye'de Siyasi Dusunce, Vol.II, Kemalizm.* Istanbul: Iletisim.

Karpat, K. (1963), 'The People's Houses in Turkey: Establishment and Growth', *The Middle East Journal,* Winter-Spring 1963.

Karpat, K. (1973), *An Inquiry into the Social Foundations of Nationalism in the Ottoman Empire: From Millets to Nations, from Estates to Social Classes,* Princeton: Centre of International Studies, Princeton University.

Kemali, A. (1992), *Erzincan: Tarihi, Cografi, Toplumsal, Etnografi, Idari, Ihsai Inceleme Arastirma Tecrubesi.* Istanbul: Kaynak (first impression 1932).

Kendal (1980), 'Kurdistan in Turkey', in G. Chailand (ed.), *People Without a Country: The Kurds and Kurdistan.* London: Zed.

Kennie, N. (1968), *An Islamic Response to Imperialism.* Berkeley/Los Angeles.

Keyder, Ç. (1987), *State and Classes in Turkey: A Study in Capitalist Development.* London and New York: Verso.

Keyder, C., ed. (1999), *Istanbul: Kuresel ile Yerel Arasinda.* Istanbul: Metis.

Keyman, F. (1995), 'On the Relation Between Global Modernity and Nationalism: The Crisis of Hegemony and the Rise of (Islamic) Identity in Turkey', *New Perspectives on Turkey,* no. 64, s. 93-120.

501

Kili, S. and Gozubuyuk, A. S. (1985), *Turk Anayasa Metinleri*. Ankara: Turkiye Is Bankasi.

Kinzer, S. (2001), *Crescent and Star: Turkey Between Two Worlds*. New York: Farrar, Straus and Giroux.

Kirisci, K. and Winrow, G. M. (1997), *The Kurdish Question in Turkey: An Example of a Trans-State Ethnic Conflict*. London: Frank Cass.

Kivilcimli, H. (1979), Ihtiyat Kuvvet Milliyet (Sark). Istanbul: Yol.

Kocabasoglu, U., ed. (2002), *Modern Türkiye'de Siyasi Düsünce, Volume 3: Modernlesme ve Baticilik*. Istanbul: Iletisim.

Koçak, C. (1995), 'Siyasal Tarih (1923-1950)', *Türkiye Tarihi*, Vol. 4, (ed.) Sina Aksin. Istanbul: Cem Yayinevi.

Kocak, O. (2001), '1920'lerden 1970'lere Kultur Politikalari', in (eds.) T. Bora & M. Gultekingil, *Modern Turkiye'de Siyasi Dusunce, Vol.II, Kemalizm*. Istanbul: Iletisim.

Kocaturk, U. (1984), *Ataturk'un Fikir ve Dusunceleri*. Ankara: Turhan Kitabevi.

Kojeve, A. (1969), *Introduction to the Reading of Hegel*. New York: Basic Books.

Kristianasen, W. (1999), 'Secular Turks in Search of Reform', *Le Monde Diplomatique*, 6 February 1999.

Kucuk, Y. (1985), *Bilim ve Edebiyat*. Ankara: Tekin Yayınları.

Kucukomer, I. (1994), *Duzenin Yabancilasmasi*. Istanbul: Baglam.

Kunt, M. (1997), 'Siyasal Tarih (1600-1789)', in (eds.) S. Aksin, et. al., *Türkiye Tarihi, vol.III: Osmanlı Devleti 1600-1908*. Istanbul: Cem.

Kuntay, M. C. (1976), *Üç Istanbul*. Istanbul: Sander.

Kutlay N. (1991), *Ittihat Terakki ve Kurtler*. Istanbul: Koral Yayinevi.

Kutlay, N. (1996), *Kurt Kimligi Olusum Sureci*. Istanbul: Belge.

Lacan, J. (1977), *Ecrits: A Selection*, Trans. A. Sheridan, London: Tavistock.

Laciner, O (1999), 'Abdullah Ocalan Operasyonu: Kurt Sorunu Cozumunde Yeni Bir Asama mi?' *Birikim*. No. 119.

Laclau, E. and Mouffe, C. (1985), *Hegemony and Socialist Strategy*. London: Verso.

Laclau, E. (1988), 'Politics and the Limits of Modernity' in Ross, A. (ed.), *Universal Abandon?* Minneapolis: University of Minnesota Press.

Laclau, E. (1994), 'Introduction' in Laclau, E. (ed.), *The Making of Political Identities*. London: Verso.

Laclau, E.(1990), *New Reflections on the Revolution of Our Time*. London: Verso.

Laclau, E. (1996), 'Why do Empty Signifiers Matter to Politics?', in *Emancipation(s)*. London: Verso.

Landau, J. M. (1981), *Pan-Turkism in Turkey*. London: C. Hurst.

Laplanche, J. & Pontalis, J. (2004), *The Language of Psychoanalysis*. London: Karnac Books.

Leledakis, K. (1995), *Society and Psyche: Social Theory and the Unconscious Dimension of the Social*. Oxford: Berg.

Lerner, A. J. (1991), 'The Nineteenth Century Monument and the Embodiment of National Time', *Millennium*, vol. 20, no. 3.

Lewis, B. (1968), *The Emergence of Modern Turkey*. London: Oxford University Press.

Makal, M. (1965), *A Village in Anatolia*. London: Vallentine, Mitchell & Co. Ltd.

Malek, A. (1981), *Social Dialectics*. Albany, NY: State University of New York Press.

Mango, A. (1999), *Atatürk*. London: John Murray.

Mardin, S. (1969), *Din ve Ideoloji*. Ankara: Ankara Universitesi Yayinlari.

Mardin, S. (1975), 'Centre-Periphery Relations: A Key to Turkish Politics?', in (eds.) E. D. Akarli *et. al.*, *Political Participation in Turkey*. Istanbul: Bogazici University Publications.

Mardin, S. (1981), 'Religion and Secularism in Turkey', in (eds.) S. Kazancigil and E. Ozbudun, *Ataturk: Founder of a Modern State*. London: Hurst.

Mardin, S. (1983), *Jon Türklerin Siyasi Fikirleri*. Istanbul: Iletisim.

Mardin, S. (1989), *Religion and Social Change in Turkey: The Case of Bediuzzaman Said Nursi*. Albany: State University of New York Press.

Mardin, S. (1991), *Turkiye'de Din ve Siyaset, Makaleler 3*. Istanbul: Iletisim.

Mardin, S,. (1991a), 'Tanzimattan Sonra Asırı Modernlesme', *Makaleler 4: Türk Modernlesmesi*. Istanbul: Iletisim.

Mardin, S. (1992), *Bediuzzaman Said Nursi Olayi*. Istanbul: Iletisim.

Mater, N. (1999), *Memedin Kitabi: Guneydogu'da Savasmis Askerler Anlatiyor*. Istanbul: Metis.

Mazici, N. (2001), 'Menemen Olayinin Sosyo-Kulturel ve Sosyo-Ekonomik Analizi', *Toplum ve Bilim*, 90.

McDowell, D. (1992), *The Kurds: A Nation Denied*. London: MRG.

McDowall, D. (1996), *A Modern History of the Kurds*. London: I. B. Tauris.

Melikoff, I. (1994), *Uyur Idik Uyardilar*, (trans.) Turan Alptekin. Istanbul: Cem Yayinevi.

Melikoff , I. (1999), 'Bektasilik/Kizilbaslik: Tarihsel Bolunme ve Sonuclari', in eds., T. Olsson, et. al., *Alevi Kimligi*. Istanbul: Tarih Vakfi Yurt Yayinlari.

Meric, C. (1978), *Umrandan Uygarliga*. Istanbul: Otuken.

Meric, C. (1985), *Bu Ulke*. Istanbul: Iletisim.

Mouffe, C. (1993), *The Return of the Political*. London: Verso.

Mumcu, U. (1992), *Kürt-Islam Ayaklanması 1919-1925*. Ankara: Tekin Yayinlari.

Mumcu, U. (1995), *Kurt Dosyasi*, Ankara: Tekin Yayinlari.

Nairn, T. (1977), *The Break-up of Britain*. London: New Left Books.

Navaro-Yashin, N. (2002), *Faces of the State: Secularism and Public Life in Turkey*. Princeton and Oxford: Princeton University Press.

Nikitin, B (1986), *Kurtler*. Ozgurluk Yolu Yayinlari: Istanbul.

Noktali, A. (1996), '1800lerden 1980e Kurt Sorunu', in *Cumhuriyet Donemi Turkiye Ansiklopedisi*. Istanbul: Iletisim.

Norval, A. (1996), 'Social Ambiguity and the Crisis of Apartheid', in (ed.), E. Laclau, *The Making of Political Identities*. London and New York: Verso.

Norval, A. (2000), 'Trajectories of Future Research in Discourse Theory', in (eds.) D. Howarth, *et. al.*, *Discourse Theory and Political Analysis: Identities, Hegemonies and Social Change*. Manchester and New York: Manchester University Press.

Ocalan, A. (1978), *Kurdistan Devriminin Yolu (Manifesto)*. Koln: Wesanen Serxwebun. (5th Impression 1993).

Ocalan, A. (1991), 'Kurdistan Isci Partisi (PKK): Abdullah Ocalan'la Gorusme', in Balli, R. (1991).

Ocalan, A. (2005), 'Talabani'ye Demokrasi Mesaji', *Ozgur Politika*. Saturday, 30 April 2005.

Ogun, S. S. (1997), 'Türk Milliyetçiliginde Hakim Millet Kodunun Dönüsümü' [The Transformation of the code of Dominant Nation in Turkish Nationalism], in Nuri Bilgin (ed.), *Cumhuriyet, Demokrasi ve Kimlik*. Istanbul: Baglam.

Okte, F. (1987), *The Tragedy of the Turkish Capital Tax*. London: Croom Helm.

Olson, R. (1991), *The Emergence of Kurdish Nationalism 1880-1925*. Austin: University of Texsas Press.

Onen, N. (2002), 'Fethi Tevetoglu', in (ed.) T. Bora, *Modern Turkiye'de Siyasi Dusunce, Vol.IV, Milliyetcilik*. Istanbul: Iletisim.

Onen, N. (2002a), 'Reha Oguz Turkkan', in (ed.) T. Bora, *Modern Turkiye'de Siyasi Dusunce, Vol.IV, Milliyetcilik*. Istanbul: Iletisim.

Onis, Z. (1993), 'The Dynamics of Export Oriented Growth in a Second Generation NIC: Perspectives on the Turkish Case 1980-1990, *New Perspectives on Turkey*, no. 9, pp. 75-100.

Onur, N. (1943), 'Kan Gruplari Bakimindan Turk Irkinin Mensei Hakkinda Bir Etud', in TTK, *Ikinci Turk Tarih Kongresi Calismalari ve Kongreye Sunulan Tebligler*. Istanbul: TTK.

Oran, B. (2000), 'Linguistic Minority Rights in Turkey, the Kurds and Globalisation', in F. Ibrahim and G. Gurbey (eds.), *The Kurdish Conflict in Turkey: Obstacles and Chances for Peace and Democracy*. New York: St Martin's Press.

505

Oran, B. (2002), 'Kurt Milliyetciliginin Diyalektigi', in T. Bora (ed.), *Modern Turkiye'de Siyasi Dusunce, Vol.IV, Milliyetcilik*. Istanbul: Iletisim.

Ortayli, I. (1995), *Imparatorlugun En Uzun Yüzyili*. Istanbul: Hil Yayın.

Ozdalga, E. (1998), *The Veiling Issue, Official Secularism and Popular Islam in Modern Turkey*. Surrey: Curzon.

Ozdogan, G. G. (2001), *'Turan'dan 'Bozkurt'a: Tek Parti Döneminde Türkçülük*. Istanbul: Iletisim.

Parla, T. (1989), *Ziya Gokalp, Kemalizm ve Turkiye'de Korporatizm*. Istanbul: Iletisim.

Parla, T. (1991), *Turkiye'de Siyasal Kulturun Resmi Kaynaklari, V.I, Ataturk'un Nutuk'u*. Istanbul: Iletisim.

Parla, T. (1991a), *Turkiye'de Siyasal Kulturun Resmi Kaynaklari, V.II, Ataturk'un Soylev ve Demecleri*. Istanbul: Iletisim.

Parla, T. (1992), *Turkiye'de Siyasal Kulturun Resmi Kaynaklari, V.III, Kemalist Tek Parti Ideolojisi ve CHP'nin Alti Oku*. Istanbul: Iletisim.

Pascal, J., 'A People Killed Twice', *The Guardian Weekend*, 27 January 2001.

Pekcan, Y. and Ozturk, S. (1995), *Tarih ve Etnografya Acisindan Nevruz*. Ankara: Tum.

Perincek, D., ed. (1996), *Turk Tarihinin Anahatlari*. Istanbul: Kaynak.

PKK (1995), *PKK (Partiya Karkeran Kurdistan) Program ve Tuzugu*. Koln: Wasenen Serxwebun.

Poulton, H. (1997), *Top Hat, Grey Wolf and Crescent: Turkish Nationalism and the Turkish Republic*. London: Hurst and Company.

Rabinow, P., ed. (1984), *The Foucault Reader*. London: Penguin.

Renan, E. (1990), 'What is a Nation?' in ed. Homi Bhabha, *Nation and Narration*. London: Routledge.

Rorty, R. (1991), 'Habermas and Lyotard on Postmodernity' in *Essays on Heidegger and Others*. Cambridge: Cambridge University Press.

Rosenfeld, H. A. (1987), *Impasse and Interpretation*. London, New York: Tavistock.

Rousseau, J. J. (1964), *First and Second Discourses*, Roger D. and Judith R. Masters, trans. New York: St Martin Press.

Rugman, J. (1994), 'Muslim Radicals Challenge Nation's Secular, European Self-Image', *The Guardian*, Saturday, April 2 1994.

Rugman, J. (1996), *Ataturk's Children: Turkey and the Kurds*. London and New York: Cassell.

Rustow, D. and Penrose, T. (1981), *Turkey and the Community*. Sussex: University of Sussex.

Safa, P. (1990), *Turk Inkilabina Bakislar*. Istanbul: Otuken.

Safa, P. (1995), *Fatih Harbiye*. Istanbul: Otuken.

Said, E. (1979), *Orientalism*. London: Routledge and Kegan Paul.

Salt, J. (1995), 'Nationalism and the Rise of the Muslim Sentiment in Turkey', *Middle Eastern Studies*, 31(1).

Saribay, A. Y. (1985), *Turkiye'de Din ve Parti Politikasi: MSP Ornek Olayi*. Istanbul: Alan.

Savran, S. (1992), *Turkiye'de Sinif Mucadeleleri*, Istanbul: Kardelen.

Saylan, G. (no date), *Türkiye'de Laiklik*. Istanbul: Yeni Yüzyil Kitapligi.

Sayyid, B. (1994), 'Sign O' Times: Kaffirs and Infidels Fighting the Ninth Crusade' in Laclau, E., ed., *The Making of Political Identities*. London: Verso.

Schmitt, C. (1976), *The Concept of the Political*. New Brunswick-N.J.: Rotgers University Press.

Selek, S. (1963), *Anadolu Ihtilali*. Istanbul.

Seyfettin, Ö. (1988), *Harem*. Ankara: Bilgi.

Seyfettin, Ö. (1993), *Türklük Üzerine Yazılar*. Ankara: Bilgi.

Shaw, S. J. and Shaw, E. K. (1977), *History of the Ottoman Empire and Modern Turkey*. Cambridge: Cambridge University Press.

Simsir, B. (1973), *British Documents on Ataturk (1919-1938), Volume 1*. Ankara: Turk Tarih Kurumu.

507

Simsir, B. (1991), *Ingiliz Belgeleriyle Türkiye'de Kürt Sorunu (1924-1938)*. Ankara: Türk Tarih Kurumu.

Stavrakakis, Y. (1999), *Lacan and the Political*. London and New York: Routledge.

Stavrakakis, Y. (2000), 'Identity, Political', in (eds.) J. Foweraker & B. Clarke, *Encyclopedia of Contemporary Democratic Thought*. London: Routledge.

Stavrakakis, Y. (2000a), 'On the Emergence of Green Ideology: the Dislocation Factor in Green Politics', in (eds.) D. Howarth, et. al., *Discourse Theory and Political Analysis: Identities, Hegemonies and Social Change*. Manchester and New York: Manchester University Press.

Stirling, P. (1981), 'Social Change and Social Control in Republican Turkey', in *Papers and Discussion, Turkiye Is Bankasi International Symposium on Ataturk*, 17-22 May 1981, Ankara: TISA.

Sumer, F. and Turhal, Y. (1986), *Tarih, Lise I*. Istanbul: Ders Kitaplari Anonim Sirketi.

Tahir, K. (1969), *Turk Romani*. Istanbul: Tekin.

Tahir, K. (1972), 'Turk Hikayeciligi Ustune', *Yansima*, June 1972.

Tanpinar, A. H. (1970), *Yasadıgım Gibi*. Istanbul: Türkiye Kültür Enstitüsü Yayınlari.

Tanpınar, A. H. (2001), *Bes Sehir*. Ankara: Milli Eg˘itim Bakanlıg˘ı Yayınları.

Tanyol, C. (1994), *Laiklik ve Irtica*. Istanbul: Altın Kitaplar.

Taylor, C. (1989), *Source of theSelf: The Making of the Modern Identity*. Cambridge, Mass: Harward University Press.

Taylor, C. (1992), *Multiculturalism and the Politics of Recognition*. Princeton: Princeton University Press.

TBMM (1920-1950), *Turkiye Buyuk Millet Meclisi Zabit Ceridesi*. Ankara: TBMM Yayinlari.

TDN (1995), 'Europe Europe, Hear Our Voice!', *Turkish Daily News*, 15 November 1995.

Tekin Alp (1998), *Kemalizm*. Istanbul: Toplumsal Dönüsüm Yayınları.

Tezcan, N. ed. (1989), *Atatürk'ün Yazdığı Yurttaslık Bilgileri*. Istanbul.

Topcu, N. (1939), 'Benligimiz', *Hareket*, May 1939.

Topcu, N. (1939a), 'Ronesans Hareketleri', *Hareket*, February 1939.

Topcu, N. (1943), 'Avrupa', *Hareket*, February 1943.

Toprak, B. (1981), *Islam and Political Development in Turkey*. Leiden: E.J. Brill

Toprak, Z. (1995), *Milli Iktisat-Milli Burjuvazi*. Istanbul: Tarih Vakfi Yurt Yayinlari.

Toprak, Z. ed. (1998), *Bir Yurttaş Yaratmak: Muasır Bir Medeniyyet Için Seferberlik Bilgileri*. Istanbul: Yapı Kredi Yayıncılık.

Toynbee, A. (1970), *The Western Question in Greece and Turkey*.

TTK (1932), *Birinci Turk Tarih Kongresi: Konferanslar Muzakere Zabitlari*. Istanbul: TC Maarif Vekaleti.

TumTurk, I. (1950), 'Komunist', *Bozkurt*, no. 5, 13 October 1950.

Tunaya, T. Z. (2003), *Islamcilik Akimi*. Istanbul: Bilgi Universitesi Yayinlari.

Tunçay, M (1981)., *Türkiye Cumhuriyeti'nde Tek Parti Yönetiminin Kurulması (1923-1931)*. Ankara: Yurt.

Tunçay, M. (2000), 'Birinci Meclis', *Toplumsal Tarih*, April 2000, no. 76, vol. 13, Tarih Vakfı, pp. 54-55.

Tura, R. (1998), 'Kemalist Devlet', www.iscimucadelesi.org.tr

Turan, O. (1969), *Turk Cihan Hakimiyeti Mefkuresi Tarihi*. Istanbul: Turan Nesriyat Yurdu.

Turkkan, R. O. (1940), 'Turkculuk Deyince Ne Anlariz', *Bozkurt*, no. 4, May-July 1940.

Turkiye Cumhuriyeti Dahiliye Vekaleti Jandarma Umum Kumandanlığı (1936), *Dersim*. Ankara.

Turkes, M. (2002), 'Kadro Dergisi', in (eds.) T. Bora & M. Gultekingil, *Modern Turkiye'de Siyasi Dusunce, Vol.III, Kemalizm*. Istanbul: Iletisim.

Türköne, M. (1991), *Siyasi Ideoloji Olarak Islamciligin Dogusu*. Istanbul: Iletisim.

Türk Tarih Kurumu (1977), *Birinci Türk Tarih Kongresi*. Ankara: TTK.

Turner, B. S. (1978), *Marx and the End of Orientalism*. London and Boston: Allen and Unwin.

Tusalp, E. (1988), *Eylül Imparatorlugu, Dogusu ve Yükselisi*. Ankara: Bilgi.

Ulken, H. Z. (1966), *Turkiye'de Cagdas Dusunce Tarihi*. Konya: Selcuk Yayinlari.

Unat, F. R. (1964), *Turkiye Egitim Sisteminin Gelismesine Tarihi Bir Bakis*. Ankara: Milli Egitim Basimevi.

Under, H. (2002), 'Ataturk Imgesinin Siyasal Yasamdaki Rolu', in (eds.) T. Bora & M. Gultekingil, *Modern Turkiye'de Siyasi Dusunce, Vol. III, Kemalizm*. Istanbul: Iletisim.

Unlu, M. and Özcan, Ö. (1987), *20. Yüzyıl Türk Edebiyatı 1*. Istanbul: Inkılap.

Ustel, F. (2002), 'Turk Ocaklari', in (ed.) T. Bora, *Modern Turkiye'de Siyasi Dusunce, Vol.IV, Milliyetcilik*. Istanbul: Iletisim.

Vincent, A. (1998), *Modern Political Ideologies*. Oxford & Cambridge: Blackwell.

Vryonis, S., Jr. (1991), *The Turkish State and History: Clio Meets the Grey Wolf*. Thessaloniki: Institute for Balkan Studies.

Weiker, W. F. (1973), *Political Tutelage and Democracy in Turkey: The Free Party and Its Aftermath*. Leiden: E. J. Brill.

White, J. (2002), *Islamist Mobilization in Turkey*. Seattle: University of Washington Press.

Yasar, H. (1988), 'Kurt Milli Meselesi Karsisinda Turk Sosyalistlerinin Tutumu', *Sosyalizm ve Toplumsal Mucadeleler Ansiklopedisi*. Istanbul: Iletisim.

Yavuz, H. (1975), *Felsefe ve Ulusal Kultur*. Istanbul: Cagdas.

Yavuz, H. (1987), *Kultur Uzerine*. Istanbul: Baglam.

Yavuz, H. (1996), *Denemeler*. Istanbul: Boyut.

Yavuz, H. (1998), 'Batililasma Degil Oryantalistlesme', *Dogu Bati*, no. 2: 100-2.

Yegen, M. (1994), 'The Archaeology of Republican Turkish State Discourse', unpublished PhD Thesis, University of Essex.

Yegen, M. (1995), 'Türk Devlet Söylemi ve Cumhuriyet Kurumları', *Mürekkep*, no. 5, 37-47.

Yegen, M. (1999), *Devlet Söyleminde Kürt Sorunu*. Istanbul: Iletisim.

Yerasimos, S. (1987), 'The Monoparty Period' in (eds.) I.C. Schick and E. A. Tonak, *Turkey in Transition: New Perspectives*. New York: Oxford University Press.

Yildiz, A. (2001), *Ne Mutlu Türküm Diyebilene: Türk Ulusal Kimliginin Etno-Seküler Sinirlari (1919-1938)*. Istanbul: Iletisim.

Yoruk, Z. (1996), 'Turk Kimligi', in *Irkcilik ve Milliyetcilik*. Istanbul: Belge.

Yoruk, Z. (1997), 'Turkish Identity from Genesis to the Day of Judgement', in ed. Kathryn Dean, *Politics and the Ends of Identity*. Aldershot: Ashgate.

Yoruk, Z. (2002), 'Politik Psise Olarak Turk Kimligi', in T. Bora (ed.), *Modern Turkiye'de Siyasi Dusunce, Vol.IV, Milliyetcilik*. Istanbul: Iletisim.

Yücekök, A. N. (1971), *Türkiye'de Örgütlenmis Dinin Sosyo-Ekonomik Tabani (1946-1968)*. Ankara: SBF Yayınları.

Yucel H. A. (1994), *Turkiye'de Orta Ogretim*. Ankara: TC Kultur Bakanligi Milli Kutuphane Basimevi.

Yumul, A. (2003), 'Araf'ta Kalanlar', *Dogu Bati*, V. 23.

Zizek, S. (1989), *The Sublime Object of Ideology*. London & New York: Verso.

Zizek, S. (1991), *For They Know Not What They Do: Enjoyment as a Political Factor*. London & New York: Verso.

Zizek, S. (2001), *On Belief*. London: Routledge.

Zurcher, E. J. (1984), *The Unionist Factor*. Leiden: Brill.

Printed in Great Britain
by Amazon